Ordering Customs

Ethnographic Thought in Early Modern Venice

Kathryn Taylor

University of Delaware

University of Delaware Press

Newark, DE

Library of Congress Cataloging-in-Publication Data

Names: Taylor, Kathryn, author.
Title: Ordering customs : ethnographic thought in early modern Venice / Kathryn Taylor.
Description: Newark, DE : University of Delaware Press, [2023] | Series: The Early Modern Exchange | "Distributed worldwide by Rutgers University Press"—T.p. verso. | Includes bibliographical references and index.
Identifiers: LCCN 2022037177 | ISBN 9781644532997 (Paperback : alk. paper) | ISBN 9781644533000 (Hardback : alk. paper) | ISBN 9781644533017 (epub) | ISBN 9781644533024 (mobi) | ISBN 9781644533031 (pdf)
Subjects: LCSH: Ethnology—Italy—Venice—History. | Venice (Italy)—Foreign relations—1508–1797. | Venice (Italy)—Ethnic relations—History—17th century. | Ambassadors—Italy—Venice—Correspondence. | Venice (Italy)—Politics and government—1508–1797.
Classification: LCC GN585.I8 T38 2023 | DDC 305.800945/311—dc23/eng/20221021
LC record available at https://lccn.loc.gov/2022037177

A British Cataloging-in-Publication record for this book is available from the British Library.

udpress.udel.edu

Distributed worldwide by Rutgers University Press

ORDERING CUSTOMS

The Early Modern Exchange

SELECTED TITLES

The Waxing of the Middle Ages: Revisiting Late Medieval France, edited by Tracy Adams and Charles-Louis Morand-Métivier

Gendering the Renaissance: Text and Context in Early Modern Italy, edited by Meredith K. Ray and Lynn Lara Westwater

Storytelling in Sixteenth-Century France: Negotiating Shifting Forms, edited by Emily E. Thompson

England's Asian Renaissance, edited by Su Fang Ng and Carmen Nocentelli

Performative Polemic: Anti-Absolutist Pamphlets and Their Readers in Late Seventeenth-Century France, Kathrina Ann LaPorta

Innovation in the Italian Counter-Reformation, edited by Shannon McHugh and Anna Wainwright

Milton among Spaniards, Angelica Duran

The Dark Thread: From Tragical Histories to Gothic Tales, edited by John D. Lyons

Women Warriors in Early Modern Spain: A Tribute to Bárbara Mujica, edited by Susan L. Fischer and Frederick A. de Armas

For my parents, Joyce Hendy and Ronald Taylor

Contents

Acknowledgments

Over the many years this project has been in my life, I have incurred numerous intellectual, personal, and material debts. One of the pleasures of completing this book is the opportunity it provides to thank those who have supported me and this work along the way.

This book has benefited from conversations—some momentary, others sustained over years—with colleagues and friends kind enough to share their ideas with me. I would like especially to thank Beeta Baghoolizadeh, Warren Breckman, Kathy Brown, Tamara Buckley, Jackie Burek, Dan Cheely, Roger Chartier, John Christman, Surekha Davies, Lizzie Di Giacomo, Heidi Dodson, Antonio Feros, Smita Ghosh, Timothy Griffiths, Paul Guernsey, Rayne Jarvis, Carina Johnson, Janine Knedlik, Noria Litaker, Alex Logue, Salar Mohandasi, Maria Murphy, Alexis Neumann, Anthony Pratcher, Alex Ponsen, Kelsey Rice, Natalie Rothman, Amanda Scott, Jen Shook, Iuliia Skubytska, Leigh Soares, Holly Stevens, Kristian Taketomo, and Stefano Villani.

My deepest professional debts are to Ann Moyer, Margo Todd, and Ann Matter. As members of the dissertation committee that oversaw the earliest incarnation of this project, all three engaged scrupulously with my work. Their incisive comments shaped and improved the project. Ann Moyer has continued to be a source of professional and intellectual guidance. I am grateful to her for this and, quite simply, for teaching me how to be a historian.

The research and writing of this book were made possible by the support of the following institutions: the Social Sciences and Humanities Research Council, the Doris G. Quinn Foundation, the Humanities Institute at the Pennsylvania State University, and within the University of Pennsylvania, the Center for Italian Studies, Department of History, and Graduate School of Arts and Sciences.

During my time in Venice, I was grateful for the hospitality of Marino Zorzi and Rosella Mamoli and for the friendship of Alessandra Trasforini and

Michela Murialdo, both of whom taught me to appreciate and wonder at the twenty-first-century incarnation of the city.

I would like to thank the generous archivists, librarians, and staff at the Archivio di Stato di Venezia, the University of Pennsylvania Libraries, Biblioteca Ambrosiana, Biblioteca Nazionale Marciana, Biblioteca del Museo Correr, and the Pontifical Institute for Medieval Studies at the University of Toronto. For their patience and generosity, I owe special thanks to Orfea Granzotto, Elisabetta Lugato, Susy Marcon, John Pollack, and Elisabetta Sciarra.

It has been a pleasure working with the University of Delaware Press. I am especially grateful to Julia Oestreich, Gary Ferguson, Meredith Ray, and the press's two anonymous readers.

It was my good fortune that the final stages of this project were completed at the University of Tennessee at Chattanooga. Within UTC's Department of History, I have found a community of creative and thoughtful colleagues and friends. I am especially grateful to Jess Arnet, Eddie Brudney, Julia Cummisky, Susan Eckelmann Berghel, Fang Yu Hu, Will Kuby, Jaclyn Michael, Irven Resnick, Kira Robison, Annie Tracy Samuel, John Swanson, Mike Thompson, and Gerda Zinner. All of these colleagues were generous with their advice and helped smooth my transition to junior faculty member.

My wider Chattanooga community has also been a source of support and inspiration. I moved to Tennessee against the backdrop of a legislative assault on LGBTQ southerners—one that seeks to exclude trans people in particular from public and private life. The tenacity of the queer and trans people I've met who make the South their home has not only moved me, but it has also taught me important lessons about resistance, resilience, and home. Special thanks are due to Tegan Alsop and Al Sachs for welcoming me with such warmth to Tennessee. And above all to Mads Ledbetter for their love and for showing me what it means to make a home in a place that doesn't always love you back.

I am grateful for the support of my family, particularly Peter Taylor, Amelie Proulx, Sandra Proulx, Gary Hendy, George Hendy, Lise Hendi, Jinkx Taylor, Caroline Taylor, and Nancy Taylor. My parents, Joyce Hendy and Ron Taylor, have been an unwavering source of love and support.

Finally, this book would not exist without Rebekah Johnston. She has championed this project from the beginning and has been my most attentive reader and critic. For this and for the years of love, support, and crucially, joy she has brought to my life, I will be forever grateful.

Abbreviations

ASVe	Archivio di Stato di Venezia
b	*Busta* (Folder)
BAM	Biblioteca Ambrosiana
BCV	Biblioteca del Museo Correr
BNM	Biblioteca Nazionale Marciana
Ital	Manoscritti Italiani
Lt	Manoscritti Latini
proc	*Processo* (Trial, Proceedings)
reg	Registro
SU	Santo Ufficio
VS	Cinque Savi alla Mercanzia

Introduction

Early modern Venice provoked endless comment on the relationship of scale between city and world. This is a book about that relationship. When observers—Venetian and non-Venetian alike—reflected on what made Venice unique, one of their preferred topoi involved playing with the contrast between city and world. Venice, they claimed, was no ordinary city but rather a microcosm of the globe. Members of the patriciate—Venice's hereditary ruling elite—were especially flattered by this image of their city, and their clients were more than happy to appeal to patrician vanity. Addressing the Venetian patrician, historian, and diarist Marin Sanudo in 1498, the printer Aldo Manuzio proclaimed that their shared home was "a place more like an entire world than a city."[1] Over a century after Manuzio's remarks, observers continued to draw on the relationship between world and city. In 1611, the English traveler Thomas Coryate invoked the image of Venice as a world in miniature in his description of the Piazza San Marco, the city's principal square. "Here," he wrote, "you may both see all manner of fashions of attire, and heare all the languages of Christendome, besides those that are spoken by the barbarous Ethnickes. . . . A man may very properly call it rather Orbis than Urbis in forum, that is, a marketplace of the world, not of the citie."[2]

If Venetians and their city provoked seemingly endless comment from outsiders, Venetian thinkers were preoccupied with describing other places and their inhabitants near and far. Early modern Venetians were keenly interested in questions of what made the inhabitants of these places and their ways of life different from one another. Sixteenth-century Venetian observers not only foregrounded these questions in a new way, but they also answered them using a new vocabulary and a new conceptual framework. There emerged in sixteenth-century Venice a growing preoccupation with cultural accounts of human difference. Manifestations of this preoccupation can be seen not only in the products of the city's active print industry, which in the sixteenth and early seventeenth centuries published a spate of books describing the customs of the world's peoples to readers, but also in the reports of far-flung diplomats, the journals of young travelers, and the briefings of harried bureaucrats.

Ordering Customs takes as its subject the production and circulation of ethnographic knowledge in sixteenth- and early seventeenth-century Venice. The term *ethnographic* may seem strange when applied to an early modern context. We are used to thinking about ethnographic writing as a product of nineteenth-century European imperialism. Indeed, the term *ethnography* itself is a product of late eighteenth-century German thought.[3] Given that the term *ethnography* first appeared long after the period considered here, a word about my use of the term is in order. I use it to refer broadly to information about human cultures and social organization that is acquired by what is claimed to be empirical observation.

The insistence on empirical observation is particularly important, given that the sixteenth and early seventeenth centuries were a period during which the means of establishing ethnographic authority was in flux. In ethnographic knowledge—as in so many other areas of early modern knowledge—there was a tension between the weight that should be placed on direct observation versus information derived from written authorities.[4] This tension was never fully resolved. Venetians themselves engaged in vociferous debates about how ethnographic knowledge ought to be made and what sort of speakers could claim ethnographic expertise. Increasingly, they decided that eyewitness authority was to be privileged. In practice, though, the lines between direct observation and secondhand reading were often blurred.

Early modern Venetians employed a range of terms and phrases to describe the subject matter of their accounts of human cultures and social organization. Ethnography's literal meaning of "writing about peoples" makes it an efficient translator of the variety of terms in use at the time, including, in Italian, *modo di vivere* (way of life), *habiti* (habits), *usanze* (use or custom), *riti* (rites), and perhaps the most common, *costumi* (customs). These terms were blazoned across the pages of sixteenth- and early seventeenth-century books, advertising their ethnographic content to readers. By the 1570s, Venetian readers could purchase books promising to treat the costumi, riti, and usanze of the French, Spanish,

Turks, Peruvians, and in the particularly ambitious formulation of one author, all the world's peoples.[5] Sixteenth-century Europeans may not have had a single name or genre for descriptions of human societies, but they understood the practice of describing those societies to be a distinct kind of activity.

Today, ethnography finds its disciplinary home in anthropology, and indeed, the practice of ethnographic fieldwork is part of what lends anthropology its distinctive disciplinary identity. There was, however, no discipline of anthropology in the sixteenth century, nor would there be for another three centuries. Although the term *anthropology* has its origins in the sixteenth century, for educated sixteenth-century Europeans, the term had none of its modern connotations.[6] In his 1506 *Commentariorum urbanorum*, the humanist Raffaelle Maffei reserved the term *anthropologia* for the volume of his work containing an alphabetical catalog of "illustrious men of all ages, languages, and peoples."[7] The study of customs came to be a feature of a variety of disciplines. Part of the story told here is how, even in the absence of recognizable modern disciplinary boundaries, customs became a discrete and valued object of study in early modern Europe. Fluid disciplinary boundaries resulted in a situation in which there existed a wide variety of practitioners of ethnography in the early modern world.

Venetian Ethnography and Its Objects

As cross-cultural contact has moved to the core of scholarly debates about the late Middle Ages and early modern period, premodern ethnographic writing has captured the attention of historians and scholars of literature alike in recent years. Our understanding of premodern ethnography has been fundamentally shaped by the geographical remit of their studies, which have favored a narrow scope for the subjects of ethnographic descriptions coupled with a broad geographical scope for the origins of those descriptions. A number of recent studies have examined the representations of a single region of the world that took shape across Europe as a whole. In recent years, for example, we have the publication of studies of "European" representations of the Americas, Asia, and the Ottoman Empire.[8] *Ordering Customs* reverses this focus. It examines a single urban information hub that served as the center for the production and circulation of ethnographic knowledge touching on all parts of the globe.

The advantages of this approach are twofold. First, the Venetian case demonstrates clearly that ethnographic description did not develop simply from European encounters with a particular new group of people, nor did it develop from a more general fascination with the exotic or the marvelous. By focusing on the representations of specific extra-European regions, recent scholarship has not fully recognized the extent to which Europeans were simultaneously applying categories of ethnographic thought to Europe—including Western Europe—itself. Venetian authors and statesmen certainly had a great deal to say about the cultural alterity, for example, of the Ottoman Turks. Yet they were no less concerned with describing and accounting for the cultural differences that they perceived between Venetians, Germans, Spaniards, and Poles. This development was no accident; it was a product of Venetian diplomatic practice, which relied on ambassadors who served in brief, successive embassies in different states and were required to report in a uniform fashion on each of those states. Over the course of the sixteenth century, the imperative for ethnographic reporting came to be ingrained in the training of the elite young men who would serve as the state's representatives abroad. To understand the rise of ethnographic observation, it is necessary to understand the world of Venetian diplomacy that formed so much of its immediate context.

Second, the focus on a single urban center of communication permits a fine-grained analysis of the dynamics of the production and circulation of early modern ethnographic knowledge. Although some aspects of Venetian ethnography can be understood as part of the development of a pan-European set of practices for describing and accounting for cultural difference, many aspects were specific to Venice. In the Venetian case, the dynamics of ethnographic knowledge production were determined by the particularities of the Venetian political system, the intellectual and career ambitions of the elite group of men from which Venice drew its ambassadors, and the politics of diplomatic speech as a performance by and for men of the political class.

The Venetian case invites us to reconsider long-standing assumptions about the relationship between ethnography and empire. It encourages us to think about ethnography not only in terms of European colonization in Asia and the Americas but also in terms of diplomacy. Indeed, some of the most astute, prolific, and influential practitioners of ethnography in the early modern world were not adventurers, conquistadors, or missionaries but rather diplomats. Scholars of modern European imperialism have left us attuned to the ways in which ethnography was thoroughly imbricated in imperial fields of power. Yet, even scholars who push the concept of ethnography backward in time have long treated early modern voyages of conquest and discovery as the primary impetus in the development of European ethnography.[9] In their accounts, early modern ethnographic thought is taken to be the product of Europeans' shock upon encountering peoples with beliefs and practices radically incommensurate with their own. A language of ethnography was thus developed to account for those differences and render them orderly.

Research on the intellectual and cultural ramifications of European imperial expansion cannot fully account for the extensive body of Venetian ethnographic literature. Venetian ethnography was produced largely outside of a colonial context and was, as a rule, more concerned with describing and accounting for cultural differences among peoples closer to Venice. The Venetian example demonstrates that Europeans were very interested in understanding other European peoples (and themselves) through ethnographic frames. Scholars have long seen the fourteenth- and fifteenth-century Italian states as the birthplace of "modern" European diplomatic practice.[10] The late-medieval Italian states pioneered the practice of resident diplomacy. They increasingly relied on permanent ambassadors who remained at their posts until recalled as opposed to temporary envoys sent for a finite period to complete a specific piece of business. Along with an expansion of resident diplomacy came new forms of diplomatic communication. Venetian diplomats, in particular, integrated ethnographic description into their official reports. The long history and broad geographical extent of Venice's diplomatic network by the sixteenth century was a key factor in the development of Venetian ethnographic writing. It is easy to miss this feature of early modern ethnographic thought when ethnography is studied solely through the lens of empire.

This immediate diplomatic context for so much Venetian ethnographic writing made Venetian ethnography fundamentally different from ethnographic reporting in colonial settings. Such writing was embedded in very different fields of power. The diplomats who so often cataloged Turkish, English, or German customs did so in a context in which they were the supplicants to the peoples hosting them rather than the imperial rulers of subjugated peoples. Venice was the center of an eastern Mediterranean empire, but its colonies did not serve as its chief laboratories for the production of ethnographic knowledge. Venetian ethnographic writing helps us think differently about the origins of early modern ethnography. In Venice, they lay in the city's commercial connections in the eastern Mediterranean, in the development of Venetian diplomatic practice, and at another level, in the daily reality of Venetians' coexistence in a religiously and ethnically diverse city.

Ordering Customs focuses on why Venetians believed the project of ethnographic observation to be a worthwhile one, the role ethnographic knowledge played in Venetian intellectual life, and the uses to which ethnographic information was put. As a result, the focus of this project is not on the content of ethnographic observation per se. To be sure, there were shifts over time in the ethnographic representations of specific societies. These shifts, which occurred in both Venice and Europe more broadly, have been explored productively by scholars in the past two decades.[11]

There are, in short, new and valuable insights into premodern ethnography, its origins, dynamics, and functions to be gained by approaching the subject through a new geographical framework. Venice is an ideal focus for such a study. By virtue of its large printing industry, its extensive diplomatic network, and its status as a major port for the movement of people and goods between the Mediterranean and northern Europe, Venice was an important center of information and communication in early modern Europe. While these very factors obviously made Venice a distinctive case within the early modern world, they also meant that the city had a unique cultural influence.

Venice and the Early Modern Information Order

Venice held a privileged position in the early modern information order. In the realm of print, its central position in both Europe and Italy in the late fifteenth and sixteenth centuries is clear. Incunable catalogs reveal that Italian printers were responsible for 35–41 percent of the volume of printed works in the fifteenth century and that Venetian printers held 40 percent of the Italian share.[12] All told, through the fifteenth century, more books were printed in Venice than in any other European city.[13] Venetian printers were also important in pioneering the printing of books not purely for local markets but for a geographically dispersed readership.[14] Through much of the sixteenth century, Venice retained this important position in publishing, particularly vis-à-vis other Italian cities. As Mario Infelise's detailed figures show, Venice's share of Italian print output peaked in the 1540s, when Venetian printers were responsible for 59.54 percent of titles. There was, however, a period of relative decline in the second half of the sixteenth century, as printers in other Italian cities expanded their local industries. By the 1590s, the Venetian share had declined steadily to 31.89 percent.[15] To put these figures in perspective, Venice's nearest Italian competitor, Rome, fluctuated between 9 and 16 percent of the Italian total during the same period. In Europe as a whole, Venice appears to have maintained its fifteenth-century role. Ugo Rozzo estimates that Venice produced fifty thousand to sixty thousand editions in the sixteenth century, out of a European total of approximately four hundred thousand.[16]

Venice's important position in the history of print production—both on the Italian Peninsula and in Europe more generally—has, of course, long been recognized. Print, however, does not exhaust Venice's role in the early modern European information order. As recent work on early modern communication emphasizes, print was but one strand in a network of communication that also included oral and manuscript transmission.[17] This is why, following Peter Burke, I deliberately refer to Venice using the more capacious phrase "center of information and communication" rather than describing it as merely a center of print.[18]

In addition to early modern printed ethnographic literature, this project draws on a wide range of archival and manuscript sources, including court records, diplomatic communication, the records of the magistracies charged with overseeing foreign merchants in the city, library inventories, and the private diaries, travel journals, and correspondence of government officials and colonial administrators. Some of these sources, such as the series of Venetian ambassadorial reports and inquisitorial court records, are well known to scholars of the period but have yet to be analyzed for what they reveal about the development of ethnographic thought; others, such as the large body of unpublished Venetian diplomatic travel journals, have received little attention. Consulting a wide range of archival and manuscript sources was necessary in order to produce a grounded history of the production and circulation of ethnographic knowledge. Although printed travel literature has served as the point of entry for many studies of the history of ethnography, treating this literature alongside manuscript and archival sources makes it possible to examine the social formations and institutional contexts in which ethnographic discourses were articulated and circulated in early modern Venice. The use of manuscript and archival sources has permitted me to address key questions that would not have been possible to address through printed sources alone, including the manner in which early modern readers acquired ethnographic knowledge and put it to use and the role that ethnographic literature played in the education of elite Venetian men. Ultimately, the production of ethnographic knowledge was closely tied to the institutions of the Venetian state, and this is partly how it is studied here—through the archival records of those institutions.

No study of early modern ethnography can afford to ignore printed works, as these interacted with, shaped, and were shaped by lived experience, empirical observation, and oral and manuscript communication. When it came to the production of ethnographic knowledge, the print-manuscript-orality interface could be as simple as a Venetian diplomatic secretary circulating his ethnographic observations in manuscript among a closed circle of Venetian elites before opting to have them printed for a wider readership. This, for example, was the case with the Venetian diplomatic secretary Benedetto Ramberti's account of Turkish customs and society, the *Libri tre delle cose de Turchi*, whose genesis will be discussed in chapter 3.

This interface, however, also worked in subtler and more complicated ways, as printed ethnographic accounts gradually came to condition their readers' horizons of expectation. Venetian travelers read widely in both print and manuscript, and they did so in an environment awash with ethnographic information. Their sense of themselves and their role as travelers and observers was inevitably conditioned by this reading. The observations relayed to a Venetian patrician regarding the inhabitants of Val Camonica, a mountain valley north of Brescia, gives us a sense of this complexity. Writing in 1518, Lodovico Querini's correspondent, Giuseppe da Orzinuovi, could think of no better way to render intelligible the customs of these far-flung Venetian subjects than by invoking, on the one hand, the cultural gulf that existed between Europeans and Indians and, on the other hand, mythological accounts of witchcraft that had been handed down to him from classical antiquity. Val Camonica, he wrote,

> is more mountain than valley, more sterile than fertile, and inhabited by people who are for the most part more ignorant than anything else, people afflicted with goiter, almost all of them with the grossest deformations and without any rule of civil life. Their customs are most frequently rustic and wild; rare are those who are familiar with, let alone observe, the commandments of the Lord. One can say that in a sense there is as much difference between these valley folk and the other inhabitants of the Brescian territory as there is between the Portuguese and the people of Colocut. Rumor has it that there have been warlocks and witches here for some years, which there used to be in the time of Medea in Thessaly, as the authorities write.[19]

In another layer of complexity, historians today are able to access Orzinuovi's observations because they were recorded in the diary of Marin Sanudo.[20] Sanudo was himself a great annotator and collector of travel writing, and his diaries reveal him to have had a keen interest in ethnographic information.[21] Although they are usually prized as a rich source for the study of governance in early sixteenth-century Venice, Sanudo's diaries also reveal much about the channels through which news and information flowed in sixteenth-century Venice and the processes by which patricians sought to evaluate the reliability of that information.[22]

As the writings preserved in Sanudo's diary suggest, the distinctive structure of Venice's social hierarchy shaped the ways in which Venetians acquired, organized, and made sense of ethnographic information. A final level of complexity was added by what Jutta Sperling deems the "synecdochical identification" of patricians and, we might add, citizens with the Venetian state.[23] When patricians and citizens outlined the social hierarchy of their city, they most often reached for a tripartite division, describing a body politic composed of nobles, citizens, and the *popolo*, or common people.[24] Patricians ruled as a caste defined by birth. Deliberative and judicial powers and the right to hold many offices—including the ambassadorial offices that became so important in the development of Venetian ethnography—were restricted to men of patrician birth. One of the by-products of this system of rule, as recent studies show, was that the ruling patricians went to great lengths to control the circulation of information in the city.[25] Although these efforts to circumscribe the flow of information were ultimately unsuccessful, they shaped how Venetians of all social locations accessed and evaluated ethnographic information in the sixteenth and early seventeenth centuries.

As scholars have long recognized, Venice played a singular role in the gathering, filtering, and repackaging of the information that western Europeans received about the Ottoman world.[26] Just as the Jesuits would serve as the major information conduit between Europe and East Asia in the later sixteenth century, Venice occupied a similar position vis-à-vis the Ottoman and Safavid worlds in the early decades of the century.[27] Owing to a centuries-long history of commercial contacts with Byzantine and then Ottoman Constantinople, Venice had denser and more enduring contacts with the Ottoman world than did other European states. Venetian merchants and diplomats were simply present on the ground in greater numbers and could draw on more durable institutions and channels of communication than could other Europeans. Before the French Crown began sending a permanent diplomatic representative to the Ottoman court in 1535, for instance, Venice was the only major state with a permanent diplomatic presence in Istanbul.[28]

Several factors determined the sixteenth-century starting point for this study, some of which are specific to Venice, others of which are demonstrably part of broader European developments. The first of these factors has to do with shifts in how Europeans understood the very meaning of customs. It was in the sixteenth century that the meaning of customs began to change to resemble our own modern anthropological conception. This shift, which will be explored in the first chapter, was in turn accompanied by a growing tendency by European thinkers to treat customs as a discrete object of study. There were, to be sure, medieval travel narratives that included descriptions of customs, but these works saw their meanings recast in an age of print.[29] At times, this recasting was the result of deliberate editorial intervention as sixteenth-century scholars began applying humanist editorial techniques to travel narratives, including those of medieval Venetian authors. In his edition of Marco Polo's *Divisament dou monde*, for example, the Venetian secretary Giovanni Battista Ramusio sought to bolster the reputation of his countryman's narrative—just as he would do for more contemporary accounts of foreign customs (see chapter 3).[30] The sheer scale of available texts played an even more important role in resituating medieval accounts. Print enabled readers and editors to amass, compare, and rearrange texts in a way that foregrounded their ethnographic content. The sixteenth century saw the first appearance of systematic and comparative treatments of customs, a development facilitated both by the greater availability of printed travel literature and the availability of that material in new formats that facilitated comparative reading.

The changing economic, political, and cultural fortunes of Venice itself also determined the chronological parameters of my study. In the early sixteenth century, as we have seen, Venice enjoyed a status as a major center of information and communication in the early modern world. Many of the same factors that made Venice such a center were present in earlier centuries. Venice's diplomatic network, however, which was so closely linked to the production of Venetian ethnographic knowledge, was largely a product of the last decade of the fifteenth century. Apart from the office of the bailo, the permanent diplomatic representative of the Venetian state to the Ottoman court, in Istanbul—a special case that will be discussed in chapter 2—Venice's permanent diplomatic missions outside of the Italian Peninsula date largely from the 1490s. Venice sent its first resident ambassador to France in 1478, to Spain and the Holy Roman Empire in 1495, and to England in 1496.[31] At the turn of the sixteenth century, Venice was unparalleled in Europe in the reach of its diplomatic network, which stretched from England to the Safavid Empire. The city's status as a center of information, coupled with the breadth of its diplomatic coverage, lent Venetian ethnographic writing a weighted influence beyond the borders of the republic.

This study ends in the early seventeenth century for a similar set of reasons. Developments elsewhere in Europe meant that, by that point, Venice no longer held a privileged position in the production and circulation of ethnographic knowledge. By the time *Ordering Customs* closes, many of the factors that had made the city a unique center of information and communication in the early sixteenth century were either no longer present or were widely shared with other cities. Just as scholars have debated the chronology and scale of Venice's economic decline, so too have they debated the nature and timeline of the decline of the Venetian print industry. Scholars are now apt to place the decline of Venetian printing further back than they once did, at the end of the long cinquecento, a period that concluded with the devastating plague of 1630.[32] What is certain is that, in relative terms, the city played a less significant role in European print in the seventeenth century than it had previously. Venice continued to be the dominant city in the Italian Peninsula for print production, but its role would be less outstanding as print production came to be more widely distributed geographically.

The city's decline as a singular center of ethnographic knowledge went beyond the print industry. Changes in the diplomatic practices of other European states also stripped Venice of its unique status. Over the course of the sixteenth century, other European powers established permanent embassies throughout Europe, including in the Ottoman Empire, where the Venetians had for so long served as privileged diplomatic operatives. With permanent embassies came myriad opportunities for ethnographic observation and reporting. The bailo was joined in Istanbul by a French resident ambassador in 1535, an English ambassador in 1583, and a Dutch ambassador in 1612.[33] As in the Venetian case, many of the major early modern French authorities on the Ottoman Empire, including Nicolas de Nicolay, Pierre Belon, André Thevet, and Guillaume Postel traveled to Istanbul on diplomatic missions. By the mid-seventeenth century, Venice had begun to lose its singular place in the early modern European information order. Even the Venetian diplomatic sources that had so long been valued by readers abroad as privileged sources of information on foreign peoples and states were read less and less outside the republic's borders.[34] Venetians, like other Europeans, would of course continue to write ethnographies and think in ethnographic terms, but they would no longer be at the fore of developments in ethnographic thought.[35]

Ordering Customs is structured thematically, with each chapter examining a different facet of the production and circulation of ethnographic knowledge in early modern Venice. The first chapter addresses the fundamental questions of what contemporaries understood the term *customs* to mean and why they deemed customs worthy of study. Over the course of the sixteenth century,

Europeans' understanding of the meaning of customs became more capacious, gradually stretching to resemble our own anthropological conception of the term. At the same time, in the Venetian context, a consensus emerged that the knowledge of foreign customs was crucial for future statesmen, particularly if they hoped to serve as diplomats.

The second chapter examines the place of ethnography in the hallmark genre of Venetian diplomacy, the ambassadorial *relazione*, or final report. In the world of early modern diplomacy, Venice was not only distinctive for the sheer number of permanent representatives it sent abroad. The republic was also unique among European states in requiring its ambassadors to deliver a relazione on the states in which they had served. The reports were widely read both within the Venetian republic and beyond its borders and served as models for other forms of ethnographic reporting. While relazioni were intended to assist statesmen in making judicious decisions in matters of foreign policy, over the course of the sixteenth century, ambassadors devoted increasing attention to ethnographic topics, including the customs, religious observances, foodways, and dress of the states in which they served. The new emphasis on ethnographic reporting was as much a product of the literary and career ambitions of ambassadors as it was a reflection of the perceived political utility of ethnographic knowledge. The shift in the nature of diplomatic reporting did not go unnoticed by contemporaries, engendering a vigorous debate about both the parameters of political knowledge and the nature and reliability of eyewitness versus textual authority.

The ambassadorial relazione serves as a clear example of the Venetian state's involvement in ethnographic knowledge making. Chapter 3 addresses the role of state in the production of ethnography more broadly, arguing that the early modern Venetian state assumed a central role in sponsoring, enabling, and conferring authority on the production of ethnographic knowledge. The question of what kinds of claims could legitimately be made regarding the cultural practices of foreign peoples and what kinds of speakers could pronounce those claims with authority was a significant one in the sixteenth century. It was also a matter in which the Venetian state found occasion to intervene. The chapter begins with a case study of the reception of Ludovico de Varthema, perhaps the most famous European traveler to India in the early sixteenth century and a self-styled authority on the customs of East Asia and the Indian subcontinent. Although many of his contemporaries cast doubts on the veracity of his written account of his travels, he enjoyed the early patronage of the Venetian state. Over the course of the sixteenth century, his reputation was gradually rehabilitated.

The revaluation of Varthema's work was the fruit of intervention by Venetian editors and printers, including those who were themselves in the employ of the state. Ultimately, this case demonstrates the ways in which the recognition of the Venetian state, coupled with Venice's status as a center of print and information, could have a lasting impact on an author's reputation. The chapter then examines the practice of diplomatic-educational travel and its textual legacy. Accompanying an ambassador on a diplomatic mission was a traditional component of the political education of young Venetian men of the governing class. As part of their educational experience, diplomatic travelers were encouraged to keep journals recording their voyages and their observations of the lands and peoples they encountered. These travel journals, like the ambassadorial relazioni on which they were modeled, came to foreground ethnographic reporting. Although diplomatic-educational travelers were not legally required to keep travel journals, their journals nevertheless enjoyed a quasi-official status, with several such journals being seized by the Venetian state for preservation in the republic's archive.

Chapter 4 examines how ethnography was read and understood in early modern Venice and its empire. The question is a central one for the study of premodern ethnography since, in the absence of a dedicated genre of ethnography, ethnographic information was embedded in a variety of genres that could be read in very different ways. Through the analysis of the material aspects of numerous manuscript and print works, I demonstrate that readers employed strategies that allowed them to read selectively for ethnographic information. These strategies left material evidence in readers' libraries in the form of marginal annotations, handwritten indexes, and commonplace books. Printers, too, increasingly strove to accommodate readers' interest in foreign customs through the inclusion of paratextual apparatuses to facilitate consultative reading. Despite the growing availability of ethnographic works in print, Venetian readers, particularly those at the highest levels of society, exhibited a decided preference for manuscript accounts of foreign customs, a tendency that is on first glance surprising given Venice's central role in the history of print. These readers favored manuscript accounts—which circulated in a circumscribed and, importantly, noncommercial form—precisely because they afforded their community of readers access to a privileged body of knowledge.

This introduction began with a discussion of the early modern image of Venice as a microcosm of the globe. The final chapter returns to this microcosmical Venice—defined by its religious and ethnic diversity—and asks what role ethnography played in its governance. It examines how the on-the-ground deployment of ethnographic knowledge shaped the fate of religious minorities in the city. Contemporaries rarely failed to remark on the religious and ethnic diversity of the city's population. The Venetian state strove to accommodate foreigners and, in some cases, even competed to attract them to the city in an effort to support their involvement in commerce. At the same time, however, the government sought to impose religious order by mandating the residential segregation of certain religious minorities. Venice has the dubious distinction of being the site of the first compulsory Jewish ghetto, the quincentennial of which was observed as I was researching *Ordering Customs*. By the end of the sixteenth century, the Venetian government had devised a similar scheme for the residential segregation of Muslim merchants from the Ottoman Empire, which was also the first arrangement of its kind in Europe. Decisions concerning the design and management of these spaces were weighed carefully by Venetian officials, who showed a great willingness to defer on these matters to individuals who claimed ethnographic expertise. The chapter then examines the role of ethnographic knowledge in the court proceedings of the Venetian Inquisition. Inquisitorial records document some of the rare instances in which a wide range of Venetians were invited to reflect on cultural difference and its significance. The tribunal's function as a forum for the articulation of cultural difference was especially pronounced in cases of contested religious identity. In such cases, witnesses were called on to speculate about the religious identity of the accused and, in the process, to cite evidence for their speculations. The analysis of these cases reveals the existence of an entirely different source of ethnographic knowledge—the reality of daily life in a religiously and ethnically diverse early modern city—that complemented, and occasionally conflicted with, traditional bodies of ethnographic knowledge.

As a midsize Mediterranean power, excluded from European empire-building in Asia and the Americas, Venice has not been a traditional starting point for the history of ethnography. Taken together, though, these chapters suggest how that history might be written differently when viewed with a new lens and from different shores. As cross-cultural contact has come to be seen as a defining feature of the early modern period, it is imperative that we examine the fundamental early modern assumptions underpinning that contact. The study of the production and circulation of ethnographic knowledge allows us to do just that. Contact between Europeans and non-Europeans was, of course, not new to the early modern period. By the sixteenth century, Venetians, like many other Europeans, had a centuries-long history of ties to peoples beyond Europe forged through commerce, diplomacy, and war. It was only in the sixteenth century, however, that Venetians began systematically producing, reading, and learning from ethnographic descriptions. What the study of the Venetian case reveals is that far from being the natural or inevitable result of cross-cultural encounter, ethnography needed to be made; it was the product of a complicated set of historical contingencies. Ethnography responded to preexisting divisions between religious, ethnic, and linguistic communities, but it also sharpened those divisions, worked to create new ones, and ultimately shaped their political significance.

CHAPTER ONE

The Study of Customs

In 1497, Andrea de Franceschi, a young assistant diplomatic secretary traveling abroad, wrote to his friend at home in Venice about the importance of observing foreign customs. "We were able to observe," he wrote, "so many varied and different sorts of people, so many ways of life of both men and women, that I doubt if I shall ever examine a more comprehensive survey. And the result of seeing such a variety of things and diversity of customs is that even men of low intelligence soon become quick-witted."[1] Franceschi proceeded to regale his friend with accounts of the local diet, dining customs, and variations in gendered comportment. If we understand the term *ethnographic* to refer broadly to information about human cultures and social organization acquired by what is claimed to be empirical observation, then Franceschi was engaging in a species of ethnographic observation and reporting. What is noteworthy about Franceschi's letter is that the twenty-four-year-old's ethnographic reflections were occasioned not by a voyage to the New World or Asia or North Africa but rather a journey from Trent to London that took him overland through Germany and the Low Countries.

Franceschi's brief comments underscore two important features of Venetian ethnographic thought. First, that the study of customs and the comparative treatment of customs were seen as serving an important didactic function, particularly for those who worked, or aspired to work, in the service of the Venetian state. Second, Franceschi's comments reveal that in the sixteenth century, the study of customs was as likely to be directed at other European peoples as it was at non-Europeans. Neither of these features was particular to Venetian ethnographic thought, but both were especially pronounced in Venice owing to the close relationship between Venetian diplomatic culture and the development of ethnographic thought.

These two features of early modern ethnographic thought are easy to miss when ethnography is studied chiefly through the lens of overseas empire. Scholars of ethnographic and travel literature were long disappointed by what they saw as the insufficiently rigorous nature of Europeans' writings about other peoples before the sixteenth century.[2] In her influential early work on the prehistory of anthropology, Margaret Hodgen notes rightly that European encounters with the wider world were not new to the sixteenth century. She does little to veil her disappointment with medieval authors for failing to draw on this firsthand information about extra-European peoples in order to create a body of anthropological literature. "One of the problems for the historian of European ideas," writes Hodgen, "is to account for the backwardness of ethnological thought [in the Middle Ages] despite sustained contact with non-Europeans."[3]

Hodgen's assessment here rests on a pair of widely held assumptions. She assumes first that the experience of encountering cultural practices different from one's own must be one of inherent shock; as an extension, the impulse to record and account for divergent practices ought to be innate and universal.[4] Second, Hodgen assumes that late medieval and early modern Europe itself was so culturally homogenous that only encounters with non-Europeans would provide such stimulus. The Venetian case reveals that neither of these two assumptions holds in any straightforward manner. Ethnographic observation was neither the natural nor inevitable outcome of cross-cultural contact. The idea that cultural differences mattered, that they ought to be described, and that they had a larger import is an idea with a history that can be productively explored. Indeed, it was often European peoples themselves, both ancient and modern, who served as the object of study in sixteenth-century ethnographic writing.

What Were Customs?

Throughout the sixteenth century, the term *custom* and its equivalents (the most common being costume in Italian and *mos* and *consuetudo* in Latin) were used in a variety of distinct yet intersecting ways—at times within the same text. The oldest and most enduring meaning of custom was primarily a juridical one, referring to the notion of unwritten law.[5] Whereas we and, indeed, most sixteenth-century authors tend to locate custom at the collective level, custom could also be used to refer to individual behavior and predispositions. When Giorgio Vasari, for example, wrote of the costumi of individual artists (usually their *buoni* or *ottimi costumi*), what he was evaluating was their mannerliness and refined behavior. Thus, we learn that Raphael had particularly "buoni & ottimi costumi" as a result of his father's decision to have him spend his early years at home rather than with a wet nurse.[6] This was also a usage that appeared frequently in Venetian ambassadorial reports when ambassadors discussed the person of the ruler. In his discussion of the future Queen Elizabeth, Giacomo Soranzo, the returning ambassador to England, reported approvingly that she was not only accomplished in Latin, Greek, French, Spanish, and Italian but was also "of modest and humane customs."[7] Over the course of the sixteenth century, the meaning of custom broadened. The juridical conception of custom persisted into the sixteenth century but became relatively less common. Gradually, the use of custom to refer to a complex of cultural practices came to supersede other concurrent usages—a development that was a function of the increasing availability and influence of ethnographic literature.

The notion of custom as a form of unwritten law derived from popular consensus that in turn served as the source for written law had a long pedigree. Gratian's *Decretum* (ca. 1150) included discussion of the sources of law, one of the most prominent of which was custom. Custom (consuetudo) was defined by Gratian as "a sort of law established by usages and recognized as ordinance when ordinance is lacking" (C.5 §1).[8] Custom, he added, "is so called because it is in common use. What is put in writing is called enactment or law, while what is not collected in writing is called by the general term 'custom'" (C.5 §3).[9] Although this usage of custom was elaborated most fully in juridical literature, it also had a place in medieval travel literature. Writing less than a century after Gratian, the thirteenth-century Franciscan envoy of Pope Innocent IV, Giovanni da Pian del Carpine, used "custom" primarily in the sense of unwritten law. Custom, for Giovanni, was not a broader category encompassing all cultural practices of a given people. His written account of his journey through the Mongol dominion tellingly includes a chapter on the Mongols' "laws and customs" ("De legibus et consuetudinibus eorum"). In it, Giovanni uses "customs" almost exclusively in a legal sense, treating the word roughly as a synonym for unwritten law. In a representative treatment of the Mongols' practice of executing adulterous men and women, for example, he writes, "[The Mongols] have this law or custom that whatsoever man or woman be manifestly taken in adultery, they are punished with death."[10] Medieval accounts such as Giovanni da Pian del

Carpine's certainly continued to be read in the sixteenth century. Indeed, in many instances, they came to reach a much wider audience through print circulation. Giovanni's account, for example, first appeared in print in Venice in 1537, where it was published by the same family of publishers who had earlier published the second Italian translation of Hernán Cortés's account of the conquest of Mexico.[11] As medieval travel accounts found a new readership, it is unsurprising that the use of "custom" to refer primarily to the realm of politics and law persisted into the sixteenth century. A continued readership for medieval writings ensured that a juridical conception of custom would continue to have purchase. Vestiges of the medieval usage can be seen in sixteenth-century geographical writing. The Aquilani geographer Giulio Cesare de Solis, for example, employed the term *customs* in his comparison of the Venetian and Ragusan legal and political regimes. The Ragusans, he wrote, "are free and live in a republican fashion; and in customs and law they conform with the great city of Venice."[12] He explicated this claim of correspondence between the two cities by noting that as in Venice, the Ragusan republic was governed exclusively by the city's nobility and that non-nobles did not concern themselves with public affairs. Clearly, de Solis understood "customs" to refer to a broad constellation of cultural practices but in a more restricted fashion to the ways in which the two republics were governed.

Custom in the sense of law can also be found in sixteenth-century Venetian diplomatic writings. It was, for example, this older juridical conception of custom that the ambassador Girolamo Lippomano drew on in his 1575 report following his mission to Poland. Since the laws of a state naturally fell within the purview of an ambassadorial report, Lippomano suggested, it followed that ambassadors should also address the customs of the state in their reports, given that "laws were nothing other than written customs."[13] Revealingly, he followed this remark up with a discussion of the idiosyncrasies of Polish statutes governing homicide, many of which were, in Lippomano's estimation, legal relics retained from "the earliest barbarian times."[14]

The innovation of the sixteenth century lay in the expansion of the meaning of "custom." In the hands of sixteenth-century authors, the term became much more capacious, eventually stretching to something resembling our own anthropological conception of the term. The Venetian subject Luigi Bassano's mid-century treatise on "the customs and particular ways of life of the Turks," provides a revealing example of the shift. Bassano divided the work into fifty-nine brief chapters, each treating a different aspect of Turkish society and culture. The content of Bassano's chapters ranged from sleep habits to bathing customs to dress and care of the body to the rituals accompanying death to games and pastimes.[15]

Why Study Customs?

In touting the benefits of their works to readers, sixteenth-century authors and editors of travel literature drew on a set of shared arguments. Firsthand experience of foreign travel, they agreed, offered the traveler innumerable moral and intellectual benefits, not least of which was the ability to observe and gain familiarity with customs different from those of his homeland. As Michel de Montaigne memorably rendered this injunction in "On the Education of Children," the ultimate purpose of travel was not "merely for the sake of recording, as our French nobles do, the exact measurements of the Holy Rotunda, or the embroidery on Signora Livia's drawers, or of noting, like some others, how much longer or broader the face of Nero is on some old ruin than on a medal of equal antiquity, but for the principal purpose of discovering the characteristics and customs of the different nations, and of rubbing and polishing our wits on those of others."[16] For many Europeans, though, opportunities to rub wits with foreigners were limited. Since the great expense and significant perils associated with travel made such journeys feasible only for the few, travelers and cosmographers offered their accounts to the legions of armchair readers at home so that they, too, might reap the benefits of travel. Sixteenth-century authors saw both moral and practical advantages to the study of customs.

Familiarity with a variety of customs, writer after writer agreed, offered the reader or traveler a mirror in which he could critically examine the customs of his own nation—a process that created opportunities for emulating the worthy customs of foreign nations. The then nineteen-year-old Andrea de Franceschi joined the Venetian mission to congratulate Frederick III on the conclusion of the recent war in Bavaria as the assistant to the mission's secretary.[17] Like many other men who traveled as part of Venetian diplomatic missions, Franceschi, whose comments on the utility of the study of custom began this chapter, kept a journal documenting his journey (see chapter 3). In it, he recorded observations on the dress, food and dining customs, linguistic particularities, and variations in gendered comportment in the regions he visited. In 1497, writing to a friend to whom he had sent a copy of his journal, Franceschi extolled the ways in which exposure to a variety of customs created the opportunity for emulation. "There can scarcely be anyone," he wrote, "who, by picking out the best and worst of all he sees, will not quickly form sensible habits of life and improved virtues. And so . . . I have decided to compile a little book containing descriptions of every town or fort that I saw, together with the ways of life and government characteristic of them."[18]

For Franceschi and other recorders of foreign customs, firsthand experience of foreign countries was the ideal way to gain familiarity with those customs, but armchair travelers like Franceschi's friend might also benefit from the study of foreign customs. Franceschi exhorted the recipient of his journal to "read it over and over again; for, if you have not had the opportunity to see for yourself and study all that this report describes, you may get the same pleasure from reading it as if you had been on the spot with us."[19] Along similar lines, Johannes Boemus, the German humanist and author of the first major printed ethnographic compendium, the *Omnium gentium mores, leges et ritus*, offered his readers the metaphor of the global variety of customs as a mirror through which they might examine and improve their own. In his address to the reader, Boemus explains that he had fashioned a collection of "customs and habits, both ancient and modern, both good and wicked," so that his readers "as though in a mirror . . . would be able to imitate the good examples and avoid the wicked."[20]

For Boemus and Franceschi, the benefits afforded by the study of customs were primarily individual rather than communal; the gains they promised would accrue to the individual reader. There was, however, also a cosmopolitan impulse in certain sixteenth-century justifications for the study and contemplation of foreign customs. For example, Nicolas de Nicolay, the French royal geographer and author of an account of his journey to Istanbul, suggested broader, social benefits. Like many other authors of travel accounts, Nicolay began his *Quatres premiers livres des navigations* with a reflection on the purpose and utility of travel. For Nicolay, one of the most laudable benefits of travel (and, by extension, the armchair experience of travel he offered readers) was the mutual knowledge and exchange of customs. This process of exchange and emulation, observed throughout history, would gradually lead to the widespread emendation of customs:[21] "Through such travel and communication, all the diverse nations of the world become tame and familiarize themselves with one another, mutually emending barbarous vices, also teaching each other true religion, virtues, and civil and political morals. . . . Through such reciprocal visitation, cognizance, and communicative alliance they remove that arrogant presumption usurped from the Greeks and Romans of holding and calling another man or another nation more barbarous than oneself and one's own nation."[22] Whatever moral gains, either individual or communal, the study of customs afforded readers, it also promised a more concrete set of benefits. A consensus emerged in the sixteenth century that effective service as a statesman required knowledge of foreign customs, particularly for those individuals whose work would take them into the world of diplomacy. Although Venetian authors and editors agreed with their European counterparts about the moral benefit of studying customs, there was a marked Venetian emphasis on the argument that the study of customs was of practical benefit to future statesmen. The axiom that experience with and knowledge of foreign customs was a necessary complement to the education of statesmen had special resonance in Venice, which was not only dependent on foreign trade but also a middling state in political and military terms. This made effective diplomacy crucial to its political and economic fortunes. The knowledge of foreign customs was of obvious benefit to future ambassadors and those who would assist them.

Olaus Magnus, the future titular archbishop of Uppsala, certainly assumed that his audience of Venetian patricians would appreciate such a connection between diplomacy, governance, and the study of customs. During his time in Venice, Olaus enjoyed the patronage of the patriarch, Girolamo Querini, in whose palace he stayed while in the city. In Venice, Olaus dedicated himself to completing his magisterial map of northern Europe, known as the *Carta marina*, and an accompanying explanatory text, which detailed the customs of northern Europeans.[23] The 1539 work would eventually form the basis for his *Historia de gentibus septentrionalibus*, which served as the authoritative work on northern Europe through the seventeenth century.[24] The *Carta marina* was a work with both deliberately Venetian and deliberately international dimensions. In Venice, Olaus and his enterprising Venetian printer, Giovanni Tommaso, published two printed vernacular commentaries on the map—the first in Italian and the second in German for export across the Alps. The *Carta marina* itself contained little text, but it did contain letters directing readers to the relevant sections of Olaus's commentary, thus rendering the map suitable for sale in different vernacular markets.[25]

Stamped by its Venetian origin, the Italian-language commentary contained a dedicatory epistle by Olaus praising the doge and senators for their wisdom in sponsoring the production of geographical knowledge. Olaus addressed the doge, Pietro Lando, and the body of senators, praising the Venetians for their commitment to the study of history and geography—the two disciplines he believed to be most intimately tied to the governance of a republic.[26] In Olaus's view, the most prudent rulers—including presumably those of the Venetian republic—were not only students of history and geography but sponsors of ethnographic knowledge in their own right. "For who," he asked, "is better suited to be placed in charge of kingdoms and nations than he who has seen for himself the customs and cities of many men. For this reason, those most ancient and prudent princes of the earth, with great care and expense, sent many envoys through diverse regions of the world, so that they might fully investigate the customs of those lands which [the rulers themselves] could not visit."[27] Here, Olaus concurred with other authorities, including many Venetian writers, that the knowledge of foreign customs ranked among the most valuable things a reader could derive from works of history. Writing just two years earlier, Francesco Marcolini, the Venetian publisher of Mafio Priuli's *Copia di una lettera venuta d'India,* made such a claim to readers. "It is the opinion of wise men," he wrote in his dedicatory epistle to the patriarch of Aquileia, Alvise Giustiniano, "that the knowledge of history, especially that history describing the life and customs of peoples, in addition to the pleasure that may be derived from it, is of the greatest utility and a thing that is a most worthy thing for every person who has his mind open to the rays of virtue."[28]

Authors and editors such as Olaus and Marcolini expertly played on the conceits of Venetian patrician identity. Venetian patricians themselves had long seen the familiarity with foreign customs as a quintessential part of patrician education, and they were apt to read these educational practices into the past. In so doing, they suggested that in an era marked by growing recognition of the importance of cross-cultural contact and an interest in the customs of others, Venetians stood as precocious forerunners of those developments. In his *De magistratibus et republica venetorum,* the Venetian ambassador and future cardinal Gasparo Contarini described the intellectual benefits and opportunities for knowledge production furnished by patricians' historical involvement in long-distance maritime trade:

> For the manner of educating noblemen was such that from their tender years through adolescence, they were under the discipline of a tutor and instructed in Latin letters according to their abilities. And from that age on (with the exception for those few who, led by their genius and nature, devoted themselves to the study of letters), all were to apply themselves to maritime and family affairs. And those others who navigated to distant shores, where they augmented their domestic affairs through the industry of trade and at the same time became experts in the habits, customs, and laws of many men.[29]

As Contarini's idealized portrait of patrician education suggests, noblemen would preferably have garnered their familiarity with foreign customs through firsthand experience of maritime travel. Even by Contarini's time, however, the patrician retreat from direct involvement in maritime commerce was well under way. Patricians and those who aspired to partake in their education norms, however, might still become experts.

Systematic and Comparative Treatments of Customs

The sixteenth century brought with it not only unprecedented opportunities for Europeans, including Venetians, to travel to distant regions but also to read about those regions. Yet travel narratives that included descriptions of the customs of foreign peoples were clearly not an invention of the early modern period. Marco Polo, John of Mandeville, and other figures—travelers whose voyages ranged from real to fictive to somewhere in between—all provided late-medieval readers with descriptions of the cultures and social organization of extra-European peoples. As we have seen, in the early sixteenth century, the concept of custom itself came to take on new meanings. Another innovation of the sixteenth century lay in the introduction of systematic and comparative accounts of customs, which treated customs as a discrete object of study in themselves. In the broadest sense, it was the advent of printing that allowed for this new way of thinking about customs. Print circulation allowed readers to collect and compare examples of travel writing both new and old at a scale that would previously have been impossible. The real boon for the comparative and systematic treatment of customs, however, came with the publication of edited collections of travel writing.

Venetians played a central role in the editing and publication of collections of travel writing. The form that a collection of travel writing could take varied considerably, from a slim, single volume octavo dealing with a single region to a multivolume, illustrated folio, with accounts spanning the entire globe. Venice saw the production of both forms. An example of the former is the *Viaggi fatti da Vinetia, alla Tana, in Persia, in India, et in Costantinopoli,* published by Antonio and Paolo Manuzio in Venice in 1543.[30] The collection contains only six accounts, five of which are Venetian in origin and deals with travels of Venetian diplomats and merchants to the east.

Venice also saw the production of a new kind of large-scale travel collection. In 1550, the Venetian humanist and secretary Giovanni Battista Ramusio published the first volume of his *Navigazioni e viaggi,* which represented the first large-scale attempt to order, compile, and provide a critical edition of the major travel accounts available at the time. In Ramusio's view, contemporary geographical knowledge had advanced so rapidly and given cause for the reevaluation of so many ancient authorities that it was necessary to assemble and create reliable editions of the most important modern travel accounts.[31] Eventually, the collection would span three volumes. Ramusio's volumes went through thirteen editions in total and proved influential. His editorial approach would later be emulated elsewhere in Europe. His collection was used as a model for other collections such as Richard Hakluyt's *Divers Voyages* (London, 1582), Theodore de Bry's *Les grands voyages* (Frankfurt, 1590), and above all, Samuel Purchas's *Pilgrimes* (London, 1625)—so heavy was Purchas's debt to Ramusio that he referred to the *Navigazioni* and Hakluyt's *Principal Navigations* as his "two libraries."[32]

The *Navigazioni* was a product of its intellectual environment not only in the humanist philological methods he employed but also in the way Ramusio obtained material for the collection. His long career as a state secretary, including a diplomatic secretary, enabled him to take full advantage of Venice's status as a clearinghouse for news and information on all parts of the globe. Like other members of the secretarial corps, he hailed from an elite subset of the citizenry: the *cittadini originari*. These citizen families shared a set of values and formed a broader elite with the patriciate with whom they were often linked through ties of marriage.[33] Indeed, Ramusio's family was linked to the patrician Navagero family through long ties of kinship.[34] Ramusio leveraged his familial and professional connections with Venetian diplomats who obtained rare texts for him when they were abroad.[35] Through his close friendship with Andrea Navagero, Venice's ambassador to Spain, he was able to obtain accounts of the Americas otherwise unavailable in Venice. Navagero's surviving letters to Ramusio dating from his diplomatic mission in Spain from 1525 to 1528 make clear that he was on the lookout for materials for Ramusio, and he reported back regularly on his successes and failures in obtaining them.[36]

Autoethnography and the Writing of European Customs

The study of the production and circulation of ethnographic knowledge in early modern Venice makes clear that early modern Europeans were just as concerned with describing, accounting for, and comparing the customs of other Europeans as they were with developing ethnographic accounts of extra-European peoples. The sixteenth and early seventeenth centuries, however, also saw Europeans write ethnographic accounts not of other European peoples but of their own nations. These were, in effect, examples of what Mary Louise Pratt terms "autoethnographic texts."[37] Pratt originally employed the term in a discussion of the writings of colonized peoples, defining authoethnographic works as those in which "colonized subjects undertake to represent themselves in ways that engage with the colonizer's terms."[38] Neither of the two Venetian-inflected works discussed here—Olaus Magnus's ethnographic account of northern European peoples and Leon Modena's ethnography of the Jews—were the products of colonial settings. Both, however, exhibit key traits of Pratt's model of autoethnographic works. Both responded to and engaged with traditions of representation of northern European and Jewish peoples authored by outsiders and were addressed largely to a broader European readership of outsiders. Both, moreover, did so using what Pratt describes as "a selective collaboration with appropriation of idioms of the metropolis"—in this case, the conventions of ethnographic writing as they developed over the course of the sixteenth century.[39]

Olaus Magnus arrived in Italy a Catholic exile from Sweden. Like many other sixteenth-century practitioners of ethnography, he spent much of his early career as a diplomat, first in the service of the Swedish crown and later of the papacy. His early diplomatic work took him to Rome, where he settled following the break of the Swedish church from Rome. His two most important works, the aforementioned *Carta marina et descriptio septemtrionalium terrarum*, published in Venice in 1539, and *Historia de gentibus septentrionalibus*, published in Rome in 1555, introduced many European readers to the history, customs, and natural history of Scandinavia. The *Historia* was eventually translated into Italian, German, English, and Dutch, and it continued to serve as the authoritative work on northern Europe through the seventeenth century. The work built on Olaus's earlier *Carta marina*, a large-scale map printed on nine wood blocks and measuring 1.25 by 1.7 meters.[40] The *Carta marina* was itself the product of Olaus's intellectual connections in Venice. While he enjoyed the hospitality of the patriarch Girolamo Querini, Olaus's circle in Venice included such important figures in the history of Venetian ethnography as the cartographer Giacomo Gastaldi and Giovanni Battista Ramusio.[41]

One of Olaus's aims in publishing the map was to correct the inaccuracies of existing Ptolemaic maps of Scandinavia.[42] The *Carta marina*, however, also contained a wealth of ethnographic information. The map and its legend, for example, contained visual depictions and brief textual descriptions of marriage ceremonies, customs surrounding the preparation of food, and religious observances. Although the text of the map was entirely in Latin, Olaus and the Venetian printer with whom he worked, Giovanni Tommaso, ensured a broad readership for the map, by simultaneously publishing separate vernacular explanatory texts destined for northern and southern European markets.[43] In addition to his detailed Latin legend, Olaus supplemented the *Carta marina* with a pair of German and Italian commentaries, which expanded on the ethnographic information contained in the map and map legend.[44] Thus, readers of the map with a knowledge of Latin who were interested in the image of four worshipers kneeling before a banner in the polar reaches of Sweden could consult the legend to learn that individuals there worshipped a red cloth suspended on a spear. Readers of the vernacular commentaries could also learn that worshippers left offerings of animal bones before the cloth.[45]

A second example of autoethnographic writing, the Venetian rabbi Leon Modena's *Historia de' riti hebraici* (henceforth *Riti*), is even more strongly marked by its Venetian origins. First published in Paris in 1637, Modena's *Riti* was the first account of Jewish customs and ritual written by a Jew for a Christian audience. While Modena's faith was integral to readers' interest in the *Riti*, the autoethnographic status of the work also necessitated a delicate balancing act. Modena reassured readers that his intention was "to relate and not to persuade."[46] In composing the work, he writes, "I truly forgot to be a Jew, and instead imagined myself a neutral relator."[47] He maintained this stance throughout the *Riti*, consistently employing the third-person plural when discussing Jews and their customs. The result was a work that Carlo Ginzburg describes as "a kind of travel account, written by a native pretending to be an outsider."[48]

Even though it was the first Jewish-authored work of its kind, the *Riti* was far from the first work to describe Jewish practices to Christians. The *Riti* was in fact an apologetic work responding to a German tradition of polemical ethnographies of the Jews, which had emerged in the sixteenth century.[49] In the sixteenth and seventeenth centuries, at least twenty-seven works by Christian authors describing Jewish religious practices were published, the vast majority of which were in German.[50] Christian writers used ethnographic examples in the service of themes and arguments that had a long history in anti-Jewish polemics, including the degenerate nature of post-biblical Judaism and Jewish hostility toward Christians. Although Christian writing on Jewish practices ranged in format from brief pamphlets to extensive treatises, nearly all such works drew an explicit contrast between biblical Judaism and rabbinic Judaism. Examining variations in specific customs over time lent exemplary weight to the argument that Jews were apostates to their own religion—an argument with its origins in the early thirteenth-century. Jeremy Cohen argues convincingly that the view of rabbinic Judaism as a departure from its biblical predecessor emerged most fully in mendicant polemic of the thirteenth century, when it eclipsed the Augustinian doctrine of Jewish witness.[51] Contrary to Augustine's claim that the Jews had remained, "stationary in useless antiquity," sixteenth- and seventeenth-century Christian ethnographers were able to offer concrete examples of the mutability of Jewish practice over time.[52] It was not the ethnographers' theological arguments that were new but the type of example that they employed in service of those arguments.

As a rabbi with extensive Christian intellectual contacts both in Venice and abroad, Modena was quite familiar with Christian ethnographic writing on the Jews.[53] He worked regularly for Christian publishers of Hebrew books in Venice.[54] Modena also taught Hebrew to Christian students, many of whom were foreigners who had come to Venice specifically to master Hebrew under the instruction of a Jew.[55] Indeed, the genesis of the *Riti* lies in Modena's relationships with English visitors to Venice. Modena began meeting regularly with English protestants in Venice in 1608. These meetings were prompted by English interest in Hebrew during the preparation of the King James Bible, completed in 1611.[56] Modena was asked to compose the *Riti* by an unnamed English nobleman, likely the English ambassador to Venice, Henry Wotton, who wished to present it to James I.[57] Thereafter, the *Riti* circulated in manuscript form in England for years before it was finally published in Paris.[58]

Modena conceived of the *Riti* as an antidote to some of the more flagrant claims made about Jewish belief and ritual. He used the long-standing charge in anti-Jewish polemics concerning the mutability of Jewish belief and practices—a charge made in most Christian ethnographies of the Jews—to argue for the social toleration of Jews. Modena in effect manipulated a charge that had long been used to promote the exclusion of Jews from Christian society and transform it into an argument for the suitability of Jews for life in Christian society. In the process, he provided Christian readers with what was then the most thoroughgoing account of Jewish customs and ritual. Moreover, he did so in a way that emphasized the diversity of custom among different Jewish communities—something that Modena, who lived in the multiethnic Jewish ghetto in Venice, was sensitive to in a way that his German Christian interlocutors were not (see chapter 5). The *Riti* was notable for the sheer variety of topics treated by Modena, who included chapters ranging from "On Dwellings and Homes," to "On Purim," to "On Weddings," to "On Menstruous and Birthing Women."[59] The comprehensive nature of Modena's account is part of what ensured its longevity. The work was published in nine Italian editions between 1637 and 1728. It was also published widely in translation, with nine French editions and English, Dutch, and Latin translations appearing by the end of the seventeenth century.

Ethnography and Antiquarianism

At their most ambitious, comparative approaches to human difference could range not only over space but also over time. The newfound interest in ethnographic descriptions of both European and extra-European peoples in the sixteenth century developed in dialogue with an interest in daily life in antiquity. Historians have long acknowledged the ways in which the model of classical ethnography served as a foundation for early modern understandings of human difference. Scholars have traced the influence that authorities such as Herodotus, Tacitus, and Pomponius Mela had on Europeans' apprehension of the unfamiliar cultural practices they encountered during the period of early modern imperial and commercial expansion.[60] Ancient categories of civility and barbarism could be, and indeed frequently were, applied to peoples whom sixteenth-century authors encountered both within Europe and further afield. What has been less readily appreciated is the extent to which ethnographic treatments of extra-European cultures informed contemporary understandings of classical antiquity. The reckoning with extra-European cultures occurred at the same time that humanists grew increasingly preoccupied with the daily life, material culture, and lived religion of antiquity. Venice in particular produced numerous comparative works on customs and dress that treated the customs of the ancients alongside those of extra-European societies, placing contemporary and ancient cultures in the same ethnographic frame. The writings of Venetian merchants, diplomats, and humanists testify to the ways in which the practices of ethnographic writing helped to shape travelers' and readers' appreciation of the cultural alterity of classical antiquity.[61]

As Michael Ryan observes, "the discovery of 'difference'—i.e., that men varied in manners, customs, and beliefs—grew out of the Renaissance experience of classical texts: It was above all the recognition of historical distance."[62] But certainly, Renaissance readers' and authors' awareness of the cultural gap that separated them from the ancients was a product not only of their familiarity with classical texts but of a growing familiarity with the material culture of antiquity. There were clear connections between the concerns of sixteenth-century ethnography and the concerns of the Renaissance antiquarianism that had emerged in the fifteenth century.[63] Antiquarianism, with its concern for the material remains of the ancient past, was predicated on a broad vision of what about that past was worth studying. Aided by material remains, antiquarians turned their attention to the heretofore neglected topics of daily life and social customs. When combined with the study of texts, the evidence provided by artifacts allowed a more detailed and comprehensive view of ancient customs than texts alone could provide.

Historiographers increasingly emphasized the need for historians to possess the skills of the antiquarian. In his 1548 *Disputatio* on history, Francesco Robortello called not only for a refinement of antiquarian skills on the part of historians but an application of those skills to recovering the customs and daily life of antiquity. "If the historian must take into account this whole long sweep of years," he wrote, "it is clear that he must be knowledgeable about all of antiquity, so far as it pertains to customs, to ways of life, to the building of cities, to the movements of peoples. Let our example be Thucydides, who in book six offers a very thorough and precise account of the antiquity of the cities and peoples of Sicily. And since the remains of old buildings and the inscriptions cut into marbles, gold, brass, and silver can help us greatly when we try to gain knowledge of ancient times, he must also master them."[64] If antiquarian studies shared with ethnographic writing a concern with customs and daily life, they were further aligned with ethnographic treatments of foreign peoples through their organizational principles. Like the most ambitious sixteenth-century treatments of customs, antiquarian studies were ordered systematically rather than chronologically. Arnaldo Momigliano long ago noted, that while what he termed "ordinary history" was chronologically ordered, antiquarian research was instead "systematic and covered the whole subject section by section: it was descriptive in a systematic form, not explanatory in a chronological order."[65] Distinctive schemes for the organization of knowledge went hand in hand with distinctive domains over subject matter. Subjects held in common by ethnography and antiquarianism—religion, political institutions, customs, private life—were by their very nature better suited to systematic than chronological or genealogical description.[66] In this respect, the study of ancient customs via the material remains of antiquity was further aligned with the study of the customs of modern peoples.

The application of antiquarian studies to questions of daily life stemmed from a real and genuine interest on the part of humanists in the lived reality of the ancients. In his essay "On Vanity," Montaigne reflects on his "perfect and lively union" with the dead—the bond that he and other men of humanist educational backgrounds shared with the ancients.[67] In the service of this union, Montaigne writes, he wishes to gain familiarity not only with the written works of antiquity through which he had first encountered the ancients but also be able to reconstruct the contours of their daily lives. "Whenever there are qualities in things which are great and awesome," he writes, "I feel awe for their ordinary ones as well. I would love to see those men talking, walking, and eating."[68]

By the end of the sixteenth century, it had become considerably easier for readers to reconstruct these ordinary qualities. The insights of antiquarian research were increasingly shared with a broad readership. Synthetic works of history, written for a readership of nonspecialists, usually in the vernacular, made information on ancient history available in novel formats and to a novel set of readers. Venice and its surrounding cities, where the large printing industry allowed a group of these men, known collectively as *poligrafi*, to make a living from writing, saw the production of many of these popular works of history.[69] One of these popularizers, for example, Guido Panciroli published a successful compendium of the most notable things known to the ancients that had been lost to the moderns and, conversely, the most notable things invented or discovered by the moderns that had been unknown to the ancients. Within two decades of its first appearance, the account had been published in French, Latin, and Italian. The work was divided into two books of unequal length, with the first, much longer, book containing chapters on the lost features of ancient culture and society and the second book containing the innovations of the moderns. Panciroli, who spent much of his career at Padua as a distinguished jurist, is often classified as a cataloger of inventions.[70] Inventions are certainly well represented in his work, and Panciroli leans particularly heavily on inventions in the second book, which deals with the moderns. There, sugar, eyeglasses, and clocks all receive their due. Panciroli, however, was equally concerned with documenting the lost cultural practices of antiquity. To this end, he included in the first book chapters on ancient marriage customs, games and pastimes, and the burial of the dead.[71] He even, as Montaigne had wished, informed readers of how the ancients had supped. Panciroli included a dedicated chapter on ancient dining customs, covering topics such as the number of major meals eaten in a day, refrigeration practices, and the giving of toasts.[72]

The most ambitious students of custom placed ancient and modern customs alike in the same frame. Here, again, Montaigne offers one of the more memorable expressions of this interpretive tendency. For Montaigne, the unfamiliarity and distance of ancient customs threw into relief the arbitrary and historically contingent nature of modern European customs. A concern for both the resemblances and divergences between ancient and modern custom marks many of Montaigne's essays, but Montaigne takes it as the subject of "On Ancient

Customs." As he explains in his introduction to the essay, he does so precisely in order to underscore "the continual changes in human affairs, [so that] our judgements on them may be more firm and more enlightened."[73] In the remainder of the essay, Montaigne proceeds to recount an eclectic array of ancient customs, ranging from bathing to dining to transportation, noting where those differ from or correspond to modern customs, both European and extra-European. Thus, the ancient Romans removed their body hair with tweezers in the manner of French women, took their meals reclining in the manner of the Turks, and kissed in greeting in the manner of the Venetians.[74]

Much has been written about the ways in which a growing familiarity with the customs of distant peoples—particularly the peoples of the New World—gave Europeans an occasion to reflect on the origins and historicity of their own ways of life.[75] For other sixteenth-century students of customs, though, it was an awareness of the diversity of contemporary customs that came to shape how they understood the culture of antiquity. This was the case with the Venetian patrician merchant Mafio Priuli, who spent many years away from Venice in the Levant and India. Priuli provides a fascinating case study of the processes through which Venetians combined knowledge of ancient and modern customs, both because his career and reading practices were shaped by distinctly Venetian currents and because his work remains largely unknown to historians. What little is known about Priuli comes chiefly from the long letter he wrote to his family from the Coromandel Coast in India in 1537. The letter reached his family in Venice in 1539 and was published shortly thereafter by Francesco Marcolini, best known as the publisher of the works of Pietro Aretino. We do know something about Priuli's voyage to India. Priuli traveled to India via Damascus, home to a stable community of Venetian merchants, where traces of his stay can be found in the correspondence of the Venetian consul.[76] We know, however, little about Priuli's life before or after he wrote the letter, which remains his only known piece of writing. His year of birth and death are uncertain as is the city in which he died. Indeed, it is unclear if Priuli ever returned to Venice before his death.[77] Pietro Donazzolo identified Mafio as the likely brother of Antonio Priuli, who was elected a procurator of San Marco, one of the highest elected offices a patrician could hold, and later in his life, elected ambassador to the Spanish court in 1560.[78] While Mafio was in India, Antonio had also contracted to form a trading company to import goods from the West Indies with two giants of sixteenth-century cosmographical and ethnographic writing: Giovanni Battista Ramusio and Gonzalo Fernández de Oviedo.[79] Priuli thus hailed from a family that was not only among the most prominent in Venice but also deeply enmeshed in the city's distinctive geographical culture.[80]

To understand the ways in which Priuli grappled with the relationship between the customs of the ancient Mediterranean and those of southeastern India, we must first understand something about his intellectual preparation for his voyage. From what he tells us of his preparation for his time in India, Priuli's training was typical of other patrician merchants.[81] Priuli belonged to a patrician culture that took seriously the didactic potential of travel and viewed travel as a serious undertaking. Commerce and diplomacy were the two great lures that drew Venetian patrician men abroad, and those traveling for either purpose were expected to prepare for their voyage through study.[82] While Priuli's motivations for traveling abroad were strictly commercial, he prepared for his voyage in the same fashion that his counterparts in public service prepared for their diplomatic voyages: through the study of works of history and geography. Like other Venetian patricians, Priuli's education would certainly have included the study of the major works of Roman history, a fact that his letter itself makes clear. The letter also reveals that he drew from both ancient and modern sources in his reading on India.[83]

Priuli's engagement with cosmographical and ethnographic literature was likely furthered during his time in Damascus, which brought him into the orbit of another key figure in Venice's geographical culture: Pietro Zen. Zen, who was then serving as consul, would later go on to serve as the Venetian bailo, or resident diplomat, in Istanbul. The Zen family had long played a central role in Venice's relations with Islamic empires to the south and east. The Zens had and would continue to serve as key figures in the production and circulation of ethnographic information on these regions in both print and manuscript. Pietro's account of his journey to Istanbul and formal reports delivered following his missions in Syria and Istanbul circulated widely in manuscript.[84] Pietro's father, Caterino Zen, had served as a Venetian envoy to Persia, and his account of his travels and Persian customs was first published by Marcolini and widely read in Venice.[85] His grandson, Nicolò, who had accompanied him to Istanbul, would also write both a history of the Ottoman-Venetian War of 1537–1540 and a widely read account asserting that members of the Zen family had made landfall in the Americas long before Columbus.[86] Given the Zen family's prominent role as mediators between Venice and points east and their history of authoring ethnographic accounts, it is likely that Priuli engaged with Zen on the questions that would come to occupy him in his letter.

From Syria, Priuli traveled to India. He reported that he brought with him from Damascus four world maps along with editions of Ptolemy, Solinus, Marco Polo, and other authorities on India, all of which he ultimately found wanting. Although he allowed that there were in fact cannibals in Sumatra as authorities claimed, little else that he had read in his books or world maps proved to be true. All the books and world maps, he wrote,

> that deal with the subject of India, they all lie and are false, and I tell you that when I left Damascus, I brought with me four world maps, Solinus, Ptolemy, and other books on India, and many of them take special delight in describing the island of Taprobane which is [also] called the island of Sumatra, which I visited. And I wished to see everything very meticulously, but by my faith I found none of the things that these books or world maps talk about, with the exception of men on the island who live on human flesh, whom we call anthropophagi.[87]

Priuli's first experience of India—like his experience of the ancient world—was thus that of a reader. During his time in India, however, Priuli began to place his experience in India and his observation of Indian culture in dialogue with what he had read concerning both the customs of India and Roman antiquity. Priuli wrote to his family explaining how witnessing Indian sacrificial rites had altered his experiences as a reader of Roman history. "And many things," he wrote, "that are written in Titus Livius about what the Romans did in their life's tests that we did not believe at the time but that now seem to me to be more than true: and every day I see new things that I myself marvel at. And when I return to you, I will not dare to recount them to you because I doubt that you will believe them."[88]

Priuli was clearly not asserting a genetic relationship between ancient Roman and modern Indian customs. He was, however, claiming that the experience of appreciating the cultural alterity of the Indians—in this case, through eyewitness experience—helped him to fully apprehend the cultural alterity of the ancient Romans. In effect, his grappling with Indian custom permitted him to stop viewing tales of Roman custom as mere exaggerations and instead prompted him to reconceive them as yet another example of the variety of human cultural difference. Priuli's experience in the Indian subcontinent afforded him a different vantage point from which to view the culture of Roman antiquity, in effect decentering it.

By the sixteenth century, an interest in the cultural differences between the ancients and moderns was closely interwoven with an interest in the cultural differences between modern peoples. Evidence of this survives not only in the published works of men such as Montaigne and Priuli but in the evidence we have of the reading strategies of ordinary readers. Readers in their notes and commonplace books recorded notes on the customs of the ancients alongside notes on the customs of modern peoples—both European and extra-European. Their willingness to do so attests to the emergence of ethnographic information as a discrete category of knowledge. Readers wove together pieces of information from disparate sources in order to create their own ethnographic compendiums that cut across geographical and chronological boundaries. One anonymous Venetian reader included an entry on ancient Roman and African women immediately following his entries on modern Indian women. On the very same page of his commonplace book, he ranged from the Hindu observance of sati, or the self-immolation of widows, to the ancient African practice of raising a dowry through prostitution, to the modesty of women's dress in ancient Rome.[89] This intermingling of ethnographic entries on ancient and modern peoples also marked the note-taking strategies of the Paduan intellectual and book collector Gian Vincenzo Pinelli, whose library and commonplace book will be discussed at greater length in chapter 4.[90]

The juxtaposition of ancient and modern customs was not simply an initiative of readers. Readers were encouraged in their habit of conceiving of ancient and modern customs within the same ethnographic frame by editors and authors who presented information on customs in novel ways. Beginning in the third decade of the sixteenth century, a growing number of ethnographic works treated both ancient and modern customs. The earliest and by far the most expansive of the sixteenth-century works to adopt this approach was Johannes Boemus's aforementioned *Omnium gentium mores leges et ritus,* first published in Augsburg in 1520. Boemus offered readers a true ethnographic compendium—one that compiled and compared the customs of a wide range of peoples, ranging broadly both geographically and chronologically.

Boemus organized his account of customs in the first instance geographically rather than chronologically. Although the work begins with a chronological outline of the variation of human custom over time—for Boemus, all cultural diversity was the result of a process of corruption of a single sacred origin—his fundamental unit of analysis was geographical. He divided the work along continental lines, with Africa, Asia, and Europe each being treated in its own book. Each book was then further divided into smaller geographical chapter units, which were in turn arranged along chronological lines. While for some regions, limited traditions of recorded history prevented Boemus from ranging into the customs of the distant past, he began each chapter with the most remote period of recorded history available to him.

Boemus's *Omnium gentium mores* was by far the widest ranging of the sixteenth-century comparative ethnographic works to treat both ancient and modern customs. Although Boemus famously opted not to treat the Americas on the grounds that information on the customs of the New World was too unreliable, he did endeavor to treat a wide range of customs within the Old World societies he included.[91] Thus, his chapter on Italian customs ranged from matters of dress, to language, to marriage and inheritance, to the reputation and esteem of different professions.[92] Boemus's was the only work in the sixteenth or early seventeenth century that took the treatment the full range of human customs ranging across time and space as its principal goal. Even though authors working in other genres, notably cosmography, would at times treat both ancient and modern customs, their works did not take the variation of human customs as their primary subject matter.[93] A handful of works, however, followed in Boemus's footsteps by attempting to provide readers with a comprehensive account of the variation through time and space of a single set of customs.

These works drew heavily from the writings of classical authorities, although they varied in relative emphasis they placed on ancient versus modern customs. They were united, however, by a commitment to joining the consideration of cultural variation in antiquity and the present in a single ethnographic frame. One of the earliest Venetian authors to write a comparative ethnographic account of a single set of customs was the polygraph Sebastiano Fausto, who in 1554 published a slim vernacular volume on the diversity of marriage customs.[94] Fausto's brief work on marriage was followed by Tommaso Porcacchi's survey of burial customs, the *Funerali antichi di diversi popoli et nationi*, first published in Venice in 1574. Porcacchi's work included twenty-three brief chapters, ranging from the burial practices of the Romans (who occupied the majority of Porcacchi's account), to the Athenians, Indians, and finally concluding with those of the early Christians.[95] Porcacchi's *Funerali* was preceded by and, indeed, drew heavily from the work of the Ferrarese humanist and papal notary Lilio Gregorio Giraldi. In 1539, Giraldi had published an account of the diversity of customs surrounding death and burial, *De sepulchris et vario sepeliendi ritu*.[96] Each chapter contained a detailed engraved illustration by the Paduan engraver Girolamo Porro with whom Porcacchi had also collaborated on his 1572 *isolario*, or island book (see chapter 4).[97]

It is no surprise that the authors of these works tended to be vernacularizers of the classical tradition. Men like Fausto and Porcacchi sought to render bodies of historical information in a form accessible to nonspecialists. As Paul Grendler notes of Francesco Sansovino, a contemporary of Fausto and Porcacchi, the problem that these men addressed was essentially one of organization, as they sought to shape their material into new forms that would be intelligible to a broad readership.[98] As Porcacchi acknowledged, all of the information on burial customs he relayed was available in works of ancient and modern histories; he presented his task as one of compiling and arranging that information. He sought to unite accounts of burial customs assembled from diverse sources and present that information in a novel format for readers. Porcacchi was evidently serious about his claim to have consulted a diverse range of sources. As he assured readers, he had drawn his information from a variety of sources and not only from "books of history." He explained that he had consulted the writings of friends, various letters, reports, diaries, and other texts written "in other circumstances and for other purposes."[99]

Ancient and Modern Cultural Change in the Costume Book

Perhaps the most distinctive and enduring early modern genre to unite the consideration of ancient and modern customs was the costume book. The costume book served as a very particular type of survey of the customs of antiquity and the modern world. Unlike other genres considered thus far, costume books were first and foremost visual genres. At their most rudimentary, they could be little more than collections of illustrations of typical national costumes with nothing in the way of text apart from captions designating each illustration. This was the case, for example, with the Venetian engraver and print dealer Ferdinando Bertelli's costume book *Omnium fere gentium nostrae aetatis habitus*, first published in Venice in 1563.[100] Costume books, however, could also be much more elaborate volumes with textual explanations accompanying and contextualizing the illustrations.

Cesare Vecellio's *Degli habiti antichi e moderni di diverse parti del mondo*, first published in Venice in 1590, was not only the most elaborate costume book of the sixteenth century; it was also the most explicit in terms of ethnographic content. The volume was also remarkable for its heft and geographical breadth. Vecellio's first edition included 415 woodcuts, most of which were produced by the German printmaker Christoph Krieger. That number would be expanded to 503 in the second edition, published in 1598.[101] The sheer heft of Vecellio's work allowed for a more variegated taxonomy than was typical of the costume book. Vecellio included not only regional variations in dress but also variations of dress according to status and profession. Thus, the nineteen entries under Paduan dress included plates and descriptions of the dress typical of doctors of law and medicine, porters, foot soldiers, young scholars, young peasant women, and "women of mediocre condition," among others.[102] By contrast, the 1594 edition of Bertelli's costume book included only six examples of Paduan dress.[103] Even in more distant regions, Vecellio made an effort to address divisions of status and profession. His plates on male Armenian dress, for example, include the dress of Armenians "of condition," merchants, and noblemen.[104]

Whereas earlier costume books such as Bertelli's had largely been collections of captioned plates, Vecellio provided readers with a true treatise on costume.[105] Indeed, the first edition of the *Habiti antichi et moderni* began with a brief essay by Vecellio on "ancient and modern dress and its origins, mutations, and variations."[106] Vecellio began the essay by discussing the mechanisms by which customs of national dress changed over time in both antiquity and the present, emphasizing the ways in which change in dress was closely tied to the historical factors that precipitated broader cultural change. For Vecellio, military conquest, the migration of populations, and the rise and fall of empires were the most potent agents of cultural change.[107] Italy in particular bore the visible marks of these processes. The linguistic, cultural, and sartorial diversity of the Italian Peninsula, which Vecellio saw as unrivaled in Europe, was a lasting testament to the depredations that Italy had endured over the centuries. He explained that he wished his discourse on costume to convey to readers a sense of "what great ruin this beautiful region of Italy has been subjected to and by what a great diversity of barbarian and northern inhabitants and predators this fertile country has been trampled and robbed." The centuries-long line of invaders, he continued, "satiated themselves and despoiled all the desirable commodities, and left as recompense nothing more than the diversity and change of language, dress, and costume."[108]

But how could Vecellio and his contemporaries know what the costumes of past centuries, let alone those of antiquity, looked like? How could they trace developments in dress over time? To be sure, by the end of the sixteenth century, there had within living memory been significant changes in dress, but many of the costumes that Vecellio discussed had their origins much further in the past. Vecellio's contemporaries whose primary interest lay in linguistic change rather than change in dress had at their disposal a textual record on which they could draw to chart that change.[109] There were, as Vecellio acknowledged, important differences between the study of linguistic change and the study of sartorial change, and he used his discourse as a space to reflect on the sources for the study of the dress of the past. Like the antiquarians on whose work he drew, Vecellio advocated the necessity of consulting a range of evidence, both textual and visual, which, in the case of dress, included scriptural evidence, histories, pictures, and sculptures.[110]

For Vecellio, the nation was the basic unit of division for the study of dress. As he explained in his address to the readers, he saw his project as that of "putting in drawing the dress of different nations of the world," and it was the unit of the nation around which the engravings and descriptions would be organized, first in books corresponding to continents and then by nation within those books.[111] In keeping with the broader usage of the term in the sixteenth century, the parameters of nation for Vecellio were somewhat elastic.[112] For Vecellio as for his contemporaries, a nation was defined by an admixture of its ethnolinguistic, religious, and juridical qualities. At times, Vecellio uses the designation to refer collectively to the inhabitants of a state, at other times a region within a state (or spanning several states), and at other times a city. Thus, the Persians, Spanish, and French constitute a nation, but so too do the Italians, Greeks, and Uskoks, as do the inhabitants of Venice, Milan, and Antwerp.[113]

The costume book was simultaneously hyperlocal in its production and self-consciously international in its imagined audience. Although the costume book was by no means a Venetian or even Italian innovation, Venice played a disproportionate role in the production of costume books, even when its predominance in the world of Italian printing is taken into consideration. Approximately one-third of the printed costume books circulating in Europe between 1540 and 1610 were the products of Venetian presses.[114] Venice and Nuremberg were the two major centers of costume book production in the sixteenth century.[115] As a primarily visual genre, the costume book crossed linguistic borders more readily internationally than other ethnographic genres. To further facilitate the international circulation, editors and engravers frequently adopted Latin as the language of the costume books, even at a time when other ethnographic works were increasingly appearing in the vernacular. The Latin of the costume books, however, was one that demanded little from readers. Readers did not require any degree of fluency in Latin in order to engage with the sort of simple textual labels such as "Italicae mulier Roma" (Roman woman), "Ungarica mulier" (Hungarian woman), or "Hispanus" (Spanish man) that served as the only textual intrusions in Bertelli's *Omnium fere gentium nostrae aetatis*.[116]

The appearance of the costume book in the sixteenth century has, like the rise of ethnographic genres more generally, been linked to the acceleration of European imperial expansion.[117] As a rule, though, costume books were much more attuned to variations of culture and dress within Europe than without. As the example of Vecellio's *Habiti antichi et moderni* demonstrates, the preoccupation with describing and accounting for the diversity of dress was not limited to the non-European world. Extra-Europeans were not the only or even the most prominent subjects of costume books. Costume books in fact typically began with the dress of the author's and/or engraver's own nation. This is the case, for example, with Bertelli's *Omnium fere gentium nostrae aetatis habitus*, which began with the dress of Venetian men and women before proceeding to the dress of other Italian states.[118] The foregrounding of local dress was also a feature of costume books produced outside of the Venetian context. The Parisian illustrator François Desprez's early costume book *Recueil de la diversité des habits* similarly began with plates and brief descriptions of French dress, and Hans Weigel's 1577 *Habitus praecipuorum populorum* began with the dress of the German nobility.[119] Vecellio's *De gli habiti antichi et moderni* in fact departed from this convention by beginning with the dress of ancient and modern Rome. Vecellio nevertheless lavished attention on the dress of his home city; entries for Venice far outnumbered those of any other nation. In Vecellio's 1590 edition, the first book covering Europe (including the European portions of the Ottoman Empire) is afforded a full 430 out of 499 leaves, an asymmetry that Vecellio explained in terms of the greater quantity and reliability of information on the dress and customs of European peoples.[120]

The sixteenth century saw a gradual shift both in how Europeans conceived of customs and the value they attributed to the study of customs. Without ever fully disappearing, an older juridical conception of customs was superseded by a conception of customs encompassing a broad complex of cultural practices. Human difference would increasingly be conceived of in terms of differences in customs. Ethnographic models provided Venetians and Europeans more generally with a framework for understanding human difference both elsewhere in Europe and at home.

There was broad agreement that the study of foreign customs was a necessary complement to the education of future statesmen. In Venice, where elite identity was so thoroughly interwoven with service to the state and public office holding, the study of customs became important in the education of patrician and citizen men. Venetian ethnographic writing would remain closely tied to the practices of governance, a theme explored in each of the following chapters. At the same time, authors and printers of ethnographic literature promised readers a broader set of moral and intellectual benefits. Studying the customs of foreign peoples offered readers a mirror in which they might critically evaluate the customs of their own nation. Through a process of critical evaluation, readers would be able to amend their own customs—emulating the worthy customs of other nations while avoiding the wicked. In the most expansive formulations, ethnographic writing promised collective benefits. The study of foreign customs might gradually improve not only the customs of the individual reader but also those of the nation.

When authors and editors invited readers to treat ethnographic writing as a mirror of customs, they were proposing an inherently comparative process. That process was at once synchronic and diachronic. Comparative treatments of customs ranged not only over space but also over time. Drawing on the insights of antiquarians, they incorporated the customs of contemporary peoples, both European and extra-European, as well as those of the peoples of antiquity. As the writing of Mafio Priuli demonstrates, that comparative exercise affected evaluations of the customs of peoples on both sides of the ancient-modern divide. The Venetian case reveals, in the first instance, that ethnographic thought and writing have a much longer history than is usually assumed. It also suggests that ethnographic writing was the product of a broader shift in how Europeans conceived of human difference, as they engaged in the project of inscribing others and, in some cases, themselves in ethnographic frames.

CHAPTER TWO

Ambassadors as Ethnographers

In 1592, the Venetian patrician and ambassador to Poland, Pietro Duodo, appeared before the steering committee of the Venetian Senate and delivered a report detailing the worship of snakes in parts of the Polish-Lithuanian commonwealth. Rural inhabitants, he reported, worshiped a black snake, keeping statues of the serpent in their homes by the hearth. One night a year, they prepared a feast for the snake, believing that how much or how little of the offering the snake had eaten by daybreak held portent for the coming year.[1] Duodo's final report of his embassy, or relazione as it was referred to in Venetian diplomatic parlance, was, like all relazioni, ostensibly intended to provide members of the Venetian government with the information they needed to rule effectively and to make judicious decisions in matters of foreign policy. It is somewhat surprising, then, that Duodo would choose to devote a significant portion of his relazione to the beliefs, religious practices, diet, and daily life of the rural populace—in short, to areas that we would see as the subject matter of ethnography.

Duodo was far from alone among Venetian ambassadors in his emphasis on ethnographic reporting. Collectively, the republic's ambassadors left behind a large body of writing. By the sixteenth century, Venice had a larger number of permanent diplomatic representatives than any other European state.[2] When Venice's temporary envoys are considered alongside its permanent representatives, its diplomatic network extended from England to Iran. All Venetian ambassadors, whether permanent or temporary envoys, were required by law to deliver a final oral and written report on the states in which they had served. Although ambassadors were required to deliver relazioni as early as the thirteenth century, written reports dating from before the beginning of the sixteenth century have not survived in significant numbers.

The delivery of an ambassadorial relazione was a major political event, and the reports were widely read both within the Venetian republic and beyond its borders. Contemporaries valued the relazioni for, among other things, the observations that they offered on the customs of princes and their subjects and for the critical detachment that Venetian ambassadors brought as foreign observers. Toward the end of the sixteenth century, Scipione Ammirato praised the Venetian relazioni in these terms, writing, "The ambassadors whom [the Venetians] send to the potentates of the world are obliged upon return from their embassies to report in the senate that which they have been able to glean of the customs of the prince and of the situation, riches, fertility and other qualities of the places and of the people where were sent. [And] they do this with much felicity, since more often than not one sees that things are more manifest to them than to the very men of that country."[3] In the hands of later historians such as Leopold von Ranke, Venetian relazioni would serve as an important source base for political and diplomatic histories of early modern Europe.[4] In more recent years, the reports have been used to trace the evolution of Venetian views on subjects ranging from Ottoman despotism to the conquest of the Americas to the changing fortunes of sixteenth-century Spain.[5]

This chapter adopts a very different approach to the relazioni, examining them instead for what they reveal about the development of contemporary ethnographic thought. Over the course of the sixteenth and early seventeenth centuries, relazioni became increasingly important as vehicles for the circulation of ethnographic information within Europe and served as models for other forms of ethnographic reporting. During that period, individuals in the service of the Venetian state came to play a growing role in the production of ethnographic information. This did not, however, always occur in expected ways or for expected purposes. While relazioni were intended to assist statesmen in making judicious decisions in matters of foreign policy, over the course of the sixteenth century, ambassadors devoted increasing attention to ethnographic topics, including the customs, religious observances, foodways, and dress of the states in which they had served. The new emphasis on ethnographic reporting was as much a product of the literary and career ambitions of ambassadors as it was a reflection of the perceived political utility of ethnographic knowledge. The shift in the nature of diplomatic reporting did not go unnoticed by contemporaries; it engendered a vigorous debate about both the parameters of political knowledge and the nature and reliability of eyewitness versus textual authority.

Venice's Diplomatic Network

The long history and broad geographical extent of Venice's diplomatic network by the sixteenth century was a key factor in the development of Venetian ethnographic writing. Scholars have long seen the fourteenth- and fifteenth-century Italian states as the birthplace of "modern" European diplomatic practice.[6] Among the late-medieval Italian states, Venice's role in the development of the consuls, often seen as the precursors to resident ambassadors, has been widely recognized.[7] The office of the Venetian bailo in Istanbul, which has the distinction of being the earliest permanent European diplomatic office in a foreign state, is particularly important in this regard. The office was created for the purpose of representing the Venetian merchant community in Byzantine Constantinople in the eleventh century, and at least initially, the bailo dealt primarily with commercial matters.[8] Following a brief interruption, the office of the bailo was reestablished in 1454 following the Ottoman conquest of the city the previous year.[9]

Although the early duties of the bailo have been described as those of a senior consul, over the course of the fifteenth century the bailo increasingly took on diplomatic and ambassadorial functions.[10] Indeed, although the office retained its consular functions, it came to be regarded as one of the most prestigious of the Venetian ambassadorial offices, rivaled only by the ambassadorship to Rome.[11] The importance of the office in the sixteenth and early seventeenth centuries can be gauged from an examination of the career trajectories of the patricians who held it. In most cases, the appointment as bailo came at the culmination of a long political career that included other lesser diplomatic and ambassadorial postings.[12] It was not normally a post awarded to mid-career patricians, as were most consulships. The career trajectory of Daniele Barbarigo who served as the Venetian consul in Alexandria a decade before being elected bailo is fairly typical in this regard.[13] Thus, without ever shedding its consular functions, the bailate was aligned with other ambassadorships in terms of the prestige of the office and the profile of the men who held it. Since evidence suggests that the growing ethnographic character of Venetian diplomatic writing was a function not only of perceived exigencies of state but also of the literary and career ambitions of the largely patrician group of men who served as

Venice's early modern diplomatic representatives, this alignment of the bailate and other ambassadorial offices is significant. Accordingly, I use the terms *ambassadorial writing* and *ambassadorial relazioni* to refer not only to the works of ambassadors proper but also to those of the bailo.

By the beginning of the sixteenth century, the Venetian state had a larger number of diplomatic representatives than any other European state. In addition to the bailo in Istanbul, Venice also had permanent representatives in the major Italian states, dating from the fifteenth century, as well as in the Holy Roman Empire, France, England, and Spain. A permanent representative in the United Provinces was added in 1610. The republic also sent temporary embassies to Poland, Mamluk Egypt, Persia, the Swiss cantons, and the Ottoman Empire. In this final case, the presence of a temporary ambassador, referred to either as an orator or extraordinary ambassador, at the Ottoman court meant that there were two Venetian diplomatic representatives in Istanbul.[14]

Genres of Diplomatic Writing

Diplomacy produced an extraordinary amount of written material. It has been estimated that half of the material from the archives of fifteenth-century Italy was produced through diplomatic activity.[15] As the care that states invested in organizing and safeguarding their diplomatic archives might suggest, information gathering was one of the chief functions of early modern ambassadors.[16]

Like their counterparts from other states, Venetian representatives regularly communicated updates on their missions and news from the courts in which they served. In the Venetian context, these letters were known as *dispacci*. Although dispacci would certainly have been filed by fourteenth- and fifteenth-century Venetian representatives, they do not survive in great quantity from before the end of the fifteenth century. The earliest surviving dispacci from Istanbul, for example, date from the 1480s.[17] For other missions, the survival rate is much worse; for example, nearly all of the Venetian dispacci from Spain written in the fifteenth and first half of the sixteenth century are now lost.[18] Venetian representatives were also required by law to deliver a final relazione.[19] The origins of the reports date to an order of 1268 issued by the Great Council requiring returning representatives to deliver a report "on whatever they might have learned and heard said which they deemed to the profit and honor of Venice."[20] The order was reaffirmed in 1425 and again in a separate decree of the Senate in 1524.[21] Both of the later decrees emphasized the timely presentation of a written copy of the relazione, suggesting that ambassadors may have been lax in this regard. The relazione was first delivered orally before the Senate or its steering committee, the Collegio. After the ambassador's presentation, a written copy would in theory be deposited into the *Secreta*, the section of the state's archive that held the most sensitive documents. In 1425, a special section of the Secreta was created for the preservation of the relazioni. Written copies of these reports from before the sixteenth century, however, do not survive in significant numbers. Even many relazioni from the first decades of the sixteenth century survive only in the form of summaries. In the case of Istanbul, for example, the earliest surviving relazione that is not in summary form is the 1503 report of the ambassador and future doge Andrea Gritti.[22]

The extant series of ambassadorial relazioni in the Archivio di Stato in Venice runs to 31 volumes. Of the reports contained in those volumes, 113 date from the sixteenth century, with 35 of those reports covering Italian states and 78 covering non-Italian states.[23] Not all surviving relazioni, though, are preserved in the Archivio di Stato—a situation that itself testifies to the illicit circulation of the reports. Although there is no unified catalog of the manuscript copies of Venetian relazioni dispersed throughout European libraries and archives, a catalog of modern editions of the reports, lists an additional 81 sixteenth-century relazioni, 48 of which are reports on non-Italian states.[24]

The relazione as it developed in sixteenth-century Venetian diplomatic practice grew increasingly distinct from other forms of diplomatic writing. Unlike dispacci, relazioni were wide-ranging synthetic accounts of a state, its ruler, and its peoples. They were not intended to serve as recapitulations of the detailed information that an ambassador had already relayed in his dispacci, nor were they intended simply to summarize the events of the mission. Venetian ambassadors and their audiences were well versed in the distinct conventions of the two forms of communication. In the final relazione of his embassy to Charles V, delivered in 1532, for example, Nicolò Tiepolo differentiates the wider-ranging synthetic relazione from the narrower, more particular communications of the dispacci, referred to here simply as *lettere*: "Everyone who returns from any legation comes before this most wise Senate, not to render account of his actions (which can be clearly grasped from his own letters written from time to time), but to report if he has learned anything about the country from which he has returned . . . worthy of being heard and pondered by the prudent senators for the benefit of the fatherland."[25] Tiepolo's passage also highlights another key distinction between the dispacci and the relazioni: while the former were simply written communications, the latter were first and foremost oratorical performances. While this difference is an obvious one, it is difficult to overstate its importance. As a nobleman, an ambassador delivering a relazione was called on to speak before an audience of his peers. In theory, this should have been his only audience. The circulation of copies of relazioni was legally prohibited in Venice, and those present for the delivery of a relazione in the Senate or Collegio were forbidden from divulging the content of the report. Despite this prohibition, it was widely known that relazioni circulated in manuscript form—many ambassadors were themselves avid collectors of the reports.[26] An ambassador would thus expect to address two audiences: a primary audience of fellow patricians in the Senate or Collegio and a secondary one of readers.

The delivery of a relazione could be a lengthy affair: the diarist Marin Sanudo recorded that the delivery of a 1527 report lasted four hours—to the great tedium of the ambassador's audience.[27] For some ambassadors, the duration of their performance was itself a point of pride. The returning ambassador to the Ottoman court, Leonardo Donà, labeled his personal copy of his 1596 relazione "Unfinished draft of the relazione that I delivered aloud for over four continuous hours in the most excellent Senate."[28] Although the written relazioni submitted by ambassadors varied in length, they grew longer on average over the course of the sixteenth century. To take the example of the series of reports published in Eugenio Albèri's nineteenth-century edition, the length of the Ottoman reports increased from an average of thirty-three pages in the first half of the century to fifty in the second half, the French reports from forty-one pages to forty-nine, and the Spanish reports from thirty to fifty-seven.[29] Before his primary audience, an ambassador could expect to be judged not only on the content of his relazione but also on his appearance and delivery. The diaries of Sanudo, himself a keen collector of the reports, illustrate the multiple grounds on which ambassadors were evaluated. Sanudo frequently remarks on the dress, posture, and voice of ambassadors.[30]

The two audiences would also have heard or read slightly different versions of the relazioni. Since the written relazione was not a direct transcription of the speech delivered in the Senate or Collegio but rather a copy submitted later by the ambassador, there certainly existed differences between the written and oral versions. Available evidence also suggests that audiences expected ambassadors to make only sparing use of notes. In his personal notes on the delivery of Pietro Duodo's relazione of Poland, for example, Leonardo Donà praised the ambassador for having delivered much of his speech from memory.[31] The expectation that an ambassador not simply read from a written copy of his report would only have amplified differences between the written and oral relazioni.

The Place of Ethnography in Ambassadorial Reporting

Scholars have debated the nature and function of ambassadorial relazioni and the extent to which they were concerned with ethnographic reporting. Given the interest of the last several decades in the history of orientalism and on Muslim-Christian encounters in the Mediterranean more generally, the focus of this debate has tended to be the series of Ottoman relazioni. Several scholars have suggested that because of their origins as state reports on political and economic affairs, the parameters of the relazione allowed only for the treatment of a narrow set of topics. In this view, even though there may have existed a broad interest in religion and culture in the Ottoman Empire, the relazione, with its political focus and ossified conventions, was not the venue to address such matters. Paolo Preto, for example, argues that the interest of ambassadors to the Ottoman court was not in dogma and history but in concrete political and social developments and their implications for the Venetian state.[32] More recently, Andrei Pippidi argues both that the generic conventions of the relazione changed little over the course of the sixteenth and seventeenth centuries and that ambassadors' reports on the Ottoman Empire remained resolutely focused on a narrow set of political topics. For Pippidi, this limited set of interests was a function of the ambassadors' shared backgrounds and intellectual horizons. The ambassadors, he argues, "were neither ethnographers nor historians; they were politicians first and last."[33] Similarly, Robert Mantran views Venetian reporting from Istanbul, including but not limited to the relazioni, as being conditioned by a narrow set of mercantile interests. On the whole, he argues, Venetians evinced little interest in matters of culture or religion in the Ottoman Empire.[34]

Other scholars, meanwhile, argue that ambassadors demonstrated a broader range of interests in their relazioni, although there are different opinions regarding how early this broadening occurred. Franco Gaeta, for example, argues that in the sixteenth century, relazioni from all states—not only those from the Ottoman Empire—took on an increasingly "encyclopedic character," which included the treatment of ethnographic information.[35] By contrast, in his edition of late seventeenth- and early eighteenth-century relazioni, Carlo Morandi argues that later relazioni differ appreciably from their better-studied sixteenth-century predecessors. In Morandi's view, later Venetian ambassadors became more preoccupied with ethnographic "curiosities," and their relazioni more erudite and "bookish" as they derived information not from firsthand experience but from secondhand reading.[36]

One way in which we might evaluate what place, if any, contemporaries saw ethnographic information as having in the relazioni is by evaluating prescriptive literature on the writing of relazioni. Unfortunately, because the use of the ambassadorial relazione was restricted to Venice, examples of this type of literature are exceedingly rare. General treatises on the office of the ambassador understandably do not address its composition. Even treatises produced within the Venetian context often omit specific advice on the composition of relazioni.[37] At least one example, however, does unequivocally state that an ambassador ought to report to the Senate on the peoples, customs, and religion of the country in which he served. The anonymous Venetian text, which bears the heading "Queste cose si ricercano per fare una relazione" (These are the things required to compose a relazione) exists as an epilogue to a brief manuscript treatise on the office of the ambassador.[38] Nothing is known about the text's author or the circumstances of its composition, although Donald Queller suggests that it most likely dates from the 1570s, by which time ethnographic reporting had already become commonplace in Venetian relazioni.[39] The author sets out four broad areas that an ambassador ought to treat in his relazione. The first, second, and fourth of these deal respectively with the state's political geography, its physical geography and natural resources, and the character of the prince, his expenditures, and his disposition toward other rulers and states.[40] The inclusion of this information is unsurprising given the purpose of the relazione. The third category, however, counsels the inclusion of ethnographic information, broadly construed. Here, the author advises that "[the ambassador] should discuss its inhabitants, showing their customs and habit. Of what color, stature or disposition they are, whether they are religious, superstitious, and other religious particulars. . . . [He should address] the natures and condition of the common people."[41]

One reason there existed so little prescriptive literature on the construction of a relazione—aside from the obvious fact that the pool of potential relazione authors, and hence of potential readers of such literature, was a limited one—is that such explicit instructions were superfluous. The relazione was a highly formulaic genre. Most patricians would have learned the conventions of the reports' content and construction by reading and hearing numerous iterations of the genre. Ambassadors themselves also increasingly included statements outlining the contents of their reports and, in the process, addressing what categories of information an ideal relazione ought to include. More often than not, this included ethnographic information, usually articulated as the treatment of the costumi of the people. In his 1531 relazione, for example, Lodovico

Falier, the ambassador to England, praised the Senate for its wisdom in instituting the practice of the diplomatic relazioni, as these kept the government informed of, among other things, "the customs and varieties of peoples."[42] Similar statements on the importance of reporting on customs of the people can be found in other relazione from the 1530s.[43]

In subsequent decades, explicit statements concerning the contents of relazioni became both more common and more elaborate. In his relazione of Spain, delivered nearly thirty years after Falier's, Marcantonio da Mula articulates a much fuller agenda. "In the final act of their legation," he writes, "it is the custom of ambassadors to report to Your Serenity and to Your Most Excellent Lordships on matters related to princes, on their families, origins, parts of their bodies, quality of their soul, the customs and operations; of their states and kingdoms, where they are located, their borders, the people, the customs and will of the people."[44] Although in the view of Da Mula and other late sixteenth-century ambassadors the range of topics that were to be treated in a relazione had expanded, reporting on the inhabitants and customs of a country remained important.

By the 1530s, there existed a shared understanding between ambassadors and their primary audience in the Senate that ethnographic reporting lay within the purview of the relazione. Once ambassadors viewed ethnographic information as having a legitimate place in the relazione, they increasingly treated it in a discrete section, bracketed from other subjects on which they reported. Although reports from the first half of the century included ethnographic information, they tended neither to gather that information in a discrete section nor to highlight its inclusion in the introduction of their relazioni. The future cardinal Gasparo Contarini, for example, included brief observations on the nature of the German and Spanish peoples in his 1525 report on the Hapsburg territories but did not foreground the discussion of customs in his preamble.[45] By 1551, the returning ambassador to England, Daniele Barbaro, not only included a discrete section on religion and customs in his relazione; he included a justification for doing so in the preamble to his report.[46]

The bracketing of ethnographic information in a discrete section was an important development and one that further set the Venetian relazioni apart from other contemporary genres that included ethnographic information, notably forms of travel literature. Travel accounts, by their very nature, were organized geographically rather than thematically and tended to present whatever ethnographic information they contained episodically. In the relazioni, by contrast, ethnographic information came to be treated as a discrete form of knowledge, to be collected and reported on alongside information about a country's geography, climate, natural resources, and state expenditures. In a genre that, from its inception, had been highly analytical and syncretic, this development was perhaps unsurprising, but its consequences were far reaching.

The Uses of Ethnographic Information to the State

Statements counseling the inclusion of ethnographic information in the relazioni raise the question of what utility that information had, or was perceived to have, for the state. Although the ethnographic sections of a relazione may seem like a departure from more concrete reporting on state expenditures, military preparedness, and political organization, some of the ethnographic reporting in the relazioni was in fact linked to perceived exigencies of state. In order to understand these links, it is necessary to delve into Venetian patricians' assumptions about the political functions of religion.

For Venetian ambassadors, as for many other early modern Europeans, the religious integrity of a state was intimately tied to its political integrity.[47] The assumption that religious divisions within a state would inevitably be accompanied by political turmoil undergirded some of the newly emphasized ethnographic reporting in the relazioni, particularly reporting on religious observances. This commonplace was articulated with great concision by Nicolò Michiel, the Venetian nobleman who traveled as part of the diplomatic retinue of the Antonio Barbarigo to Istanbul and wrote an account of his journey in 1558.[48] He begins his discrete section titled "On the Religion of the Turks" by declaring, "A prince cannot rule his state if there is no religion among the people; and the more the people are observant of ceremonies, the more obedient they will be to their prince and the more obstinate they will be in the defense of his faith."[49] In what follows, he gives a wide-ranging account of religious observances modeled on the relazione and touching on mosque architecture, ritual ablution, and the practice of salat.[50] Since ambassadors shared with their primary audience an assumption that multiconfessional states were inherently weak, ethnographic reporting on religious diversity was not necessarily extraneous to the avowed political focus of the relazione. Instead, keeping the doge, his counselors, and the Senate informed about the religious beliefs and practices of the state in which the ambassador had served was seen as essential to a full understanding of the political prospects of that state.

The deeply held view that there existed a link between religious change and political disorder shaped Venetian ambassadors' accounts of the Reformation in their relazioni. Daniele Barbaro served as the Venetian ambassador to England to congratulate Edward VI on his coronation. Barbaro's relazione, delivered in 1551, has an extensive section treating ethnographic material, particularly as it relates to changes in religious observance in England. Barbaro, who upon his return from England was elected patriarch of Aquileia, structures his treatment of religion in a unique way: the section is organized according to the seven sacraments, and Barbaro outlines for his audience novelties and retentions in the observance of each of the sacraments. Notably, he prefaces this section with a statement on the political importance of religious observance. Barbaro offers a dim assessment of the prospects for English political integrity given the religious transformations the country had undergone over the past two decades. "Religion," he declares, "is as the heart of the man, the thing on which life depends; it is an optimum means, as can be seen in all republics and governments, and especially in monarchies, of moderating men's minds and making them know God, the giver of states, and of victory, but this cannot happen in the English case, because nothing is more inconstant than their decrees regarding religion, for today they do one thing and tomorrow another."[51]

A slightly different formulation of the relationship between religious observance and political loyalty occurs in the relazione of Giovanni Michiel, delivered in 1557. Michiel was sent as ambassador to England in 1553, six years after Daniele Barbaro, for the occasion of Mary I's accession to the throne. Like Barbaro, Michiel prefaces his treatment of religion in England with a statement about the political import of religious observance. The English, he states,

> satisfy their duty as subjects toward their prince by living as he lives, believing what he believes, and in short doing whatever he commands, making use of religion for external show to avoid incurring his displeasure rather than from any internal zeal. They would do the same with the Mohammedan or Jewish religion, were their king to show belief in those religions and will it thus. They would accommodate themselves to anything, but more willingly to those religions that give them hope, either of the greatest license and liberty in their mode of life, or of some profit.[52]

Whereas Barbaro placed his emphasis on internal piety as a moderating force conducive to political stability, Michiel instead emphasizes the importance of subjects' external observance of the faith of their ruler. Even in the absence of any "internal zeal" for Mary's Catholic faith, the English people could still be expected to act as loyal subjects provided they adhered externally to the faith. Indeed, Michiel declares that he is ultimately skeptical about the prospect of Mary's younger subjects ever truly "returning" to the Catholic faith, since they are too young to remember a time before the English Reformation. He reports that owing to the religious upheaval of the previous decades, there are no truly pious Catholics to be found in England under the age of thirty-five.[53] In spite of this, he remains optimistic about the prospects for political tranquility in England given that the English have demonstrated a propensity to adhere to the faith of their ruler.

Ambassadors returning from France, England, the Holy Roman Empire, and Poland sought to describe changes in religious observance and to enumerate the effects of those changes on the body politic. Michele Soriano, for example, the Venetian ambassador to France from 1559 to 1561, describes in his relazione the wide-ranging effects of the Reformation in France. The spread of Protestantism, according to Soriano, has "removed the fear of God from the people," with deleterious effects to public order and the authority of the king.[54] One of the principal ways in which religious change acts on the political integrity of the state is by altering the customs of the people. Thus, in Soriano's words, "[In addition to removing the fear of God], the other bad effect wrought by this alteration of religion is the destruction of the policy and order of the government, because from this alteration is born the change of customs and of the usual way of life, which leads to contempt of the laws, and of the authority of the magistrates and, finally, also of the prince."[55] This statement echoes that of his relazione delivered three years prior in which he discussed the situation in England. In his earlier report, too, Soriano emphasizes the role of religious change in altering the customs of the people along with their obedience to their sovereign. This process, he argues, has been observed not only in England but also in Asia, Africa, and large swaths of Europe.[56]

Whereas for Soriano, it was religious change and the attendant alteration of customs that precipitated political instability, for other ambassadors, particularly those reporting from large, multiethnic empires, the existence of ethnic and cultural diversity could itself be seen as a source of political instability. This is evident, for example, in the surviving summary of the relazione, which likely dates from 1578, of Vincenzo Tron, ambassador to Emperor Maximilian II and his successor Rudolf II.[57] It is unclear whether the surviving summary was made by someone present for the delivery of Tron's relazione, or whether the summary served as a sort of outline of the speech made by Tron himself.[58] Whatever the origins of the surviving summary, however, it is clear that Tron devoted a great deal of his attention in his report to cultural differences between the emperor's Hungarian, German, and Bohemian subjects. Tron in fact suggests that the empire's cultural and linguistic diversity—and not only its religious diversity—is a source of weakness. The summary of the relazione notes that Tron reported that "just as all these peoples of Germany are different in language, so too are they discordant in many areas of nature and customs."[59] Tron proceeds to enumerate the deficiencies of each of the three peoples in broad terms. The Hungarians, for example, are brave but seditious; the Germans avaricious, distrustful, and proud; the Bohemians prone to heresy and overly credulous.[60] In fact, Tron sees little common cultural ground between the three principal nations of the empire. He does report that the three nations share a common propensity for excessive drinking, which the summary renders with memorable concision: "Common defect of drinking: the poor when they can, the rich at all times."[61] Beyond this, though, they share only the opinion that their own nation is the best and their contempt for all other nations, which in Tron's view makes the empire especially difficult to govern.[62]

A similar logic informed the relazioni of Venetian ambassadors to Istanbul. Within the Venetian diplomatic network, the Ottoman Empire was unparalleled in terms of its religious and ethnic diversity. Accordingly, the body of Ottoman relazioni came to display an even greater preoccupation with the challenges of governance in a multiconfessional state. In presenting the Ottoman religious landscape, they increasingly came to focus not only on the sultan's Christian and Jewish subjects but also on religious divisions within Islam. This kind of reporting was almost entirely absent in the surviving fifteenth- and early sixteenth-century relazioni delivered by Venetian baili and ambassadors. The earliest Venetian diplomatic reports on confessional differences within Islam were in fact delivered by envoys in Persia. The focus of these reports was obviously very different from those of the relazioni of later baili and ambassadors in the Ottoman Empire; the purpose of the earlier reports was not to discuss the challenges of governing the multiconfessional Ottoman Empire but rather to contextualize divisions between the Ottoman and Safavid Empires.

In part, the absence of reporting on religious diversity within the Ottoman Empire in the earliest surviving relazioni may be the result of the smaller number of subject peoples under Ottoman rule in the first decades of the sixteenth century. This is not a fully satisfactory explanation, however, because even those relazioni delivered in the immediate aftermath of the Ottoman conquest of Mamulk Egypt and Syria in 1516–1517, for example, fail to report on any religious and cultural differences between the Ottomans and their new subjects. Alvise Mocenigo and Bartolomeo Contarini, the two ambassadors sent in 1517 to congratulate Selim I on his military victories in Egypt, make no mention of religious difference in their reports. Their accounts instead deal almost exclusively with military and fiscal affairs.[63] In contrast, for Venetian representatives in the second half of the century, religious and cultural differences between the Ottomans and their Arab and "Moorish" subjects in Africa would become a major theme of the relazioni.

While in the second half of the sixteenth century, Venetian baili and ambassadors sought to describe the state of religious and ethnic diversity in the Ottoman Empire in order to draw attention to potential weaknesses in the Ottoman state, in so doing, they both drew on and helped to develop an increasingly elaborate religious and ethnic taxonomy of the Muslim world. They did so at a time when cognizance of confessional diversity within the Islam elsewhere in western Europe was not particularly developed.[64] Even within Venice, with its significant—albeit usually transient—Muslim population, this awareness was lacking. For example, Pietro Ioly Zorattini's work on the Venetian Pia Casa dei Catecumeni, the Jesuit-run institution for housing and instructing converts, has revealed a truncated view of Islam among members of the congregation. Despite dealing with a largely Muslim body of catechumens, officials at the institution tended to view Islam as a monolithic whole and evinced little awareness of the existence of diverse juridical and theological schools.[65]

By contrast, Venetian baili and ambassadors showed a much greater interest in divisions within Islam. Marcantonio Barbaro, the younger brother of Daniele Barbaro, served as bailo from 1568 to 1573. Barbaro's unusually long term as bailo was the result of the outbreak of the War of Cyprus in 1570 and his subsequent detainment under house arrest. In his report to the Senate, delivered after the Ottoman-Venetian negotiation of peace in 1573, Barbaro emphasized that religious and cultural differences among Ottoman subject peoples in Europe, Africa, and Asia ultimately posed a significant challenge to Ottoman rule. "All of their subject peoples," he reports, "are their enemies, and especially in the westernmost part, which not only borders the Christian princes but is also entirely inhabited by people of the [Christian] religion; nor do they lack enemies in the eastern part of their empire, since there the Turks are of the Persian sect, and the Moors too have many differences in their law with those of the Porte."[66] Barbaro's three-part typology of Islam (Moorish, Persian, Turkish) would become common in late sixteenth-century Venetian reports on the Ottoman Empire.[67]

However, whereas Barbaro is content simply to note the existence of religious differences between subjects without elaborating on the substance of those differences, subsequent baili and ambassadors would provide much greater detail in their relazioni. Sixteen years later, for example, the returning bailo Lorenzo Bernardo outlined the same tensions between the sultan's various Muslim subjects but elaborated on the origins of those divisions and their ramifications. "Today," he reported,

> religion among them is very divided, with nearly all of Asia following the Persian religion, according to the doctrine of Ali, the disciple of Mohammed, their common prophet. And those who follow that opinion are called *chisillas*, that is red crest, by the Turks because they usually wear on their head a certain red band to make themselves known to others. Furthermore, in Africa there are Arabs and Moors who, although they are Mohammedans like the Turks, are of a different opinion in many things, and each of them holds their own opinion to be true. The Arabs do not wish to enter the mosques of the Turks of Europe to pray, holding them to be of a corrupt and, as they say, bastard religion.[68]

In his relazione delivered in 1592 following his return to Istanbul, Bernardo provides his audience with even more detail about religious and ethnic divisions within the Ottoman Empire.[69] In his second report, he explicates the ethnoreligious category of "Turks of Europe" introduced in his 1590 report. He explains that the category is not of his own invention but rather, one employed by the sultan's Arab subjects, who use it or the alternative "Turks of Greece" to refer to the powerful group of Ottoman officials who were converts from Christianity to Islam. Converts, the Arabs charge, are opportunistic social climbers with little grasp of the Muslim faith. Bernardo, for his part, makes clear that he shares this assessment, as did many other Venetian officials in Istanbul.[70] He reports that he himself has met many converts in Istanbul who are irreligious and hold religion itself to be an invention of men to aid in governing the people.[71]

Finally, ambassadors also presented ethnographic information relating to divisions within Islam to help contextualize military conflicts between the Ottoman Empire and the Persian Safavid Empire. Venice intermittently pursued a military alliance with the Safavids against the Ottomans, making the Persian-Ottoman rivalry of particular interest to members of the Senate.[72] Because the republic did not have a permanent representative to the Safavid court, Venetian-Persian diplomatic contact was episodic, with activity peaking during periods of war with the Ottoman Empire. An envoy was sent to the Safavid court during each of the three sixteenth-century Venetian-Ottoman wars, all three of whom delivered relazioni.[73]

There was great interest in Venice in the news of the military victories of Shah Ismail Safavi (r. 1501–1524), particularly since these came at the time of the Second Ottoman-Venetian War. Gathering information on the newly proclaimed shah became a priority of the Signoria.[74] The diaries of Marin Sanudo, for example, contain more than a hundred reports on Ismail that reached Venice between 1501 and 1504.[75] The earliest state reports on the political import of confessional differences within Islam came not from the baili or ambassadors to the Ottoman court but from Costantino Lascari's 1502 relazione following his mission to Iran. Despite failing to negotiate a military alliance with the shah, Lascari reports that the Persians are well disposed toward Venice. They are also sworn enemies of the Ottomans, since the Persians, he reports, view the Ottomans as "heretics to the faith of Mohammed and usurpers of the states of many Muslim lords."[76] Lascari proceeds to explain the religious differences between the Persians and Ottomans in terms derived from the early history of Christianity: "The shah is very devoted to his sect, which is a certain Catholic religion in their own way, in disagreement about the opinion of its prophet Mohammed and his disciple Omar. The shah adhered to the opinion of Ali, who was also a disciple of the prophet. Yet in the article of their faith they were dissidents as one can say the Aryans were in the time of Saint Peter at the other pontiffs, since, although they were Christians, they were also heretics."[77]

Not all later Venetian diplomats were as convinced as Lascari that religious differences were ultimately at the root of the Ottoman-Safavid imperial rivalry. Giacomo Soranzo, the two-time ambassador to the Ottoman Empire, diligently rehearsed the nature of the confessional divisions in both his relazioni but made clear that he saw territorial disputes rather than religious differences as the true source of the conflict.[78] Diplomatic reporting on religion in the Persian Empire was among the most pragmatic of all the ethnographic information presented in the relazioni. Just as diplomatic efforts in Persia were concentrated during periods of Venetian military conflict with the Ottoman Empire, so too were baili and ambassadors to Istanbul more likely to dwell on Ottoman-Persian religious differences during periods of war. Reporting tended to arise during times of war either between the Ottomans and Venetians or between the Ottomans and Persians.

Ethnography and the Relazione beyond Considerations of State

As every ambassador noted in his address before the Senate or Collegio the primary purpose of the relazione was to provide members of the government with the information they needed to make judicious decisions in matters of foreign policy. Given contemporary understandings of the parameters of matters of state, some of the ethnographic reporting by Venetian ambassadors was clearly connected to this purpose: information on new religious observances could serve as an index to a state's prospects for political integrity; an understanding of the divisions between Sunni and Shi'a Islam was seen as important in assessing Persia's potential as an anti-Ottoman ally. The ethnographic reporting of Venetian ambassadors, however, was not always connected to considerations of state, even when this concept is taken at its most capacious. Several ambassadors, particularly in the late sixteenth and early seventeenth centuries, began reporting on a variety of topics related to dress, custom, belief, and daily life without connecting these to the interests of the Venetian state, either explicitly or implicitly.

Vincenzo degli Alessandri's 1574 relazione following his mission to Persia, for example, describes the sleeping arrangements, physical appearance, and dress of the Persian people. "The Persians," he reports,

> are for the most part poor people. In the cities and towns, they do not use many adornments. Everyone sleeps on the ground, and those who are of some condition use a mattress on top of carpeting, the others use only felt. The women are, for the most part, all ugly, but of beautiful features and noble complexions, although their clothing is not as close-fitting as that of the Turks. They are accustomed, however, to dressing in silk and wearing on their heads a caftan, allowing the face to be seen by those they wish and concealing it from those they do not wish to see it.[79]

Here, Alessandri presents a patchwork of ethnographic information, one that in many ways resembles the unfocused ethnographic accounts found in contemporary travel literature. Significantly, he does not articulate any relationship between the information he presents and the interests of the Venetian state.

Ottoman relazioni, too, were subject to a similar proliferation of ethnographic information, particularly as it became more common for ambassadors to include discrete sections on religion in their reports. Several late sixteenth- and early seventeenth-century representatives to the Ottoman court included in their reports lengthy discussions on the historical evolution of Islamic thought and religious observance. As with Alessandri's digression on Persian dress and sleeping arrangements, these discussions were not connected in any clear way to the contemporary interests of the Venetian state. The accounts of the baili and ambassadors presented Islam as a syncretic religion, which selectively and strategically combined elements of Christianity and Judaism. One of the first representatives to present such an account was Gianfrancesco Morosini, who served as bailo from 1582 to 1585.[80] While Morosini opts to keep his treatment of the historical origins of Islam quite short, the subject would receive more attention in the relazioni of his successors. Leonardo Donà, who served as ambassador for the coronation of Mehmed III, offered one of the more elaborate treatments of the subject. He signals his intent to address religion in the introduction of his relazione.[81] "The religion of the Turks," Donà reports, "was extracted by those who in the beginning invented it artificially with the goal of ruling from the old Mosaic law of the Jews and from that of Christ our redeemer, picking and leaving aside from each of them that which conferred with their intention and which they judged would easily be received by the souls of their followers."[82]

Nearly identical passages on the syncretic nature of Islam appear in the relazioni of Agostino Nani and Simone Contarini, delivered respectively in 1603 and 1612.[83] Donà pointed to the worship of a single deity, the precepts of charity and almsgiving, and the practices of fasting as elements derived from Christianity and Judaism.[84] Nani and Contarini would add circumcision and abstention from pork to Donà's list of appropriations from Judaism.[85] To these borrowed customs, Donà continued, Muslims added certain liberties to their religious law which made the religion particularly attractive to "sensual" persons, thereby seducing them away from competing religions.[86] While Donà declined to specify these liberties, his successors were less circumspect. Nani listed among these concessions the sanctioning of men taking multiple wives and the sexual use of slaves. In addition to attracting converts, Nani speculated that these concessions may historically have served the double purpose of facilitating repopulation following outbreaks of plague.[87]

When ambassadors and baili gave an account of the syncretic origins of Islam, they were not being particularly innovative; they were certainly not, as early modern champions of the relazione would have it, presenting information derived from observation and firsthand experience. They were, however, placing a new emphasis on an old idea. Fifteenth-century humanists had also attempted to explain Islam's ability to attract converts in terms of its supposed promises of carnal pleasure.[88] In his letter to Mehmed II (1461), for example, Pius II explains Mohammed's early success in attracting converts in such terms: "His discovery did not disappoint in this regard, for it was pleasing, and thus in a little while it grew and was received by many peoples of many languages because its foundation was pleasure."[89] In the sixteenth century, the charge that religious obligations might be made less onerous in order to attract converts had of course been made in the context of the Reformation.[90] It was a mainstay of Catholic polemic and also appeared frequently in Venetian ambassadors' accounts of the Reformation in their relazioni. In language anticipating Simone Contarini's, Giovanni Michiel, the ambassador to England under Mary I, claimed that many of the queen's subjects were understandably reluctant to reembrace Catholicism, having enjoyed for twenty years' freedom from the obligations of sacramental confession, religious abstention from meat, and strict prohibitions on consanguinity.[91] Such resemblances underscore the extent to which the experience of the European Reformation served as a key model for understanding religious change elsewhere.

Nor was the idea that Islam had borrowed heavily from other religions particularly novel.[92] The idea of Islam as a Christian heresy or at least a religion that drew from Christian heresies was one with a long history. In his eighth-century *De haeresibus*, John of Damascus both addressed what he termed the "heresy of the Ishmaelites" as a Christian heresy and attributed the development of its doctrine to Mohammed's instruction by an Arian monk.[93] In the Latin Christian tradition, the idea of Arian influence would come to be eclipsed by Nestorian influence, but the broad outlines of earlier accounts remained the same.[94] This was the case, for example, with Peter the Venerable's *Summa totius haeresis saracenorum* (ca. 1143–1144), which was included in the paratext of the first printed Latin translation of the Qur'an, published in Basel in 1543.[95]

Christian authors continued to write polemical accounts of Islamic syncretism in the fifteenth and sixteenth centuries. In his *Utilissma consultatio de bello turcis inferendo*, Erasmus had asserted that Islam was derived from a mixture of Judaism, Christianity, Arianism, and paganism.[96] In the fifteenth century, the charge was also found in Nicholas of Cusa's *Cribratio Alkorani*, although there the influence was attributed to Nestorianism rather than Arianism.[97] In other fifteenth-century iterations still, notably the *Commentaries* of Pius II, Islam was seen as having borrowed from both Arian and Nestorian Christianity.[98] In the sixteenth-century Venetian context, this view also circulated widely in mid-century printed ethnographic literature on the Turks and Islam. Two of the more notable examples are the Venetian subject Luigi Bassano's account of Turkish customs and the anonymous preface attached to the Italian edition of the Qur'an printed in Venice in 1547.[99] Donà, who kept particularly detailed notes on his library, certainly owned a copy of Bassano's *Costumi*, and it is likely that his successors would also have read these works.[100] At the very least, they would certainly have been familiar with Donà's relazione.

In their relazioni, however, Donà, Nani, and Contarini do not simply repeat late-medieval commonplaces about the origins of Islam. Indeed, they omit the most damning part of medieval accounts—namely, that Islam had borrowed not simply from Christianity but from Christian heresies. They instead shift their emphasis from the theological significance of the Muslim syncretism to its political significance, emphasizing religion as a tool of Ottoman rule. In the process, they also displaced the culpability for the borrowing from Mohammed himself, as Nicholas of Cusa and Pius II do, to a more nebulous group of actors, thereby suggesting a contemporary as opposed to merely historical relevance.[101] In so doing, the baili and ambassadors were displaying their erudition and mastery of the relevant historical source while also shaping their accounts to conform to the generic parameters of the relazione.

The Limits of Autopsy

Ethnographic observations in the relazioni were thoroughly mediated through their authors' textual engagement, whether that came in the form of engagement with printed works of history and geography or with the manuscript works of their predecessors. This textual engagement left traces in ambassadors' libraries and notebooks as well as in the relazioni themselves, making it possible to reconstruct diplomatic reading practices (see chapter 4). But ambassadors' ethnographic observations were also mediated through the work of flesh-and-blood intermediaries on the ground. The ability of ambassadors to carry out the work of diplomacy and information gathering, including the work of ethnographic observation, hinged largely on the labor of intermediaries.

Ambassadors brought with them large household staffs and retinues, and members of ambassadorial households from secretaries to diplomatic interpreters to physicians all served as important information brokers.[102] In a handful of instances, there is evidence that secretarial "mediation" extended to ghostwriting relazioni, although this does not appear to have occurred in the case of ambassadorial reports.[103] Linguistic difference alone necessitated ambassadors' reliance on linguistic intermediaries. In Istanbul, for example, only one Venetian bailo after the 1550s learned Turkish.[104] There, Venetian baili and ambassadors were heavily reliant for information gathering on the specialized corps of diplomatic interpreters, or dragomans, who in turn came to play an important role in systematizing knowledge of the Ottoman Empire.[105]

Ambassadors' intelligence-gathering functions meant that they were viewed with deep suspicion by their host states. Just as foreign ambassadors did in Venice, Venetian ambassadors abroad often found their mobility and access to local informants restricted, thereby compounding their reliance on intermediaries.[106] In Venice, the Council of Ten required Venetians to obtain a license before meeting with foreign ambassadors, and foreign states reciprocated with their own limitations on the social activities of ambassadors.[107] Ambassadors were also tied to the courts at which they represented Venice. While this sometimes involved following an itinerant court, it more often meant staying put. Leonardo Donà complained that spending most of his embassy at Philip II's new capital in Madrid placed him at a disadvantage compared to his predecessors who had traveled with itinerant courts. His stationary post in land-locked Madrid, for example, left him ill-equipped to gather intelligence on maritime trade, a matter of crucial importance to the Venetian government.[108] In their relazioni, then, ambassadors sought to report on the peoples and customs of a state as a whole, while in practice they saw only narrow and rarefied bands of the states in which they served. These restrictions, too, limited ambassadors' ability to engage in firsthand observation and made inevitable the reliance on intermediaries in the collation of ethnographic information.

By design, though, this human mediation left few traces in the relazioni as ambassadors crafted their reports to maximize their own singular authority as a speaker. In their reports, ambassadors sought both to display their own erudition and position themselves as brokers of exclusive information. There was a potential tension between these two objectives since the display of erudition through engagement with written authorities could undermine an ambassador's claim to the exclusivity of his report. If the logic of the relazioni left some room for acknowledging the mediation of textual authorities, there was little room for rendering visible the mediation of the ambassador's subordinates.

Venetian audiences were closely attuned both to the question of textual mediation in the relazione and to the related issue of ethnographic reporting exceeding the bounds of information pertinent to governance. In certain quarters of the Venetian patriciate, the proliferation of ethnographic reporting in ambassadorial reports was a matter of some controversy. At issue was whether certain ambassadors had strayed too far from matters of clear relevance to the state and were treating the relazione as a vehicle for the display of their own erudition. One of the common ways of articulating such a complaint was by charging that ambassadors were duplicating in their reports information that could be found "in books." This concern can be seen first and foremost in the relazioni themselves. Several ambassadors took pains in the openings of their reports to emphasize that their own reports would not duplicate information that their audience could readily find in books. As early as 1561, for example, Giovanni Michiel, the returning ambassador to the court of Ferdinand I, offered such a disclaimer.[109] Michiel explained that because so much had been written about Germany by historians and geographers, no one could help but be somewhat informed about the country through his own reading. Accordingly, his report would refrain from addressing topics that appealed merely to the curiosity of his audience and would instead deal only with matters "worthy of being known by men of state."[110] Statements such as Michiel's were, of course, a means for ambassadors to flatter their audience in the Senate by appealing to their breadth of knowledge. While still operating within the decorous parameters of a relazione, such statements disavowing vanity and appealing to curiosity were also an implicit rebuke to the ambassadors who had delivered relazioni before them.

While it would have been outside the parameters of the relazione for an ambassador to single out particular ambassadors and their relazioni for censure, one ambassador did just that in his personal notes. In 1592, the future doge Leonardo Donà wrote what was effectively a review of Pietro Duodo's relazione of Poland.[111] The document is unique in that commentary on particular relazioni usually exists in the form of marginal annotations in manuscript copies of those reports rather than as a separate text. Commentaries on individual ambassadorial relazioni are also rarely as sustained as Donà's. Writing in the same evening in which Duodo had delivered his report and commenting on the ambassador's oratorical performance, Donà evidently made his on the basis of Duodo's oral delivery of the relazione rather than a written copy.[112] Donà, a prodigious collector of relazioni, also had in his possession a copy of the text of the relazione, presumably obtained at a later date.[113] Although Donà does summarize the key points of Duodo's relazione, the document differs from usual summaries of relazioni in that it also critically evaluates the content and the delivery of the ambassador's report.[114]

Even though he appreciated Duodo's skill as an orator, writing that Duodo's delivery was graceful and his memory impressive, Donà was on the whole critical of the relazione.[115] Duodo had reported on a number of subjects that were, in Donà's view, insufficiently related to affairs of state. Much of Duodo's relazione, he writes, is "more fitting to history than to a relazione, in which considerations of state are more appropriate than other curiosities that can best be seen in books."[116] Although the category of "curiosities" is a broad one that could encompass ethnographic as well as nonethnographic material, the portions of the relazione that Donà singles out for criticism suggest that he was referring primarily to Duodo's ethnographic reporting. Donà, for example, is especially censorious of Duodo's treatment of Polish idolatry: "He said that in certain parts of the kingdom some people are idolaters . . . that they worship a certain serpent and other fabulous things, which can also be read in books."[117] Since Duodo's itinerary did not take him to northwestern Lithuania, where he claimed the most pronounced vestiges of Lithuania's pagan past could be found, his report almost certainly drew on what he had read. Donà may have detected echoes of the accounts of Lithuanian serpent worship contained in Martin Kromer's and Olaus Magnus's histories, the latter of which he owned in multiple editions.[118] Donà was himself intimately familiar with the genre of the relazione. Like many Venetian patricians, he had studied written copies from a young age; he had also, by 1592, delivered several relazioni of his own.[119] Donà's report on the Ottoman Empire, delivered four years after Duodo's relazione, would, of course, include its own lengthy section on religion which was, arguably, only tangentially related to "considerations of state."

In the early seventeenth century, statements disavowing curiosities and the repetition of information that could be found in books became commonplace in ambassadorial relazioni themselves. Tommaso Contarini began his 1610 relazione of the Dutch republic by claiming that he would limit himself to the most essential topics, leaving aside any material that his audience could readily find in works of history.[120] It is worth noting that Contarini remains true to his word. When, for example, he discusses the local population's penchant for beer—a recurring topos in Venetian reporting on northern European states—he does so only in the context of examining tax revenue collected from beer.[121] The returning bailo Cristoforo Valier makes a similar statement in the introduction to his 1616 report, claiming that he will omit "description, history, the treatment of completed business, and superfluity of words, the end of the relazione being utility and not ambition; I shall attend only to real and necessary matters."[122] Valier's is one of the clearest statements that personal ambition might lie at the heart of the proliferation of extraneous material in the relazione, including ethnographic information. Here, the suggestion that other ambassadors used their relazioni to further their own ambitions is made not only explicitly but in a public forum.

Statements such as Contarini's and Valier's reveal some of the tensions at work in the crafting of a diplomatic report. To fully appreciate these tensions, it is necessary to recall the context in which ambassadors delivered their relazioni. The delivery of an ambassadorial report was one of the most important acts of a Venetian patrician's career; the performance was an occasion for the ambassador to display his acumen and clarity of judgment, his learning, eloquence, and experience.[123] An ambassador would expect to have his performance and the text of his speech closely scrutinized by a body of his peers—Leonardo Donà's notes on Duodo's relazione reveals just how closely. The nearly universal acclaim with which some relazioni, such as Lorenzo Bernardo's report on the Ottoman Empire and Vincenzo Querini's on the Holy Roman Empire, were received demonstrates just how important a successful performance could be for a patrician's reputation.[124] Within the relatively confined political world of the Venetian patriciate, an ambassador's performance mattered greatly. Given the expectations of his audience, an ambassador needed to display his erudition. At the same time, he needed to avoid the appearance of using his relazione and the major audience it delivered to further his own ambition.

Nonambassadorial Relazioni

Ambassadors were not the only officials charged with the delivery of oral reports and the filing of written copies of their relazioni. From 1524, the Senate extended the obligation to all public officials stationed outside of Venice, whether in foreign or subject territories.[125] This included consuls representing Venetian merchant communities in cities such as Alexandria, Aleppo, and Cairo as well as administrators in Venice's mainland and maritime territories—the *terraferma* and *stato da mar*. Reports by administrators in Venice's subject territories form the largest body of Venetian relazioni, outnumbering both ambassadorial and consular reports. The modern edition of reports from the terraferma alone includes over a thousand reports.[126] Consular and imperial relazioni differ appreciably in style and content from the ambassadorial relazioni. These reports were shorter and more focused on quotidian details than those of ambassadors. They were, on the whole, less synthetic than ambassadorial relazioni. Although ethnographic reporting took on a greater prominence in ambassadorial relazioni over the course of the sixteenth century and indeed came to be expected by audiences and readers, nonambassadorial relazioni remained relatively untouched by these developments. Within the relazioni, ethnographic reporting was largely the preserve of ambassadors.

The prestige of the office of ambassador helps to explain the relative absence of ethnographic reporting in nonambassadorial relazioni. The platform of consuls and of most officials in the stato da mar and terraferma was simply not at the same level as that of the ambassadors. As a rule, they were younger men at earlier stages of their careers. The delivery of their reports was not met with the same interest as the delivery of ambassadorial relazioni, and judging by the number of extant manuscript copies, the contents of their reports were not scrutinized as closely after the performance. The relative importance attached to ambassadorial and nonambassadorial relazioni can also be gauged by their length. The four-hour performances to which ambassadors treated their audiences, however, almost unheard of in relazioni delivered by other officials. More typical of consular and other nonambassadorial relazioni was Domenico Molin's brief relazione of Damascus, which spans only two folios.[127]

The absence of ethnographic reporting in consular relazioni also reveals that simply reporting on an "exotic" locale was not sufficient to mandate ethnographic reporting. Several examples from the relazioni of Venetian consuls illustrate this point. In addition to the bailo in Istanbul, who provided both ambassadorial and consular functions, there were several other consuls representing Venetian merchant communities throughout the Ottoman Empire, all of whom were expected to deliver relazioni.[128] As a rule, consuls in the Ottoman Empire did not dwell on ethnographic information in their relazioni in the same way the bailo did. This was true of the consul Domenico Molin's 1548 relazione of Damascus, which focused entirely on commercial affairs.[129] Forty-five years later, at a time when, as we have seen, ambassadors were devoting more attention to ethnographic material in their own reports, the consul Tommaso Contarini's 1593 relazione on Syria was still devoted almost entirely to commercial affairs.[130] While this is perhaps attributable to Contarini's particular aversion to extraneous information in relazioni for which, as we have seen, he expressed a distaste in his later ambassadorial relazione, the reports of Contarini's successors are marked by the same absence of ethnographic reporting. This is true, for example, of Giorgio Emo's 1599 relazione on Syria.[131] Ethnographic reporting was simply not part of the genre of the consular relazione.

Part of the difference between ambassadorial and nonambassadorial relazione can be explained by the different scopes of the offices. The duties of a consul were much more narrowly commercial than those of an ambassador or of the bailo in Istanbul. Toward the end of the sixteenth century, the consul in Syria, Alessandro Malipiero, described the principal duty of his office as the "care and protection of the commerce of merchandise in which Venetian merchants deal in those parts."[132] It is understandable, then, that their relazioni would be less expansive than those of their ambassadorial counterparts. It was not unusual for a patrician to serve as a consul or rector earlier in his career before becoming an ambassador, and the men who did so understood well the differing conventions of the two types of relazioni. Daniele Barbarigo, for example, served as the Venetian consul in Alexandria a decade before serving as bailo from 1562 to 1564. His 1554 report on Alexandria is fairly typical of a consular relazione; if anything, it runs a little long.[133] In it, Barbarigo limits his discussion almost entirely to commercial affairs. Like many other relazioni, Barbarigo's contains a résumé toward the beginning of his report, outlining the subjects to be treated. Barbarigo's summary, with its promise to treat "le cose del Signor Turco" (the affairs of the Ottoman sultan), actually suggests a more expansive relazione than was typical for consuls.[134] In the course of the report, however, it becomes clear that these "cose" are entirely commercial. His relazione following his return as bailo from Istanbul is very different in nature. To begin with, the later relazione is four times longer than his earlier report on Alexandria, allowing Barbarigo to treat a more expansive range of topics.[135] Although more restrained in its ethnographic content than later Ottoman relazioni, Barbarigo's relazione still addresses Muslim prohibitions on alcohol, the practice of pilgrimage to Mecca, and religious conversion in Portuguese Goa.[136] The patrician's two reports, separated by only a decade, reveal the extent to which ethnographic reporting was the prerogative of the more senior figure of the ambassador.

Ethnographic information did not consistently feature in reports from either the terraferma or the stato da mar, which, as scholars of Venetian imperial administration have shown, were dominated by matters of military preparedness and agricultural capacity.[137] Even in the stato da mar where Venice ruled over territories confessionally divided between Greek and Latin Christians, administrators rarely addressed questions of religion. Gerassimos Pagratis, editor of the series of relazioni from Venetian Corfu, notes that there was not only scant discussion of Corfiot religious observance in the reports; there was little attention paid to the inhabitants of the island at all.[138] Officials in the stato da mar and terraferma alike discussed local residents largely in terms of their material needs—food insecurity and the status of communal granaries were perennial preoccupations of Venetian administrators—and their productive capacity.[139] Their reports described not peoples with customs but populations that might be counted on to fight or increase the territory's productive capacity.

Just as ambassadors did in their reports, Venetian imperial officials outlined the contents of the reports in their preambles, in the process indicating what material they thought such a relazione ought to cover. Zuane Barbarigo, the returning patrician governor, or *provveditore*, of Zante (Zakynthos), divided his short 1542 report on the territory into four distinct sections: the provisioning of naval galleys, arquebusiers, "the city," dealing with Zante's fortifications rather than its inhabitants, and "grains," covering both agricultural productivity and taxation.[140] Nowhere in this scheme were Venetian subjects on the island and their customs treated. While over the course of the sixteenth century the ambassadorial relazione grew to include a discrete section covering ethnographic information, there was no parallel development in nonambassadorial reports. Eight decades after Barbarigo's return from Zante, his successor, Paulo Basadonna, delivered a report that was considerably longer and more expansive in the topics it treated but without the section on the peoples and their customs that had by then become standard in ambassadorial reports. Basadonna divided his 1622 report into distinct sections and included a summary of the sections at the end, functioning as a sort of table of contents. Among the fourteen sections were treatments of the demographic toll of the plague, the state of the currant harvest, and munitions supplies, but nowhere did Basadonna address the customs of Zante.[141]

The absence of systematic ethnographic reporting did not stem from a lack of interest in the comparative study of customs but rather from the parameters of the genre and the scope of imperial officials' duties. Officials in the stato da mar and terraferma with a demonstrated interest in customs routinely omitted ethnographic information from their official relazioni. A case in point is the report of Giovanni Battista Giustiniano, who served as corepresentative, or syndic, Venetian Dalmatia and Albania. In addition to his official relazione, Giustiniano also left behind a travel journal in which he recorded his observations of each of the cities he visited. In the journal, he consistently remarked on the customs, language, and dress of the inhabitants. Like other visitors to the region, he was especially interested in the gendered nature of both bilingualism and the adoption of Italian dress (see chapter 3). Most men, he noted, spoke Italian in addition to their native language, and many elite men had also adopted Italian dress. Women, meanwhile, were uniformly Slavic in both their dress and language.[142] Although Giustiniano clearly drew on his travel journal in composing his relazione, none of his ethnographic observations made their way into the report.[143]

This pattern held through the early seventeenth century. It can be observed in the relazione delivered by Ottaviano Bon following his service as *provveditore inquisitore di terraferma*, a post that saw him travel throughout Friuli and the Trevigiano to monitor public representatives. Bon's office differed from other imperial posts in that it was typically held by established patricians who had already carved out successful political careers. In this respect, it resembled the office of ambassador. Indeed, some patricians, including Bon, held the position after having served as ambassadors. The inquisitors' relazioni, as Matteo Melchiorre notes, were more substantial and wider ranging than those of typical officials in the terraferma or stato da mar.[144] Nevertheless, their reports did not develop to include a discrete section on customs, nor did they typically incorporate ethnographic information even in a nonsystematic fashion. Bon's report, delivered in 1612, contained no ethnographic reporting on the areas he had visited.[145] In keeping with the scope of his office, Bon's focus was instead on matters of finance and defense. Less than a decade earlier, though, while serving as bailo in Istanbul, Bon had authored one of the most widely circulated accounts of Ottoman customs written by any Venetian ambassador: the *Descrizione del serraglio* (see chapter 4). His wide-ranging discussions of religious observances, foodways, marriage customs, and pedagogical practices show just how closely Bon was attuned to matters of customs. Given their inclusion of ethnographic reporting in their other writings, Bon, Giustiniano, and their contemporaries were clearly interested in the study of customs. At the same time, they were well versed in the distinct parameters of Venetian institutional genres. That they omitted ethnographic information from official relazioni is not a sign that they saw no value in the study of customs but rather that ethnographic reporting fell outside the purview of their reports.

Over the past two decades, diplomatic history has increasingly attended to the diversity of early modern diplomatic actors who operated outside the ranks of diplomatic corps.[146] Whereas historians of early modern diplomacy were long preoccupied with tracing the origin of the resident ambassador, historians now recognize that early modern diplomacy was driven not only by official diplomatic representatives but by the mediation of a range of nonambassadorial actors.[147] While the figure of the Venetian ambassador was at the heart of the "old" diplomatic history, the study of the crafting and reception of the relazioni reminds us that by design, Venetian ambassadors played multiple roles.[148] Far from being professionalized members of a permanent diplomatic corps, they were at once temporary diplomatic representatives and members of a patriciate called on to perform before their peers. As such, their reports were shaped by a variety of considerations, including a desire to secure their own intellectual reputations and advance their political careers.

If the relazione's primary audience of patricians was a confined one, its secondary one was considerably larger. It was through this secondary readership reached through the manuscript and, later, print circulation of the reports that the relazioni came to serve as models of ethnographic reporting. While some relazioni appeared in print in a series of works published under the title *Tesoro politico*, works either modeled on or borrowed from the reports predate the first publication of the *Tesoro* in 1589.[149] Despite the Venetian prohibition on their circulation, the reports traveled quickly in manuscript form. The Ferrarese diplomat Giulio Raviglio Rosso's 1560 history of Mary Tudor's reign borrowed heavily from the Venetian ambassador Giovanni Michiel's relazione on England, delivered only three years earlier.[150] In the same decade, the Venetian historian and publisher Francesco Sansovino drew from two Venetian relazioni in composing his biography of Charles V.[151] Francesco Marcaldi, the author of a series of short descriptions of European states, used Venetian relazioni as key sources in his 1588 and 1589 reports on the Ottoman Empire and Naples, which themselves circulated widely in manuscript.[152] Although most of the reworkings of the relazioni were written by Italian authors, the reports did have a transalpine reach. Beginning in the late sixteenth century, the relazioni would serve as models by northern European authors in the tradition of the *ars apodemica* for instructing travelers how to fruitfully observe and document the customs and political life of foreign states.[153]

Venetian relazioni were prized as models of reporting and sources of information on foreign states partly because they offered authoritative eyewitness accounts of those states without any of the troubling questions of reliability that clung to published forms of travel literature. Lazzaro Soranzo, whose description of the Ottoman Empire, *L'Ottomano*, took its structure and a great deal of its content from Venetian relazioni on the Ottoman court, put this plainly.[154] In his preface, Soranzo contrasts books of geography and cosmography with the relazioni. The former, he argues, abound with falsehoods because their authors repeat commonplaces from old works without seeing the lands they write about for themselves.[155] The Venetians in their wisdom not only sent shrewd and "perceptive" ambassadors trained in the observation of foreign states; they required those ambassadors to deposit written reports "with great trust and secrecy in an archive appointed for this purpose," thus allowing the reports to be of service to present and future statesmen.[156]

Although the relazione was certainly a genre resistant to innovation, its conventions were far from static. Over the course of the sixteenth century, ambassadors came to devote increasing attention to ethnographic subjects in their reports. A consensus emerged that the ideal relazione should address the religion and customs of the people in a given state. It is difficult to establish firmly when this consensus emerged, largely owing to the fragmentary nature of the early sixteenth-century documentation, itself a product of ambassadors' own laxity in complying with legislation requiring them to file written copies of their reports. Certainly, by the 1530s, audiences would not have been surprised to hear an ambassador speak about ethnographic topics in his address before the Senate or Collegio. Over the course of the century, ambassadors' treatment of ethnographic material continued to change as it came to occupy a more important place in the relazione. Increasingly, ethnographic content was treated in a discrete section of the relazione.

As every patrician knew, the central purpose of the relazione was to provide members of the government with the knowledge of foreign states that they needed to govern wisely. An ambassador was to present, in the words of the ambassador Giovanni Michiel, matters "worthy of men of state."[157] At first glance, it is thus somewhat surprising that ethnographic reporting would come to play such an important role in the relazione. Part of this development stemmed from contemporary understandings of what information was pertinent to matters of state. Rather than being extraneous, ethnographic reporting could be seen as eminently useful to men of state. Not all of the ethnographic reporting in the relazioni, however, fell into this category, particularly in the later decades of the sixteenth century. If ethnographic reporting was useful to men of state, it could also evidently be useful to the ambassador himself, allowing him to craft a more impressive, erudite, and engaging relazione. If an ambassador went too far, however, he was liable to be accused of dealing in mere curiosities or worse, matters found in books. All ambassadors, of course, consulted books in constructing their reports, but the charge points to the animating fiction of the relazione: that ambassadors presented information derived from observation and firsthand observation, filtered through the lens of their political acumen. This was the base on which their authority rested; it is why contemporaries read them and put faith in their claims. It is why, somewhat improbably, a body of legally protected government documents, created by and for a closed group of patricians, became important vehicles for the circulation of ethnographic knowledge.

CHAPTER THREE

Ethnography and the Venetian State

The early modern Venetian state's involvement with the production of ethnographic knowledge was not confined to institutional genre of the relazione. The state sponsored, enabled, and conferred authority on the production of ethnographic knowledge. The questions of what kinds of travelers could serve as ethnographic authorities and what kinds of claims they could make were urgent ones in the sixteenth century. They were also questions in which the Venetian state found occasion to intervene. The early reception of Ludovico de Varthema, the most famous early sixteenth-century European traveler to India and a self-styled authority on the customs of the Indian subcontinent, serves as a case study of the ways in which the early modern Venetian state sponsored and conferred authority on the production of ethnographic knowledge. Although many contemporaries cast doubts on the veracity of his *Itinerario* (first published in Rome in 1510), Varthema enjoyed the early patronage of the Venetian state. Varthema's reputation was gradually rehabilitated through the work of sixteenth-century Venetian printers and editors, such as Giovanni Battista Ramusio, who were themselves in the employ of the state. Ultimately, the case demonstrates the ways in which state recognition, coupled with Venice's status as a center of print and information, could dramatically reshape an author's reputation.

In addition to mediating ethnographic truth claims, the Venetian state also enabled the production of ethnographic information through its sponsorship of diplomatic activity. Over the course of the sixteenth century, ethnographic observation became an increasingly important component of the written genres associated with the culture of Venetian diplomacy. The ambassadorial relazione is certainly the best known and the most distinctive genre of Venetian diplomatic culture; it is not, however, exhaustive of the category. Venetian ambassadors, like their counterparts from other states, were accompanied on their missions by large retinues. In Venice, members of these diplomatic parties were encouraged to keep journals of their voyage. Diplomatic travel journals developed in tandem with the relazione. In the case of ambassadors who kept their own journals, their observations furnished material that they might later develop in their relazioni. In the case of young men who accompanied an embassy as part of their political education, the relazione loomed large as both a model of political reporting and a guide to what about a given society was worth observing. As ambassadors devoted more attention over the course of the sixteenth century to ethnographic reporting in their relazioni, this shift was also reflected in their travel journals and those of the young men who sought to learn from them. Collectively, the body of Venetian travel journals helps us to understand the origins of the methodization of observation in travel. They help answer the questions of how travelers learned what was worth observing and how those observations were systematized.

Finally, I turn to two ethnographic accounts of Ottoman customs, Benedetto Ramberti's *Libri tre delle cose de Turchi* and Ottaviano Bon's *Descrizione del serraglio*, both of which emerged out of the world of Venetian diplomacy, albeit at very different moments. The two accounts, both written by functionaries of the Venetian state, achieved a much wider circulation than most ambassadorial relazioni or diplomatic travel journals. Taken together, they reveal the ways in which the parameters of Venetian ethnography expanded over the course of the sixteenth and early seventeenth centuries as diplomats sought to move beyond the uses of ethnographic reporting prescribed in the relazione.

Ludovico de Varthema: The State, Print, and Eyewitness Authority

Like other early modern states, Venice relied on its diplomatic network to gather news and intelligence.[1] The long history and geographical breadth of its diplomatic network left Venice exceptionally well positioned to gather intelligence from far-flung regions. In the early sixteenth century, however, there were regions of great strategic and commercial interest to which the state's regular diplomatic network did not extend, notably Persia and India. To address these intelligence shortfalls, the Venetian government relied on merchants and other travelers to deliver news on regions of strategic interest.

The diaries of the Venetian patrician Marin Sanudo serve as an invaluable source for this early period. As Pierre Sardella noted many decades ago, Sanudo's diaries reveal the extent to which Venice's status as a commercial hub made it an important center for the circulation of news in the Mediterranean and beyond in the early sixteenth century.[2] Sanudo records in his diaries numerous instances in which merchants, soldiers, and other travelers arriving in the city report either formally or informally on the customs, trade, and recent military and political events in the regions they had visited. In February of 1508, for example, Sanudo noted the arrival in the city of an unnamed Frenchman who had accompanied Shah Ismail on the battlefield, likely in southeastern Anatolia.[3] The man reported on the religion of the Persians, the character and appearance of Shah Ismail, and Persian military progress against the Ottomans, although where and before what audience he reported is left somewhat ambiguous in Sanudo's diary.[4] The timing of the Frenchman's arrival would also have made his report particularly valuable. The period 1507–1508 was a moment of intense interest in the figure of Ismail as European observers speculated about his chances of conquering Anatolia.[5] In the decades that followed, nondiplomatic travelers whose routes took them through Venice would continue to serve as valuable sources of information. In April 1522, Sanudo recorded that German merchants who had recently arrived in the city had been reporting attacks on Portuguese outposts in India, the news of which Sanudo believed boded well for Venetian merchants.[6]

Sanudo's diaries also make clear that the Collegio occasionally engaged travelers to deliver reports on regions of interest. In November 1523, Antonio Pigafetta, a Vicentine who had participated in and documented the Magellan-Elcano circumnavigation of 1519–1522, spoke in the morning before the Collegio about India and later the same afternoon addressed the doge, Andrea Gritti, and a smaller audience. His report on India, according to Sanudo, left all who heard it "stupefied."[7] Although Sanudo does not specify what exactly Pigafetta discussed, his language in the passage is suggestive. When describing the reports of other travelers, Sanudo tends to employ the language of wonder for descriptions of foreign customs while omitting it in cases where only commercial matters were discussed.[8] In a similar audience in 1530, Giovanni Francesco Giustinian, a Venetian patrician and merchant, who had returned to Venice after nine years abroad, addressed the doge, the Collegio, and the heads of the Council of Ten about India.[9]

The most famous traveler to make an appearance before a Venetian governing body was undoubtedly Ludovico de Varthema. Originally from Bologna,

Varthema boarded a ship from Venice to Alexandria in 1500 and did not set foot in Italy again for over seven years. During that period, Varthema traveled through Mamluk Egypt and Syria, Persia, India, and at least in his own account, as far as Java. Scholars, however, have raised significant doubts about the authenticity of entire portions of Varthema's journey, notably his claims to have traveled to both the interior of Persia and beyond the Coromandel Coast in India to Bengal and then the Moluccas and Java.[10] Varthema spent much of his journey living as a Muslim. From Damascus, where he shed his identity as Ludovico and adopted the name Yunus, he went on to join a Mamluk party on pilgrimage to Mecca and Medina. Indeed, today he is often remembered as the first western European to pen an account of the hajj. Little is known about Varthema's life before he left Europe, and indeed, much of our knowledge of Varthema's biography comes from his own account of his journey, first published in Rome in 1510.[11] This first Italian edition was followed by a Latin translation a year later and, by the end of the century, additional translations in German, Dutch, and Czech. Varthema's background and profession are unknown, although the knowledge of military techniques he demonstrates in his account and the ease with which he found work as a mercenary abroad have led some scholars to speculate that he may have had a military background.[12]

Varthema's journey was bookended by stays in Venice. The city was one of the first that he visited upon his return to Italy. Sanudo records that on November 5, 1508, Varthema was paid by the Collegio to deliver a report of what he had observed during his voyage. The entry in its entirety reads: "Today in the Collegio, following lunch, [there appeared] a Bolognese man, who had come from Calicut [Kozhikode]. He reported many things about those parts, such that everyone was left stunned by the rites and customs of India. And by the Collegio he was given twenty-five ducats for his report."[13] Sanudo's entry here, as in so many other places, is tantalizingly brief. A few things can be surmised from the report, however. The first is the perceived value of Varthema's testimony. Twenty-five ducats was undeniably a large sum for a single appearance before the Collegio and was, in fact, the highest amount that the Collegio was permitted to award in such cases.[14] To put the figure in perspective, Varthema's compensation was worth more than half the annual salary of a chancellery notary in Venice.[15] Given the generous level of compensation, we can assume that Varthema reported on matters of particular interest to the Collegio. In his six years of travel, of course, Varthema had visited numerous locations, but as Sanudo's entry suggests, Varthema did not report on his journey in its entirety. Sanudo mentions only that Varthema reported on India and specifically the city of Calicut. The likely explanation for this particular focus is that members of the Collegio, uneasy about the relatively recent Portuguese circumnavigation of Africa and its potential economic effects on Venetian trade, desired recent news from the important trading center of Calicut.[16]

It is difficult to overstate the apprehension with which news of Portuguese activity in India was met by Venetian merchants and magistrates. When news of Pedro Álvares Cabral's return from Calicut in 1501 first reached Venice several years earlier, another patrician diarist, Girolamo Priuli predicted nothing less than the republic's downfall: "If this voyage from Lisbon to Calicut continues as it has begun, there will be a shortage of spices for the Venetian galleys, and their merchants will be like a baby without milk and nourishment. And in this, I see clearly the ruin of the city of Venice."[17] Given this context, it is easy to see why Varthema's address would focus on India and on Calicut in particular. The perceived value of his report was derived not only from its geographical subject—the important trading city of Calicut—but also from its timeliness, since Varthema had returned to Europe via Lisbon just months before his appearance.

While Sanudo's laconic entry in his diary leaves many questions unanswered, what it makes clear is that Varthema leaned heavily on ethnographic detail in his address to the Collegio. What Sanudo emphasized in the entry is Varthema's treatment of the "rites and customs" of India and the audience's response to that treatment. This ethnographic treatment was in keeping with what we know of how Varthema presented his voyage in other venues. His address to the Collegio in return for compensation was not anomalous. Following his return to Europe, Varthema capitalized on his voyage with residencies at various courts and, shortly after the return, the publication of his *Itinerario*. One of these residences took him to Marino in 1509, where his audience included Agnese da Montefeltro, to whom the printed *Itinerario* would be dedicated, and her daughter, the young Vittoria Colonna. After departing from the court, Varthema wrote to Vittoria Colonna offering her a manuscript copy of his *Itinerario* and praising her for having listened attentively and thoughtfully to him in Marino. His letter also gives an indication of the contents of his address, recalling the account he gave at Marino of "the remote parts and southern and eastern peoples, the places, and their customs."[18]

The episode of Varthema's report before the Collegio and the later reception history of his *Itinerario* raise important questions about the ways in which the perceived reliability of eyewitness reporting was bound up with the recognition of the state. Varthema, like many other authors of travel accounts, faced accusations of exaggeration, embellishment, and outright fabrication.[19] If modern scholars have cast doubts on the veracity of entire portions of his itinerary, Varthema's contemporaries also found much of his account difficult to believe. Johannes Boemus, the author of the influential ethnographic synthesis *Omnium gentium mores, leges et ritus,* first published in 1520, pointed to Varthema as an example of a sensationalist travel writer who appealed to the baser instincts of his readers. In a letter to Sigismund Grimm, the Augsburg editor and printer of the first edition of the *Omnium gentium mores,* Boemus voiced his apprehension about the reliability of Varthema and other contemporary authors of travel accounts.[20] Boemus underscored the importance of drawing information from trustworthy authorities rather than from "trifling peddlers and roving liars, who, in order to be admired and accepted by the common people, generally lie in a most wicked and shameless way, so that one must distrust not only them but nearly all others who write or repeat anything of theirs."[21] Boemus included Varthema among this pack of "peddlers and liars" and thus, understandably, declined to draw on Varthema's account in his study.

Another of Varthema's prominent sixteenth-century detractors was Garcia da Orta, a Portuguese physician, who spent nearly all of his career in Goa. His botanical treatise, the *Coloquios dos simples e drogas,* first published in Goa in 1563, became a standard reference on medicinal plants following the appearance of a Latin translation in 1567. It would also become a standard reference for Varthema's later critics.[22] In the treatise, Orta issued a strong attack on the credibility of the *Itinerario.* "As for Ludovico Vartomano," he writes, "I have spoken here and in Portugal with men who knew him in India, and said that he went about in the dress of a Moor, and that he returned to us and did penance for his sins. They told me that he never went beyond Calicut and Cochin, nor did we then frequent the seas which we now navigate. As for what he says about Sumatra, he never was there. . . . From this you will see how little he is to be trusted as regards anything in India."[23] As Joan-Pau Rubiés notes, Orta's criticism in this passage hinges in part on what *kind* of traveler Varthema was—a feature it shares in common with Boemus's earlier attack on Varthema's credibility.[24] Varthema did not enjoy the backing of any state in his travels, nor did he fit into any of the established categories of late-medieval extra-European travel. He was not a diplomat, a pilgrim, or a merchant. This created for Varthema problems of credibility, which were only compounded—as Orta's comment about Varthema's Moorish dress suggests—by his having lived for so many years as a Muslim.

Varthema's reputation fared considerably better in Venice than elsewhere in Europe. Venetian presses were responsible for a disproportionate share of editions of the *Itinerario*. Of the twenty-nine stand-alone editions of Varthema's account that appeared between 1510 and 1600, eight were the products of Venetian presses. Editions of Varthema's *Itinerario* also found their way into influential private libraries in the city and its territories. Copies were held in the libraries of Leonardo Donà and Gian Vincenzo Pinelli.[25] Figures regarding the publishing history of the *Itinerario* itself, however, can obscure the true reach of Varthema's account. A proper assessment of the Venetian role in promoting Varthema's *Itinerario* cannot fail to take into account its inclusion in Giovanni Battista Ramusio's influential compilation of travel writing, the *Navigazioni e viaggi*.

Ramusio fatefully included Varthema's account in the first volume of his *Navigazioni e viaggi*, published in Venice in 1550. In reading his brief introduction to the text, unsuspecting readers would have no idea that Varthema's *Itinerario* had such a troubled reputation. Ramusio in fact praised Varthema for describing India and the Spice Islands in a level of detail surpassing all ancient authorities.[26] Ramusio's editorial decision to draw attention to Varthema's account of the Spice Islands, in effect vouching for the authenticity of the most distant, and most contested, leg of his journey is particularly significant given that by the time the *Navigazioni e viaggi* appeared, contemporaries had already raised doubts about whether Varthema had ever actually visited the islands. Ultimately, Ramusio's decision to include the *Itinerario* in his collection helped to bolster Varthema's authority and ensured the continued circulation of his account into the second half of the sixteenth century and beyond. When examining only stand-alone Venetian editions of Varthema's *Itinerario*, there is a major gap in the second half of the sixteenth century. During this half-century gap, however, the account appeared in four separate editions of Ramusio's collection.[27] It was not only Ramusio's editorial approach but also his selection of texts that proved influential. Samuel Purchas, for example, not only included Varthema's *Itinerario* in his collection, he also cited Ramusio as his source for the account.[28]

Ramusio's history of engagement with Varthema's *Itinerario* in fact began before his decision to edit the text for the *Navigazioni e viaggi*. Two decades earlier, in the aftermath of Varthema's appearance before the Collegio, Ramusio had used the *Itinerario* as an authoritative source on the customs of the Middle East. In a highly unusual case, Ramusio, in his capacity as a secretary to the Senate, was charged with investigating and reporting to the Collegio on a Jewish messianic preacher and self-declared prince who had been causing disruption in Venice.[29] Marin Sanudo evidently took an interest in the case and included a copy of Ramusio's report in his diary.[30] The preacher, referred to in Ramusio's report as David Ebreo but better known today as David ha Reuveni, had arrived in the city in the autumn of 1530 and taken up residence outside the Jewish ghetto.[31] In Venice, Reuveni presented himself as the brother and emissary of a Jewish king in Arabia who wished to see the Jews return to Jerusalem. Before arriving in the city, however, Reuveni had spent time in Portugal, France, Rome, and Modena, and the story he presented had shifted over time.[32] Members of the Venetian government were, understandably, wary about the appearance of such a figure in the city and skeptical about his claims of royal lineage.[33] Ramusio was thus charged with interviewing Reuveni and delivering a report on the veracity of his claims. It seems likely that Ramusio was chosen for the task because of his linguistic ability.[34] Ramusio does not note the language in which he questioned Reuveni, nor does he note the presence of an interpreter, but according to all other reports, Reuveni spoke only Arabic and Hebrew.[35] Ramusio's demonstrated expertise in contemporary travel literature and the customs of eastern peoples also made him a natural candidate for the assignment.[36]

Ramusio's "methodology" for his task involved interviewing Reuveni at length and then assessing the validity of his claims by reading them against cosmographical and travel literature. He leaned especially heavily on Varthema's *Itinerario* in this process.[37] Given Sanudo's comments on Reuveni and the apprehensions of other Venetian patricians, it is likely that Ramusio was expected to unmask Reuveni as a fraud. Instead, Ramusio was clearly quite taken with the preacher, finding him "very learned in Jewish law" and was intrigued by Reuveni's claims of having visited the court of Prester John.[38] By 1530, Ramusio was already assembling material for what would become the *Navigazioni e viaggi*, and one can only imagine how delighted he would have been to have the opportunity to speak with a "native informant" who had not only traveled through Arabia, Persia, Ethiopia, and Egypt but also claimed to have met with Prester John himself.

Ramusio found Reuveni's claims credible for the most part. In evaluating Reuveni's credibility, Ramusio drew from Varthema's account of a tribe of Jewish warriors in the Arabian Peninsula in order to verify the story that Reuveni had presented to Venetian authorities. Ramusio begins his report by situating Reuveni within the context of his Arabian tribe:

> Above the mountains dividing Arabia Deserta from Arabia Felix and Arabia Petra, not many days away from Mount Sinai, there is a great

> multitude of Jews, numbering about 300,000 souls, who live according to the manner and customs of the Arabs, that is they go through the fields riding bareback with [only] a cotton saddle on the flesh of the horse and they carry a pole for a lance . . . and every time that the caravan of the Moors, which brings spices from Mecca and the port of Aden toward Damascus and Aleppo stops there (it being necessary for the caravan to stop for a day near the mountain to take water since it then has to pass through the sandy desert), those Jews armed in the aforementioned manner, attack the caravan, often with the neighboring Arabs.[39]

This bears remarkable similarity to Varthema's description in his *Itinerario* of a tribe of mountain-dwelling Jews whom he encountered while traveling with a Mamluk caravan between Damascus and Medina:

> We found a mountain, which appeared to be ten or twelve miles in circumference. In this mountain there dwell four or five thousand Jews, who go naked and are five or six spans in height with a feminine voice, and they are more black than any other color. And they eat no meat besides mutton, and eat nothing else. They are circumcised, and confess that they are Jews; and if they can get a Moor into their hands, they skin him alive. At the foot of the mountain we found a tank of water, which is water that falls in the rainy season. We loaded with water 16,000 camels, which left the Jews ill-pleased; and they went about that mountain like wild goats, and on no account would descend into the plain, because they are mortal enemies of the Moors.[40]

The similarities in the two accounts are readily apparent—so apparent that Miriam Eliav-Feldon has speculated that Reuveni, too, may have been familiar with Varthema's work. As Reuveni modified the account he gave of himself through the 1520s and 1530s, his story hewed ever closer to the details of the *Itinerario*.[41] The location of the Jewish kingdom is roughly identical in the two accounts, located at a strategic point on the road between Damascus and Medina.[42] In both accounts, the foothills of the mountains are an important resting point for caravans traveling to and from Medina and points beyond. The two accounts also align in terms of their depiction of the way of life of the Jews. Varthema, like Ramusio, reports that the Arabs in the plains surrounding the mountain ride their horses without full saddles.[43] In both accounts, the Arabian Jews are warrior-like and seem to live off the profits of banditry. The reports obviously differ considerably in the number of Jews they report living in the mountains, but we know that Reuveni had often reported in his visits to European courts that his brother commanded 300,000 subjects.[44] Reuveni's physiognomy, described by Ramusio in the report to the Collegio, must also have reassured Ramusio, given that it corresponded roughly with Varthema's description. Reuveni, he reported, looked like an Arab "because in the form of his person and in his color he shows himself to not be from our lands. He is very lean and slender and similar to the Indians of Prester John."[45] Reuveni, then, presented a reasonable approximation of Varthema's slight, dark-skinned Arabian Jews.

Not every detail in Reuveni's story as mediated by Ramusio corresponds exactly to those presented in Varthema's *Itinerario*, but given the nature of Ramusio's report, it is difficult to interpret at which points Ramusio is quoting Reuveni, where he is paraphrasing him, and where he is adding his own commentary. Assessing the relative responsibility of the two parties in crafting the narrative, however, is less important than the criteria that Ramusio used to assess its veracity. For Ramusio, the correspondences between Reuveni's and Varthema's account of the territory, customs, and physiognomy of the Jewish tribe were numerous and substantial enough that he was unwilling to dismiss Reuveni's story out of hand.

What Ramusio and later editors of travel compendiums were selling readers was not their own eyewitness experience but their expertise as cultural arbiters. Their work involved collating and evaluating the testimony of potentially unreliable eyewitnesses—precisely the same work that Ramusio had been asked to perform for the Venetian Collegio in his report on Reuveni. That Ramusio would put such stock Varthema's *Itinerario*, an account that, as we have seen, was dismissed in many quarters as the work of a charlatan, is in some respects surprising. It can be explained in part by Varthema's early recognition by the Venetian state, in the form of the audience and compensation he was granted by the Collegio. In 1530 when Ramusio delivered his report on Reuveni, there were still many influential Venetians alive who remembered well Varthema's earlier reception by the Collegio. Marin Sanudo, who recorded both Varthema's 1508 address to the Collegio and Ramusio's 1530 report in his diaries, was just one of these men.[46] If travelers like Varthema, who wrote accounts of customs based—at least purportedly—on eye-witness experience, faced challenges in establishing the veracity of their claims, the recognition of the state could have a lasting effect on their reception by lending credibility to those claims. The Venetian Collegio was certainly not the only authority to sanction Varthema's narrative, but because of the city's outsized role in the production and circulation of print, the vagaries of Varthema's reception in Venice had a lasting effect on the *Itinerario*'s broader reception. Ultimately, the tangled history of Varthema's reception that I have traced here highlights the ways in which the state and its agents might act as brokers of authority and credibility—in some instances reshaping an author's reputation.

Making Statesmen, Writing Culture: Ethnography and Diplomatic Travel Journals

Venetian diplomacy, like most state activities, mandated the production of volumes of written documents. Ambassadorial relazioni remain the best-known textual products of Venetian diplomacy, but there was another more nebulous body of writing that grew out of Venetian diplomatic practice: the diplomatic travel journal. These journals, written by members of an ambassadors' retinue or, less frequently, by an ambassador himself, followed a similar developmental trajectory as the relazioni. Forty such journals written by members of Venetian diplomatic retinues survive from the sixteenth century and another twelve from the first two decades of the seventeenth century. Over the course of the sixteenth and early seventeenth centuries as ethnography occupied an increasingly prominent position in ambassadorial reports, diplomatic travel journals also came to emphasize ethnographic reporting, although they did so in ways that did not align entirely with those of the relazioni.

Ambassadorial relazioni can give the impression of an embassy as a relatively spare affair. Ambassadors typically offer some evaluation of the performance of their secretaries and interpreters, but the large retinue that traveled with them goes unmentioned. Certainly, Venetian ambassadors, like their counterparts from other states, took with them a large number of servants. In the Venetian case, beyond the ranks of servants, secretaries, and notaries, however, ambassadors were also accompanied by a small group of noblemen and citizens, often relatives, whose official role as part of the embassy was not clearly defined. To date, the culture and composition of early modern diplomatic retinues, either in the diplomatic practice of Venice or that of other states has not received a great deal of attention. There are no studies specifically dedicated to the phenomenon, although it was clearly an established feature of early modern diplomatic culture.[47] Diplomatic envoys to Venice, whether from other western European states or from farther afield, routinely arrived in the city with retinues of twenty or more men.[48] As Maria Pia Pedani notes, the ballooning size of Ottoman retinues to the city, for which Venice assumed much of the cost, was one of the reasons that the Venetian government requested a reduction of the frequency of Ottoman missions to the city in the seventeenth century.[49]

Certainly, one of the functions of large diplomatic retinues was to impress upon members of the court to which they were sent the power and splendor of the state that they represented. In Venice as in other states, however, diplomatic travel also served as an important part of the training of young elite men. In his account of the 1551 French mission to the Ottoman court, for example, Nicolas de Nicolay lists fifteen noblemen in the retinue without defined functions, two of whom were the nephews of the ambassador Gabriel d'Aramon.[50] For many young Venetian noblemen, accompanying an ambassador on a diplomatic mission was also an important component of their political education. In the political world of early modern Venice where patrician men did not typically assume significant offices before their mid-forties, "young" was, of course, a relative term, and these political educations could be quite protracted.[51] Diplomatic-educational travel was a particularly common feature in the background of future ambassadors.[52] To take just a few examples, at the age of twenty, the future bailo Lorenzo Bernardo accompanied Giovanni Capello, a relative on his mother's side, on his embassy to France in 1554.[53] Francesco Contarini, who would later serve as ambassador to Florence, France, England, Rome, and the Holy Roman Empire and as bailo, similarly traveled to Spain and Portugal at the age of twenty-six in order to observe, in his words, "the customs of the people" and "their form of political and civil life."[54]

Diplomatic-educational travel was not limited to patricians. Elite Venetian subjects also accompanied diplomatic missions. Marino Cavalli recounted how the Friulian Panfilo Strassoldo profited from his experience accompanying the ambassador Andrea Navagero to the court of Charles V. When Panfilo relocated to Rome following the voyage, he was reckoned "so courteous a gentleman" that he was made bishop of Ragusa in under three years.[55] Diplomatic-educational travel was especially important in the training of future secretaries. By the sixteenth century, men belonging to the cittadini originari (an elite subset of the citizenry who could prove multiple generations of legitimate Venetian birth) held a monopoly on secretarial appointments within the state bureaucracy.[56] For cittadini originari advancing on their secretarial *cursus honarum*, an appointment as ambassadorial secretary paralleled the function of an ambassadorship in the political careers of the patriciate.[57] For patricians and citizens alike, diplomatic postings were significant appointments in themselves and important stepping-stones that promised even more prestigious appointments in the future. Venetian embassies could not function without secretaries, and it was not uncommon for two secretaries—a lead and an assistant (*coadjutor*)—to be attached to a mission. In practice, the large size of Venice's network coupled with the limited number of chancellery secretaries meant that service abroad was more of a certainty for secretaries than for politically active patricians.[58] Secretarial families were thus eager to prepare their sons for diplomatic service, and as with patricians, diplomatic-educational travel was the favored vehicle for doing so. An unofficial diplomatic apprenticeship could take place before official entry into the chancellery. Young men from secretarial families accompanied family members on embassies and at times were even entrusted with delicate tasks such as the drawing up of dispacci.[59]

The question of the relationship of the travel journals to the state is a complicated one. The journals were certainly the product of Venetian diplomatic culture, but unlike the relazioni and dispacci, their production was not mandated by state ordinances. Obviously, at the most fundamental level, the journals' existence hinged on the Venetian state's extensive diplomatic network. The state also provided the broader cultural context, insofar as a majority of the journals were written by Venetian patricians or citizens in the course of their political preparation for future service to the state—preparation that took the form of a model of educational travel that was itself an established part of Venetian political culture. Beyond this, however, the journals themselves were considered writings of the state and, in some instances, were seen as belonging *to* the state.

The location in which the journals are preserved today tells us something about how they were understood by contemporaries. Several of the diplomatic travel journals are held in the Archivio di Stato in the section reserved for ambassadorial relazioni, where they were placed following the orders of the Council of Ten in 1601.[60] The section of the archive was instituted in 1425 for the preservation of relazioni in the same Senate order that required all ambassadors to submit written copies of their reports.[61] It is the section reserved for relazioni, for example, that holds the travel journal the Venetian patrician Nicolò Michiel, who accompanied the bailo Antonio Barbarigo in 1556, as well as the journal of a young nobleman from Foligno, who accompanied the ambassador Giacomo Soranzo in 1582.[62] Both journals are held alongside ambassadorial relazioni from the same state, in both cases the Ottoman Empire. Similarly, the folder containing relazioni of Persia, also contains an anonymous account of the 1572 voyage of the Venetian envoy Vincenzo degli Alessandri.[63] This alignment of the relazioni and travel journals suggests that, like the relazioni, travel journals were understood not only as potentially pertinent to the interests of the state but, in a very real sense, as being of the state.

The circuitous route by which some diplomatic travel journals came to be held in the archive also reveals the extent to which the journals straddled the boundary between public (in the sense of being of the state) and private writing. As Filippo de Vivo's work on the circulation of political information in early modern Venice has shown, Venetian magistrates were perpetually concerned with preserving the secrecy of state documents.[64] While magistrates were ultimately fighting a losing battle, they did periodically seize materials from private libraries in their efforts to uphold the integrity of Venetian state secrecy. Several diplomatic travel journals were seized from the library of Gian Vincenzo Pinelli under the order of the Council of Ten, the magistracy charged with, among other things, state security and the maintenance of public order. The 1601 sequestration illustrates just how capacious the category of state documents could be.

The story of the sequestration and, indeed, of the fate of Pinelli's library is a complicated one. Pinelli had arrived in Padua in 1558 as a student, although he never completed a degree. He spent the rest of his life in the Padua, where he assembled one of the largest private libraries in sixteenth-century Italy.[65] Following Pinelli's death in August 1601, the executor of his estate arranged to have the library transferred to Pinelli's heir in Naples. Before the library could be shipped to Naples via Venice, however, the Council of Ten ordered that portions of it be seized. The council's concern was that Pinelli's library contained public materials that should not be shipped to his heirs but rather, consigned to the Cancelleria secreta, the archive held in the Ducal Palace and overseen by the Council of Ten.[66] Pinelli's executor (and later biographer), Paolo Gualdo, understandably protested the council's decision to break up the library.[67] One of Gualdo's principal strategies involved arguing that the parameters of what the Council of Ten considered public writings were overly capacious. In so doing, he pointed to the widely known permeability of the archive. Since the council was concerned only with writings related to state interests, Gualdo argued that relazioni and similar writings should not be seized given that no private library was so "abject" that it did not contain these writings and since ambassadors themselves were known to distribute copies.[68]

Gualdo's protests were ultimately unsuccessful. By the end of the month, the council ordered by unanimous vote that the secretaries of the Cancelleria secreta should create an inventory of the library so that writings pertaining to matters of state could be separated from private materials. The latter would then be consigned to Pinelli's heirs.[69] The text of the Council of Ten's order sets out the parameters of the sequestration, stating clearly that only "public writings" should be kept in the archive of the Cancelleria secreta:

> It being the case that the majority of the writings belonging to the deceased Gian Vincenzo Pinelli and brought here from Padua by the heads of this council pertain to diverse matters of state with few others pertaining to private matters, or learning, and others not pertinent to the public interest, it is ordered that the trunk containing of all these writings be brought and held in the secreto of our Senate, where the secretaries assigned to the secreto will make a new inventory of all those writings that are public and on matters of state and arrange them such that they are able to find with said inventory those few writings concerning private matters, and if they are of little significance, that they be set aside and consigned to the heirs of the aforementioned Pinelli.[70]

After drawing up the inventory, the secretaries seized almost 200 writings in total. Given the clarity of the instructions issued by the council, the materials that the secretaries opted to seize is revealing. As might be expected, the sequestered materials included numerous ambassadorial relazioni, including seven from Spain, twelve from the Holy Roman Empire, two from England, one from Poland, seven from France, and seven from the Ottoman Empire.[71] Although the fact that Pinelli's library in particular was singled out for the state seizure of such writings when they were commonly found in the libraries of Venetian patricians is remarkable, the fact that relazioni were targeted once the decision to investigate the library had been finalized is not, given the clear legal prohibitions on their circulation.[72] More surprising is that seized alongside the relazioni were at least six diplomatic travel journals. The sequestration as it was actually carried out suggests a broad conception indeed of "public" writings.

The alignment of the diplomatic journals with the considerations of the Venetian state was not something that occurred only retrospectively via state seizure of writings. Some journal authors positioned their own activity as eyewitnesses and recorders as a patriotic one. This was the case with Nicolò Michiel, who accompanied the newly elected bailo Antonio Barbarigo on his journey to Istanbul in 1556.[73] Michiel is explicit about the utility he saw his account as having to the state. He begins his journal with a vigorous endorsement of the personal and public benefits of educational travel:

> Knowing what great utility experience usually brings to men in their actions, I resolved on my own to seize the first opportunity I had to see and know diligently the court and customs of some prince of great force and power. . . . I thought that for a Venetian gentleman who had it in his heart to strive always in the exercises of his fatherland, it was in every

> way necessary not only that he understand the customs and know the forces of the Turks, but also that he try to see with his own eyes whatever was possible.[74]

Not coincidently, this appeal to the utility of eyewitness experience, including the experience of foreign customs, also served as the animating rationale of the relazione. For Michiel, patrician educational travel yielded public benefit not only in the long term, by shaping wiser and more judicious decision makers, but also in the short term. The journal itself would convey the insights he gained about the Ottoman Empire. Here, too, he shows his indebtedness to the model of the ambassadorial relazione, with its disavowal of any traffic in curiosities. Michiel notes that he too will decline to speak of things that merely satisfy "the curiosity of men" and will instead focus on those things that might educate and instruct men in the conduct of state affairs.[75] Ultimately, Michiel's journal came to be included in the republic's archives via the sequestration of portions of Pinelli's library, when it was incorporated into the section reserved for relazioni.[76] Michiel, of course, could not have predicted this turn of events, but one imagines that it would not have displeased him to have his journal sit alongside ambassadorial relazioni.

Michiel's statements raise the important questions of for whom and for what purposes such journals were written. There is no single or straightforward answer to this question. One of the reasons for this is that the journals were more varied than the relazioni in terms of the age and social location of their authors, who ranged from young Venetian noblemen such as Michiel, to citizen secretaries, to ambassadors themselves. Some of the journals, such as the numerous journals of the ambassador Leonardo Donà, do not seem to have been intended to be read by anyone but the author himself. Donà, for example, includes no forms of address to potential readers as Michiel does.[77] Other journals, like Michiel's, were clearly intended for a readership of fellow patricians. In certain instances, we can identify a wider circle of intended readers, including members of both the citizenry and patriciate. This is the case with the Venetian ambassador and humanist Andrea Navagero's journal of his voyage through France and Spain in the 1520s, written during his embassy to Charles V. Navagero shared his journal with his friend and frequent correspondent Giovanni Battista Ramusio. Navagero's journal posthumously reached a much wider readership when, through the promotion of Ramusio and his son, it came to the attention of the Venetian printer Domenico Farri, who published the account in 1563.[78]

The material form of the journals themselves, which ranged in length from three to sixty-six leaves, also suggests something about their readerships and the uses to which they were put. Some of the journals survive in rough copies with corrections, suggesting that they were intended for personal use and not for a wider readership. This is the case, for example, with the journals of Leonardo Donà. Many more, however, survive in clean, formal copies made in a neat, uniform hand, suggesting that they were intended for—or at the very least found—a broader readership. The copy of Michiel's journal seized from Pinelli's library is typical in this regard. Some of these copies we know were made by someone other than the author himself. The nobleman and future patriarch of Venice Giovanni Tiepolo copied in his own hand a journal made during Antonio Donà's 1618 embassy to England.[79] Similarly, Leonardo Donà had in his library a copy of an anonymous journal from Girolamo Lippomano's 1573 embassy to France made in his own hand.[80]

Although the journals do not address themselves to a uniform set of readers, what they share is an investment in both the value of eyewitness experience and in the didactic function of travel. As Michiel's journal makes clear, the truth claims of the diplomatic travel journal, like so many other forms of travel writing, rested on eyewitness experience. At first glance, it can thus seem somewhat surprising that even though the journals are predicated on the value and utility of eyewitness experience, their authors all tend to "see" exactly the same things, focusing on a similar set of topics. Ultimately, though, this feature was neither an accident nor the symptom of a discrepancy between the ideals of diplomatic-educational travel and its practice. It was, instead, an intended effect of the very practice of educational travel. Diplomatic travel and the journals that emerged from the practice were designed to teach men of affairs what about a foreign state was worth observing and how those features ought to be observed. In keeping travel journals, patricians and other members of diplomatic retinues honed this skill.

Diplomatic travelers were, of course, no more blank slates than the ambassadors whom they accompanied and whose relazioni they emulated. Just as ambassadors were expected to have studied extensively in preparation for their missions and the delivery of their relazioni, so too were the men who accompanied them on their embassies expected to have read in order to reap the full benefits of travel. In a 1569 memoir written for his sons, Giovanni Carlo Scaramelli, a citizen who spent much of his career as a Venetian diplomatic secretary, advised his sons to prepare for their own secretarial careers by studying histories, both ancient and modern, as well as "books of cosmography."[81] Beginning in the late sixteenth century and continuing into the seventeenth century, northern European humanists would also emphasize the necessity of such preparation for travel in the ars apodemica, the body of texts that sought to lay out a method for secular travel.[82] Scattered didactic notes for travelers and, of course, evidence from Venetian travel journals themselves, make clear that this too was a norm for travelers south of the Alps. Tommaso Porcacchi, the Venetian historian and author of a frequently reprinted *isolario*, advised an English correspondent preparing for a journey to the Ottoman Empire in 1564 that he needed to read in advance of his journey in order to profit from it. That way, Porcacchi writes, "with your books you will be able to enjoy appropriate entertainment, and while discovering . . . an island or a place on the mainland, I know you will be a diligent investigator of the most notable things."[83]

Diplomatic travelers apparently took advice such as Porcacchi's to heart. Their journals reveal just how thoroughly interwoven the practices of reading, observation, and recording were. Evidence from the journals themselves also makes clear that diplomatic travelers read extensively in preparation for their journeys. In their travel accounts, the journal authors engage repeatedly with written authorities. In his account of his 1512 voyage to Cairo with the Venetian ambassador Domenico Trevisan, Zaccaria Pagani frequently contrasts what he has observed with what he has read and heard about the city and its inhabitants. After all Pagani had read about Cairo, the experience of seeing the city with his own eyes was ultimately something of a disappointment. It was physically smaller and less impressive than he had been led to believe (he reckoned it was only twice the size of Padua).[84] Given the reports he had heard about the great number and gracious manners of the city's inhabitants, he was also disappointed on this count. Although it is true that Cairo has a large population, Pagani writes, "it is not as great as people say; it is believed to be a million and a half, but it is not even half of this, and most of the inhabitants are scoundrels and people with no manners."[85]

Pagani's wording in this passage leaves the source of the reports ambiguous; it is unclear whether he has *heard* reports of Cairo's large population and reputation for civility (and, if so, from whom), or whether he has read them. In other journals, however, diplomatic travelers engage explicitly with written texts. Travelers, particularly those who accompanied a bailo or ambassador to the Ottoman court, were often eager to correct what they saw as the misinformation about Turkish religious practices and customs that circulated readily at home. Nicolò Michiel, for example, wanted to lay to rest the misconception that the Ottomans had turned the church of Hagia Sophia into a stable.[86] The Turks, he writes, "have adapted it to a mosque according to their custom, although some have written that this Lord has turned it into a stable for horses, which is entirely false."[87] In a similar vein, Aurelio Santa Croce, who accompanied the bailo Antonio Barbarigo in 1573, sought to dispel widespread reports that Jews could not convert to Islam without first becoming Christian.[88] "It is not true," he writes, "that a Jew may not turn Turk if he does not first become Christian, although it is true that the Turks hold the Jewish religion in less esteem than the Christian and that they also hold in higher regard a Christian who turns Turk than a Jewish Turk."[89]

That diplomatic travelers would use their journals to correct ethnographic falsehoods is, of course, not entirely surprising. One of the conceits of diplomatic travel and of the journals that were part of its complex of practices was that such travel afforded men valuable firsthand experience of foreign states, peoples, and customs. This firsthand experience was a necessary supplement to the knowledge that could be gained from books, which could be unnuanced, sensationalistic, outdated, or simply false. Such an appeal to the value of firsthand experience was also one of the central premises behind the ambassadorial relazione, a genre with which the journals share much in common. I use the word *supplement* intentionally here, since firsthand experience was never intended to replace reading and study. Although it is true that certain early modern travelers offered vigorous endorsements of the supremacy of eyewitness authority over other forms of authority (Ludovico de Varthema's exhorted his readers remember that "the testimony of one eyewitness is worth more than ten hearsays"), more moderate formulations were much more typical.[90] The extensive preparation of ambassadors and diplomatic travelers for the journeys is a testament to this. As we have seen, one of the ways in which travelers, diplomatic and otherwise, were taught to see was via the mediation of and engagement with written authorities. Thus, repetition and appropriation were ultimately more common modes of engagement with written texts than was outright refutation.

In the most extreme cases, journal authors display their engagement with the world of written ethnography by appropriating material from these texts wholesale. Nicolò Michiel, for example, borrows a lengthy passage from Giovanni Antonio Menavino's *Cinque libri della legge, religione, et vita de' Turchi* dealing with the sources of Islamic law.[91] Menavino, the son of a Genoese merchant, was captured at the age of twelve near Corsica along with his father and taken to Istanbul where he was presented to Sultan Bayezid II. He served as an *icoglan*, or personal page, to Bayezid until the sultan's death in 1512, at which point he briefly entered the service of Bayezid's son Selim I. After escaping and returning to Italy sometime around 1514, he wrote his account, which was completed by 1519, although not published until 1547.[92] Thus, when Michiel traveled as part of the embassy to Istanbul in 1556, Menavino's account was a relatively recent work. It also had the advantage of being one of the more comprehensive and theologically literate ethnographic treatments of Turkish society and culture available at the time. This was largely a function of the nature of Menavino's experience at the Ottoman court. Because of his personal service to the sultan, Menavino was educated in the seraglio, where he not only learned Arabic and Turkish but also received instruction in Islamic law and theology.[93]

The borrowed passage in Michiel's journal reads as follows: "The Turkish law is principally based in the commandments of a book called *Mus'haf* [codex or volume], which they say was sent from God through the angel to Mohammed, to which they bear such honor that they do not touch it without first having washed and with a cloth covering their hands, as it is a sacred thing."[94] The sentence begins with a direct borrowing from Menavino, followed by a slightly truncated paraphrase of his account of the reverence accorded the Qur'an.[95] Michiel goes on to list what he refers to as "the eight commandments" of the Qur'an, which are also listed in the corresponding section of Menavino's account.[96] Menavino offers a detailed exposition of each of the eight commandments, which Michiel opts not to include in his journal. He signals the omission, however, by writing that while the commandments all have "their own expositions; if I were to write them, I would be too longwinded and would stray from my purpose."[97]

Although it is relatively easy to see why a traveler like Michiel would turn to written authorities in order to embellish his journal with information on Muslim religious law that he would otherwise have had difficulty accessing, other examples of borrowing in the diplomatic travel journals are on the surface more difficult to assess. This is the case with the anonymous journal author who accompanied the ambassador Giacomo Soranzo's party to Istanbul in 1575. The author, who identified himself as a young man, was part of a large retinue of forty men who accompanied Soranzo.[98] The author clearly adopted much of his account of dress and customs in Ragusa (Dubrovnik) from an obscure twenty-year-old report on the government of the city.[99] The authorship, origins, and purpose of the 1555 report are all something of a mystery.[100] Nor is its location in the archive of much assistance here. The report is held within the Commemorali, a miscellaneous section of the archive not linked to any particular Venetian magistracy, containing material such as letters of permission issued to ambassadors and other state representatives, ducal privileges, and varied writings on foreign states.[101] The 1555 report's particular collection within the Commemorali was likely originally a private sixteenth-century collection of political and diplomatic documents, although its exact provenance is unknown.[102]

The correspondences between the account of the anonymous 1575 traveler and that of the 1555 report are numerous and sustained. At times, the correspondences are word for word. The 1575 diarist had clearly not only read the report but either possessed a copy or could at least make frequent reference to one. The instances of borrowing are too numerous to rehearse in their entirety, but a few examples will illustrate the point. Like many other diplomatic travelers, the anonymous author reports intermittently on features of local languages in his journal. In the late sixteenth century in particular, diplomatic travelers often noted shifts in spoken language in border areas and commented on the hybrid linguistic forms that emerged in these regions. Traveling between France and Savoy in 1572 while returning to Venice, Costantino Garzoni, a cousin of the Venetian ambassador to Spain, noted in his journal that the Italian of the inhabitants was so commingled with French as to render it almost unintelligible.[103] Other diplomatic travelers remarked on the similar gradual shift from Italian to German when traveling north en route to Vienna. Upon reaching Trent, for example, Leonardo Donà, notes in his journal the linguistic divide in the city: "All of the city speaks Italian, although there is one quarter inhabited by Germans and called the German Quarter that speaks the German idiom together with Italian. The Germans consider this a city of Germany, but it is not, either in its language or its site, which is located on this side of the Alps."[104] As he continues north, Donà also notes the first time he reaches a city that is majority German-speaking and the first time he reaches a city that has an entirely German-speaking population.[105]

Although the discussion of local vernaculars was common in late sixteenth-century diplomatic travel journals, the anonymous author's discussion of language is both more sustained and more incisive than that of most other diplomatic travelers. Borrowing heavily from the 1555 report, he included observations on the gendered nature of multilingualism in Ragusa. Like many other visitors to the region, he noted that most men were functionally bilingual, being able to communicate in both their native Serbo-Croatian dialect and in Italian, albeit a highly idiosyncratic Italian.[106] This quality of the men's Italian was noted by a range of travelers, Venetian and non-Venetian alike; the French traveler and royal geographer Nicolas de Nicolay wrote that the Italian of the Ragusans was even more "inelegant" than that of the Venetians.[107] The women, meanwhile, could speak only their native language; as a result, Serbo-Croatian served as the language of the home. In Ragusa, the journal author reports, "the women use the Dalmatian language, which others in Dalmatia use in speaking, but the men use both this and the Italian language, the latter with foreigners and the former among themselves; though their native language is Slavic with corrupted vowels, with some of them using many Tuscan and Venetian vowels and others using Lombard and Puglian vowels."[108] With the exception of its initial reference to the language spoken by the women of Ragusa as "the Dalmatian" rather than "the Slavonic" language, the wording of the journal is nearly identical to that of the report.[109]

Crucial to understanding the journal author's heavy reliance on the twenty-year-old report is the length of time he spent in Ragusa. The Venetian party spent only one day in the city, and the actual time he spent in the city itself would have been shorter than this suggests.[110] Since the party had arrived by sea, they spent the night on their galley, a practice that was not unusual.[111] Tellingly, the author's account of the party's activities in Ragusa occupies only two paragraphs in his lengthy entry on the city. Neither of these paragraphs suggests that he or the other young members of the party met with any Ragusans. Yet despite the brevity and constraints of his stay in Ragusa, the author's account of the city occupies a fifth of the space of his journal. Although he spent only a day in the city, he manages to treat issues of Ragusan language, customs, and dress. In addition, he offers a detailed account of the Ragusan republic's system of governance, also derived largely from the 1555 report.[112] Any attempt to address this range of topics on Ragusan culture and society would necessarily involve turning to existing accounts in order to supplement, as it were, his own eyewitness experience.

Underlying the strategies of reading and appropriation in the journal of Nicolò Michiel and the anonymous journal of 1575 were a set of shared motives and practices. Venetian educational travel was predicated on the value of first-hand experience and observation, but religious divisions, the grueling pace of diplomatic travel, a lack of fluency with local languages, and restrictions on the movement of members of ambassadorial parties all placed limits on what diplomatic travelers were able to observe. Ultimately, diplomatic travelers turned to written sources in the crafting of their journals, both printed and manuscript, for many of the same reasons ambassadors did in the crafting of their relazioni; they sought to include information in their writings that was expected and useful but that they personally had no opportunity to experience. This was in no way a violation of the norms or ends of the diplomatic travel journal but rather an expected part of the practice of diplomatic-educational travel as it developed over the course of the sixteenth century. As their journals attest, diplomatic travelers came to emphasize ethnographic reporting in the same period that ambassadors did in their relazioni. That these developments occurred simultaneously was of course no accident. The diplomatic travel journals and the relazioni were closely linked since the men who traveled as part of diplomatic missions were meant to learn from the conduct and writing of the older and more experienced ambassadors they accompanied.

Benedetto Ramberti's *Libri tre delle cose de Turchi*

The vast majority of diplomatic travel journals remained unpublished; they were intended only for private use or for a very limited readership. One work that began its life as a diplomatic travel journal, Benedetto Ramberti's *Libri tre delle cose de Turchi*, warrants separate consideration, both for its form and the wide readership it reached. Whereas many travel journals found a limited audience through manuscript circulation, Ramberti's account provides an instance of the norms of Venetian diplomatic observation reaching a much wider European readership. Ramberti, born around 1503 to a Venetian citizen family, spent most of his career as a secretary in the service of the Venetian state. After Pietro Bembo was made a cardinal and relocated to Rome, Ramberti assumed an important role in the city's intellectual life when he took over as librarian of the Biblioteca Marciana in 1542.[113] He began his secretarial career at a relatively young age, becoming a secretary to the Council of Ten in 1525. Seven years later, he was made secretary to the Senate. Ramberti's secretarial career brought him into the world of Venetian diplomacy. In 1530, he traveled to the Diet of Augsburg with Venice's ambassador to Charles V. During his period of employment as secretary to the Senate, Ramberti accompanied his cousin Daniele de' Ludovici who was sent as a Venetian envoy to Istanbul in 1534.[114] As Ramberti explains in a manuscript account of his voyage, Ludovici was sent to smooth Venetian-Ottoman relations following a mistaken peacetime attack on an Ottoman ship that left the Ottoman captain dead.[115]

Like many other diplomatic travelers, Ramberti kept a journal of his voyage to Istanbul, which eventually became the first book of the *Libri tre*. Ramberti's was one of only three of the sixteenth-century Venetian diplomatic travel journals to appear in print during the period. The edition was first published in 1539, by the Aldine press, with another Venetian edition following two years later. The work's inclusion in anthologies, however, was likely more important to its continued circulation than the appearance of individual editions. Ramberti's work was included in an Aldine collection of travel literature, printed in 1543 and again in 1545.[116] It was also included in the first edition of Francesco Sansovino's *Historia universale dell'origine et imperio de Turchi*, although it was omitted from all subsequent editions of the collection.[117] Outside of Venice, the work also appeared in both French and English translation by 1542.[118] In all of these editions, the work appeared without attribution to Ramberti, although he is often named as the author in manuscript copies of the account.[119]

Ultimately, Ramberti's *Libri tre* enjoyed a relatively brief but influential print run. Between 1539 and 1560, it appeared in five editions, all printed in Venice with none translated out of Italian, although it does not appear to have been reprinted after that. It still appeared in influential private libraries at the end of the century. Pinelli's library in Padua, for example, contained both print and manuscript copies of the work.[120] Leonardo Donà, meanwhile, included two printed editions of the work in his inventory of his library. He had also evidently read the account closely enough to be able to speculate about its authorship: his notes next to the entry for the 1541 edition refer to the work as a "report by an uncertain author," but he also notes the author must have been connected to Daniele de' Ludovici.[121] Despite the absence of any printed translations, Ramberti's account was evidently read elsewhere in Europe. Nicolas de Nicolay used Ramberti's *Libri tre* as an important source for his hybrid travel account and costume book, *Les quatre premiers livres des navigations*, first published in 1567. Nicolay drew particularly heavily from the *Libri tre* in crafting his account of Ragusa; his treatment of women's dress, for example, is a direct translation of Ramberti's description.[122]

As with relazione, the distinctive generic conventions of the diplomatic travel journal shaped its authors' presentation of ethnographic material. Like other travel accounts, Venetian diplomatic travel journals were organized geographically rather than thematically with an entry for each major stop along the party's route. As a result, they tended to present the ethnographic information they contained episodically rather than systematically. Diplomatic travelers who wished to provide lengthier or more involved accounts of customs within their journals often did so by departing from the traditional form of the travel journal. We have already seen two examples of this: Nicolò Michiel interrupted his narrative account of his journey to Istanbul with a discrete section on "The Religion of the Turks" that drew heavily from published accounts of Turkish religious observances. The anonymous author who accompanied Giacomo Soranzo to Istanbul in 1575 achieved a similar effect by departing from his usual short entries for each of the cities he visited to include a lengthy ethnographic section on the customs and governance of Ragusa. Ramberti's *Libri tre* took this separation even further while still remaining a recognizable product of Venetian diplomatic culture.

One characteristic that differentiates Ramberti's account from either the ambassadorial relazioni or the diplomatic travel journal was his purpose in writing. Ambassadors and many journal authors articulated their purpose in terms of the benefit that the information they provided would bring to public officials. Their project, at least in its stated aims, was a patriotic one. Ramberti, however, frames his project and, by extension, his imagined community of readers, in slightly more expansive terms:

> Now that I have finished with the exertion of my long voyage and find myself at leisure, I shall briefly record those things that seem to me worthy of memory; so that if fortune or time cause a mutation in [the Ottoman] state, as is their nature and as they have done to the states of Alexander the Great, of the Romans (lords of the world), and in our own time to the state of the [Mamluk] sultan, all of which with their infinite greatness have left only their names to posterity, I will be able to leave an account of the customs, forces, government, and laws of that nation for those who have not seen it.[123]

His project, then, is that of leaving, in the words of one scholar, a "political-ethnographic" monument for a future in which the Ottoman Empire might no longer exist.[124]

The first of Ramberti's three books contained the account of his voyage from Venice to Istanbul and reads very similarly to other diplomatic travel journals. As is the case with other journals, the ethnographic information Ramberti presents in the first book is episodic and not systematic. Ramberti notes, although not consistently, the religion, marriage customs, dress, and architectural features of the cities through which his party passes. His descriptions of each city are generally brief, with many lasting no more than two sentences. Major cities such as Ragusa and Edirne, however, receive longer treatments. As with some of the other diplomatic travel journals we have seen, for example, Ramberti includes a relatively lengthy account of the customs and government of Ragusa, addressing (and serving as a source for) many of the same topics that would be treated by later diplomatic travelers.[125] The second book, as Ramberti explains it, describes the Ottoman court, the size of the state, and its expenses.[126] Ramberti also reserves his treatment of the history and built environment of Istanbul for the second book. The book is largely devoid of any discussion of customs, although Ramberti does briefly note the religious and ethnic diversity of the city's population.[127]

It is in the final book that Ramberti groups most of his ethnographic information. In the third book, Ramberti promises his readers information "pertinent to the perfect understanding of [the sultan's] state."[128] He offers no other description of the final book in the introduction, although toward the beginning of the third book itself, Ramberti signals his shift away from the subject of the sultan's court, which he treated in the second book, and toward material "pertinent to the complete understanding of the customs of the nation, their way of life, and their government."[129] The actual contents of the final book are instructive. Ramberti begins by addressing religion, including the sources of religious law and rituals accompanying conversion, then proceeding to address dress, pastimes, marriage, and sexual customs. Finally, near the end of the third book, he departs from ethnographic material, and offers a description of the person and character of Suleiman I.

In the ordering and the presentation of his material in the *Libri tre*, Ramberti clearly draws on the norms of Venetian diplomatic observation, particularly those found in the ambassadorial relazione. Ethnographic material on the Turks is grouped into a discrete section within the third book and is presented as facilitating a more complete understanding of the Ottoman state. Ramberti diligently avoids presenting ethnographic material as mere curiosities and, in so doing, adopted one of the central rhetorical strategies of the relazione. There are several points in the *Libri tre* where Ramberti explicitly links his ethnographic material to considerations of the state. To take one example, he offers a political analysis of the ways in which Islamic occasionalism is exploited for military advantage by Ottoman commanders. After explaining the measures that the sultan and his commanders must take to combat the indolent natures of Turks in order to make them suitable soldiers, Ramberti allows that certain elements of Muslim belief work in the Ottomans' favor. "One advantage that they have," he explains, "is that they care nothing of death because they are convinced that the day of everyone's death is written before him. This opinion, however, is found only among the common people, and they do not have much to lose in dying. But those who hold offices and who are rich, rarely or never put themselves in danger, and they hold their lives dear, while maintaining the aforementioned persuasion in their soldiers."[130] In this instance, Ramberti draws a connection between elements of the Muslim belief system and its military and political ramifications in a clear and explicit fashion.[131]

Not all of the ethnographic material in the final book of the *Libri tre*, however, is so clearly framed in terms of its political import. Ramberti also, for example, includes a short description of Turkish dress, where he described women's habits of painting their fingernails and men's habits of dying their beards.[132] Readers could also learn the names of the hours of prayer and read a description of the ritual of conversion.[133] Clearly, then, not all of the ethnographic material that Ramberti included was tied to political considerations—at least not in any straightforward manner. Without denying the *Libri tre*'s obvious appeal to the curiosity of its readers, it is also worth taking Ramberti at his word when he claims that he intends in the final book to present material that will afford readers a more "perfect" or "complete" understanding of the Ottoman state. The way in which he structures and presents his material suggest that this perfect understanding of the state included within it an understanding of the customs and way of life of its inhabitants. This represented in many ways an expansion of the parameters of what might count as political information. In this key respect, Ramberti's *Libri tre* also participates in the same project as that of the Venetian ambassadors and their treatment of ethnographic information in their own relazioni.

The Two Relazioni of Ottaviano Bon

The hallmark genre of Venetian diplomacy was undoubtedly the relazione. Yet one of the most widely circulated texts by a Venetian ambassador or bailo, judging by the number of extant copies, was not a relazione at all but an independent account of daily life in Istanbul focused on the Ottoman court. The account was written by the patrician Ottaviano Bon, who served as the Venetian bailo in Istanbul from 1604 to 1609. Bon's account circulated in manuscript under various titles, the two most common being the *Relazione del serraglio* and the *Descrizione del serraglio*. For the sake of clarity, I use the latter title to distinguish the account from the relazione that Bon delivered in accordance with his duties as bailo. For Venetian patricians, diplomatic service was always a temporary office rather than a permanent career, although as we have seen, many patricians came to hold multiple ambassadorial posts. Given the varied natures of their careers, patricians accordingly cultivated a wide variety of skills and interests, and many ambassadors had literary careers and ambitions that took them far beyond their relazioni. Gasparo Contarini, for example, came to be remembered primarily for his *De magistratibus et Republica*

Venetorum, a work he began during his time as an ambassador, rather than for his ambassadorial relazioni.[134] Ultimately, this was also the case with Ottaviano Bon, whose literary reputation rested on the *Descrizione*. Bon's *Descrizione* exemplifies the ways in which, by the early seventeenth century, the ethnographic writing facilitated by the Venetian state and carried out by its agents moved beyond the generic and conventional constraints governing the treatment of ethnographic material in the relazione.

The antecedents of Bon's work do not lie in the diplomatic travel journal. Unlike Ramberti's *Libri tre*, Bon's *Descrizione* contains no account of his journey to Istanbul; it is strictly an account of social and cultural institutions in Istanbul. If Bon or a member of his party kept a journal of their voyage to Istanbul, it does not appear to survive today. Bruno Basile, the editor of the *Descrizione*, has suggested that Bon may have found a model for the work in his friend and mentor Leonardo Donà's *Libreto di alcune memorie tenute nell'ambasceria mia di Costantinopoli*, a hybrid journal and commonplace book that Donà kept during his 1595 mission to Istanbul.[135] In contrast with Bon's *Descrizione*, however, Donà's notes on his Istanbul embassy were nowhere near a polished work intended for circulation. The "libreto" was in effect a private notebook containing Donà's notes drawn from his reading in preparation for both his mission itself and the drafting of his final relazione and scattered observations he recorded during his mission (see chapter 4). To give an idea of the variety of its contents, the manuscript, written entirely in Donà's hand, combines Donà's brief account of his voyage to Istanbul, his notes on Paolo Giovio's *Commentario de le cose de' Turchi*, his notes on four late sixteenth-century Venetian relazioni, and tellingly, a copy of his final relazione itself.[136]

The *Descrizione*, however, was not entirely without precedent. It shares many similarities with the Venetian secretary Marcantonio Donini's *Tre dialoghi delle cose dei Turchi*. Although the *Tre dialoghi* has been dated to the 1560s, it was likely written in the 1580s, by which time Donini had served as secretary to four baili.[137] In the dialogue, Donini includes himself as one of the two interlocutors and positions himself as an expert on Turkish affairs on account of his extended diplomatic service in Istanbul (the dialogue begins with a lengthy résumé of his secretarial appointments). He responds to the questions of his interlocutor who, conveniently, knows almost nothing of Turkish society and culture. The use of the traditional format of the dialogue between the magister and idiota allows Donini to cover a great deal of ground, as his interlocutor poses questions ranging from what a mosque is and whether there are many of them in Istanbul to how the Turks bury their dead.[138]

Unlike Donini's *Tre dialoghi*, which appears to have survived only in a single manuscript copy, Bon's *Descrizione* was widely read. As scholars suggest, prurient readers may have been drawn to the work by Bon's inclusion of titillating details about the lives of women and slaves in the seraglio.[139] Without denying that this was part of the text's appeal, it is important to note that Bon's ethnographic reporting in the *Descrizione* is not limited to the seraglio. Despite the emphasis on the institution of the seraglio in the title, Bon treats Turkish society and culture more broadly. Approximately three-fifths of the account is devoted to the seraglio, while the remainder addresses broader aspects of culture beyond the seraglio. The sheer range of ethnographic topics Bon included is impressive. After concluding his discussion of the seraglio, Bon treats, in order, foodways and fasting; marriage, divorce, and inheritance; the treatment of slaves; weddings; points of Muslim doctrine; the practices of prayer and pilgrimage; circumcision; the rituals surrounding death and burial; women's religious observances; and finally, confessional divisions within Islam.

What is absent in the *Descrizione* is the sort of extended analysis of political, military, and economic affairs that one would expect to find in an ambassadorial relazione. Bon indeed provides this in his relazione, delivered following his return to Venice in 1609. A comparison of the *Descrizione* and the relazione reveals a very different deployment of ethnographic information. In the relazione, ethnographic detail is offered in order to contextualize political insights. In the *Descrizione*, the relationship is reversed. Thus, as one might expect, Bon addresses the subject of Ottoman rule in Europe and Africa in his relazione, drawing attention to the religious and cultural differences that existed between the Ottomans and their far-flung subjects.[140] Like other baili and ambassadors we have seen, Bon saw these differences as rendering Ottoman control over their empire tenuous. In the *Descrizione*, by contrast, Ottoman provinces and vassal states in Greece, Egypt, and Transylvania are discussed in terms of the variety that they provide to the Turkish diet.[141] The parameters of the relazione had certainly expanded over the course of the sixteenth century but clearly not enough to accommodate the sorts of fine-grained descriptions of daily life that Bon sought to capture in his *Descrizione*. In effect, Bon avoided potential controversy about the inclusion of "curiosities" in ambassadorial relazioni by producing two separate but related texts based on his observations as bailo: the *Descrizione* and the relazione.

There is plainly much separating Bon's *Descrizione* from the generic parameters of the ambassadorial relazione. One feature that the *Descrizione* and the relazioni share, however, is a common set of discursive mechanisms for advancing truth claims. Both the *Descrizione* and the relazioni relied on an assumption of the supremacy of eyewitness observation. In the case of the relazioni, the very practice of requiring ambassadors to deliver such reports was predicated on the value of eyewitness observation. Since this assumption underlay their claims, ambassadors generally did not need to insist further on their role as empirical observers. In his *Descrizione* (although not in his relazione), Bon forcefully and elaborately insists on his role as an observer. He emphasizes his own authority as an eyewitness via an account of how he gained access to the Topkapı Palace, claiming that he leveraged his friendship with Ahmed I's head gardener in order to gain access to the palace while the sultan was away hunting. Escorted by his friend through a service entrance, he was then able to see with his own eyes numerous chambers of the palace, various baths, "and other very exquisite and curious things" normally off-limits to foreign dignitaries.[142]

The *Descrizione* also reveals the extent to which the parameters of ethnographic knowledge had expanded by the first decade of the seventeenth century. Topics treated only superficially or in passing by Ramberti in the 1530s come to occupy significant portions of Bon's account. Education, language, and the study of letters, for example, are addressed only briefly by Ramberti. In the *Libri tre*, education—or rather, the lack thereof—arises merely to illustrate a claim about Turkish idleness. The Turks, Ramberti claims, are an idle people; the absence of a Turkish tradition of studying letters serves as one of his illustrations for this claim.[143] In Bon's account, by contrast, education receives a much fuller treatment, occupying a discrete section of the *Descrizione*. He reports on the education of boys and girls in the seraglio. In keeping with his lifelong interest in education initiatives for the Venetian nobility, Bon displays a special interest in the Enderun Mektebi, or Palace School, the elite institution that trained Ottoman military and civilian administrators.[144] In its level of detail, his description of the curriculum of each of the four levels of instruction surpasses even that of Giovanni Antonio Menavino, a former pupil at the school.[145] Bon also uses his account of the Palace School as an occasion to treat the different social registers of the Turkish language, explaining that in their second level of study, pupils begin the study of Arabic, Persian, and Tartar literature, the study of which is meant to inflect their spoken and written Turkish. As a result, the form of Turkish learned in the Palace School is so rarified that its graduates are readily identifiable by their speech alone.[146]

The Venetian state shaped the production and reception of ethnographic literature in a variety of ways not previously recognized. In an age in which accounts of distant places, peoples, and their customs were contested and liable to be met with incredulity, the backing or recognition of the state did much to confer authority. This authority could extend far beyond institutional genres such as the relazione that were the recognizable products of state activity. As the complicated reception history of Ludovico de Varthema illustrates, early modern Europeans hotly contested what kinds of ethnographic claims could be made and what kinds of speakers were eligible to make them. Varthema's case also demonstrates the ways in which the recognition of the Venetian state, coupled with Venice's status as a center of print and information more generally, could have a lasting impact on an author's reputation and the status of his work.

The ambassadorial relazione's status as the most celebrated genre of Venetian diplomacy can obscure the variety of the literary output of ambassadors and their retinues. As part of their extended political educations, men raised on ambassadorial relazioni were encouraged to try their hand at a related genre, the diplomatic travel journal. The practice of diplomatic-educational travel was undoubtedly an elite undertaking, but it was one that cut across lines of estate. Patricians, citizens, and subjects could all be found accompanying diplomatic missions. As scholars of early modern travel literature have noted, one of the functions of the travel journal, diplomatic or otherwise, was to teach travelers what elements of a foreign society were worth observing and how these should be observed. This general claim holds true in the case of Venetian diplomatic travel journals, although the Venetian journals remained a distinct species of travel writing that grew out of a particular practice of diplomatic-educational travel. One of the features that distinguished the journals was their deep indebtedness to the model of the ambassadorial relazione. At the same time, for some Venetian diplomats, both the relazione and the diplomatic travel journal presented constraints on ethnographic reporting, leading them to seek other ways of presenting ethnographic material in a more detailed and systematic manner.

For all the diversity that existed in the writings that emerged from Venetian diplomatic culture, there was a certain uniformity in the value they placed on ethnographic reporting. Observers, be they ambassadors or less senior members of their retinues, were encouraged to "see" and remark on a similar set of features, many of which were ethnographic in nature. Observers could be expected to remark on, for example, dress and religious observances whether they were reporting on Spain, England, or the Ottoman Empire. Underpinning the uniformity in Venetian diplomatic writings was a common assumption that cultural differences were worth noting and an implicit method, developed over the course of the sixteenth century, suggesting which differences travelers should note and how those differences should be recorded.

CHAPTER FOUR

Reading Ethnography in Early Modern Venice

In 1552, the returning bailo Bernardo Navagero described Venice as a city awash in information about the Turks. So many things about the Turks, he lamented, "have not only been said by many people, but also written about and printed, so that with little money everyone can see them."[1] By the time Navagero made his complaint, Venetians could purchase descriptions not only of the Turks but of many other of the world's peoples. How did Venetians read and make sense of this literature? The question is an important one in the study of ethnography since, in the absence of a dedicated genre of ethnography, ethnographic reporting was embedded in a variety of early modern genres that could be read in very different ways. An ambassadorial relazione, for example, could be read for information on customs and religious observances, but it could just as easily be read for up-to-date political or military information. Similarly, readers might approach the travel journals documenting the voyage of an ambassador seeking information on the dress, diet, and language of local populations, but they might also turn to such journals for practical information on the distances between major cities and the conditions of the roads connecting them.

Given the mixed nature of early modern ethnographic writing, particularly Venetian ethnographic writing with its close connections to the broader world of diplomatic and political writing, it is essential to assess why readers turned to these writings and what they made of them. Analysis of the material aspects of numerous manuscript and print works shows that readers employed strategies that allowed them to read selectively for ethnographic information. These strategies left evidence in readers' libraries in the form of marginal annotations, handwritten indexes, and commonplace books. The situation in print was no different. Dedicated works of ethnography were few and far between in the sixteenth and early seventeenth centuries, but ethnographic information embedded in other genres was plentiful. Over the course of the sixteenth century, printers strove increasingly to accommodate readers' interest in foreign customs through the inclusion of paratextual apparatuses to facilitate consultative reading.

At the same time, despite the growing availability of ethnographic works in print, Venetian readers at the highest levels of society exhibited a decided preference for manuscript accounts of foreign customs—a tendency that is on first glance surprising given Venice's central role in the history of print. These readers instead favored manuscript accounts, which circulated in a circumscribed and, importantly, noncommercial form, precisely because they afforded their community of readers access to a privileged body of knowledge.

Literacy, Books, and Reading in Early Modern Venice

The investigation of how ethnography was read in Venice might begin by addressing the fundamental question of who in Venice read and what they read. In Venice, however, as in other early modern cities, there are significant challenges in establishing reliable figures on literacy and book ownership. Paul Grendler estimates that in the late sixteenth century, approximately 33 percent of boys and 12–13 percent of girls in the city attained basic literacy—a rate that put Venice on par with other major northern and central Italian cities.[2] Grendler's figures have the advantage of being based on school attendance rather than on rates of signing. Studies of literacy based on signing inevitably underestimate overall literacy rates given that reading was taught before writing and are doomed to underestimate rates of female literacy in particular since girls' education was much less likely to progress to the writing stage.[3] Furthermore, the figures are based on attendance at a wide variety of schools, including not only formal schools but also the Schools of Christian Doctrine that were so important in teaching rudimentary vernacular literacy to girls.[4]

At the same time, scholars have increasingly come to emphasize literacy as a hierarchy of skills. In so doing, they have highlighted a vast spectrum that existed between complete illiteracy and the ability to read and write with facility in either Latin or the vernacular.[5] Studies of artisanal literacy in Italian cities suggest that many more individuals fell somewhere in the middle of this spectrum than studies of either school attendance or signing would suggest. Armando Petrucci conclude that there existed a high degree of what he terms "functional semi-literacy" among the population of male artisans in early sixteenth-century Rome. Moreover, Petrucci emphasizes the centrality of informal, noninstitutional spaces such as the home, the workshop, and self-directed study in the acquisition of basic literacy skills.[6] These broad patterns have also been observed in sixteenth-century Venice, where Richard Mackenney suggests that regardless of their level of formal instruction, few artisans or shopkeepers in the city were completely illiterate.[7] Given the noninstitutional nature of many artisans' "instruction" in reading and writing, attempts to measure literacy through school attendance rates will necessarily fail to capture a large swath of the population's engagement with the written word.

For a city that was not only a major printing center but also enjoyed a relatively high rate of literacy by early modern standards, Venice does not appear to have had especially high rates of book ownership. Based on the analysis of 600 notarial acts, Isabelle Palumbo-Fossati's study of book ownership in late sixteenth-century Venice places the rate of book ownership at the higher end. She finds that books were included in 30 percent of Venetian inventories from the second half of the century.[8] To put this figure in perspective, Peter Clark's study of inventories from Kent finds that in 1560, books were included in 15 percent of inventories, while studies of Amiens from 1503 to 1576 and Paris from 1540 to 1610 find books present in 20 percent and 25 percent of inventories, respectively.[9] A similar study by Marino Zorzi based on household inventories find even lower rates of book ownership, with books present in only about 15 percent of households.[10] More recently, Sarah Ross's comprehensive study of Venetian inventories reveal similar rates of ownership, finding books mentioned in 18 percent of inventories.[11]

In Venice as in other cities, behind these population-wide figures, there existed marked differences between the book-owning habits of individuals of different social locations.[12] Whereas Palumbo-Fossati finds that books were present in the inventories of only 12 percent of non-noble and noncitizen households, they were present in 70 percent of patrician inventories.[13] Certain professional identities were also strongly correlated with book ownership. Highly literate professionals, including notaries, lawyers, and physicians, owned books at a much higher rate (60 percent in Palumbo-Fossati's figures) than other non-nobles and noncitizens.[14] The libraries of these professionals, particularly those of physicians, were also larger on average than other libraries.[15] Professional identity was to some extent correlated with the types of books individuals owned. The notarial acts of wealthy, nonpatrician merchants were less likely to include books than other professional groups, but they were more likely to include books of cosmography and travel literature.[16] Given that so much of Venice's long-distance trade was directed toward the eastern Mediterranean and beyond, the professional rationale for merchants' interest in geographical works is clear.

As a source for the study of early modern reading habits, household inventories, of course, have some limitations. The first of these has to do with the inherent bias of testaments and other household inventories toward recording items of value. Ephemeral printed matter and other works of cheap print rarely made their ways into inventories.[17] The invisibility of cheap print, it should be noted, is not a problem confined to testaments and household inventories. It also presents itself in contemporary catalogs of private libraries. Even the most diligent library owners often neglected to include ephemeral printed works in the surviving inventories of their libraries. The inventories produced in the late sixteenth century by Leonardo Donà, who took special care in the documentation of his library, do not come close to fully documenting the extent of his collection. Although Donà's efforts to inventory his own library were not undertaken to facilitate inheritance and thus should not have been explicitly concerned with the monetary value of the books, Donà's decisions about what to include or exclude do seem to have been governed by considerations of prestige. For example, in the section of his inventory devoted to voyages of exploration in "the Indies" he included his Latin folio edition of Pietro Martire d'Anghiera's *Decades* of the New World but omitted the copy of the inexpensive pamphlet he owned documenting the then-recent Spanish voyage of exploration in Australia.[18] Donà clearly deemed this slight ephemeral pamphlet informative enough to preserve among his papers on Spain, its empire and its peoples, but not important enough to include in the record he created of his library and its holdings.

Reading Ethnography in Print

The other obvious limit of a quantitative approach to the history of reading based on inventory records, no matter how complete those records are, is that the mere fact of book ownership reveals little about how readers made sense of their books. Here, I would like to turn to the physical presentation of the texts and to the various supplementary texts and information that surrounded them for the insights they offer into how readers approached, or were expected to approach, texts. Scholars have noted the phenomenon of the gradual expansion of paratexts in printed books over the course of the sixteenth century.[19] In the case of ethnographic literature, broadly construed, these accrued paratexts increasingly directed readers' attention to information on customs, beliefs, and religious practices. Editors, of course, anticipated certain modes of reading a given text and designed paratexts that would be conducive to those modes of reading. Paratextual interventions, though, were more than simply reflections of the kinds of readers and modes of readings envisaged by editors; they were also a means of guiding those readers' engagement with a text. Thus, an edition of a travel narrative with dozens of entries listed in the index under "customs" not only suggested that its editor anticipated that readers of the narrative would be interested in ethnographic material; it also signaled to readers that information of foreign customs was one of the more important things that they ought to take away from the text.

There is ample evidence of paratextual interventions shaping the way in which early modern readers engaged with a given text. Take the case of the Italian translation of the Qur'an published in Venice by Andrea Arrivabene in 1547 as *L'Alcorano di Macometto*. Arrivabene's edition included an elaborate paratext consisting of marginal annotations and prefatory texts on the life of Mohammed and the history and customs of the Ottoman Empire by authors such as Giovanni Antonio Menavino and Luigi Bassano.[20] Indeed, the inclusion of a set of printed marginal annotations highlighting what the Venetian Senate deemed the Qur'an's "theological contradictions" was a condition of the privilege that body granted for the edition.[21] One of the more famous readers of the *Alcorano* was Leon Modena (1571–1648), the Venetian rabbi who himself wrote an account of Jewish ritual aimed at a Christian readership.[22] As Howard Adelman notes, Modena read the *Alcorano* with an eye toward assembling material relevant to Jewish apologetics.[23] In particular, he was interested in material that positioned Judaism and Islam as closely aligned while distancing the two religions from Christianity. It is safe to assume that Modena's was not an approach to the Qur'an that would have been anticipated by either Arrivabene or the senators who insisted on the expansion of the paratext. Not all readers, of course, were as idiosyncratic in their approach to the *Alcorano* as Modena. In the copy held in the Marciana, an anonymous reader, taking his cues from the marginal annotations, supplemented the already ample marginal apparatus mandated by the Senate with his own set of manuscript annotations drawing attention to contradictions between the Qur'an and the Bible.[24] Modena, though, did make extensive use of the supplied paratext. His reading of the

Alcorano focused heavily on the prefatory material that accompanied the translation. In the five pages of notes that Modena made based on his reading of the *Alcorano*, he made no distinction between the text of the Qur'an itself, the commentary, and the prefatory texts.[25]

The state-mandated set of marginal annotations and the inclusion of multiple prefatory framing texts certainly make *Alcorano di Macometto* an extreme case when it comes to the sixteenth-century use of paratexts. A more common and subtle means of shaping readers' engagement with a printed text came in the form of indexes and other interventions that facilitated nonlinear consultative reading.[26] Indexes, tables, and other paratextual interventions designed to facilitate consultative reading proliferated over the course of the sixteenth century. They were also important selling features of early modern printed books. As Ann Blair notes, advertisements of indexes appeared with growing frequency on sixteenth-century title pages.[27] A sufficiently detailed topical index meant that a reader could take a continuous narrative—for example, that of a travel account—and read it discontinuously with a particular eye to gathering ethnographic information.

The subtle paratextual changes that appeared in successive editions of Tommaso Porcacchi's isolario, or island book, *L'isole piu famose del mondo*, is illustrative of the ways in which editors strove to accommodate readers' interest in ethnographic topics and, through the same means, guided readers to pertinent ethnographic information. First published in Venice in 1572, Porcacchi's isolario went through three editions in the sixteenth century with two final editions in the early seventeenth century, all printed in Venice and all involving members of the Gagliano family of printers.[28] Isolarii were manuscript or printed atlases consisting of maps of islands, usually accompanied by a description of each island.[29] The curious genre flourished in the Mediterranean region between the fifteenth and seventeenth centuries. Venice, perhaps unsurprisingly, was the major center of isolario production, although Florence, which had no equivalent maritime tradition of its own, was also an important early center of manuscript production.[30] In Porcacchi's isolario, as in other examples of the genre, each island was accompanied by a map and a brief account of its geographical features, its history, and the customs of its inhabitants.

Because of their discontinuous nature, isolarii in particular invited consultative reading. An isolario had no overarching narrative, no sustained argument, and no temporal organization; it was, in essence, an encyclopedia of islands, organized geographically rather than chronologically. A reader's appreciation of an entry on Corfu did not hinge on having read the entry on Elba. Thus, an index in an isolario, unlike, for example, an index in a travel narrative, served not so much to enable readers to work around or ignore the continuous nature of the text as to enhance the already discontinuous nature of the text. Ethnographic information had long been a component of the genre of the isolario, but information on customs, dress, and religion was always included alongside other forms of information. For example, in 1526, nearly a half century before the publication of Porcacchi's work, another isolario author and engraver, Benedetto Bordone, petitioned the Venetian Senate for a ten-year privilege for a book that he described as encompassing "all the islands of the world," treating their "ancient and modern names, locations, customs, histories, fables, and all other pertinent information."[31] When the isolario was finally published two years later, the wording of Bordone's petition was incorporated almost verbatim into the extended title of the work, which advertised Bordone's treatment of the islands' "histories, fables, and ways of life."[32] Bordone's own framing of his project to the Senate conveys the inherent diversity of the genre. Given the mixed nature of all isolarii, the pertinent question in addressing how they might have been read ethnographically revolves around the degree to which ethnographic information was emphasized and what options readers were given via paratextual interventions for consulting that information.

The significant changes to which Porcacchi's *L'isole piu famose* was subjected between its first and second editions are indicative of the ways in which authors and printers drew readers' attention to ethnographic material in their texts and facilitated consultative ethnographic reading more generally. Between the first and second editions of Porcacchi's isolario, the text underwent several revisions, including the addition of sixteen new islands. There was also a significant expansion of the work's index, which in the 1576 edition came to include numerous new entries under the headings of "customs" (*costumi*), "inhabitants" (*habitatori*), "faith" (*fede*), and "dress" (*vestimenti*). The last three terms were entirely absent from the index of the first edition, while the number of entries under the heading "customs" grew from six to twenty-one.[33] The proliferation of ethnographic entries in the index was not simply a reflection of the new material incorporated into the text. Most of the new entries in the 1576 index in fact directed readers to material that had already been included in the first edition. The actual descriptions, for example, of England, Sicily, Gotland, Majorca, and Minorca remained unaltered between the first and second editions, but each received an entry on the customs of its inhabitants in the index of the second edition.[34] In the second edition, ethnographic information was, to be sure, slightly more abundant, but that information was foregrounded in a much more emphatic way by the paratext.

A similar process is apparent in other Venetian works published in multiple editions over the course of the sixteenth century. Francesco Sansovino's *Dell'historia universale dell'origine et imperio de Turchi*, an anthology of contemporary writings on the Turks and Islam more generally, appeared in five editions in the sixteenth century, with another two in the following century. Much like an isolario, Sansovino's anthology included both ethnographic and nonethnographic material. Thus, accounts focused primarily on customs, such as Menavino's *Cinque libri della legge, religione, et vita de' Turchi* and Bassano's *Costumi et modi particolari de la vita de' Turchi*, sat alongside accounts of military engagements that were largely devoid of ethnographic content. The contents of the anthology changed with successive editions as texts were added or, in rarer cases, removed. As with Porcacchi's isolario, though, the expansion of ethnographic material in the index outstripped that of the text. Even texts that remained stable across editions, such as Theodoro Spandugino's *Delle historie et origine de principi de Turchi* (significantly, published by Sansovino under the altered title *De costumi de Turchi*) were treated to new index entries drawing readers' attention to ethnographic material. The 1573 edition, which advertised its expanded alphabetical index as a selling feature in the title, included a number of index entries for Spandugino's work that were absent in the first 1560 edition. Among these new were entries on Turkish sleeping arrangements ("Dormire de turchi qual sia & in che modo"), women's dress and sequestration ("Donne & habito loro: & usanza nell'andar fuori"), and practices of charity ("Limosine differenti de turchi, & quanto differenti alle nostre").[35]

The Circulation and Reading of Ambassadorial Reports

In the late sixteenth and early seventeenth centuries, observers began noting the relative ease with which Venetian ambassadorial relazioni could be purchased or consulted abroad. Orazio Busino, the chaplain to the Venetian ambassador in London, recorded in his journal in 1618 that relazioni could be consulted readily in Oxford in the then-recently founded Bodleian Library. The library, he wrote, was "filled with innumerable and very rare books on all the sciences and in every language, including a folio volume full of Venetian reports, despite the state's injunctions to secrecy."[36] Two years earlier, a Venetian diplomatic secretary had reported the existence of a manuscript volume (possibly the same one that Busino had noted) containing fourteen relazioni in an unnamed Oxford library.[37] His report was forwarded to the Inquisitors of State, the magistracy established in 1539 to investigate the illicit disclosure of political secrets, indicating the seriousness with which such breaches were viewed by the Venetian state.[38]

Foreign agents were also able to purchase relazioni in Venice itself at a significant but not prohibitive cost. In 1610, an agent of the Duke of Mantua wrote to the duke from Venice, informing him that a copy of a recent relazione of England could be purchased for ten ducats. The agent reported that the relazione consisted of "a narration of the customs and qualities of the king and queen and their children, where the king's forces extend, the situation of the island and other curious things."[39] Outside of Venice, it appears that copies of relazione were available at a considerably lower cost. While serving as ambassador to Rome in 1598, Leonardo Donà compiled a two-page-long list that he titled "relazioni that can be bought in Rome."[40] The list includes fifty-three Venetian relazioni on a number of states, including France, the Holy Roman Empire, Persia, and the Ottoman Empire. Reports on the Ottoman Empire were the most widely available (with a total of eight relazioni for sale), followed closely by reports on France and Rome (with six relazioni each).[41] In Rome, Donà reported, relazioni were available even more cheaply than in Venice, with the going rate being fifteen paoli, or about one-tenth the ten-ducat rate quoted by the Mantuan agent.[42]

Donà's list raises important questions about why exactly foreign readers sought out Venetian relazioni. The obvious reason, of course, is that foreign agents valued the reports as a source of up-to-date political and military intelligence. Indeed, the concern of Venetian diplomats abroad and the Inquisitors of State about the availability of relazioni abroad would seem to confirm this suspicion. Yet if this were the only or even primary reason that international readers sought out Venetian relazioni, we would expect the Roman market to be dominated by the most recent reports. Most of the relazioni listed for sale by Donà, however, were decades old. The oldest, a report from 1527, was more than seventy years old, and one-third of the reports that can be dated were over forty years old.[43] Donà's list includes only one relazione that was less than a decade old. Whatever the "news appeal" of the relazioni, it is clear that readers valued the reports as more than simply sources of information on current affairs.[44]

The late sixteenth and early seventeenth centuries marked the high point of foreign interest in Venetian relazioni. Over the course of the seventeenth century, demand for the reports slackened abroad. By the late seventeenth century,

Venetian relazioni were no longer a requisite component of foreign diplomats' information diet. This shift was especially notable in the case of Venetian reports on the Ottoman Empire, since Venice had long been a key broker of information on the Ottoman Empire in western Europe.[45] Foreign diplomats and others who sought information on the Ottomans increasingly turned to homegrown sources. In his study of the circulation of information between Istanbul, London, and Paris in the late seventeenth century, John-Paul Ghobrial notes the absence of copies of Venetian relazioni in the papers of contemporary French and English ambassadors.[46] Late seventeenth-century ambassadors continued to prepare for their missions in ways strikingly similar to those of their predecessors, both inside and outside of Venice.[47] They read widely, keeping notebooks with excerpts on the politics and customs of the state to which they were assigned, but outside of Venice, the writings of Venetian ambassadors no longer played a central role in their mission preparation.[48] In part, this turn away from Venetian sources—particularly Venetian sources on the Ottoman Empire—was a function of the growing availability of other sources as European states expanded their diplomatic networks. Whereas at the beginning of the sixteenth century, Venice was unique among western European states in having a permanent diplomatic representative in Istanbul, by the end of the century this was no longer the case. The new geopolitical realities of the seventeenth century meant that Venetians were simply no longer in the position of being privileged brokers of information on the Ottoman Empire.

Within Venice and its territory, the circulation of relazioni proceeded along very different lines. Outside of Venice, entrepreneurial scribes sold copies of Venetian relazioni for varying rates. Although there were certainly exceptions, relazioni within Venice were much less likely to be the objects of commercial transaction.[49] The reports were objects of noncommercial social exchange among members of the patriciate. For young Venetian noblemen, the practice of socialization through and around the relazioni began young. As part of their broader practical education in rhetoric, patrician boys practiced and attempted to perfect the norms of diplomatic discourse in preparation for a presumed political career. Traces of this preparation can be seen in the early seventeenth-century exercise book belonging to the young patrician Benedetto Soranzo. The book, which Soranzo began keeping at the age of seventeen, consists of a set of short exercises in which he wrote mock letters assuming the role of a Venetian ambassador.[50] Soranzo's "embassy" changed from week to week; he wrote alternately as the Venetian ambassador to Spain, France, Rome, Savoy, and the Holy Roman Empire.[51]

At a slightly older age, young patricians could take part in the reading and discussion of relazioni in informal academies. One such academy's minute book, recording the group's weekly meetings between 1599 and 1602, reveals that individual members occasionally brought copies of ambassadorial relazioni to share with their peers.[52] On these occasions, the academy departed from its usual debate format to discuss the ambassadorial report.[53] Given the terse nature of the minutes, it is impossible to say what exactly the young men made of the relazioni or to what extent their discussions focused on the reports' ethnographic content. The academy's activities, however, are suggestive of the ways in which the sharing and collective reading of relazioni were important elements not only of the political education of young Venetian noblemen but also of their socialization as patricians. In a context in which the defining quality of nobility for men was participation in government and, as a corollary, in which a particular social group was so closely identified with the state, it was inevitable that political education and socialization as patricians would be closely linked.

While the minute book of the academy of young noblemen provides an example of the intimate sharing of relazioni on a small scale, the sharing of a given ambassadorial report could be a much more widespread and much more deliberately orchestrated phenomenon. One such case involved the state investigation of Ottaviano Bon for what appears to have been the carefully managed leak of his relazione following his 1617 embassy to France. By this point in his career, Bon was an experienced diplomat, having served in several major embassies including as bailo in Istanbul (see chapter 3). In 1617, Bon was one of the two Venetian ambassadors who negotiated and signed a peace treaty in Paris following the two-year-long War of Gradisca between Venice and the Austrian Hapsburgs. The treaty proved unpopular among Venetian patricians, and Bon was held responsible for what were seen as the treaty's unfavorable terms for the republic. The backlash prompted Bon to "retire" to Padua.[54] From Padua, Bon used his relazione as a vehicle to justify his actions during the negotiations and then took measures to circulate the report in Venice in an effort to rebuild his political reputation.[55]

The wide diffusion of the Bon's relazione was brought to the attention of the Inquisitors of State. Initially, the inquisitors were uncertain of the nature of the circulating document. It was not immediately apparent to them that the document was in fact Bon's relazione as opposed to a private statement of opinion designed to rehabilitate Bon's reputation. In total, the inquisitors' investigation uncovered the names of nineteen men who had read or received copies of Bon's relazione and nine more who had discussed its contents.[56] Through questioning a number of patricians who possessed or had read copies of the relazione, the Inquisitors of State had determined that Bon, working closely with his brother Filippo in Venice, was the ultimate source of the circulating copies of the report. Once this was determined, the Council of Ten dispatched a messenger to Bon's home in Padua ordering Bon to present himself before the inquisitors in Venice within three days. Bon, incensed, appeared a week later.[57]

The case and Bon's testimony in particular reveal some of the ordinarily tacit assumptions about what latitude an ambassador had to share his work with a readership of fellow patricians. As Bon reminded the inquisitors, frequently and with great irritation, he was an experienced ambassador with many years of service to the republic behind him. In his long political career, he had frequently shared copies of his relazione with his allies (*parenti*) in the Senate in order to elicit their opinions and strengthen his own writing.[58] Bon clearly saw nothing wrong or unusual in what he had done. He acknowledged that at some point, he and his brother had lost control of the circulation of the relazione, as the original recipients shared it with other readers who in turn shared it with others. This was, he allowed, an unfortunate development but one that was entirely predictable given the enthusiastic readership that existed for ambassadorial relazioni. "What happened to me," he explained to the Inquisitors of State, "was what happens in all cases with relazioni, since they are curious and desired things."[59]

Although the very fact that a formal investigation of a former ambassador was conducted might indicate an official zero-tolerance policy regarding the social circulation of relazioni, the Inquisitors of State's line of questioning suggests a more complicated dynamic. One of the inquisitors' central concerns was that the work that Bon had circulated was not in fact a relazione at all but rather, a statement of private political opinion designed to sway the opinions of other Venetian patricians. The question of whether Bon's piece was a relazione might seem like a strange one. The obvious solution to the matter, of course, would have been to check the piece that Bon had circulated against the copy of his relazione preserved in the archive. Bon, however, had never submitted a written copy of his relazione for preservation. This, he claimed, was part of the reason that he had initially shared the relazione—in order to receive feedback so that he might improve the report before depositing it in the archive.[60]

Evincing a sophisticated understanding of the generic conventions of the relazione, the inquisitors repeatedly asked Bon to defend the work's very status as a relazione. For example, if the piece were in fact a relazione, why, they wanted to know, did it not employ the first person, as relazioni typically did? Bon, for his part, responded that since he had been one of two Venetian ambassadors involved in the treaty negotiations, it seemed appropriate to employ the third person in his relazione so as not to render invisible the contributions of his colleague Vincenzo Gussoni.[61] To the inquisitors, Bon's departures from the conventions of the relazione gave his writing the appearance of having been written "to give news to the world" rather than to inform the doge and senators.[62] The Inquisitors of State were in a sense correct—Bon's relazione did not read like a typical relazione. Furthermore, it was highly unusual to use the platform of the relazione as Bon did to justify his actions as an ambassador. In the absence of an archival copy against which it could be compared, it is not surprising that the work's status as a relazione was initially met with incredulity.

A second major concern of the inquisitors was that as a result of the actions of Bon and his brother, the relazione had ended up circulating well beyond the confines of the Venetian patriciate. When Bon attempted to justify his sharing of the report as the ordinary action of an ambassador seeking the opinion of his relazione's audience of senators, the inquisitors challenged him. Because of Bon's indiscretion, they objected, the report "was placed not only in the hands of senators but also of people who are neither members of the Senate nor even among the number of the nobles of this republic."[63] This course of events, Bon claimed, was unintended but predictable. It is difficult to escape the conclusion that had the circumstances around the circulation of Bon's relazione been more typical—had it resembled a standard relazione instead of an exculpatory political screed and had its circulation been limited to the patriciate—Bon's actions would never have come to the attention of the authorities, let alone been the subject of a formal investigation.

Print and Manuscript

Print, as many early modern observers would attest, was one of the defining inventions of their age. Print had rendered the contemporary world unrecognizable from that of the ancients.[64] It divided the Christian world from the Muslim.[65] Today, Venice's outsized role in the production of printed works is also one of the principal reasons that the city is justifiably seen as a center of information and communication in the early modern world. As the enduring circulation and influence of Venetian relazioni underscores, however, print alone does not exhaust the city's role as a center of information, including ethnographic information. Many Venetian ethnographic writings, particularly those works emanating from the world of Venetian diplomacy, circulated in manuscript.[66] Any attempt to grapple with the contemporary significance of these writings needs to take seriously the fact that they circulated overwhelming in manuscript and through noncommercial means. They did so, moreover, in a world in which the information order was increasingly dominated by print and in which printed works were commercially available to anyone who could afford to pay for them. Scholars are now apt to emphasize the continuities that existed between manuscript and print as forms of textual transmission.[67] It is fair to say that the consensus view of the information order of the fifteenth through seventeenth centuries is, in the words of David McKitterick, a "mixed world of print and manuscript."[68]

At the same time, there has been a persistent assumption among some scholars that because relazioni and other Venetian diplomatic writings circulated primarily in manuscript, their influence was necessarily limited.[69] The evidence suggests instead that ambassadorial relazioni were influential and sought after in part because their circulation was limited and controlled. The readership of the relazioni was undeniably a circumscribed one, although perhaps not as circumscribed as Venetian authorities would have liked. As historians of the book have noted, when compared with print circulation, scribal circulation clearly excluded many potential readers, but it was also more strongly inclusive of those readers who had access to a given text; in an age of print, manuscript circulation took on a meaning that it did not have before and, indeed, could not have had before.[70] Examples such as the testimony gathered during the formal investigation of Ottaviano Bon illustrate the ways in which being able to receive, or simply even read, a work not widely owned fostered a sense of privilege, exclusiveness, and even intimacy. Then as now, the exclusive and inclusive qualities were linked; a text could be inclusive and work to forge links between its community of readers precisely because access to it was exclusive.

Venice was an environment where information was plentiful and where Venetians of a range of social locations sought to socially position themselves via the texts they owned and read.[71] In this context, patricians and those in their orbit fancied themselves an information elite. Access to the exclusive, scribally circulated relazioni was thus deeply imbricated with how they positioned themselves socially. Venetian patricians, quite simply, appreciated having access to a purportedly exclusive body of knowledge—so much so that they even when the material they presented to their peers in their relazioni was culled from printed sources, they still strove to present themselves as the bearers of novel and privileged information. Typically, this manifested itself in a rhetorical strategy disavowing the repetition of material that their audience could readily find "in books." Statements such as those by the Venetian ambassador to France, Lorenzo Priuli, who claimed in his 1582 report that he would "leave aside the consideration of many things, curious though they might be . . . since they are ordinary things that can be drawn from various books and readily circulating information" were not uncommon.[72]

When ambassadors vowed so ostentatiously not to trade in the material contained in printed books, they not only made a claim for the novelty of the information they presented in their relazioni; they also drew on and reinforced a distinction between a commercial information order accessible to increasingly large segments of the population and the closed information order of the Venetian patriciate. Unsurprisingly, patricians viewed the former with a good deal of apprehension. Elite Venetians' views of print as disreputable in the decades following the introduction of printing in the city in 1469 have been well documented. Martin Lowry shows that the commercial nature of print in particular lent it an air of disreputability.[73] As the protests of ambassadors in their relazioni make clear, however, patrician views of print remained in some respects apprehensive long after the printing industry was well established in the city.

Typically, ambassadors' apprehensions about the commercial nature of print were implicit in their more general promises not to traffic in the information found in books. In some instances, however, the contrast between the inclusive commercial information order and the exclusive information order of the patriciate was made explicit. This is the case, for example, in the preamble to the returning bailo Bernardo Navagero's 1553 relazione, introduced at the beginning of this chapter. He explained that he would refrain from wasting the senators' time by describing elements of the Ottoman Empire that had already been described in widely available printed works.[74] In Navagero's own formulation, the information he conveyed to the senators was literally invaluable, existing outside of and, indeed, positioned in contrast to a disreputable commercial information order, where the bars for admission were low.

Statements such as Navagero's articulating an underlying wariness about print help to contextualize contemporary debates around the presentation of ethnographic material in the relazioni introduced in chapter 2. The problem, in the view of Navagero and a host of his contemporaries, was that if an ambassador merely repeated and padded his report with ethnographic details culled from books—from sources that anyone could read—then the relazioni were no longer as exclusive. They no longer afforded their community of readers, composed in theory exclusively of Venetian patricians, access to a privileged body of knowledge.

Reading as an Ambassador: The Library and Embassies of Leonardo Donà

Although some relazioni leaned more heavily than others on material gathered through study, all ambassadors read and studied extensively in preparation for their missions. The line dividing the work of the diplomat from the work of the scholar was not a firm one for Venetians. Congratulating a friend appointed ambassador to England, Gasparo Contarini wrote that the life of a diplomat "is most beautiful and honorable, most similar to a life of studies; or rather, it is more important."[75] Diplomats were at once readers and purveyors of information about the states in which they served. The library and papers of the ambassador and future doge Leonardo Donà, today preserved largely intact, provide a rare glimpse into the ways patricians made use of their libraries in the preparation for and execution of their duties. Although Donà offers an instructive case study, there is no reason to believe he was exceptional in his activities. Indeed, he hewed closely to the prescriptions enjoined on patricians preparing for diplomatic offices, keeping journals of his travels, reading widely on foreign customs, and studying the writings of his predecessors. Donà's library reveals the sheer diversity of sources on which Venetian patricians relied in preparing for diplomatic missions and in forming their visions of the cultural practices of other peoples more generally. Donà drew his notes from Venetian state documents, including ambassadorial relazioni and dispacci, travel journals written by fellow patricians, historical and geographical works in Latin and the vernacular, and ephemeral printed works describing recent events. But even though Donà and other patricians were willing to collect and consult a range of sources, they clearly did not value all of these sources equally. Donà's library gives us a sense of the great weight he placed on the ambassadorial relazioni of his predecessors, which he, like many other patricians, assiduously collected and carefully read.[76] His attentive reading of the reports in turn left evidence in his library as Donà annotated or excerpted information from relazioni, repurposing it and making it his own.

In the case of the Ottoman Empire, where he served as ambassador in 1595, Donà turned to printed sources primarily for historical information and to the relazioni of his predecessors for information on both customs and recent political developments. One of his notebooks on the Ottoman Empire, for example, contains several pages of notes and excerpts from Paolo Giovio's *Commentario de le cose de' Turchi*, first published in 1532. From Giovio, Donà copied verbatim an introductory account of the origins of the Ottoman dynasty followed by his own summaries, at times greatly truncated, of Giovio's biographies of each of the Ottoman sultans.[77] Much more copious, however, and more varied in the information they contained are Donà's notes and summaries of Venetian relazioni.

As Donà's preparation for his mission suggests, no ambassador arrived in Istanbul—or in any other mission for that matter—a blank slate. In the case of the Ottoman Empire, Donà and other diplomats brought with them a set of assumptions not only about Ottoman cultural alterity but also about what cultural differences were worth nothing and how they should be recorded. Even Donà's notebooks written during his time in Istanbul in late 1595 and early 1596 reveal a constant interplay between what he heard and observed on a daily basis and what he had read in preparation for his mission.

The first of the two notebooks consists of a series of brief, unrelated notes on a variety of political and ethnographic topics. Donà titled this notebook "Libretto primo di alcune memorie tenute nell'ambasceria mia di Costantinopoli giornalmente."[78] The "giornalmente" of the title is somewhat misleading since the vast majority of the entries are undated. Although Donà's title might suggest a diary, the notebook functions as more of a journal-cum-commonplace book. Donà kept similar notebooks in preparation for and during his earlier diplomatic missions. He titled his corresponding notebook from his time as ambassador in Spain "Observations concerning the Province of Spain, Its Kingdoms, and Its Income and Expenses, 1570–1573." He organized the notes in the Spanish notebook in a strictly thematic (as opposed to chronological) fashion under subject headings. Whereas Donà's Ottoman notebook relied on a set of marginal indexing notes to facilitate consultative reading, his Spanish notebook included a separate, dedicated index page. In addition to the numerous entries on royal expenditures we would expect given the title, Donà also included a great deal of ethnographic material under the headings "customs of Spain," "women's customs," "Moors of Spain," "Judaizers of Spain," and "Old and New Christians of Spain, including Portugal."[79]

Donà's organization of the entries in his Ottoman notebook was somewhat looser. The notes have a clipped quality throughout, and several of the entries are not written in complete sentence form. To give an impression of the sheer concision of the notes and variety of topics they treat, Donà ranges in a single page from Islamic prohibitions on printing, to the familial ties between the deceased Sultan Murad III and the third vizier, to the Muslim veneration of Christian holy sites in Jerusalem, and finally to the institution of salat, or the five daily recitations of prayer.[80] Donà later went over the notebook adding marginal annotations that served an indexing function, thereby making an already concise series of notes even easier to read in a consultative manner. The form of the notebook and the nature of its contents strongly suggest that Donà intended it to be a repository of raw material that he would later develop into other, more systematized writings. Indeed, some of the material in the notebook was eventually incorporated into his relazione. This material included Donà's observations on the relationship between the deceased Sultan Murad III and the third vizier; the tensions that existed between "native" and "renegade" Turks; the status of Tartars in the Ottoman Empire; and the practice of salat.[81]

In several of the entries, Donà in turn shows a clear engagement with the relazioni of his predecessors as well as with authoritative works on Ottoman history and culture. Through his reading, Donà departed from Venice with a sense of the debates to which he might contribute. Take, for example, his treatment of printing—or rather, the absence of printing—in the Ottoman Empire. As Paolo Preto notes, the absence of print in the Ottoman world was a favorite topic of Venetian authors, for whom it served as an example of a broader privation of learning in the empire.[82] The ultimate reason for the absence of print, however, was a matter of some debate among Venetians. Unlike several of his predecessors, Donà did not ultimately include any mention of printing in his final relazione, but he did see fit to include the topic in his notebook. "The Turks," Donà noted succinctly, "do not permit the printing of books in their state, the reason for which some said was so as not to take away the livelihood of the many who live from copies written by hand."[83] Here, Donà presented the assessments of his recent predecessor Lorenzo Bernardo, who had reported in his 1592 relazione that the absence of printing in the Ottoman Empire ultimately stemmed from the vested interests of the many who made their living from producing manuscripts.[84] Bernardo's assessment was shared by the anonymous author of the prefatory material of the Venetian edition of the Qur'an.[85] Donà for his part believed that a more accurate explanation lay in religious prohibitions against touching "writing which contains the name of God and their law."[86]

Donà's use of the writings of his diplomatic predecessors and other authoritative works on Islam and the Ottoman Empire as scaffolding for his own observations was the result of both tradition and necessity. Linguistic difference mandated this state of affairs. Like the other sixteenth- and early seventeenth-century Venetian baili and ambassadors to the Ottoman court, Donà could neither read nor speak the Turkish necessary for political negotiations or the Arabic that would have allowed them to engage with the sources of Islamic theology.[87] Although ambassadors from other European states were occasionally able to function in Turkish, the structures of Venetian diplomacy mitigated against this. Donà's English counterpart in Istanbul, Edward Barton, for example, was able to function quite comfortably in Turkish. After meeting Barton, Donà recorded in his notebook that in a complete departure from Venetian practice, Barton was skilled in the Turkish language.[88] Although it was not uncommon for Venetian patricians to serve in multiple embassies over the course of their careers, there was no true patrician diplomatic corps. An ambassadorship was one office among many that a patrician could expect to hold in his career in public service. It would simply not have been a practical investment of time or resources for a young nobleman to spend years learning Turkish to prepare for the remote possibility that he might one day be elected to serve in a brief mission in Istanbul.[89]

As a result, in their negotiations with Ottoman officials, Donà and other the Venetian ambassadors and baili were utterly dependent on the Venetian corps of diplomatic interpreters, or dragomans. The use of diplomatic interpreters was also a feature of other missions, but in none of Venice's permanent missions was the ambassador's reliance on those interpreters as extreme as in Istanbul, where diplomats could not rely on a common knowledge of Latin. Marino Cavalli, one of Donà's predecessors, underscored just how complete an ambassador's reliance on linguistic intermediaries could be. In a book of advice on the management of an embassy written for his son, he outlined a hierarchy of linguistic dependency based on the state to which the ambassador had been assigned. Cavalli advised that in addition to the official interpreters, at least two other members of the ambassador's household should be fluent in the local language, adding that this was less of a concern in the case of missions to France and Spain, where the ambassador could rely on a shared knowledge of Latin or Italian, but critical in missions to Germany. In the case of missions to Istanbul, the linguistic requirements were even more demanding. "In Constantinople," he wrote, "there is no doubt that [the ambassador's men] must know the Slavic, Greek, and Turkish languages, otherwise men are like mutes and suffer in the extreme; indeed, it will not be possible to go there, to remain there, or to do anything at all."[90]

Like other ambassadors, Leonardo Donà read widely in preparation for his embassies. Ambassadors' reading taught them that customs, broadly construed, were an important aspect of any state, to be duly scrutinized and recorded alongside matters such as state expenditures, natural resources, the ruler's character, and so on. This in turn guided how they read and, crucially, how they observed. Although it is obvious that visitors to Istanbul, or for that matter any other city, did not arrive as blank slates, Donà's notebooks from his time in Istanbul reveal just how thoroughly interwoven the practices of reading, observation, and recording were for early modern ambassadors.

The Library of Gian Vincenzo Pinelli

While Venetian ambassadors were heirs to a tradition that encouraged ethnographic reading and observation, they were far from the only readers who read with an eye to assembling ethnographic material. The examination of the library and notebooks of Gian Vincenzo Pinelli reveals a set of reading practices very similar to Donà's but pursued for very different ends and, given the vast resources at Pinelli's disposal, with a much broader range of material. Pinelli was born in Naples in 1535 to a family of noble Genoese origin. He moved to Padua in 1558 to pursue legal studies at the university and remained in the city until his death in 1601. During his time in Padua, Pinelli assembled what has been reckoned to be one of the largest private libraries of its day in the Venetian state, a project facilitated by both his access to the Venetian book market and his correspondence with intellectuals throughout Europe.[91] Although volumes of his correspondence and notes survive today, Pinelli never published anything; the building of the library was, in effect, his life's work. What fame he enjoys today rests on his library and his association with the vast network of intellectuals he counted among his correspondents. Pinelli's library was unique, but his reading practices were not. Much like the library of Donà, it is the very qualities that render Pinelli's library unusual—its size, the care with which its contents were cataloged, and the fact that through an accident of history it has been preserved largely intact—that make it possible to reconstruct its owner's ordinary reading practices.

Although they were part of a private collection, Pinelli's materials were accessible to scholars. Scholars have come to appreciate the important role that private libraries played in cultural exchange in sixteenth-century Italy.[92] Pinelli's library was no exception. He frequently welcomed visitors to his library. Guests at Pinelli's home and library included Galileo, Paolo Sarpi, Justus Lipsius, Sperone Speroni, and the cardinals Robert Bellarmine and Cesare Baronio.[93] Pinelli's circle also included numerous Venetian patricians and ambassadors, among whom were Girolamo Lippomano, Giacomo Contarini, Pietro Duodo, and Ottaviano Bon.[94] Even the gradual building of his collection was, to some extent, a collective endeavor. Due to poor health, Pinelli seldom left Padua, which encouraged him to rely on his vast network of correspondents to help him locate and obtain editions for his library. Indeed, much of his surviving correspondence is devoted to researching, locating, and obtaining copies of books.

Surviving inventories of the library attest to the breadth of Pinelli's collection. The two major surviving inventories were both produced after Pinelli's death.[95] Neither of the inventories is complete and each has its particular shortcomings. In the interval between Pinelli's death and the production of the first inventory, an unknown number of volumes was stolen from the library. The Council of Ten then compounded this loss by seizing from the library those manuscripts deemed to be of public interest (see chapter 3).[96] The first inventory, produced in Venice in 1604 and now held in the Marciana, was made as a record of the estate inherited by Pinelli's nephew in Naples. (Pinelli was never married and died without children.) The inventory does not record complete publication information for Pinelli's printed books and frequently omits authors' names. Those responsible for the inventory were clearly unable to read Greek and as a result, were unable to inventory Pinelli's substantial collection of Greek books and manuscripts. The second inventory was produced in Naples in 1609 by agents of Cardinal Federico Borromeo, who had purchased Pinelli's collection at auction with the intention of adding it to the recently founded Biblioteca Ambrosiana. This second inventory provides much more complete publication information but includes approximately 1,000 fewer printed books than the Venetian inventory—a reflection of losses sustained in transit.[97] While the contents of the library were being shipped from Venice to Pinelli's heir in Naples, the ship carrying them was attacked by pirates and a third of the cases of books and manuscripts were destroyed.[98]

The sheer size of Pinelli's library and the variety of its contents make it difficult to offer any general statements about Pinelli's relative interest in ethnographic material based on inventories of the library alone. Works of ethnographic literature, both in print and manuscript, were certainly well represented in his collection. The two major inventories of Pinelli's collection made shortly after his death make clear that he owned copies, and often multiple editions, of all of the major sixteenth-century works of Venetian ethnographic literature, including Ramusio's *Navigazioni e viaggi*, Benedetto Ramberti's *Libri tre delle cose de turchi*, Lazzaro Soranzo's *L'Ottomano*, and Francesco Sansovino's collection of writings on Turkish customs and history.[99] His collection of printed books also included numerous Italian translations of Spanish and Portuguese writings on the East and West Indies, for the most part published in Venice, as well as some editions in the original Spanish.[100] These print accounts of the Indies were supplemented by a vast collection of manuscript copies of Jesuit relations and correspondence from China, Japan, and the Americas, including autographed letters by Matteo Ricci.[101] Finally, as we know from the Council of Ten's efforts to recoup such documents, Pinelli was also an avid collector of Venetian diplomatic writings, including relazioni and travel journals, many of which contained a great deal of ethnographic information. In short, the library included all the ethnographic works we would expect it to as well as some we would not. In a library, though, that before the depredations following its owner's death contained approximately 10,000 printed titles and 830 manuscripts, it is difficult to offer any conclusive statements about the relative significance of those works.[102]

Pinelli certainly valued Venetian state documents as sources of information. It is clear that he obtained copies of ambassadorial relazioni and other Venetian documents through a variety of channels, although some of the sources through which Pinelli obtained such documents offer more questions than answers. One of Pinelli's important contacts in Venice was Filippo Pigafetta, who was himself an author of ethnographic literature and occasional papal diplomat. Pigafetta had acted as a papal legate to the Persian court in the 1570s, where he was charged with negotiating an anti-Ottoman alliance. Like other such European missions to Persia, Pigafetta's was ultimately unsuccessful. Pigafetta would go on to publish an authoritative account of the history of the Kingdom of Kongo in 1591, based largely on information provided by the Portuguese traveler Duarte Lopez.[103] Although Pigafetta, originally from Vicenza, was not a Venetian patrician, this clearly did not impede his access to copies of state documents. On several occasions, he wrote to Pinelli from Venice offering to send him copies of ambassadorial of relazioni.[104] In other instances, he merely informed Pinelli of their contents.[105] It is likely that Pinelli's relationships with Venetian patricians, including several diplomats, also allowed him to obtain diplomatic writings through more "orthodox" channels.

Pinelli's scheme for organizing diplomatic writings provides some indication of what information he sought from the reports. Pinelli arranged his collection of occasional manuscript writings into bundles or *mazzi*. Each individual document was given an alphanumeric shelf number. The letters referred to the mazzo to which the document was assigned, while the number referred to its place within the mazzo. Venetian diplomatic materials were organized not on generic, authorial, or institutional lines but on geographical ones. Thus, the Venetian relazioni on England in Pinelli's collection were grouped into mazzo F, but included alongside them were a variety of other texts on England, such as the anonymous "Della natura degli inglesi," which addressed a range of ethnographic topics, including English dress, physiognomy, diet, and education.[106] Similarly, mazzo Q contained Venetian diplomatic writings on the Ottoman Empire, including relazioni and diplomatic travel journals, as well as writings from other sources treating religious observances and the Ottoman military.[107] This was different from how Pinelli treated other institutional writings. His Jesuit materials, for example, were arranged along institutional lines with no regard for geography. Thus, mazzo CC contained all of Pinelli's Jesuit letters and reports from China, Japan, and the Americas; however, it also included short pieces on the martyrdom of the English Jesuit Edmund Campion.[108] At an organizational level at least, Pinelli's choices suggest that he viewed Jesuit writings as sources of information on, in the first instance, the Society of Jesus itself. Pinelli did in fact have a series of mazzi dedicated to Venice and its empire (FF, parts 1–4), but this is not where he kept Venetian diplomatic writings.[109] Venetian diplomatic writings were instead filed alongside ethnographic, geographical, and political writings of various provenances as sources of information on the states they took as their subjects.

Pinelli did not consistently annotate the materials held in his library, and even in cases where he did, the results are not always revealing. Frequently, his annotations merely correct scribal errors or, in rarer instances, provide indexical marginal annotations. On rarer occasions still, he used his annotations to what he perceived as lacunae in the text, as for example when he criticized the author of a diplomatic travel journal to Egypt for not providing basic facts about the size, population, and available food supplies of Cairo—the sort of standard information that he expected to find in such accounts.[110] The absence of substantial annotations in Pinelli's books and manuscripts, however, does not mean that he did not engage in significant ways with their content. Also preserved among Pinelli's manuscripts in the Ambrosiana is a commonplace book. The manuscript, written entirely in Pinelli's hand, is organized around thematic headings with an alphabetical index and marginal cross-references to facilitate navigation. In these respects, Pinelli's commonplace book is a fairly typical example of the genre. There are, however, some idiosyncrasies, notably in the language of the entries. Although the commonplace book was typically a collection of quotations (usually in Latin) collected from authoritative sources and chosen largely for their exemplary stylistic qualities, Pinelli wrote nearly all of his entries in Italian, even in cases where his source material would likely have been in Latin.[111] He did not usually list the authors or sources from which he had drawn his entries, nor were most of the entries direct quotations. Whatever uses Pinelli envisioned for his commonplace book, he apparently did not view it as a repository of eloquence.

Significantly, Pinelli included in the book a dedicated heading titled "Customs and Habits" (*Costumi e habiti*).[112] Pinelli clearly viewed ethnographic information as belonging to a discrete category of knowledge. The material he assembled on customs in the course of his reading was also obviously something to which he wished to be able to return and make reference. Although Pinelli's arrangement of ethnographic information into a discrete section clearly reflected broader changes in the valuation of ethnographic knowledge, it also involved intervention on the part of Pinelli as reader. Pinelli did not live at a time when there were many wide-ranging and comparative treatments of customs available in print. Pinelli and other likeminded readers thus had to make their own ethnographic compendiums, cobbling together ethnographic information from a wide variety of sources and genres. Pinelli's commonplace book does not just reflect a broader shift in the valuation of ethnographic knowledge; it is an instance of enacting that shift.

The wide geographical, chronological, and topical range of the entries that Pinelli included under "Customs and Habits" is itself significant. Pinelli's commonplace entries reveal an expansive vision of what and whose practices and beliefs might be included under the rubric of customs. The entries dealt with both European and non-European customs and ranged from to naming practices in Ragusa to women's beauty regimes in England to Turkish bedroom decor and sleeping arrangements to the tonal qualities of the Chinese language.[113]

Pinelli's entries included within their ethnographic frame not only Europe more generally but also Italy itself. Among the several entries dealing with language, Pinelli included several notes on the differences between various regional Italian dialects and accents.[114] Later, in an insight almost certainly derived from his reading of Jesuit correspondence, Pinelli added an entry on Mandarin, noting that in that language, the same word spoken with different intonations could have a variety of different meanings.[115] It is worth noting, however, that geographical range of the commonplace book, broad as it was, was not without its limits. None of the hundred-plus discrete entries under the "Customs and Habits" heading treat the Americas. Given the broader contents of Pinelli's library, this absence is difficult to account for. It cannot be attributed a more general lack of interest in the Americas that some scholars have attributed to sixteenth-century Veneto readers (or European readers as a whole).[116] Pinelli possessed numerous works on the Americas, both in print and manuscript, and his correspondence reveals that he took an active interest in acquiring such materials for his collection.[117]

Although the organization of the section was loose, without any coherent chronological or geographical order, Pinelli did order some of his entries thematically, grouping entries on customs related to dress or funerals from various parts of the world in order to facilitate cross-cultural comparison. The section, for example, concludes with brief statements concerning the nature of kingship in both Sri Lanka and France.[118] Pinelli's collected entries on marriage customs are even broader in scope. They range not only geographically but also chronologically, with Pinelli treating the marriage customs of ancients and moderns alongside one another. The section's brief entries move rapidly from a comparison of the ways in which Genoese and Neapolitans contract their dowries, to French courtship customs, to the customs governing ancient Roman marriage and inheritance, to a comparison Babylonian marriage auctions (as reported by Herodotus) and the contraction of marriages in medieval Venice.[119] "In Babylon and in Venice in ancient times," Pinelli writes, "every year all of the women of marriageable age would be gathered, and the beautiful were auctioned, the mediocre were married off without money, and the ugly were married off with the money gained from [the auctioning of] the beautiful."[120] This final entry exemplifies not only the clipped quality of Pinelli's notes but also his penchant for bringing together customs that were similar in form even if separated by vast chronological and geographical distances.

Gian Vincenzo Pinelli and Leonardo Donà exemplify a mode of reading focused on extracting and repurposing ethnographic information in a text. Their reading practices help answer the question of how contemporaries made sense of the growing body of information on all parts of the globe available to them. Their notes, correspondence, journals, and commonplace books make clear that ethnographic information was clearly one of the things they read for. The point is not that ethnographic knowledge was the only thing they read for, nor perhaps even the most important, but it was in their minds a discrete category of knowledge. Both men believed they needed a deep familiar with this category of knowledge, albeit for slightly different reasons. Donà's ethnographic reading was closely conditioned by the Venetian diplomatic tradition to which he was heir. That tradition had taught him that the study of customs and the practice of statecraft went hand in hand. It had also taught him that the work of the diplomat and the work of the scholar were closely aligned. Pinelli, an unpublished polymath and book collector, never sought to put ethnographic knowledge to such practical ends. For him, foreign customs were simply one of the many subjects in which an educated man needed to be conversant.

Pinelli and Donà offer instructive case studies, but they were clearly not alone in their reading. Their mode of reading was one both anticipated and spurred on by printers and editors, who over the course of the sixteenth century incorporated evermore elaborate paratextual apparatuses to the books they produced. In so doing, they not only allowed readers to easily locate and extract ethnographic information from a text; they also signaled to those readers that ethnographic information was something to which they ought to devote their attention. In a context in which readers had ready access to a growing body of ethnographic literature in print, however, the circulation of ethnographic information in manuscript remained vital well into the seventeenth century. The distinctive reading practices and communities that emerged around ambassadorial reports underscore the continued significance of manuscript circulation. For the privileged few able to access them, the sharing and collective reading of relazioni and related writings was an important act of corporate identity. These readers—largely but not exclusive patrician—valued the reports precisely because of their exclusive nature.

CHAPTER FIVE

Ethnography, the City, and the Place of Religious Minorities

Venice enjoyed a reputation not only for the mere presence of religious minorities but also for the religious toleration its government extended to those minorities. In his *History of Italy,* William Thomas, who visited the city in the mid-1540s, marveled at the ease with which non-Catholics could escape both private and official censure: "He that dwelleth in Venice, may recon himself exempt from subjection. For no man there marks another's doings. . . . If thou be a Jew, a Turk, or beleevest in the devil (so thou spread not thyne opinions abroad) thou art free from all controllement. . . . For eating of flesh in thyne own house, what day so ever it be, it maketh no matter. And generally of all other things, so thou offend no man privately, no man shall offend the[e]: which undoubtedly is one principal cause, that draweth so many strangers thither."[1] For some observers, this aspect of Venetian society was something to be commended. For many Venetian citizens and patricians, the toleration of religious minorities was emblematic of the city's liberty and celebrated as part of the myth of Venice.[2] For other observers, as Thomas's passage suggests, the situation was far from an unalloyed good. Few, however, failed to remark on the presence and treatment of religious minorities in the city.

The lives of these "strangers" were shaped by ethnographic knowledge. Venice was certainly an important center for the production and transmission of ethnographic information that had been gathered, at least in its original form, outside of the city. Ethnographic knowledge, though, also had important applications within Venice, particularly in the governance of religious minorities. The city itself served not only as a backdrop against which ethnographic information was deployed in the service of managing religious minorities but also as a laboratory for the production of ethnographic knowledge.

The Venetian state strove to accommodate and, in some cases, even competed to attract foreigners, including non-Catholics, to the city in an effort to support their involvement in commerce.[3] At the same time, however, communities of religious minorities were not welcomed in the city without restriction. One of the means through which the state sought to impose religious order was by mandating the residential segregation of certain religious minorities. Venice has the distinction of being the site of the first compulsory Jewish ghetto, established in 1516. By the end of the sixteenth century, the Venetian government had devised a scheme for the residential segregation of Muslim merchants from the Ottoman Empire, which was also the first arrangement of its kind in Europe. Decisions about the design and management of these spaces were weighed carefully by Venetian officials, who showed a great willingness to defer to individuals who claimed ethnographic expertise in their deliberations.

The deployment of ethnographic evidence, however, was not only the province of self-proclaimed experts. As the records of the court proceedings of the Venetian Inquisition reveal, ordinary Venetians routinely drew on ethnographic information in their appearances before the tribunal. Collectively, this evidence suggests the existence of a much wider breadth of ethnographic thinking than might be assumed given the relatively limited pool of authors and readers of ethnographic literature in early modern Venice. Inquisitorial records provide records of one of the rare instances in which a wide range of Venetians was invited to reflect on cultural difference and its significance. This occurred particularly in cases where the very religious identity of the accused was in question. In such cases, witnesses were called on to speculate about the religious identity of the accused and, in the process, to cite evidence for their speculation. The analysis of these cases reveals the existence of an entirely different source of ethnographic knowledge—that of the reality of daily life in a religiously and ethnically diverse early modern city—that complemented and occasionally conflicted with traditional bodies of ethnographic knowledge.

Ethnography and Urban Planning: Managing Religious Minorities in Early Modern Venice

A changing economic landscape in the late fifteenth and sixteenth centuries had profound effects on Venice's demographic profile. Maritime trade had long been central to both the city's economy and to the collective identity of Venetian citizens and patricians. A legal prohibition on the ability of noblemen to engage in trade, of the sort that existed in other jurisdictions, would have been anathema in Venice.[4] The tight bond between political belonging and participation in maritime trade was also enshrined in legislation. Access to the lucrative trade with the Levant was restricted to two juridically defined groups: patricians and an elite subset of the citizenry, who possessed what was known as citizenship *de intus et extra*. This grade of citizenship could be acquired by newcomers to the city but only after they had resided and paid taxes in Venice for a period of twenty-five years. Venice made the economic privileges of citizenship considerably more difficult to acquire than did other commercial centers. In Paris, for example, a foreigner could acquire citizenship after a year and a day of residency, while in Amsterdam, no distinction existed between native and foreign-born merchants.[5] Venetian laws governing commerce and the acquisition of citizenship were designed to protect the economic interests of patrician and citizen merchants by excluding foreign traders from the market.

This arrangement proved economically sustainable for the state, which derived much of its revenue from customs dues and taxes on trade, so long as there were sufficient numbers of patricians and citizens de intus et extra willing to engage in overseas trade.[6] By the sixteenth century, however, this was no longer the case, and the system came under considerable stress.[7] The retreat of the nobility from maritime trade was a process that began in the fifteenth century but became more pronounced in the sixteenth century.[8] Although the causes of this shift are complicated and the subject of considerable debate, there is consensus that investment in land offered several advantages over investment in maritime trade. Higher food prices in the sixteenth century made agriculture more profitable, land ensured smooth patrimonial transmission, and maritime trade, at least in the Mediterranean, was becoming more expensive and more dangerous.[9] Ultimately, the declining participation of Venetians, and of Venetian patricians in particular, in maritime trade created the conditions for the state-sanctioned expansion of communities of religious minorities in Venice. In an effort to stem the loss of Venice's share of maritime trade, the government encouraged the settlement of foreign merchants and granted them communal trading privileges. If trade could not remain in the hands of Venetian noblemen and citizens, at least it could remain in Venice.

The commercial rationale for the presence of foreigners in the city shaped the ways in which those communities would come to interact with the Venetian state, resulting in an arrangement in which the magistracy that effectively functioned as Venice's board of trade assumed a great deal of authority over the day-to-day lives of religious minorities in the city. Against the backdrop of concerns over increasing competition for trade, the magistracy of the Cinque Savi alla Mercanzia was established in 1507 as a temporary body to provide advice on matters of trade.[10] It was made a permanent body ten years later. Members were elected from the ranks of the Senate, in theory, on the basis of their prior experience with overseas trade. The 1507 capitulary specified that those elected from the Senate to serve as savi should be "experienced both in navigation and in trade."[11] While the Savi's primary functions were consultative and included providing recommendations and policy proposals to the Senate and its steering committee, the Collegio, they also acted as a civil tribunal in commercial matters.[12] The scope of their jurisdiction was gradually expanded through the sixteenth and early seventeenth centuries and came to encompass all areas of commerce, including commercial insurance, the regulation of commercial brokers, the appointment of Venetian consuls, and the supervision of foreign consuls in Venice.

When it came to the consultation of ethnographic authorities, the Cinque Savi's most significant area of jurisdiction included authority over merchants who were Ottoman subjects. This included authority over *Ebrei Levantini*—the term used in Venice and other Italian port cities to refer to Ottoman-subject Jewish merchants—once the Levantine presence in the city was formalized in 1541. The exercise of this authority required the Savi to weigh in on matters of daily life in the Ghetto Vecchio, an annex of the ghetto established in 1541 for the exclusive use of Levantine Jews. Tedeschi Jews, as the older community of German and Italian Jews was collectively known, were technically prohibited from residing in the Ghetto Vecchio. What emerged, then, over the course of the sixteenth century was a situation in which Venetian patricians selected primarily for their commercial experience were asked to make decisions regarding the management of religious minorities in the city involving everything from the sale of wine, oil, and other foodstuffs in the ghetto to the architectural layout of the residential quarters of Ottoman merchants. These decisions were not made in a haphazard fashion; the magistrates took their deliberative role seriously. They engaged in research, conducted site visits, and most of all, consulted authorities. In weighing decisions regarding the day-to-day life of religious minorities, the Savi showed a great willingness to defer to those who claimed ethnographic expertise.

A case in point is the Fondaco dei Turchi—one of the more monumental products of the Cinque Savi's consultation of ethnographic authorities.

Although the Fondaco's final location on the Grand Canal was not established until 1621, planning for a segregated residence for Ottoman merchants began in the 1570s. The Savi heard evidence for both the distinctiveness of "Turkish" culture and for the internal cultural diversity of the Ottoman Empire at every stage of the planning process.[13] The former was employed as a justification for the very establishment of a segregated residence for Ottoman merchants, while the latter was employed as a justification for segregating different nations of Ottoman subjects *within* the Fondaco. Ethnographic evidence delivered by two public dragomans, the official interpreters employed by the Cinque Savi to assist Ottoman merchants in the city, would eventually determine the architectural layout of the Fondaco's final location, which featured separate wings for Balkan and Anatolian merchants as well as internal barriers to impede movement between those wings. Michele Membré, who served as public dragoman until his death in 1594, drew a distinction between "Asian" or "Anatolian" Turks and "Bosnian and Albanian" Turks in his report on the creation of a fondaco. By the time of Membré's death, however, a final location for the Fondaco had not yet been secured. His successor as public dragoman, Giacomo de Nores, offered recommendations based on the final location of the Fondaco. De Nores recommended the creation of separate residential quarters within the Fondaco for "Asiatic Turks" on the one hand and "Bosnians and Albanians" on the other hand since the two nations were "of diverse natures and customs." De Nores's recommendation of the creation of separate quarters was accepted by the Cinque Savi.[14]

Commerce, Governance, and Practical Ethnography: Levantine Jews and the Board of Trade

While the creation of the Fondaco dei Turchi had a lasting impact on Venice's built environment, many of the cases involving religious minorities in which the Cinque Savi were called to intervene were quite mundane, dealing with matters of day-to-day life in the ghetto. In these cases, too, the Savi often heard and weighed the merits of ethnographic evidence. In 1596, for example, the magistrates were called on to give their opinions on a petition by the community of Levantine Jews regarding the supervision of the baking and sale of bread in Ghetto Vecchio. The petition requested that the community be permitted to appoint a Jewish deputy to supervise Christian bakers in the baking of bread destined for the ghetto, presumably to ensure that neither nonkosher ingredients nor implements that had been in contact with such ingredients were used in preparing the bread.[15] The deputy would also be responsible for the sale of bread within the ghetto, although he would not operate his own bakery. Without Jewish bread vendors in either the Ghetto Nuovo or the Ghetto Vecchio, Jews were forced to leave the ghetto to buy bread from Christian bakers. The issue was clearly one of some concern to the Levantine community, who submitted at least two petitions requesting bread sales, the first in 1594 and another two years later.[16] The Venetian guild of bakers strongly objected to the Levantines' proposal. The bakers sent a representative to speak before the Cinque Savi, urging the board to recommend against the petition on the grounds that increased competition would do irreparable damage to their members' business. They argued that the presence of a Jewish deputy selling bread in the ghetto would be particularly harmful to bakers operating in Cannaregio, the district of the city in which the ghetto was located.[17] The Levantines' petitions, meanwhile, highlighted a number of ills that the sale of bread within the ghetto would remedy. Many Levantine Jews, the petitioners claimed, were ignorant of Italian and could thus not easily conduct business with local bakers.[18] Furthermore, foreign Jews knowing little about "the customs of the city" were placed at "notable and evident danger" by being forced to leave the ghetto to buy bread.[19]

More significantly for the Cinque Savi, the Levantine supplicants also emphasized the importance of bread in the observation of Jewish law. The Savi clearly found the appeal to Jewish law the more serious of the petitioners' claims, and their written opinions address it explicitly. For the Cinque Savi, the emphasis on the ritual requirement for the supervision of baking was significant because it invoked the privileges granted to the Levantine nation. In the initial 1541 *condotta*, or charter, issued to the Levantines, the Venetian government offered protections for the observance of Jewish law. These provisions were renewed in subsequent charters, and other Italian cities courting Levantine merchants would offer similar provisions in their own condotte.[20] The very first article of the 1589 Venetian charter—the operative charter at the time the Levantines made the request—stated unequivocally that in the ghetto granted them for their use they could "use and observe their rites, precepts, and ceremonies and keep synagogues according to their custom, secure for [the duration of the charter] that they will not be molested on account of religion by any magistracy."[21] The decision faced by the board was thus in part an ethnographic one. The Savi's recommendations would hinge on the question of whether the *absence* of a Jewish baker in the ghetto violated the privileges granted in the condotta, or put differently, whether Jews in fact had a legitimate religious need for their own baker.

The question divided the five members of the board. Two of the Savi, Daniele Pasqualigo and Lorenzo Capello, were clearly persuaded by the Levantines' petition. They were skeptical of the bakers' claim that the proposal would harm guild members, since the bread sold in the ghetto would ultimately continue to be produced by Christian bakers, albeit with rabbinical supervision. Pasqualigo and Capello readily accepted the Levantine's ritual claims. They stated in their written opinion that the supervision over the baking of bread was necessary "for the observance of their ceremonies," and they noted that in recognition of the economic benefit that the nation brought to the city, the state had already granted the Jews permission to have butchers and vintners operate in the ghetto for precisely the same rationale.[22] Indeed, one of the two men, Pasqualigo, had in a previous term on the board dealt with a petition from a Jewish wine merchant seeking permission to sell Cretan wine "fatto alla hebraica" in the ghetto.[23]

A three-member majority, however, recommended against granting the request on the grounds that the Levantines did not in fact have a need legitimately grounded in Jewish law to supervise the baking of bread. For the majority, the petition was just another in the Levantines' long line of flimsily grounded attempts to extract collective concessions from the state. "Every other day," they stated in their opinion, "these Jews go about procuring new things."[24] The supervision of the baking of bread, they reasoned, could not possibly be a legitimate religious requirement since the Levantines' German and Italian coreligionists in the neighboring Ghetto Nuovo had been living and buying bread for decades without similar privileges. The Levantines, they wrote, had thus acted "under pretext of ceremonies that are not observed by the other Jews of this city, and though they live under the very same law, they go about trying to introduce the practice of bread being distributed and sold in their way and through this means trying to have a new bakery established in the ghetto."[25] The majority predicted that if the measure were approved, Jews would abandon established bakers in favor of the Jewish bread vendor in the ghetto, both for the sake of convenience and "to support their own nation."[26] Since they did not view the supervision of baking as a legitimate requirement of Jewish law, they advised that the economic toll on the bakers would be too great to justify the measure. Although strongly opposed to the petition, the majority added at the end of their opinion that if the Levantines' were granted their request, the Jewish deputy should at least be placed in a bakery close to the ghetto, since it was local bakers who stood to lose the most business.[27]

In other instances, the Savi turned to ethnographic authorities to help resolve questions of the communal privileges of religious minorities. One such case occurred in 1624 when the board was called on to weigh in on a case touching on both Venetian sumptuary law and the traditional dress of Jews in the Safavid Empire. That year, the Savi intervened following the arrest of a Persian Jewish merchant for violating Venetian sumptuary law. The merchant had arrived in the city wearing a striped rather than solid-yellow head covering and was promptly arrested by agents of the Ufficiali al Cattaver. The case can only be understood against the backdrop of a complicated jurisdictional conflict between the Cinque Savi and a much older magistracy, the Ufficiali al Cattaver, whose members also laid claim to certain areas of jurisdiction over the city's Jewish population, including the enforcement of sumptuary law. Jews in Venice, like in many other Italian cities, were required to wear distinguishing clothing.[28] Although earlier (seldom enforced) late fourteenth- and early fifteenth-century legislation had required Jews to wear yellow badges attached to their clothing, during the last decade of the fifteenth century, Venetian authorities introduced new measures requiring Jewish men in the city to wear distinguishing hats.[29] Jews were required to wear yellow hats, thereby rendering them distinct from black-hatted Christian men. During the early seventeenth century, many Venetian Jews abandoned yellow hats in favor of red ones, although Levantine Jews continued to wear yellow hats or turbans, as they also did in both Ottoman and Safavid territories.[30]

In Venice, the enforcement of Jewish sumptuary law had long been the responsibility of the Ufficiali al Cattaver. The magistracy was established in the thirteenth century with a jurisdictional focus on tariffs, auctions, and other commercial matters.[31] As the magistracy's remit shifted over the following centuries, its members came to oversee the Ghetto Nuovo, the lending activities in the pawnshops of its Tedeschi residents and, through an extension of this purview, the enforcement of Jewish sumptuary law. What emerged, then, was a fractured jurisdictional landscape in which one magistracy, the Cinque Savi alla Mercanzia, played an important role in the day-to-day lives of Levantine and Ponentine Jews, while another, the Ufficiali al Cattaver, oversaw their Tedeschi neighbors but was also responsible for the enforcement of sumptuary law for all Jews, regardless of nation. This situation, predictably, created conflicts between the two magistracies. The Cinque Savi, for example, complained frequently that the Cattaveri were not doing enough to ensure that Tedeschi Jews from the Ghetto Nuovo refrained from taking up residence in the Ghetto Vecchio, which had been set aside for the exclusive use of the Levantine Jews.[32] The Cinque Savi had also objected in earlier cases in which the Cattaveri had arrested Levantine merchants for failing to properly wear distinguishing headgear.[33]

It was against this backdrop that the leaders of the Levantine community appealed the arrest of the Persian Jewish merchant, referred to only as Giosef in the records of the Cinque Savi. Giosef had in fact been wearing the sort of distinguishing headgear mandated by Venetian law. He arrived in Venice wearing the yellow turban favored by other Levantine Jews, but the yellow of his turban was striped rather than solid—a variation that the Cattaveri interpreted as a violation of the law. The leaders of the Levantine nation subsequently appealed to the Cinque Savi to have Giosef released from prison. His ultimate fate, which is not recorded in the records of the Cinque Savi, is unknown.

In this case, unlike that of the Levantine request for greater oversight of bread production, the four members of the board present were unanimous in their recommendation that the Levantines' request be granted. In their written opinion, delivered on May 10, 1624, ten days after Giosef's arrest, the Savi objected to the arrest on two grounds. The first was technical. The law, they wrote, was in fact silent on the question of whether the hats or turbans could be striped. In practical terms, they added, a striped turban would serve its purpose just as well as a solid one and would "not have any effect or make any difference, since with these cloths [the Jews] remain distinct and recognized by Christians."[34] Their second objection was ethnographic. The Savi appealed to the sartorial customs of Persian Jews, whom they maintained traditionally wore striped rather than solid turbans. In support of this claim, the board drew on a report made to them by the public dragoman Giacomo de Nores and by Persian merchants in the city, all of whom agreed that Persian Jews did in fact wear striped turbans. In their written opinion to the Senate, the Savi relayed that "from the report of dragoman Nores and of the Persians in this city, we understand that the Persian Jews in their own country wear striped cloths on their heads, and it seems that last year ten Persian Jews arrived in this city with their merchandise always wearing the same striped hats on their heads: it therefore seems to us that this arrest is without a crime."[35] The speaker here was as important as his pronouncement. As a Cypriot who had been enslaved following the Ottoman conquest of Cyprus, De Nores had spent his formative years in the Ottoman Empire. During his enslavement, De Nores had spent an extended period at the Ottoman-Safavid frontier—a fact that he had emphasized in his petition to be appointed public dragoman.[36] De Nores was known for his familiarity with Persian and Ottoman customs—indeed, the claim to such knowledge was part of the reason he was appointed to the post of public dragoman.[37] Further bolstering the board's opinion was the fact that De Nores had consulted Persian merchants in the city about the sartorial customs of Persian Jews. The Savi were clearly eager to ground their opinion in the firsthand knowledge of De Nores and the community of Persian merchants in the city.

The board's recommendation that Persian Jews be left unmolested for wearing variations of distinguishing Jewish headgear is likely a decision that its members would have reached even in the absence of De Nores's report. The Cinque Savi was a magistracy devoted first and foremost to the promotion of trade. The recommendation was consistent with the board's long history of promoting trade and its treatment of Levantine Jews as privileged agents of trade. It was also consistent with the Savi's traditional stance toward the Cattaveri in areas of ambiguous jurisdiction regarding Levantine Jews. For the board, then, De Nores's report was valued less for its determining role in the board's decision-making process than as an instrument that might persuade a broader community of patricians of the soundness of their judgment. What it reveals is that, at least for Giacomo de Nores and the patricians under whom he worked, ethnographic knowledge played an important role in the governance of religious minorities.

Ethnographic Testimony before the Venetian Inquisition

Jews and Muslims in Venice could find themselves subject to a very different form of governance by the Inquisition. Ethnographic evidence also came to play a significant role in the proceedings of the Venetian tribunal of the Holy Office, where it was used to discern the religious identity of those being investigated. In their role as witnesses before the tribunal, Venetians of a variety of social locations drew on ethnographic information in order to condemn or, less frequently, exculpate the accused. Some of these witnesses were, like De Nores, individuals who by virtue of their biographies could claim specialized knowledge of the customs and lived religion of religious minorities in the city. Many more, however, were not. Evidence from the records of the Venetian Inquisition indicates that a wide range of Venetians were familiar with the customs and lived religion of their non-Catholic neighbors and were adept at deploying that knowledge strategically before the tribunal. The same evidence suggests, moreover, that that familiarity was born of the daily reality of working and living in close proximity to the city's communities of religious minorities.

The cases in which testimony about customs and lived religion featured most prominently as evidence were those involving charges of Judaizing and the analogous charge of Mohammedanism (*maomettanismo*).[38] Although Muslims and Jews were not ordinarily subject to the Inquisition's authority, Christians—including those who had lived portions of their lives as Muslims or Jews—could be investigated for excessive fraternization with Muslims and Jews and for adherence to Muslim or Jewish customs. Judaizing and Mohammedanism, to be sure, always represented a minority of the total cases heard in Venice—well under 1 percent in the tribunal's first four decades of operation.[39] Once the Inquisition was revived in the city in 1540, the Venetian tribunal, like others throughout the Italian Peninsula, instead devoted itself to the prosecution of Protestantism.[40]

For the first seven years of its operation, the inquisitor and the papal nuncio acted alone without the participation of any representatives of the state on the tribunal; from 1547, they were joined by three Venetian patricians. The presence of lay representatives and attention to secular concerns in inquisitorial proceedings was not unique to Venice. In all jurisdictions outside the Papal States some sort of compromise between state interests and Roman interests had to be negotiated. In Venice, the interests of the government were represented in inquisitorial proceedings by the presence of three government-appointed noblemen known as the *tre savii sopra l'eresia* or, more simply, as the *assistenti*, who served for two-year terms.[41] These three men worked alongside the papal nuncio and the inquisitor, who from 1542 was appointed from Rome by papal brief.[42] Also present at inquisitorial proceedings was the Venetian patriarch or his vicar-general, who represented the authority of the diocese.

It was before this body of men representing distinct and, at times, competing interests that witnesses offered testimony. Historians have long been attuned to the ways in which inquisitorial testimony was shaped by questioners as much as by witnesses. Most trials took on what Carlo Ginzburg calls a "monologic" character: witnesses and defendants supplied answers that echoed the questions put to them by the tribunal.[43] These echoes are found in both the form and substance of witness testimony. Rarely would witnesses challenge the frameworks contained within the inquisitors' questions. Given how crucial the questions put to witnesses were in forging the documentary record, it is unfortunate that the trial records leave opaque which of the various members of the tribunal was responsible for posing those questions. Anne Schutte suggests that all members of the tribunal might have posed questions, with the inquisitor acting as the principal questioner and the nuncio and patriarch (or their deputies) and the assistenti occasionally adding questions of their own.[44] Since notaries, however, almost never recorded the identity of the questioner, it is impossible to attribute any question to a particular speaker with certainty. Accordingly, in the discussion that follows, I have opted to attribute lines of questioning to "the tribunal" collectively.

There are, to be sure, limits to what can be learned about Venetians' cognizance of Judaism and Islam through the trial records of the Inquisition. The tribunal's lines of questioning shaped the responses they received from witnesses. The question of to what extent ordinary Venetians understood the basic tenets of Islam and Judaism is difficult to answer because questions about belief were rarely put to witnesses. Those same witnesses, however, certainly knew, or thought they knew, what Islam and Judaism *looked* like. That is to say, they professed to know what Jewish and Muslim customs looked like.

The tribunal's seeming lack of interest in questions of belief was in many ways a practical and understandable response to the inherent challenge of detecting and prosecuting heresy. Heresy was, at its core, a crime of belief, and as such, it was a uniquely elusive crime. As the Spanish jurist Diego Simancas wrote in his 1575 *De catholicis institutionibus*, "a heretic is not one who lives badly but who believes badly."[45] The body of inquisitorial manuals and other ancillary literature that was produced to guide inquisitors in their task was replete with practical suggestions in how inquisitors might interpret the external signs of heresy. Through attention to behavior and participation in ritual life, the manuals' authors asserted, inquisitors could render the invisible crime of heresy visible. The *Repertorium inquisitorum*, an inquisitorial manual-cum-dictionary first published in 1494, articulated this relationship succinctly under its entry for *exteriora*: "The exterior reveals the interior, and through it the interior is judged."[46]

Inquisitors' manuals reveal a very different use for "practical ethnography": the detection of heretics. There were, however, limits to the detail and scope of the information they provided. A case in point is the *Directorium inquisitorum*, the most widely used manual in the context of the Roman Inquisition. Like many other manuals, it was originally produced in a Spanish context. Although the manual was originally written by Nicolau Eymeric as a guide for late fourteenth-century Catalan inquisitors, it was used in the early period following the establishment of the Roman Inquisition in the absence of any manuals written specifically for the sixteenth-century Italian context.[47] The jurist Francesco Peña sought to update Eymeric's work for its new context through his commentary on the *Directorium inquisitorum*, first published in 1578. Following its publication, Peña's commentary, which was published with Eymeric's original text, became the standard manual through the early seventeenth century.[48] Although the manual went through numerous editions in the sixteenth century, updated material was slow to be incorporated.[49] What new material there was still rested on Eymeric's fourteenth-century frame. As a result, even with the incorporation of Peña's additional commentary, the *Directorium inquisitorum* did not fully reflect the new religious, political, and geographical realities faced by the tribunals of the Roman Inquisition. As late as the 1607 edition, for example, readers could learn the signs by which they might recognize Waldensians and Manicheans among them but would learn nothing specific about the detection of Lutherans, Calvinists, or crypto-Muslims.[50]

Of the groups whose distinctive signs and behavior they did treat, the *Directorium inquisitorum* and other manuals had the most to say about the Judaizers. Eymeric had listed eight signs by which Judaizers might be recognized: they rarely entered churches; they frequented Jewish quarters; they associated with Jews more generally; they avoided the company of Christians; they ate with Jews during their holidays; they abstained from pork; they ate meat on Fridays; they worshiped on Saturdays; and on Sundays, they labored secretly in their homes.[51] To these, Peña added a final sign in his commentary: Judaizers would use a Jewish name rather than, or in addition to, their Christian name.[52] In practice, members of the Venetian tribunal pursuing suspected cases of Judaizing did not confine themselves to Eymeric and Peña's truncated list of signs. In trying to assess a suspect's Jewish identity, they routinely inquired about a range of practices not touched on in the manuals, ranging from the manner in which suspects prepared their meat to what dress they wore.

Ordinary Venetians, too, professed to know what Jewish customs looked like. The records of the Venetian inquisitorial tribunal are replete with instances of Venetians taking it upon themselves to investigate neighbors, acquaintances, and business associates whom they suspected of Judaizing. In many ways, these informal investigations by neighbors paralleled the official investigations of the tribunal. Typically, neighbors began scrutinizing the behavior of suspected Judaizers on the basis of *fama*, or reputation within the community. Fama also carried legal weight and could serve as the basis for the tribunal to initiate an investigation.[53] Like the inquisitors before whom they testified, ordinary Venetians sought visible, material evidence of Judaizing; they were looking in effect for participation in Jewish customs. A disproportionate number of those individuals investigated for Judaizing in Venice had either migrated to the city from the Iberian Peninsula or were of Iberian ancestry. Many of the most enthusiastic delators, or denouncers, of crypto-Jewish behavior were, like the individuals they accused, also Iberian migrants. As Brian Pullan suggests, their

Iberian backgrounds made them more sensitive to the "problem" of Judaizing and its signs.[54] There were also, however, many Venetians with no personal or ancestral connection to the Iberian Peninsula who served as assiduous delators and witnesses against suspected Judaizers. These witnesses' testimony was often spontaneous, offered without any apparent prompting from the inquisitor or other members of the tribunal. Collectively, their statements reveal an understanding of Jewish customs derived not from inquisitors' manuals or other textual sources of ethnographic knowledge but rather from the daily reality of living alongside Jews in a religiously and ethnically diverse city.

Two cases from the mid-1580s illustrate the phenomenon. In 1584, the tribunal received a denunciation against a Neapolitan named Pacifico for Judaizing. One of the key witnesses against Pacifico was Giovanni Scarpogiato, a pearl worker who had rented Pacifico a room in his home in the Cannaregio parish of Santa Sophia. Scarpogiato told the tribunal that it was widely known "through general saying" that his Christian neighbor Pacifico had converted from Judaism.[55] Without any encouragement from the tribunal, Scarpogiato added that once he learned of Pacifico's conversion, he began watching his neighbor closely paying special attention to Pacifico's activities on the Jewish Sabbath. Through his careful observation, he came to realize that Pacifico never worked or tended to his business on Saturdays.[56]

The following year, a much more involved case saw the tribunal question several residents of the parish of San Leonardo, which lay directly to the south of the ghetto. In a trial lasting over two years, the tribunal investigated the household of Filipe de Nis, a wealthy Portuguese merchant residing in Venice, for Judaizing. Filipe had rented a large house from the patrician Francesco Contarini for the extraordinary annual sum of 130 ducats. To put the figure in perspective, only 20 percent of Venetian patricians during the period rented homes in the 100–200-ducat price range, and 70 percent of all rents in the city were under 30 ducats per year.[57] Filipe and his household did not live inconspicuously, and their activities were observed with great interest by their neighbors. Over the course of the trial, it was revealed that members of the household had gone by various names: Filipe was also known as Solomon Marcos, and at least in Venice, members of the household used the additional surname Filippi. The most damning evidence in the trial came in the later stages during the questioning of members of the Filippi household. The early stages of the investigation, however, began with a denunciation by a priest in the parish church of San Leonardo, and it was at the parish level that the tribunal began its investigation.[58] The primary question the tribunal put to residents of the parish was not an especially leading one: Did they know of anyone in the parish who lived in a Lutheran or Marrano manner, or in some variations, did they know the Filippi family and could they speak to whether the family lived "Christianly." As the tribunal learned, rumors that the Filippi were Marranos had long circulated in the parish, arousing the close scrutiny of neighbors. Using the open prompt given to them by the tribunal, witnesses cited a range of ritual activity as evidence drawn from their own "investigations" of the Filippi.

The first of these witnesses, Cecilia, a thirty-six-year-old Friulian widow who shared a landlord with the Filippi family, was asked if she knew of anyone in the parish who lived in a Lutheran or Marrano manner.[59] She immediately identified the members of the Filippi household, volunteering that after hearing rumors that the family were Marranos, she observed that when the Ave Maria sounded at sunset, members of the household neither kneeled, nor doffed their hats, nor said the prayer as other Christians did.[60] Like the witness in the 1584 investigation of Pacifico, Cecilia was clearly confident in her own ability to identify the signs of Judaizing, and she took it upon herself to do so in response to rumors circulating in the neighborhood. She could, moreover, identify and interpret these signs of Judaizing voluntarily and without coaching by members of the tribunal.

Later that same day, the tribunal summoned Dominica, another resident of the parish, for questioning. Dominica, a boatman's wife, also shared a common landlord with the Filippi. Dominica, too, took it upon herself to observe the family closely. When asked directly whether the Filippi kept images of Christ or saints in their home, she replied that although she herself had never visited the family's home, she had watched the laborers unpack their belongings by barge when the Filippi first arrived, noting that the boat contained no sacred images.[61] In addition to revealing the numerous opportunities for surveillance bred by the city's built environment, Dominica's testimony also pointed to a familiarity with kosher slaughtering practices absent even in the inquisitors' manuals. When asked who in the Filippi household was responsible for the preparation of food, she responded, "That Mooress they have in the house, and when they bring chickens home they always bring them in alive, and on Fridays, they always bring a great many chickens home."[62] Here, of course, Dominica was suggesting that the family consumed meat at prohibited times—in this case, on Fridays—as she had done at other points in her testimony.[63] She may also have been suggesting that they observed the Sabbath dinner. By emphasizing, however, that members of the household slaughtered animals themselves at home, with all the secrecy that that entailed, she also alluded to the family's observance of Jewish dietary law in addition to their flouting of Catholic dietary law.[64]

Five days later, the tribunal questioned Giovanni Battista Guato, the rector of the church of San Geremia, which lay directly to the west of the parish of San Leonardo. San Geremia was the second of three parishes bordering the ghetto. Unlike many of the other witnesses in the case, Guato was not a resident of the parish of San Leonardo. His residence adjoining the church of San Geremia, however, lay directly across a canal from the Filippi's rented home—a vantage point that afforded him a view through the family's window. Like many other witnesses, Guato was aware of the rumors that the Filippi lived as Jews. Without any prompting from members of the tribunal, Guato described a scene that he had witnessed through his window many times:

> Across from my residence, on the other side of the canal, there live some people who are said to be Marranos. I don't know them by name but if I saw them, I would know them by their faces, especially the man who is head of the house. I noticed many times that about an hour before sunset on Friday evenings, they would light some lamps that had seven or eight openings and made seven or eight lights and they would immediately close the windows. But even with the glass windows shut, you could see the lamps until morning because they don't have blinds. During the day you couldn't see them, but on Saturday evenings, you could see that the lights were still burning. And I never saw the lights on other days of the week—only on Friday evening through Saturday evening. And I also noticed that in the house of those people, whom I take to be merchants, the other days of the week Christians and Jews frequent the house, but on Saturdays only Jews and not Christians frequent the house, especially women who go to visit the women of the house.[65]

It is worth noting that when questioned by the tribunal, the Filippi's servant, Luna (the "Mooress" of Dominica's testimony), freely admitted that everyone in the household lived as Jews but denied that the family had lit any lights during the observance of the Sabbath.[66] Whatever we make of the veracity of Guato's testimony, it clearly reveals the key role ethnographic evidence assumed in cases of disputed religious identity—for both members of the tribunal and the Venetians who testified before them. Guato had more than a passing familiarity with Jewish observances of the Sabbath: he knew what Shabbat candles were, identified them with Jewish ritual, knew that they were not extinguished but allowed to burn out, and crucially, saw their presence as a detail that would be of interest to the tribunal.[67]

Witnesses were certain they knew what Jewish ritual looked like, but the question of how they came by that certainty is a thorny one. Witnesses did not as a matter of course cite sources that would allow historians to reconstruct the genealogy of their certainty. Contextual clues, though, suggest a plurality of forms of ethnographic knowledge. Operative in the courtroom were both a literate ethnographic knowledge and a local knowledge grounded in the material and social reality of the city. Literate ethnographic knowledge might be brought to bear on the proceedings through inquisitors' manuals or through the testimony of educated witnesses like Guato. Guato's ecclesiastical education would certainly have left him with some familiarity of Jewish ritual. The specificity of most witnesses' ethnographic testimony was unlikely the product of engagement with written ethnographic works. Such works were almost certainly not a factor with the three other witnesses in the Filippi case. Indeed, Scarpogiato's status as a pearl worker and Dominica's status as the wife of a boatman make it unlikely that they ranked among the 26 percent of men and 0.2 percent of women in the city who received any formal education.[68] Yet all of these witnesses evinced a familiarity with Jewish custom.

That familiarity cannot be attributed to formative experiences outside of Venice. Although it is true that the most avid and astute delators and witnesses in Judaizing trials were Spanish and Portuguese migrants, none of the witnesses discussed here were of Iberian origin. Inquisitorial records typically list the birthplace of foreign-born witnesses. Cecilia, as the notary recorded, was from Friuli, while Giovanni Scarpogiato, Dominica, and Giovanni Battista Guato's places of birth were not specified, suggesting they were natives of Venice. The particular urban geography of these cases cannot be discounted. The witnesses were united by the fact that they lived in close proximity to the ghetto. The Venetian ghetto did not cut off contact between Jews and other inhabitants of the city, nor was it ever designed to do so. The rationale for the presence of the Jews in Venice—both the Tedeschi on the one hand and the Levantines and Ponentines on the other hand—was essentially commercial. The Tedeschi presence rested on their provision of pawn-broking services, the Levantine and Ponentine on their role in ensuring the city remained a central node in Mediterranean trade.[69] The very presence of Jews in the city was thereby predicated on the assumption of Christian-Jewish contact. The records of the Venetian

Inquisition are themselves replete with numerous examples of the ordinary daily contact between Jews and their neighbors that testify to the porous nature of the ghetto.

The ghetto facilitated not only contact in general but observation in particular, including a species of quotidian ethnographic observation. The establishment of the ghetto created a space—the first of its kind in early modern Europe—in which Jews were both mandated to live in concentrated residential segregation and contractually granted the right to observe, in the language of the charter, their "rites, precepts, and ceremonies."[70] In the same way that scholars have described later grand tourists flocking to the Venetian ghetto in order to observe Jews in their "native environment," so too did the ghetto facilitate the more quotidian observation of Jews by their Christian Venetian neighbors.[71] In short, one of the reasons that Christian Venetians—particularly those living and working in close proximity to the ghetto—knew what Jewish customs looked like is the ghetto had created a space in which Jews and Jewish customs became part of their daily reality. This local ethnographic knowledge did not exist in opposition to literate knowledge, nor was it shared only by Venetians of a particular social location. Local knowledge cut across social location, and as the example of Leon Modena's *Historia de' riti hebraici* demonstrates, it could leave a distinctive imprint on written ethnographic works (see chapter 1).

While the ghetto allowed Venetians to observe and acquire a passing familiarity with the lived religion of their Jewish neighbors, this does not mean that Christian Venetians welcomed, valued, or were even tolerant of Jewish customs. Many scholars have come to embrace an image of early modern Venice as a multicultural, pluralist, and above all, cosmopolitan society. This image of Venice is in many ways a reflection of a broader celebration of Mediterranean pluralism and cosmopolitanism. Although early modernists have begun to address the subject of cosmopolitanism, in the case of Venice, cosmopolitanism is not at present so much a research question as it is a historiographical assumption.[72] When applied uncritically or without definitional precision, there is a tendency for the seemingly neutral use of the term *cosmopolitan* as a description of the demographic fact of the city's religious and ethnic diversity to shade into the suggestion that Venetians were somehow multiculturalists avant la lettre. If nothing else, the testimony of Pacifico and Filippe de Nis's neighbors before the Inquisition should serve as a warning against any sort of facile interpretation of Venetian cosmopolitanism; we are, after all, aware of these individuals' cognizance of Jewish ritual and custom because they deployed that knowledge to aid in the prosecution of their neighbors. Familiarity, even a familiarity born of a policy of official toleration, did not necessarily beget tolerance.[73]

Accounts of Muslim Customs before the Inquisition

Whereas Christian witnesses offered testimony revealing of their cognizance of Jewish custom, assessing Christian Venetian's cognizance of Muslim customs via the records of the tribunal is a much more challenging task. Witnesses were simply less likely to be called on to testify about individual behavior during investigations for Mohammedanism. This was largely a function of the very different patterns of prosecution of Muslims and Jews in sixteenth- and seventeenth-century Venice. In the sixteenth century, prosecutions related to Judaizing far outnumbered those related to Mohammedanism. In the seventeenth century, the pattern was reversed, as denunciations and prosecutions for Judaizing slowed and those for Mohammedanism became more prevalent. This was a function of both shifting patterns of migration and the signing of a charter in 1589 that offered Iberian Jews who had formerly lived as Christians protection from prosecution by the Inquisition in Venice.[74] In the period spanning 1547–1585, there were thirty-four cases of Judaizing and only ten of Mohammedanism. From 1586 to 1630, however, there were twenty-seven cases of Mohammedanism and only sixteen of Judaizing.[75]

This shift in the target of denunciations was accompanied by an increasing prominence of summary procedures at the expense of full formal trials—a notable trend not only in Venice but in inquisitorial tribunals throughout the Italian Peninsula.[76] From the beginning of the seventeenth century, summary procedures outnumbered formal trials. Indeed, in Venice, the earliest investigation for Mohammedanism did not occur until 1573, by which time the shift toward summary procedure was already well under way.[77] In the case of the charge of Mohammedanism, summary procedures were the result of a more or less voluntary appearance of a convert from Islam to Catholicism before the tribunal. Many of these converts had in fact been born to Christian parents but had lived periods of their lives as Muslims, often as a result of enslavement.[78] In the late sixteenth century, these converts began presenting themselves to the tribunal in order to give a brief account of their life and be granted reconciliation with the church. These "voluntary" appearances by converts depart from the paradigmatic inquisitorial trial in many respects: there were no denunciations, no witnesses called, and no drawn-out interrogations. More often than not, the cases were concluded on the same day in which they began; indeed, the cases were concluded so quickly that it was not uncommon for the tribunal to hear and resolve multiple converts' cases via summary procedure during a single session.[79] Although summary cases are rich sources for the study of conversion, they offer little in the way of ethnographic testimony by the converts' Venetian neighbors.

Ethnographic evidence, however, played an important role in the handful of nonsummary procedures involving accusations of Mohammedanism. The most common pattern in these cases involved the accused himself or herself offering exculpatory ethnographic testimony. This testimony was designed to correct the assumptions of members of the tribunal—assumptions that were themselves ethnographic in nature—having to do largely with received ideas about Islamic dress and habits of the body (particularly circumcision, the wearing of hair, and beards). In challenging the assumptions they confronted before the Inquisition, the accused individuals insisted on Islam as a heterogeneous religion whose manifestations varied by region and social location.

This dynamic is evident in one of the earliest investigations for Mohammedanism, the 1586 case of Mustafa Balirai, a forty-year-old escaped slave born in Istanbul.[80] Before his flight to Venice, he had served a Christian Spaniard for six years. Balirai, who had reportedly arrived in Venice wearing the black hat worn by Christian men, was arrested after having negotiating passage to Istanbul aboard a Turkish merchant vessel. In preparation for the voyage, the Turks had given Balirai Turkish-style clothing and a turban, presumably to render him less conspicuous during the return voyage. Although Balirai's Turkish clothing raised the tribunal's suspicions, the adoption of Turkish-style dress by Christians traveling between Venice and Istanbul was not itself unusual. Travelers often adopted Turkish-style dress believing it would offer a measure of protection in case of attack on the voyage.[81] For example, Carlo Ranzo, who accompanied the Venetian embassy of Giacomo Soranzo to Istanbul in 1575, noted that the party departed in Turkish dress.[82] In a later inquisitorial investigation for Mohammedanism, a Venetian physician returning from Istanbul in 1631 drew the suspicion of his neighbors when he continued to wear the Turkish dress from his voyage for several days after his arrival in the city. Accounts of how long he wore Turkish dress in Venice ranged from one to fifteen days, after which time he apparently kept the clothing to rent out during carnival.[83]

Dress was a potent marker of religious identity, and as such, it became a central question in cases of contested religious identity.[84] As in many of the cases of Judaizing, Balirai's case hinged on whether he was truly a Christian. If, as he initially claimed, Balirai were not a Christian, then he would not have been guilty of any crime that fell within the tribunal's jurisdiction. While the tribunal eventually discovered that Mustafa had in fact been baptized in Genoa and taken the name Battista, Balirai began the interrogation by maintaining that he was and always had been a Muslim despite his former master's many attempts to convert him. During interrogation, members of the tribunal used Balirai's variations in dress to cast doubt on his claim of unwavering religious identity. The abjuration Balirai eventually signed, which thoroughly conflated his abandonment of Christian dress with his abandonment of the Christian faith, serves as a reminder of the potent link that existed between dress and religious identity: "I took off my Christian garb. Dressing myself in Turkish garb, having myself shaved, and placing the turban on my head, I boarded the ship to go to Constantinople. And appearing before this Holy Tribunal, I repudiated the faith of Christ many times with my own mouth saying that I have always been a Turk, for which I am remorseful and repentant and for which I ask the pardon of God and of this Holy Office, and I also ask for absolution for apostasy of the faith."[85]

In the initial stages of questioning Balirai, at issue for the tribunal was the perceived discrepancy between Balirai's appearance and his religious identity during the period following his arrival in Venice when he had not yet taken up recognizably Turkish patterns of dress and grooming. Even in the indirect discourse with which the tribunal's questions were recorded, the tribunal's expectation of a one-to-one correspondence between identity and appearance on the other is clearly articulated: "And it was said to him that slaves are shaved yet he has a very large beard and that the fact of his having come with a beard dressed as a Frank shows that he had become Christian."[86] In response, Balirai explained that he had not served as a galley slave but rather in the home of his former master. This, he claimed, was why his appearance had not differed demonstrably from that of a Christian man when he arrived in the city: unlike galley slaves, Muslim domestic slaves did not typically have clean-shaven faces.[87] In asserting this claim, Balirai suggested that members of the tribunal lacked a sufficiently nuanced understanding of the distinctive forms slavery might take. Instead, he offered the members of the tribunal what he clearly saw as a plausible and, crucially, exculpatory rejoinder about the varied ways in which dress could be indexed to religious identity. Balirai's strategy ultimately failed: he was condemned by the tribunal to galley service. It nevertheless reveals how individuals who appeared before the Inquisition sought to martial ethnographic evidence to their own ends.

Cases with the same broad outlines as Balirai's would continue to be heard sporadically for decades. A nearly identical case four decades later saw three Spanish men accused of Mohammedanism advance ethnographic claims in order to prove that they were truly Muslims and therefore outside the jurisdiction of the tribunal in the face of strong evidence suggesting otherwise. Like Balirai, the three men had apparently arrived in Venice dressed as Christians and were detained when they were found preparing to depart for Istanbul in Turkish dress. All three identified themselves as Moriscos and, at least initially, denied ever having been baptized or having truly lived as Christians. The question was put to one of the three men, Bartolomeo Derera, who also went by the name Mustafa and was originally from Seville, plainly: How could he prove that he was Muslim and not Christian given that he had the "signs" (in this case, a wooden cross and a rosary found among of his effects) and dress of a Christian?[88]

Derera responded by positioning himself as a member of the "Granadine" nation—that is to say, a descendant of the Granadine Moriscos who had been forcibly resettled throughout the territories of the Crown of Castile following the War of Alpujarras (1568–1570).[89] Like Balirai, he claimed that the apparent discrepancy between his dress and his religious identity was not a true discrepancy at all but rather, was characteristic of the lived religion of the members of his nation. "All Granadines," he claimed,

> go about [in Christian dress], because if they did otherwise they would be punished, and some of us carry relics and forcibly hear mass on Sundays in order to appear Christian, [but] I am not Christian. . . . I don't know what the Christian faith is. It is true that the Granadine Turks are forced to baptize themselves, but they use the following trick: they send a child to be baptized multiple times, pretending that he is an unbaptized child. And my mother told me that I was never baptized but that she instead used this trick and sent another child to be baptized in my place.[90]

Derera insisted throughout his testimony that his actions were not individual aberrations but rather, were components of a well-established tradition of Morisco religiosity. When asked if he was circumcised, he explained that he was not but that "no Morisco was circumcised because they all live as Christians."[91] When the tribunal insisted during a separate interrogation that Derera had lied when he claimed that he was not a Christian, he maintained that he had merely observed Christian ceremonies "in the manner that other Granadines lived."[92] As in the earlier investigation of Balirai, the tribunal was clearly unimpressed with Derera's ethnographic account of the Granadine observance of Islam; the tribunal found him vehemently suspect of heresy and was condemned to three years of galley service.[93] In an echo of the language from Balirai's case, the tribunal's final judgment emphasized Derera's culpability in voluntarily adopting Turkish dress and patterns of grooming, equating his abandonment of Christian dress with his abandonment of the faith.[94]

Derera's and Balirai's cases illustrate the most typical deployment of ethnographic evidence in cases of Mohammedanism: both men offered testimony about distinctive regional customs in order to clear their names. The opposite dynamic, however, was also possible: accusers with an unusual personal or professional familiarity with Islam could use that knowledge to incriminate suspects. The phenomenon paralleled that of Iberian migrants serving disproportionately as delators against Judaizers; individuals with specialized knowledge of the Muslim customs were, on the one hand, more attuned to the "signs" of Mohammedanism and, on the other hand, able to use that knowledge to craft credible accusations against those they wished to see convicted.

Few individuals in Venice had as much firsthand knowledge of Islam as the group of commercial agents who served as brokers and interpreters for Ottoman and Persian merchants in the city. Commercial brokers, referred to in Venetian as *sanseri,* were overseen by the Cinque Savi alla Mercanzia and were responsible for mediating between local and foreign merchants and for collecting the appropriate taxes and duties from those merchants.[95] As a class, the brokers serving Ottoman and Persian merchants, the *sanseri dei turchi,* had an obvious professional interest in the religion and customs of their clients and could lay claim to a certain expertise in these matters. As numerous witnesses would attest before the Venetian Inquisition, the profession was one especially riven by rivalry and competition. Their professional familiarity with the customs of the Ottoman and Safavid worlds also left brokers well positioned to level convincing accusations of Mohammedanism against professional rivals.

These and other factors combined to make investigation for heresy an occupational hazard for commercial brokers. At the most obvious level, the commercial brokers' work brought them into close and frequent contact with Muslim merchants in the city. Linguistic competence in Turkish and/or Persian was a requirement of their appointment as brokers, and many brokers had acquired that competence while living significant periods of their lives as Muslims outside the boundaries of Latin Christendom.[96] The challenge faced by brokers, however, was more fundamental than this. As studies of linguistic and cultural intermediaries in the Mediterranean have made apparent, individuals with the backgrounds and skill sets of the brokers were valued by the Venetian state for their perceived ability to move between the worlds of Latin Christendom and Islam—an image that the brokers themselves assiduously cultivated.[97] That same propensity for movement, however, which served as an advantage in their professional lives, proved a serious liability before the Inquisition, which was nothing if not an institution that insisted on fixity of religious identity.

A pair of related cases that emerged from the professional world of Venetian commercial brokers illustrates the point. The accused in the first of these trials was Teodoro Dandolo or, as he was more commonly known in Venice, Teodoro Persico or Tartaro. Born in Bukhara, today located in Uzbekistan, Teodoro migrated to Aleppo sometime around 1600, where he first met his future patron, the Venetian consul Vincenzo Dandolo.[98] Encouraged by Dandolo, Teodoro relocated to Venice in order to receive baptism, after which time he adopted the name Teodoro Dandolo. He then leveraged his connection to the patrician Dandolo family along with his knowledge of Turkish, Persian, and Arabic to obtain an appointment as a commercial broker by the Cinque Savi alla Mercanzia. In 1618, 1620, and again in 1623, Teodoro was accused of Mohammedanism by a group consisting largely of his professional rivals. In the investigations that followed, the tribunal judged him lightly suspect of heresy in 1621 and vehemently suspect in 1624.[99]

The trials saw the use of both exculpatory and inculpatory ethnographic testimony. Teodoro's accusers and most of the principal witnesses against him were all either brokers or men who lived their lives in the orbit of Venetian commercial brokers. Some of the testimony against Teodoro was generic in the sense that it did not draw on witnesses' specialized knowledge of the Muslim customs and lived religion. Witnesses consistently testified, for example, that Teodoro ate meat indiscriminately on Fridays and during Lent, that he rarely confessed or communed, and that he failed to doff his hat before religious processions. All of these were accusations that could be and, indeed, were made routinely against individuals accused of other crimes, including Judaizing and Lutheranism.

Some witnesses, however, drew on more specialized knowledge in their testimony. For example, several attributed Teodoro's religious prevarication to his presumed Tartar ethnicity. Benedetto Soriano, a vendor who had first met Teodoro at the Catechumen House where Teodoro had been a neophyte, testified that the Tartars had a reputation for religious dissimulation.[100] When asked if he believed Teodoro to be a good Christian, he replied that he did not "because with the Turks he makes himself Turkish, with the Jews he makes himself Jewish, and with the Christians he makes himself Christian, and all Tartars behave like this in their dealings with others."[101] Benedetto's son, Giovanni Battista Soriano, also interpreted Teodoro's actions through the lens of his Tartar ethnicity. He volunteered that when he saw Teodoro fail to doff his cap before a crucifix or kneel for the sounding of the Ave Maria at sunset, he assumed that this was an expression of Teodoro's contempt for Christianity—a contempt shared by those of the Tartar nation.[102]

Teodoro, for his part, tried unsuccessfully to employ ethnographic testimony in an exculpatory fashion. In an odd and ultimately ill-fated strategy, Teodoro sought to minimize the differences between Christian and Muslim belief in order to suggest that even if he were a Muslim (a charge that he vehemently and consistently denied), he would never have uttered the heretical statements of which he was accused since they would also contravene Islamic belief and sensibilities. One of the many charges made against Teodoro by his professional rivals was that he had disparaged the Gospels. When asked about this remark by the tribunal, Teodoro denied having uttered it and claimed that he would never have done so since "Persians and Turks also believed in the Gospels."[103] He persisted in this strategy throughout his trials. Three years later, when Teodoro was asked if he had ever disparaged the Christian faith while sharing meals with his Muslim associates in Venice, he claimed that he had not and that he would never have done so since the Qur'an itself "named the glorious Virgin Mary and the Holy Apostles with much praise."[104]

Less than three years after the conclusion of his final trial, Teodoro was involved in another investigation for Mohammedanism, this time as a delator. In this later and more straightforward case, Giovanni Battista Flaminio, a commercial broker who, like Teodoro, worked with both Ottoman and Safavid merchants, was accused by a group of men made up largely of his fellow brokers of Mohammedanism. Flaminio, not incidentally, had also served as a witness against Teodoro in the earlier case.[105] Like many other commercial brokers for Ottoman and Persian merchants, Flaminio was himself a convert to Christianity. At the time of the 1627 accusation, Flaminio had served as a broker for Ottoman merchants in the city for sixteen years.[106] The written delation against Flaminio listed eight witnesses, at least four of whom were commercial brokers.[107]

At the heart of the delation was the charge that during a lengthy voyage in which Flaminio had accompanied several Christian merchants to Persia, he had married a Muslim woman and converted to Islam. Having returned to Venice, the delators charged, he continued to associate excessively with Persian Muslims, eating with them and demonstrating a "predilection" for their rites and customs.[108] Anticipating that if the investigation were to proceed, the tribunal would surely call on a physician to see if Flaminio were circumcised (and would presumably find him uncircumcised), Flaminio's accusers took pains to assure the tribunal that there were provisions in Islamic law for conversion without the requirement of circumcision. Third on the numbered list of accusations in the written delation was the claim "that many times Turks exempt from the requirement of circumcision were those who want to turn Turk secretly."[109]

The testimony of commercial brokers before the Inquisition reveals some of the ways in which ethnographic information could be used in early modern Venice. The Venetian government's promotion of commerce meant tolerating the presence of foreigners, particularly as sixteenth-century Venetian patricians gradually abdicated their traditional role in maritime trade. Many of those foreigners brought with them customs and religious practices that differed markedly from those of the city's Catholic majority. For the election of the doge Lorenzo Priuli in 1556, the orator Luigi Groto wrote that the volume and variety of merchandise brought to Venice from throughout the world was so great that "it is difficult to tell if Venice is in the world or if the world is in Venice."[110] Men like Teodoro Dandolo and Giovanni Battista Flaminio were themselves part of the official infrastructure for that "world in Venice." In producing ethnographic writing, Venetian authors most often turned their eyes outside of Venice itself. But ethnographic information also had a place in the streets, courtrooms, and magistracies of sixteenth- and early seventeenth-century Venice.

In managing the presence of ethnoreligious minorities in the city, Venetian officials were willing to heed the advice of those who could lay claim to specialized knowledge of foreign customs. They did so in part because they had to. The conditions under which the state allowed communities of ethnoreligious minorities to settle in the city laid the groundwork for this state of affairs. So long as the Venetian state afforded religious minorities the privilege of observing their rites and customs, the magistrates charged with overseeing those communities would have to make judgments about the validity of customs.

Magistrates were also willing, however, to consider ethnographic claims even in cases that did not touch directly on the privileges extended to minority communities. This was the case with the protracted period of official planning that led to the establishment of the Fondaco dei Turchi. For Venetian magistrates, it simply passed as common sense that effectively managing the presence of ethnoreligious minorities in the city involved some consideration of those groups' customs. As the interactions between Christian Venetians and their neighbors in and around the Venetian ghetto reveal, however, ethnographic information was not only the preserve of self-proclaimed experts. The records of the Venetian Inquisition provide a glimpse of the ways in which ordinary Venetians, too, were keen observers of the customs of their neighbors. They drew on a local ethnographic knowledge grounded in the material and social reality of their city and were adept strategists in the deployment of that knowledge.

Conclusion

Ethnographic writing was central to how early modern Venetians engaged with the world around them. In Venice—a state whose economic fortunes were closely linked to maritime trade and whose political fortunes as a middling power were dependent on diplomacy—there was a broad consensus that a knowledge of foreign customs was essential for those who would enter careers of public service. In a context in which elite identity was so thoroughly interwoven with service to the state and public office holding, this meant that the study of customs would become ingrained in patrician education.

Venetians contributed to a broader European project of cultural observation, but they did so via particularly Venetian institutions and in the context of particularly Venetian social formations. One of the distinctive features of Venetian ethnographic writing was the outsized role that diplomats played in its production. Venetian diplomats developed unique forms of ethnographic observation and reporting. In Venice, the ambassador was an influential figure, and his office was one of the highest that a patrician could hold. This lent a weight to ambassadors' writings, and their reports in turn served as key sources through which young Venetian men absorbed both ethnographic information and the norms of ethnographic observation.

Within Venice itself, ethnographic information had implications at the level of policy. In executing their duties, the patricians and civil servants charged with overseeing communities of religious minorities in the city routinely considered accounts of customs. Beyond the ranks of the patriciate and civil service, assessing Venetians' cognizance of ethnographic information becomes a more complicated task. A range of Venetians, however, had their ethnographic observations preserved inadvertently. As records of Venetian inquisition demonstrate, given the proper venue, they too could deploy ethnographic information deftly.

When sixteenth-century Venetians looked outward at the world around them, they increasingly saw a world divided not in theological terms but in cultural ones. Thus, in the writings of Venetian diplomats, the Ottoman Turks were not only, or even primarily, a people defined by their theological distance from Latin Christians but by their cultural difference from Venetian observers. It is not that theological questions were of no interest to them but rather that the particularities they observed in Turkish daily life were accorded a new salience. Turks, they rehearsed again and again, ate seated cross-legged on the ground, eschewed games of chance, and were unduly preoccupied with the care of the body to the point of vanity. Similarly, what the Venetian rabbi Leon Modena offered Christian readers was not a systematic mapping of Jewish belief but rather an account of Jewish cultural practices largely shorn of any reference to belief systems.

Ethnographic writing helped to usher in a new form of difference, one that emphasized cultural distinctiveness. As scholars of Jewish history have noted, the sixteenth century saw a shift in focus in Christian discourse on the Jews from theological questions to a broader complex of cultural practices.[1] A parallel shift occurred in Latin Christian representations of Ottoman Muslims.[2] Venetian works such as Modena's played no small part in this transformation, the effects of which were not limited to Christian discourses on Jews or Muslims but were much wider reaching. Jews and Muslims had, of course, long been Europe's "others." For these groups, the novelty that ethnography brought with it was one of shifting emphasis. Venetian authors, though, reflected on the cultural distinctiveness of many peoples, including European peoples, most of whom had not been the subject of a long tradition of written reflections on their difference.

The question of who benefited from the emphasis on cultural difference at the expense of other forms of difference is a complicated one. It is also one without a single answer. At the most fundamental level, the assertion that there existed firm cultural boundaries dividing the world's peoples benefited those who laid claim to the specialized knowledge to mediate across those boundaries. Individuals who claimed ethnographic expertise by virtue of their experience, skills, erudition, or some combination thereof, found receptive audiences among members of the Venetian government. In Venice, as we have seen, these experts ranged from famous travelers such as Ludovico de Varthema to the professional interpreters overseen by the Cinque Savi alla Mercanzia. Meanwhile, for the patricians who served as the Venetian republic's ambassadors, ethnographic reporting could bolster their reputations before an audience of their peers by allowing them to craft more impressive, erudite, and engaging relazione. In inquisitorial trials, ethnographic information benefited inquisitors and members of the tribunal by rendering heretics legible. At the same time, the consensus that customs rendered legible an individual's "true" religious identity meant that ethnographic information could be used to diverse ends by those who appeared before the tribunal, to either condemn or exonerate the accused.

Early modern Venetians, like other Europeans, had available to them various categories of difference. The influence of ethnographic writing and the implications of Europeans' growing emphasis on cultural difference at the expense of other forms were wide ranging, and their effects would not be felt fully until long after the period here considered. Ethnographic writing's greatest effects were wrought in the work it did to transform Europeans' understanding of three categories: religion, ethnicity, and race. As closely linked as these categories are today, they were even more thoroughly intertwined in the early modern period.

In the first instance, ethnographic writing helped pave the way for the comparative study of religion by contributing to the development of a concept of generic religion—that is to say, the idea of religion not as a binary concept of true or false religion but as a cultural category that belonged generically to all peoples.[3] By 1613, Samuel Purchas in his *Pilgrimage*—a work whose "Catalogue of Authors" was replete with Venetian authors, including Giosafat Barbaro, Francesco Sansovino, Giovanni Battista Ramusio, and numerous Venetian ambassadors—offered just such a generic definition of religion. "Religion is here described generally," he wrote, "professing the inward observation and ceremoniall outward worship of that which is esteemed a higher and divine nature."[4] Scholars have persuasively traced the linkages between late seventeenth- and eighteenth-century ethnography and the Enlightenment project of the comparative study of religion, but the Venetian case demonstrates that the origins of this shift can be located much earlier.[5]

Ethnographic writing also worked to elaborate the meaning of the category of ethnicity. Medieval authors certainly afforded customs a constitutive role in the definition of nations. In his well-known formulation, Regino of Prüm wrote that "the various nations of peoples differ in descent, customs, language and law."[6] Early modern ethnography was in this sense a project of inscribing boundaries. The practice of cataloging the cultural traits of European and extra-Europeans that began in the sixteenth century worked to reify and harden ethnic boundaries.[7] Finally, later ethnographic writing would contribute much to an incipient notion of race. Venetian authors of the sixteenth and early seventeenth centuries were relatively unconcerned with questions of physiognomy, the somatic differences between peoples, and heritability of traits both physical and cultural. But their successors were certainly preoccupied with these questions, as were many of their contemporaries elsewhere in Europe.[8]

Sixteenth- and early seventeenth-century Venetian ethnography made significant contributions to these developments. Venetians furnished European readers not only with ethnographic information but, perhaps more importantly, with models of ethnographic reporting that would be emulated elsewhere. This was partly a function of the city's vibrant print industry, which helped to ensure a broad readership for Venetian authors. It can also be seen, however, in the influential manuscript circulation of Venetian diplomatic writings, most notably the ambassadorial relazione, a distinctively Venetian genre that came to find a wide and influential readership well beyond the borders of the Venetian state.

We have also seen that there existed significant tensions over the proper way to make ethnographic knowledge. These tensions fell into three broad categories: questions related to what kind of speaker had the authority to claim ethnographic expertise; questions related to the relative weight that should be placed on direct observation versus written authorities; and among written sources, the relative weight that should be given to accounts that circulated in a circumscribed manner versus those that were widely available. The tangled reception history of Ludovico de Varthema's work reveals just how fraught the questions of who could serve as an ethnographic authority and what kinds of claims such an individual could make were in the sixteenth century. Varthema's case fell toward the beginning of the period considered here, but the issues it raised were not fully resolved by the early seventeenth century. Venetian ethnography was marked by these tensions and Venetian authors contributed to the debates surrounding them.

Venetian authorities were largely in agreement on the value of eyewitness experience when it came to ethnographic testimony. Indeed, an assumption of the value of eyewitness experience undergirded many of the characteristic Venetian genres and institutional practices tied to the production of ethnographic knowledge. But the category of eyewitness authority was not itself unitary. Venetians were, on the one hand, deeply invested in a form of eyewitness authority that was seemingly divorced from any consideration of the subject position of the author. On the other hand, through the early seventeenth century, much Venetian ethnographic reporting was produced by and for a closed group of elites. Within this context, the identity of the speaker, his reputation, and his personal relationships with his readers were of great import.

Venetian ethnographic writing helps us recast what we know about the development of European ethnography and about European discourses of human difference more generally. Most scholars have treated European imperial expansion and the attendant encounters between Europeans and peoples in Asia and the Americas as the catalyst for systematic European reflections on human difference in the sixteenth and seventeenth centuries. Venetian ethnography, though, was embedded in very different fields of power. Venetian authors of ethnographic writing worked almost exclusively outside of a colonial context and they took a much wider range of peoples as their object of study. Theirs was a resolutely Old World ethnography oriented toward Europe and the Mediterranean.

Although Venetian ethnographic knowledge was forged within a distinctive set of power relations, it too, like colonial ethnography, was mobilized in the exercise of power. Ethnographic knowledge in Venice had a very practical set of applications, informing how the Venetian state would govern juridically defined communities of ethnolinguistic minorities. Early modern travel literature, it has been argued, "integrated the non-Christian and non-European into the mental worlds of many people from different countries and of diverse social standings."[9] While this was undoubtedly true, travel literature was far from the sole agent of mental integration. In Venice, non-Christians and non-Europeans were integrated into the mental worlds of many Christian Venetians simply by virtue of sharing a city with them. Interactions between Christian and non-Christians in that shared city were structured by ethnographic knowledge, but they also served as a source for knowledge production.

Early modern Venetians played a largely unrecognized role in the creation of European ethnography. Part of the reason their role has gone unrecognized is that most Venetian producers of ethnographic knowledge did not resemble the sort of figures we expect to find at the origins of European ethnography. Many of them did not publish their ethnographic observations, nor would they ever have thought to do so. Seldom did they seek to employ ethnographic knowledge in the exercise of imperial authority. Part of what this book has shown, though, is that we should not expect to find a single kind of early modern ethnographer. There existed a wide range of practitioners of ethnography in the early modern world. By widening our documentary search, we can find producers, readers, and users of ethnographic knowledge well beyond a restricted list of authors of travel literature. Ultimately, that ethnographic knowledge worked to transform Venetians' and other Europeans' understanding of peoples in Europe and farther afield and, indeed, of themselves.

Notes

Introduction

1. Angelo Poliziano, *Opera* (Venice: Aldo I Manuzio, 1498), a1v.

2. Thomas Coryate, *Coryats Crudities* (London: William Stansby, 1611), 171–172.

3. On the early use of the term in its original German Enlightenment context, see Han Vermeulen, "The German Invention of Völkerkunde: Ethnological Discourse in Europe and Asia, 1740–1798," in *German Invention of Race*, ed. Sara Eigen and Mark Larrimore (Albany: State University of New York Press, 2012), 123–145; Han Vermeulen, *Before Boas: The Genesis of Ethnography and Ethnology in the German Enlightenment* (Lincoln: University of Nebraska Press, 2015), 269–356.

4. For an analysis of how similar debates took shape in the realm of natural history, see Daniela Bleichmar, *Visible Empire: Botanical Expeditions and Visual Culture in the Hispanic Enlightenment* (Chicago: University of Chicago Press, 2012), 43–77; for how similar questions of authority took shape in the realm of cartography, see Surekha Davies, *Renaissance Ethnography and the Invention of the Human: New Worlds, Maps and Monsters* (Cambridge: Cambridge University Press, 2016), 3–11.

5. Some of the more notable examples published in Venice or—in the case of Luigi Bassano's account of Turkish customs—written by Venetian authors included Andrea Navagero, *Il viaggio fatto in Spagna, et in Francia . . . con la descrittione particolare delli luochi, et costumi delli popoli di quelle provincie* (Venice: Domenico Farri, 1563); Luigi Bassano, *I costumi et i modi particolari de la vita de Turchi* (Rome: Antonio Blado Asolano, 1545); Pedro de Cieza de León, *Cronica del gran regno del Perù: Con la descrittione di tutte le prouincie, costumi, e riti: Con le nuove città edificate, & altre strane & marauigliose notitie: parte prima*, trans. Agostino di Cravaliz (Venice: Camillo Franceschini, 1576); and Johannes Boemus, *Gli costumi, le leggi et l'usanze di tutte le genti*, trans. Lucio Fauno (Venice: Michele Tramezzino, 1542).

6. Tricia M. Ross, "Anthropologia: An (Almost) Forgotten Early Modern History," *Journal of the History of Ideas* 79, no. 1 (January 2018): 1–22; John H. Rowe, "Ethnography and Ethnology in the Sixteenth Century," *Kroeber Anthropological Society Papers* 30 (1964): 1.

7. "Secundus tomus Anthropologiam habet hominum clarorum omnium temporum, linguarum, gentium . . ." Raffaele Maffei, *Commentariorum urbanorum libri XXXVIII* (Rome: Ioannem Besicken Alemanum, 1506), +2r.

8. David Abulafia, *The Discovery of Mankind: Atlantic Encounters in the Age of Columbus* (New Haven, CT: Yale University Press, 2008); Kim M. Phillips, *Before Orientalism: Asian Peoples and Cultures in European Travel Writing, 1245–1510* (Philadelphia: University

of Pennsylvania Press, 2014); Andrei Pippidi, *Visions of the Ottoman World in Renaissance Europe* (New York: Columbia University Press, 2013).

9. Giuliano Gliozzi, *Adamo e il nuovo mondo: La nascita dell'antropologia come ideologia coloniale: dalle genealogie bibliche alle teorie razziali (1500–1700)* (Florence: La nuova Italia, 1977); Anthony Pagden, *The Fall of Natural Man: The American Indian and the Origins of Comparative Ethnology* (Cambridge: Cambridge University Press, 1982); John Huxtable Elliott, "The Discovery of America and the Discovery of Man," in *Spain and Its World, 1500–1700: Selected Essays* (New Haven, CT: Yale University Press, 1989), 42–64; Stuart B. Schwartz, ed., *Implicit Understandings: Observing, Reporting and Reflecting on the Encounters between Europeans and Other Peoples in the Early Modern Era* (Cambridge: Cambridge University Press, 1994); William M. Hamlin, "Attributions of Divinity in Renaissance Ethnography and Romance; or, Making Religion of Wonder," *Journal of Medieval and Renaissance Studies* 24, no. 3 (1994): 415–447; Abulafia, *The Discovery of Mankind*; Guy G. Stroumsa, *A New Science: The Discovery of Religion in the Age of Reason* (Cambridge, MA: Harvard University Press, 2010); Carmen Nocentelli, *Empires of Love: Europe, Asia, and the Making of Early Modern Identity* (Philadelphia: University of Pennsylvania Press, 2013).

10. For an overview of this historiography, see Catherine Fletcher, *Diplomacy in Renaissance Rome: The Rise of the Resident Ambassador* (Cambridge: Cambridge University Press, 2015), 5–8.

11. Olivia Remie Constable, *To Live like a Moor: Christian Perceptions of Muslim Identity in Medieval and Early Modern Spain*, ed. Robin Vose (Philadelphia: University of Pennsylvania Press, 2018); Lucette Valensi, *The Birth of the Despot: Venice and the Sublime Porte*, trans. Arthur Denner (Ithaca, NY: Cornell University Press, 1993); Larry Wolff, *Venice and the Slavs: The Discovery of Dalmatia in the Age of Enlightenment* (Stanford, CA: Stanford University Press, 2002); Nocentelli, *Empires of Love*; Palmira Brummett, *Mapping the Ottomans: Sovereignty, Territory, and Identity in the Early Modern Mediterranean* (Cambridge: Cambridge University Press, 2015); Abulafia, *The Discovery of Mankind*; Pippidi, *Visions of the Ottoman World in Renaissance Europe*; Micah True, *Masters and Students: Jesuit Mission Ethnography in Seventeenth-Century New France* (Montreal: McGill-Queen's University Press, 2015); Yaacov Deutsch, *Judaism in Christian Eyes: Ethnographic Descriptions of Jews and Judaism in Early Modern Europe*, trans. Avi Aronsky (Oxford: Oxford University Press, 2012); Michael Gaudio, *Engraving the Savage: The New World and Techniques of Civilization* (Minneapolis: University of Minnesota Press, 2008); Pompa Banerjee, *Burning Women: Widows, Witches, and Early Modern European Travelers in India* (New York: Palgrave Macmillan, 2003).

12. Mario Infelise, "Book Publishing and the Circulation of Information," in *A Companion to Venetian History, 1400–1797*, ed. Eric R. Dursteler (Leiden: Brill, 2013), 651.

13. Peter Burke, *A Social History of Knowledge: From Gutenberg to Diderot* (Cambridge: Polity Press, 2000), 162.

14. Angela Nuovo, *The Book Trade in the Italian Renaissance*, trans. Lydia G. Cochrane (Leiden: Brill, 2013), 118.

15. Mario Infelise, *I padroni dei libri: Il controllo sulla stampa nella prima età moderna* (Rome: Laterza, 2014), 61.

16. Ugo Rozzo, *Linee per una storia dell'editoria religiosa in Italia (1465–1600)* (Udine: Arti Grafiche Friulane, 1993), 21–22.

17. Rosa Salzberg, *Ephemeral City: Cheap Print and Urban Culture in Renaissance Venice* (Manchester: Manchester University Press, 2014); Brian Richardson, *Manuscript Culture in Renaissance Italy* (Cambridge: Cambridge University Press, 2009); Filippo De Vivo, *Information and Communication in Venice: Rethinking Early Modern Politics* (Oxford: Oxford University Press, 2009); D. F. McKenzie, "Speech-Manuscript-Print," in *Making Meaning: "Printers of the Mind" and Other Essays*, ed. Peter D. McDonald and Michael Felix Suarez (Amherst: University of Massachusetts Press, 2002), 237–258; Julia Crick and Alexandra Walsham, "Script, Print, and History," in *The Uses of Script and Print, 1300–1700*, ed. Alexandra Walsham and Julia Crick (Cambridge: Cambridge University Press, 2004), 1–26.

18. Peter Burke, "Early Modern Venice as a Center of Information and Communication," in *Venice Reconsidered*, ed. John Martin and Denis Romano (Baltimore: Johns Hopkins University Press, 2008), 389–419.

19. "L'è una valle in capo del teritorio brexano a li confini verso li todeschi, dove vanno li nostri beccari ogni anno ad fornirsi per la terra nostra de castroni, la quale per nome publico se chiama Valle Camonica; luogo però più montano che pianura, luogo più sterile che fructuoso, et abitato da gente per la mazor parte più ignorante che altramente, gente gozuta, quasi tutta deforme al possibile senza alcuna regola del vivere civile. De costumi più presto rusticani et silvestri, dove rari sono che sappiano, non dirò che servano li comandamenti de Iddio, dove se puole quodammodo dire che tanta differentia è da questi vallicoli a li altri brexani, quanto da portogalesi et queli de Colocut, dove fame è che zà qualche anno sono stati strioni et strie, le quale solevano esser al tempo de Medea in Tessaglia, come scriveno gli auctori." Marin Sanudo, *I diarii (1496–1533)*, ed. Rinaldo Fulin, Federico Stefani, Nicolò Barozzi, Guglielmo Berchet, and Marco Allegri (Venice: F. Visentini, 1879–1903), vol. 25, coll. 602.

20. The protracted witchcraft investigations and trials in the Bresciano were evidently of great interest to Sanudo, who copied numerous accounts of the trials into his diaries. On the prosecution of witchcraft and heresy around Brescia in the late fifteenth and early sixteenth centuries, see Stephen D. Bowd, *Venice's Most Loyal City: Civic Identity in Renaissance Brescia* (Cambridge, MA: Harvard University Press, 2010), 174–191.

21. Sanudo had in his private library manuscript copies of the writings of Giovanni Lascari on the Ottoman Empire, of Matteo da Bergamo on India, numerous Venetian diplomatic reports on the Ottoman Empire, as well as an anonymous Portuguese account of India and the customs of its peoples. Biblioteca Nazionale Marciana (hereafter BNM), Manoscritti Italiani (hereafter Ital.), classe VI, 277 (5806); BNM Ital. VI, 276 (8398).

22. On the value of Sanudo's diaries for the study of news in early modern Europe, see Pierre Sardella, *Nouvelles et spéculations à Venise au début du XVIe siècle* (Paris: A. Colin, 1948).

23. Jutta Sperling, "The Paradox of Perfection: Reproducing the Body Politic in Late Renaissance Venice," *Comparative Studies in Society and History* 41, no. 1 (January 1999): 8.

24. Brian Pullan, "'Three Orders of Inhabitants': Social Hierarchies in the Republic of Venice," in *Orders and Hierarchies in Late Medieval and Renaissance Europe*, ed. Jeffrey

Howard Denton (Toronto: University of Toronto Press, 1999), 147–168; James S. Grubb, "Elite Citizens," in *Venice Reconsidered*, ed. John Martin and Denis Romano (Baltimore: Johns Hopkins University Press, 2008), 339–364.

25. De Vivo, *Information and Communication*; Ioanna Iordanou, "What News on the Rialto? The Trade of Information and Early Modern Venice's Centralized Intelligence Organization," *Intelligence and National Security* 31, no. 3 (April 2016): 305–326; Infelise, *I padroni dei libri*, 154–182.

26. Gino Benzoni, "Il 'farsi turco,' ossia l'ombra del rinnegato," in *Venezia e i Turchi: Scontri e confronti di due civiltà*, ed. Anna Della Valle (Milan: Electra, 1985), 91–133; Paolo Preto, *Venezia e i Turchi*, 2nd ed. (Rome: Viella, 2013); Marina Formica, *Lo specchio turco: Immagini dell'altro e riflessi del sé nella cultura italiana d'età moderna* (Rome: Donzelli Editore, 2012), 21; Robert Mantran, "Venise, centre d'informations sur les turcs," in *Venezia, centro di mediazione tra Oriente e Occidente, secoli XV–XVI: Aspetti e problemi*, ed. Hans Georg Beck, Manoussos Manoussacas, and Agostino Pertusi, 2 vols. (Florence: L. S. Olschki, 1977), 1:111–116; Valensi, *Birth of the Despot*; E. Natalie Rothman, "Dragomans and 'Turkish Literature': The Making of a Field of Inquiry," *Oriente moderno* 93, no. 2 (January 2013): 390–421; Brummett, *Mapping the Ottomans*, 56–57.

27. On the Jesuit role as the major channel of communication between Japan and western Europe, see Burke, *A Social History of Knowledge*, 59; and Steven J. Harris, "Mapping Jesuit Science: The Role of Travel in the Geography of Knowledge," in *The Jesuits: Cultures, Sciences, and the Arts*, ed. John W. O'Malley, Gauvin Alexander Bailey, Steven J. Harris, and T. Frank Kennedy (Toronto: University of Toronto Press, 1999), 212–240. On the Venetian role in the circulation of information on Persia in the late fifteenth and early sixteenth centuries, see Laurence Lockhart, "European Contacts with Persia, 1350–1736," in *The Cambridge History of Iran*, ed. Peter Jackson and Laurence Lockhart (Cambridge: Cambridge University Press, 1986), 6:377–378; Palmira Brummett, "The Myth of Shah Ismail Safavi: Political Rhetoric and 'Divine' Kingship," in *Medieval Christian Perceptions of Islam*, ed. John Victor Tolan (New York: Garland, 1996), 331–360; Margaret Meserve, "The Sophy: News of Shah Ismail Safavi in Renaissance Europe," *Journal of Early Modern History* 18, no. 6 (2014): 579–608; and Giorgio Rota, *Under Two Lions: On the Knowledge of Persia in the Republic of Venice (ca. 1450–1797)* (Vienna: Österreichischen Akademie der Wissenschaften, 2009), 14–25.

28. Garrett Mattingly, *Renaissance Diplomacy* (New York: Dover, 1988), 154; Ayla Göl, "Europe, Islam and the Pax Ottomana, 1453–1774," in *International Orders in the Early Modern World: Before the Rise of the West*, ed. Shogo Suzuki, Yongjin Zhang, and Joel Quirk (London: Routledge, 2013), 34–54.

29. For recent treatments of medieval ethnography, see Shirin A. Khanmohamadi, *In Light of Another's Word: European Ethnography in the Middle Ages* (Philadelphia: University of Pennsylvania Press, 2013); Phillips, *Before Orientalism*.

30. On Ramusio's effort to reshape Marco Polo's reception, see Surekha Davies, "The Wondrous East in the Renaissance Geographical Imagination: Marco Polo, Fra Mauro and Giovanni Battista Ramusio," *History and Anthropology* 23, no. 2 (June 2012): 215–234; Elizabeth Horodowich, *The Venetian Discovery of America: Geographic Imagination in the Age of Encounters* (Cambridge: Cambridge University Press, 2018), 71–76.

31. Mattingly, *Renaissance Diplomacy*, 85, 132.

32. Nuovo, *The Book Trade in the Italian Renaissance*, 422.

33. The office of the bailo had its origins in the eleventh century. On the early history of Venetian missions in Istanbul, see Bruno Simon, "I rappresentanti diplomatici veneziani a Costantinopoli," in *Venezia e i Turchi: Scontri e confronti di due civiltà*, ed. Anna Della Valle (Milan: Electa, 1985), 56–69; Antonio Fabris, "From Adrianople to Constantinople: Venetian-Ottoman Diplomatic Missions, 1360–1453," *Mediterranean Historical Review* 7, no. 2 (1992): 154–200.

34. John-Paul Ghobrial, *The Whispers of Cities: Information Flows in Istanbul, London, and Paris in the Age of William Trumbull* (Oxford: Oxford University Press, 2013), 62.

35. On eighteenth-century Veneto scholars' engagement with the broader Enlightenment study of customs, see Wolff, *Venice and the Slavs*, 126–172.

Chapter 1 The Study of Customs

1. "Experti fuimus tot varios et diversos hominum mores, tot vivendi modos, tot virorum feminarumque cultus perspeximus, ut nesciam an usquam amplius talia sim circumspecturus: ex quo fit quod harum rerum varietate et moreum dissimilitudine homines vel hebetes ingenio excultiores promptioresque celerrime efficiuntur." Andrea de Franceschi, *Two Italian Accounts of Tudor England: A Journey to London in 1497; A Picture of English Life under Queen Mary*, ed. Cesare V. Malfatti (Barcelona, 1953), 2.

2. For a more neutral assessment of changes in the treatment of extra-European peoples in late medieval and sixteenth-century cosmography, see Matthew McLean, *The Cosmographia of Sebastian Münster: Describing the World in the Reformation* (Aldershot, UK: Ashgate, 2013), 45–142.

3. Margaret T. Hodgen, *Early Anthropology in the Sixteenth and Seventeenth Centuries* (Philadelphia: University of Pennsylvania Press, 1964), 80.

4. Judith Modell, "From Ethnographies to Encounters: Differences and Others," *Journal of Interdisciplinary History* 27, no. 3 (Winter 1997): 481–495.

5. On the evolution of the juridical conception of custom, see Donald R. Kelley, "'Second Nature': The Idea of Custom in European Law, Society, and Culture," in *The Transmission of Culture in Early Modern Europe*, ed. Ann Blair and Anthony Grafton (Philadelphia: University of Pennsylvania Press, 1990), 133–137.

6. Giorgio Vasari, *Le vite de piu eccellenti architetti, pittori, et scultori italiani da Cimabue insino a' tempi nostri* (Florence: Lorenzo Torrentino, 1550), 636.

7. "È di costumi modesti ed umani." Eugenio Albèri, ed., *Relazioni degli ambasciatori veneti al Senato* (Florence: Società editrice fiorentina, 1839–1863), p. ser. I, 3:43.

8. Gratian, *The Treatise on Laws: Decretum DD. 1–20*, trans. Augustine Thompson and James Gordley (Washington, DC: Catholic University of America Press, 1993), 5.

9. Gratian, *The Treatise on Laws*, 5–6.

10. "Hoc autem habent in lege sive consuetudine, ut occident viros & mulieres, si quando inveniantur in adulterio manifeste." Giovanni da Pian del Carpine and Willem van Ruysbroek, *The Texts and Versions of John de Plano Carpini and William de Rubruquis, as Printed for the First Time by Hakluyt in 1598, Together with Some Shorter Pieces*, ed. C. Raymond Beazley (London: Hakluyt Society, 1903), 78, 111.

11. Giovanni da Pian del Carpine, *Opera dilettevole da intendere, nella qual si contiene doi Itinerarii in Tartaria, per alcuni Frati dell'ordine minore, è di S. Dominico, mandati da*

Papa Innocento IIII nella detta Provincia de Scithia per Ambasciatori, non più vulgarizata (Venice: Giovanni Antonio de Nicolini da Sabio, 1537).

12. "Sono liberi, & vivono à Republica; & di costume, & leggi si conformano con l'eccelsa Città di Venetia." Giulio Cesare De Solis, *Descrittione di molte isole famosissime nella quale breuemente si narrano le cose principali di quelle* (Padua: Lorenzo Pasquati stampatore della magnifica Vniuersita dei legisti, 1596), 32v.

13. "Ma come sogliono i costumi d'un paese facilmente corrispondere alle leggi, non essendo le leggi altro che costumi scritti." Albèri, *Relazioni*, p. ser. I, 6:284.

14. "Hanno alcuni statuti che ritengono della prima barbarie." Albèri, *Relazioni*, p. ser. I, 6:284.

15. Bassano, *I costumi et i modi particolari de la vita de' Turchi*, 1r–7v, 33r–34r, 48r-v.

16. Michel de Montaigne, *The Complete Essays*, trans. J. M. Cohen (London: Penguin, 1993), 58.

17. Andrea de Franceschi, "Itinerario di Germania dell'anno 1492," ed. Enrico Simonsfeld, *Miscellanea di storia veneta* Ser. II, 9 (1903): 279.

18. "Ex quo fit quod harum rerum varietate et morum dissimilitudine homines vel hebetes ingenio excultiores promptioresque celerrime efficiuntur; nemo enim fere existit qui ex his omnibus quae cernimus a pravis optima quaeque secernens bonas vivendi disciplinas optimasque virtutes brevi non adipisceretur. Qua mob rem quum ita sit . . . constitui de uno quoque situ urbis aut oppida a me visi, nec minus de moribus et vivendi aut gubernandi consuetudine ex itinere labellum conficere, qui interdum voluptati amicis nostris et qui illum legerint futurus sit." Franceschi, *Two Italian Accounts of Tudor England*, 73.

19. "Mitto igitur ipsum ad te ut legas et iterum relegas, quoniam si praesens ea videre et pertractare non potuisti quae volumine inseruntur, at lectura eandem prope excipies voluptatem quam si coram nobiscum affuisses." Franceschi, *Two Italian Accounts of Tudor England*, 74.

20. "Tum veteres, tum recentes, bonos item & malos, indifferenter, ut ipsis tanq[uam] praesentissimis atq[ue] optimis exemplis perspectis vitam instituendo laudabiles sanctosq[ue] emulabundus secteris, culpabiles & obscoenos factu vitabundus praetereas." Johannes Boemus, *Omnium gentium mores leges et ritus* (Augsburg: Sigismund Grimm and Marcus Wirsung, 1520), ivr.

21. It should be noted that for Nicolay, as for many other sixteenth-century neo-Stoics, this amendment of customs would also be accompanied by the universal adoption of Christianity. On this aspect of Renaissance Stoicism, see Derek Benjamin Heater, *World Citizenship and Government: Cosmopolitan Ideas in the History of Western Political Thought* (New York: St. Martin's, 1996), 48–59.

22. "Par telles peregrinations, & communications toutes les nations diverses du monde se apprivoisent & familiarizent les unes aux autres, se emendent mutuelleme[n]t les vices barbares, se enseignent pareilleme[n]t la vraye religion, les vertus & honnesterez morales, civiles & politiques. . . . Par telle reciproque visitation, congnoissance & communicative alliance, en ostant celle arrogante presumption usurpée des Grecs & Romains, de tenir & appeler un autre homme, ou autre nation plus barbare que soy ou la sienne." Nicolas de Nicolay, *Les quatre premiers livres des Navigations et peregrinations Orientales* (Lyon: Guillaume Rouillé, 1568), 3–4.

23. On the production of the *Carta marina*, see Leena Miekkavaara, "Unknown Europe: The Mapping of the Northern Countries by Olaus Magnus in 1539," *Belgeo. Revue Belge de Géographie*, no. 3–4 (2008): 307–324.

24. Olaus Magnus, *Historia de gentibus septentrionalibus, earumque diversis statibus, conditionibus, moribus, ritibus, superstitionibus* (Rome: apud Giovanni Maria Viotti in aedibus Sanctae Brigittae, 1555).

25. Olaus Magnus, *Carta marina et descriptio septemtrionalium terrarum ac mirabilium rerum in eis contentarum diligentissime elaborata anno domini 1539* ([Venice]: Thomas de Rubis, 1539); Olaus Magnus, *Ain kurze auslegung und verklerung der neuen mappen von den alten Göttenreich und andern nordlenden sampt mit den uunderlichen dingen in land und uasser darinnen begriffen biss her also klerlich nieintuuelt geschriben* (Venice: [Giovanni Tommaso], 1539); Olaus Magnus, *Opera breve, la quale demonstra, e dechiara, overo da il modo facile de intendere la charta, over delle terre frigidissime di settentrione: oltra il mare germanico, dove si contengono le cose mirabilissime de quelli paesi, fin'a quest'hora non cognosciute, ne da greci, ne da latini* (Venice: Giovanni Tommaso, 1539).

26. "Serenissimo Principe, & Illustrissimi Signori, quelli li quali sono posti allo administrare le republiche, sono stati consueti di metter li loro studii, massimamente in doe cose: cioe nella historia, & nella Geographia: dalle qual cose si considano de poter cavare non picola prudentia, nel governar bene le republiche sue." Magnus, *Opera breve*, Aiv.

27. "Perchè chi è più atto ad essere preposto alli regni & alle natione, che quello, che ha per se visto li costumi, & le città de molti huomini? Per la qual cosa quelli antiquissimi, & prudentissimi Principi delle terre, mettevano gran cura, & facevano grande spese mandavano molti nuncii per diverse regioni dil mondo: accio che pianamente investigassero li costumi de quelle terre, alle quali non potevano andare." Magnus, *Opera breve*, Aiv.

28. "È openione di uomini sapienti che la cognizione della istoria, e massime quella dove si descrive il vivere e i costumi delle genti, oltre il piacere che se ne trae, sia di grandissima utilità e cosa anche degna di ciascuna persona che ha l'animo acceso dei raggi della virtù." Mafio Priuli, *Copia di una lettera venuta d'India, indrizzata al magnifico M. Costantino di Priuli nella quale si leggono cose maravigliose e varie di quelli paesie, scritta nel 1537 - ricevuta nel 1539* (Venice: Tip. di Alvisopoli, 1824), 15.

29. "Hic enim mos institue[n]di patricios homines semper fuit a teneris annis, ut usq[ue] ad pubertatem sub paedagogi disciplina degerent, ac latinis literis imbuerentur, pro cuiusque captu. Ab ea aetate, praeter paucos quosdam qui literarum studiis se manciparant genio naturaque ducti, omnes fere rei maritimae ac familiari operam darent. Ac alii quide[m] navigabant ad longinquas oras, ubi mercaturae industria rem domesticam augebant, simulque efficibantur periti morum, ac consuedudinis legumque multorum hominum." Gasparo Contarini, *De magistratibus & republica venetorum* (Paris: ex officina Michel de Vascosan, 1543), 102.

30. Giosafat Barbaro et al., *Viaggi fatti da Vinetia, alla Tana, in Persia, in India, et in Costantinopoli: Con la descrittione particolare di citta, luoghi, siti, costumi, et della porta del gran Turco* (Venice: nelle case haer. Aldo I Manuzio, 1543).

31. Giovanni Battista Ramusio, ed., *Primo volume delle navigationi et viaggi* (Venice: appresso gli heredi di Lucantonio Giunti, 1550), *iir-v.

32. Brummett, *Mapping the Ottomans*, 56.

33. Anna Bellavitis, "'Per cittadini metterete': La stratifiazione della società veneziana cinquecentesca tra norma giuridica e riconoscimento sociale," *Quaderni storici* 30, no. 2 (1995): 359–383.

34. Massimo Donattini, "Ramusio, Giovanni Battista," in *Dizionario Biografico degli Italiani,* 2016, https://www.treccani.it/enciclopedia/giovanni-battista-ramusio_(Dizionario-Biografico).

35. Toni Veneri, "Giovanni Battista Ramusio, molto più di uno spettatore. Le quinte delle 'Navigationi et viaggi,'" *Italica* 89, no. 2 (2012): 163–177.

36. Tommaso Porcacchi, ed., *Lettere di XIII huomini illustri* (Venice: appresso gli heredi Giovanni Maria Bonelli, 1571), 330r, 338v–339.

37. Mary Louise Pratt, *Imperial Eyes: Travel Writing and Transculturation,* 2nd ed. (London: Routledge, 2007), 7–11; Mary Louise Pratt, "Arts of the Contact Zone," *Profession* 91 (1998): 173.

38. Pratt, *Imperial Eyes,* 9.

39. Pratt, "Arts of the Contact Zone," 173.

40. Magnus, *Carta marina.*

41. John Granlund, "The Carta marina of Olaus Magnus," *Imago Mundi* 8, no. 1 (1951): 35; Massimo Donattini, "Giovanni Battista Ramusio," in *Christian-Muslim Relations: A Bibliographical History,* ed. David Thomas and John A. Chesworth (Leiden: Brill, 2014), 6:539.

42. Miekkavaara, "Unknown Europe," 10.

43. Miekkavaara, "Unknown Europe," 12.

44. Magnus, *Ain kurze auslegung und verklerung der neuen mappen*; Magnus, *Opera breve.*

45. "Alcuni adorano per loro Idio, un panno di colore rosso levato in altro sopra un'hasta: & offeriscono li ossi delli animali aquistate, o a cacciare, o a pescare." Magnus, *Opera breve,* Aiiiv.

46. "Ho inteso di refferire, e non di persuadere." Leon Modena, *Historia de gli riti hebraici* (Paris, 1637), 6.

47. "Nello scriver, in verità, che mi son scordato esser Hebreo, figurandomi semplice e nutrale relatore." Modena, *Historia de gli riti hebraici,* 5–6.

48. Carlo Ginzburg, "Provincializing the World: Europeans, Indians, Jews (1704)," *Postcolonial Studies* 14, no. 2 (2011): 137.

49. On the apologetic designs of the *Riti,* see Mark R. Cohen, "Leone da Modena's Riti: A Seventeenth-Century Plea for Social Toleration of Jews," *Jewish Social Studies* 33, no. 4 (1972): 287–321; Howard Adelman, "Success and Failure in the Seventeenth-Century Ghetto of Venice: The Life and Thought of Leon Modena, 1571–1648" (PhD diss., Brandeis University, 1985), 454–459; Rafael Arnold, "Neutral or Natural Relater? Some Remarks on Rabbi Leone da Modena's Historia de Riti Hebraici," *Zutot* 4, no. 1 (2004): 107–112; Natalie Zemon Davis, "Fame and Secrecy: Leon Modena's Life as an Early Modern Autobiography," *History and Theory* 27, no. 4 (December 1988): 116–117; Stephen G. Burnett, *From Christian Hebraism to Jewish Studies: Johannes Buxtorf (1564–1629) and Hebrew Learning in the Seventeenth Century* (Leiden: Brill, 1996), 86–89.

50. Deutsch, *Judaism in Christian Eyes,* 48.

51. Jeremy Cohen, *The Friars and the Jews: The Evolution of Medieval Anti-Judaism* (Ithaca, NY: Cornell University Press, 1982), 68–69; Jeremy Cohen, "Scholarship and In-

tolerance in the Medieval Academy: The Study and Evaluation of Judaism in European Christendom," *American Historical Review* 91, no. 3 (June 1986): 594–608.

52. Cohen, "Scholarship and Intolerance," 595.

53. For overviews of Modena's Christian contacts, see Cecil Roth, "Leone Da Modena and the Christian Hebraists of His Age," in *Jewish Studies in Memory of Israel Abrahams*, ed. George Alexander Kohut (New York: Press of the Jewish Institute of Religion, 1927), 384–401; Howard Adelman, "Rabbi Leon Modena and the Christian Kabbalists," in *Renaissance Rereadings: Intertext and Context*, ed. Maryanne Cline Horowitz, Anne J. Cruz, and Wendy Ann Furman (Urbana: University of Illinois, 1988), 271–286.

54. Adelman, "Rabbi Leon Modena and the Christian Kabbalists," 271.

55. Benjamin J. Kaplan, *Divided by Faith: Religious Conflict and the Practice of Toleration in Early Modern Europe* (Cambridge, MA: Harvard University Press, 2007), 298.

56. Adelman, "Success and Failure," 401.

57. Howard Adelman, "Leon Modena: The Autobiography and the Man," in *The Autobiography of a Seventeenth-Century Venetian Rabbi*, ed. Mark Cohen (Princeton, NJ: Princeton University Press, 1988), 29. The Modena-Wotton connection was first suggested by Cecil Roth in "Leone da Modena and England," *Transactions of the Jewish Historical Society of England* 11 (1928): 206–215.

58. Abraham Melamed, "English Travelers and Venetian Jewish Scholars: The Case of Simone Luzzatto and James Harrington," in *Gli Ebrei e Venezia: Secoli XIV–XVIII*, ed. Gaetano Cozzi (Milan: Edizioni Comunità, 1987), 512.

59. Modena, *Historia de gli riti hebraici*, 9–10, 79–81, 85–88, 89–90.

60. The literature on the influence of classical authorities on early modern ethnography is vast. For an introduction to the topic, see Hodgen, *Early Anthropology*, 17–48; Anthony Grafton, *New Worlds, Ancient Texts: The Power of Tradition and the Shock of Discovery* (Cambridge, MA: Belknap, 1992), 42–47; Peter Mason, "Classical Ethnography and Its Influence on the European Perception of the Peoples of the New World," in *The Classical Tradition and the Americas: European Images of the Americas and the Classical Tradition*, ed. Wolfgang Hasse and Meyer Reinhold (Berlin: de Gruyter, 1994), 135–172; Sabine MacCormack, "Limits of Understanding: Perceptions of Greco-Roman and Amerindian Paganism in Early Modern Europe," in *America in European Consciousness*, ed. Karen Ordahl Kupperman (Chapel Hill: University of North Carolina Press, 1995), 79–129.

61. For a detailed discussion of revaluations of the cultural alterity of classical antiquity, see Kathryn Taylor, "Ancients and Moderns in Sixteenth-Century Ethnography," *History of European Ideas* 46, no. 2 (February 2020): 113–130.

62. Michael T. Ryan, "Assimilating New Worlds in the Sixteenth and Seventeenth Centuries," *Comparative Studies in Society and History* 23, no. 4 (October 1981): 520.

63. On this topic, see Arnaldo Momigliano, *The Classical Foundations of Modern Historiography* (Berkeley: University of California Press, 1990), 54–79; Peter Burke, "From Antiquarianism to Anthropology," in *Momigliano and Antiquarianism: Foundations of the Modern Cultural Sciences*, ed. Peter N. Miller (Toronto: University of Toronto Press, 2007), 229–247.

64. "Si seriem hanc annorum quam longissime debet respicere historicus, patet totius antiquitatis, quae ad mores, ad victum antiquorum, ad urbium exaedificationes; ad populorum commigrationes spectant, bene peritum esse debere. Thycydides nobis exemplo sit, qui libro sexto omenm antiquitatem urbium ac populorum totius Siciliae diligentissime ac

verissime explicat. Et quoniam ad hanc antiquitatem cognoscendum multum nos iuvant vetustorum aedificiorum reliquiae; atque aut marmoribus, aut auro, aere, et argento incisae literae haec quoque teneat oportet." Francesco Robortello, *De historica facultate* (Florence: Lorenzo Torrentino, 1548), 25–26.

65. Momigliano, *The Classical Foundations of Modern Historiography*, 61.

66. Arnaldo Momigliano, "Ancient History and the Antiquarian," *Journal of the Warburg and Courtauld Institutes* 13, no. 3/4 (1950): 287, 311.

67. Michel de Montaigne, *The Complete Essays*, trans. M. A. Screech (London: Penguin, 2003), 1127.

68. Montaigne, *Complete Essays* (2003), 1128.

69. On the *poligrafi*, see Paul F. Grendler, "Francesco Sansovino and Italian Popular History 1560–1600," *Studies in the Renaissance* 16 (1969): 139–180; Claudia Di Filippo Bareggi, *Il mestiere di scrivere: Lavoro intellettuale e mercato librario a Venezia nel Cinquecento* (Rome: Bulzoni, 1988).

70. On Panciroli's career as a jurist, see Paul F. Grendler, *The Universities of the Italian Renaissance* (Baltimore: Johns Hopkins University Press, 2002), 97.

71. Guido Panciroli and Flavio Gualtieri, *Raccolta breue d'alcune cose piu segnalate c'hebbero gli antichi, e d'alcune altre trouate da moderni* (Venice: presso Bernardo Giunti, Gio. Battista Ciotti, & compagni, 1612), 287–302, 303–314, 318–331.

72. Panciroli and Gualtieri, *Raccolta breue*, 238–252.

73. Montaigne, *Complete Essays* (2003), 332.

74. Montaigne, *Complete Essays* (2003), 332–333.

75. Pagden, *The Fall of Natural Man*; David Boruchoff, "Indians, Cannibals, and Barbarians: Hernan Cortes and Early Modern Cultural Relativism," *Ethnohistory* 62, no. 1 (January 2015): 17–38; William M. Hamlin, "On Continuities between Skepticism and Early Ethnography; Or, Montaigne's Providential Diversity," *Sixteenth Century Journal* 31, no. 2 (2000): 361–379.

76. Giuliano Lucchetta, "Viaggiatori e racconti di viaggi nel Cinquecento," in *Storia della cultura veneta: Dal primo Quattrocento al Concilio di Trento*, ed. Girolamo Arnaldi and Manlio Pastore Stocchi (Vicenza: Neri Pozza, 1980), 2:446; On the Venetian presence in Syria, see Vera Costantini, "Dalla laguna al deserto: I rapporti tra Venezia ed Aleppo," *Levante* 49 (2002): 15–31; Maria Pia Pedani Fabris, "Venetian Consuls in Egypt and Syria in the Ottoman Age," *Mediterranean World* 18 (2006): 7–21.

77. Luca Campigotto, "Veneziani in India nel XVI secolo," *Studi Veneziani* 22 (1991): 78; Pietro Donazzolo, *I viaggiatori veneti minori, studio bio-bibliografico* (Rome: Società geografica italiana, 1927), 106–107.

78. Donazzolo, *Viaggiatori veneti*, 106, 115–116.

79. The contract signed by Ramusio and Antonio Priuli lists Priuli as a "procurator di Santo Marco," leaving little doubt concerning his identity. Biblioteca Ambrosiana (hereafter BAM), S 99 sup., 182r. On the partnership between Ramusio, Priuli, and Oviedo, see Margaret Small, "Displacing Ptolemy? The Textual Geographies of Ramusio's Navigazioni e Viaggi," in *Mapping Medieval Geographies: Geographical Encounters in the Latin West and Beyond, 300–1600*, ed. Keith D. Lilley (Cambridge: Cambridge University Press, 2014), 161; Stephanie Jed, "The Tenth Muse: Gender, Rationality, and the Marketing of

Knowledge," in *Women, "Race," and Writing in the Early Modern Period*, ed. Margo Hendricks and Patricia A. Parker (London: Routledge, 1994), 202.

80. For introductions to sixteenth-century Venetian geography, see Marica Milanesi, *Tolomeo sostituito: Studi di storia delle conoscenze geografiche nel XVI secolo* (Milan: Unicopli, 1984), 25–170; Eugenia Bevilacqua, "Geografi e cosmografi," in *Storia della cultura veneta: Dal primo Quattrocento al Concilio di Trento*, ed. Girolamo Arnaldi and Manlio Pastore Stocchi (Vicenza: Neri Pozza, 1980), 2:355–374.

81. On the education of Venetian patricians, see Ugo Tucci, "The Psychology of the Venetian Merchant in the Sixteenth Century," in *Renaissance Venice*, ed. J. R. Hale (London: Rowman & Littlefield, 1973), 346–378; Ugo Tucci, "Il patrizio veneziano mercante e umanista," in *Venezia, centro di mediazione tra Oriente e Occidente, secoli XV–XVI: Aspetti e problemi*, ed. Hans Georg Beck, Manoussos Manoussacas, and Agostino Pertusi (Florence: L. S. Olschki, 1977), 1:335–357; Erin MagLaque, "Humanism and Colonial Governance in the Venetian Ageaen: The Case of Giovanni Bembo," *Journal of Early Modern History* 19, no. 1 (January 2015): 45–70.

82. On the role of travel and travel accounts in the education of Venetian patricians, see Deborah Howard, "The Status of the Oriental Traveler in Renaissance Venice," in *Re-orienting the Renaissance: Cultural Exchanges with the East*, ed. Gerald Maclean (New York: Palgrave Macmillan, 2005), 29–49; Kathryn Taylor, "Making Statesmen, Writing Culture: Ethnography, Observation, and Diplomatic Travel in Early Modern Venice," *Journal of Early Modern History* 22, no. 4 (August 2018): 279–298.

83. Priuli, *Copia di una lettera*, 21–24.

84. An edition of Zen's travel account based a copy held by the Venetian diarist Marin Sanudo would eventually be published. Pietro Zen, "Itinerario di Pietro Zeno oratore a Costantinopoli compendiato da Marino Sanuto," ed. Rinaldo Fulin, *Archivio veneto* XXII (1881): 104–136; On the circulation of Venetian diplomatic reports, see De Vivo, *Information and Communication*, 63–70.

85. Nicolò Zen, *De i commentarii del viaggio in Persia di m. Caterino Zeno* (Venice: Francesco Marcolini, 1558).

86. On Nicolò Zen's writings, see Horodowich, *The Venetian Discovery of America*, 143–172.

87. "E solamente vi dirò che quel libro di Marco Polo da Venezia, Solino, Tolomeo, e quanti libri che scrivono, Pomponio Mela, e tutti li Nappamondi, che si fanno de le cose di questa India, tutti mentono, e sono falsi, e questo vi dico che quando mi partii da Damasco, portai con me quattro Nappamondi, e Solino, e Tolomeo, e altri libri, che dicono di questa India, e massime che molti si dilettano in iscriver di questa isola Taprobana, che qua si chiama l'isola di Samatria. dove io sono stato dentro, e ho voluto vedere il tutto molto minutamente, ove per mia fè non trovai cosa che dicano quei libri, nè Nappamondi. se non che dentro ha uomini, che vivono di carne umana, che da noi si dicono Antropofagi." Priuli, *Copia di una lettera*, 21–22.

88. "E tante cose, che si scrivono in Tito Livio, che facevano i Romani delle prove delle vite, che noi non le credemo, adesso mi paiono più che vere: e ogni giorno veggo più cose nuove, di modo, che, io stesso mi maraviglio, e quando sarò con voi, non le oserò dire, perchè dubiterò che non le crediate." Priuli, *Copia di una lettera*, 24.

89. "Encyclopaedia historica et filosophica, latine et italice," University of Pennsylvania, ms. codex 326, 84v.

90. BAM, O 150 sup., 62r–64v.

91. Klaus Vogel, "Cultural Variety in a Renaissance Perspective: Johannes Boemus on 'The Manners, Laws and Customs of All People' (1520)," in *Shifting Cultures: Interaction and Discourse in the Expansion of Europe*, ed. Joan-Pau Rubiés and Henriette Bugge (Münster: Lit Verlag, 1995), 20–24.

92. Boemus, *Omnium gentium mores leges et ritus*, LXVr–LXXr.

93. The German cosmographer Sebastian Münster, for example, has long been acknowledged for his inclusion of ethnographic description. For discussions of the place of ethnographic knowledge in his *Cosmographia*, see Margaret T. Hodgen, "Sebastian Muenster (1489–1552): A Sixteenth-Century Ethnographer," *Osiris* (1954):504–529; McLean, *The Cosmographia of Sebastian Münster*, 249–294.

94. Sebastiano Fausto, *Delle nozze trattato del Fausto da Longiano in cui si leggono i riti, i costumi, gl'instituti, le cerimonie etc. di diversi antichi popoli aggiuntivi e precetti matrimoniali di Plutarco* (Venice: Plinio Pietrasanta, 1554).

95. Tommaso Porcacchi, *Funerali antichi di diversi popoli, et nationi; forma, ordine, et pompa di sepolture, di essequie, di consecrationi antiche et d'altro, descritti in dialogo da Thomaso Porcacchi da Castiglione Arretino. Con le figure in rame di Girolamo Porro padouano* (Venice: Simone Galignani, 1574), 7–61, 79–85, 107–109.

96. Lilio Gregorio Giraldi, *De sepulchris et vario sepeliendi ritu* (Basel: Michael Isengrin, 1539).

97. The ethnographic content and publication history of Porcacchi's *isolario* will be discussed in chapter 4. Tommaso Porcacchi, *L'isole piu famose del mondo* (Venice: Simone Galignani & Girolamo Porro, 1572).

98. Grendler, "Francesco Sansovino and Italian Popular History 1560–1600."

99. "In questo modo raccolsi io già due libri di Essempi simili d'Historie: de' quali mi trovo haver un altro libro in apparecchio: & dopo essi o dato alla stampa anchora alcune altre cosette, da me in cosi fatta maniera osservate, & raccolte. Ne solamente da' libri dell'Historie, nelle quali consuo tutto il mio studio; ma ancora da gli scritti de gli amici, da diverse lettere, relationi, diarii, informationi varie, fatte ad altrui instantia, & per altrui richiesta; ho tolto molte cose, che molto m'hanno giovato, & gran lume havranno apportato, & credo che apporteranno a chi l'ha vedute, o a chi farà per vederle." Porcacchi, *Funerali*, a2r.

100. Ferdinando Bertelli, *Omnium fere gentium nostrae aetatis habitus* (Venice: Ferdinando Bertelli typis excudebat, 1563).

101. Cesare Vecellio, *Habiti antichi et moderni di tutto il mondo*, trans. Sulstatius Gratilianus (Venice: appresso haer. Melchiorre I Sessa: Giovanni Bernardo Sessa, 1598).

102. Vecellio, *Habiti*, 1598, 121v–122, 139v–140, 125v–126, 123v–124, 172v–174.

103. Pietro Bertelli, *Diversarum nationum habitus* (Padua: apud Alciato Alciati & Pietro Bertelli, 1594), plates 13–18.

104. Cesare Vecellio, *De gli habiti antichi, et moderni di diverse parti del mondo* (Venice: Damiano Zenaro, 1590), 439v–441, 444r–v.

105. Margaret F. Rosenthal and Ann Rosalind Jones, "Vecellio and His World," in *The Clothing of the Renaissance World: Europe, Asia, Africa, the Americas: Cesare Vecellio's*

Habiti Antichi et Moderni, ed. Margaret F. Rosenthal and Ann Rosalind Jones (London: Thames & Hudson, 2008), 20.

106. Vecellio, *Habiti*, 1590, 1r–12v.

107. Vecellio, *Habiti*, 1590, 1v–2r.

108. "Mi è parso far questo breve discorso, acciò si conosca à quante grandi rovine sia stata sottoposta questa bella regione dell'Italia, et da quanta diversità di habitatori, & predatori Oltramontani, & Barbari sia stato calpestato, & derobbato questo fertilissimo paese; satiandoli, & servendoli di tutte le commodità desiderabili, per premio delle quali non ha ricevuto altro da loro, che diversità, & mutationi di lingue, d'Habiti, & di costumi." Vecellio, *Habiti*, 1590, 5v.

109. Damiano Acciarino, "De Re Vestiaria: Renaissance Discovery of Ancient Clothing," *La rivista di Engramma*, no. 154 (2018): 111–140.

110. Vecellio, *Habiti*, 1590, 2r.

111. Vecellio, *Habiti*, 1590, a6r.

112. On the parameters of the concept of nation in the late Middle Ages, see Cary J. Nederman, *Worlds of Difference: European Discourses of Toleration, c. 1100–c. 1550* (University Park: Pennsylvania State University Press, 2010), 85–97; Robert Bartlett, *The Making of Europe: Conquest, Colonization, and Cultural Change, 950–1350* (Princeton, NJ: Princeton University Press, 1993); For the early modern period, see Patrick Geary, "Power and Ethnicity: History and Anthropology," *History and Anthropology* 26, no. 1 (January 2015): 8–17; Eric Dursteler, "Identity and Coexistence in the Eastern Mediterranean, ca. 1600," *New Perspectives on Turkey*, no. 18 (1998): 113–130.

113. Vecellio, *Habiti*, 1590, 385v, 281r, 274r, 348r–v, 6v, 42r, 193r, 360v.

114. Formica, *Lo specchio turco*, 33.

115. Margaret F. Rosenthal, "Clothing, Fashion, Dress, and Costume in Venice (c. 1450–1650)," in *A Companion to Venetian History, 1400–1797*, ed. Eric R. Dursteler (Leiden: Brill, 2013), 893–894; Ulinka Rublack, *Dressing Up: Cultural Identity in Renaissance Europe* (Oxford: Oxford University Press, 2010), 161; Daniel Defert, "Un genre ethnographique profane au XVIe: Les livres d'habits," in *Histoires de l'anthropologie (XVI–XIXe siècles)*, ed. Britta Rupp-Eisenreich (Paris: Klincksieck, 1984), 25–41.

116. Ferdinando Bertelli, *Omnium fere gentium nostrae aetatis habitus* (Venice: Ferdinando Bertelli typis excudebat, 1569), plates 5, 10, 47.

117. Odile Blanc, "Images du monde et portraits d'habits: Les recueils de costumes de la Renaissance," *Bulletin du bibliophile*, no. 2 (1995): 221–261.

118. Bertelli, *Omnium fere gentium nostrae aetatis habitus*, 1563.

119. François Desprez, *Recueil de la diversité des habits qui sont de present en usaige, tant es pays d'Europe, Asie, Affrique et illes sauvages* (Paris: Richard Breton, 1562); Hans Weigel and Jost Amman, *Habitus praecipuorum populorum tam virorum quam feminarum singulari arte depicti: Trachtenbuch* (Nuremberg, 1577).

120. Vecellio, *Habiti*, 1590, 432v–433.

Chapter 2 Ambassadors as Ethnographers

1. Eugenio Albèri, ed., *Relazioni degli ambasciatori veneti al Senato* (Florence: Società editrice fiorentina, 1839–1863), 1st ser., 6:233.

2. On the development of the system of resident ambassadors in the fifteenth-century Italian states, see Catherine Fletcher, *Diplomacy in Renaissance Rome: The Rise of the Resident Ambassador* (Cambridge: Cambridge University Press, 2015), 15–35; Isabella Lazzarini, *Communication and Conflict: Italian Diplomacy in the Early Renaissance, 1350–1520* (Oxford: Oxford University Press, 2015), 31–48; Mattingly, *Renaissance Diplomacy* (New York: Dover, 1988), 78–93; Matthew S. Anderson, *The Rise of Modern Diplomacy 1450–1919* (London: Longman, 1993), 2–11.

3. "Avendo gli Ambasciatori, ch'essi mandano à Potentati del mondo, quest'obbligo di riferir in Senato, tornati che sono dalle loro Ambascerie, ciò che han potuto cavare de' costumi del Principe, e del sito, ricchezze, fertilità, ed altre qualità de'luoghi, e degli uomini, ove sono stati mandati: il che fanno con tanta felicità, che si vede, il più delle volte cose esser più a loro manifeste, che agli stessi uomini del paese non sono." Scipione Ammirato, *Discorsi del signor Scipione Ammirato sopra Cornelio Tacito. Nuovamente posti in luce con due tavole, una dei discorsi, e luoghi di Cornelio sopra i quali son fondati, l'altra delle cose più notabili* (Florence: Filippo II Giunta, 1594), 304.

4. On Ranke and later historians' use of the Venetian relazioni, see Gino Benzoni, "Ranke's Favorite Source: The Venetian Relazioni: Impressions with Allusions to Later Historiography," in *Leopold von Ranke and the Shaping of the Historical Discipline*, ed. Georg G. Iggers and James M. Powell (Syracuse, NY: Syracuse University Press, 1990), 45–57; Filippo De Vivo, "How to Read Venetian Relazioni," *Renaissance and Reformation/Renaissance et réforme* 34, no. 1–2 (2011): 26–29. For a more recent use of the reports as a source for political history, see Stefan Halikowski Smith, "Gasparo Contarini's Relazione of November 1525 to the Venetian Senate on the Divergent Dynamics of the Spanish and Portuguese World Empires," *Mediterranean Historical Review* 32, no. 2 (July 2017): 189–235.

5. Lucette Valensi, *The Birth of the Despot: Venice and the Sublime Porte*, trans. Arthur Denner (Ithaca, NY: Cornell University Press, 1993); Giovanni Stiffoni, "La scoperta e la conquista dell'America nelle prime relazioni degli ambasciatori veneziani (1497–1559)," in *L'impatto della scoperta dell'America nella cultura veneziana*, ed. Angela Caracciolo Arico (Rome: Bulzoni, 1990), 351–364; Catherine Fletcher, "Mere Emulators of Italy: The Spanish-Italian Diplomatic Discourse, 1492–1550," in *The Spanish Presence in Sixteenth-Century Italy: Images of Iberia*, ed. Piers Baker-Bates and Miles Pattenden (Aldershot, UK: Ashgate, 2015), 11–28; Federica Ambrosini, "Venetian Diplomacy, Spanish Gold, and the New World in the Sixteenth Century," in *The New World in Early Modern Italy, 1492–1750*, ed. Elizabeth Horodowich and Lia Markey (Cambridge: Cambridge University Press, 2017), 47–60.

6. The classic study is Garret Mattingly's *Renaissance Diplomacy*, originally published in 1955. "Diplomacy in the modern style," Mattingly writes, "permanent diplomacy, was one of the creations of the Italian Renaissance." Although Mattingly's account has been criticized for its teleological framework and its lack of attention to the role of the Ottoman state in the development of diplomatic procedure, in the absence of a new synthesis on European diplomacy in the period, its broad contours have remained intact. The chapter of Matthew Anderson's more recent history of European diplomacy that treats the fifteenth and sixteenth centuries, for example, is largely a recapitulation of Mattingly's account. Mattingly, *Renaissance Diplomacy*, 47; Anderson, *The Rise of Modern Diplomacy 1450–1919*, 1–40; For a critique of Mattingly's teleological approach, see John Watkins, "Toward a New Diplomatic History of Medieval and Early Modern Europe," *Journal of Medieval and Early Modern*

Studies 38, no. 1 (2008): 1–14; For reassessments of the Ottoman role in the development of European diplomacy, see Daniel Goffman, "Negotiating with the Renaissance State: The Ottoman Empire and the New Diplomacy," in *The Early Modern Ottomans: Remapping the Empire*, ed. Virginia Aksan and Daniel Goffman (Cambridge: Cambridge University Press, 2007), 61–74; A. Nuri Yurdusev, "The Middle East Encounter with the Expansion of European International Society," in *International Society and the Middle East: English School Theory at the Regional Level*, ed. Barry Buzan and A. Gonzalez-Pelaez (Basingstoke, UK: Palgrave Macmillan, 2009), 70–91; Tijana Krstić and Maartje van Gelder, "Introduction: Cross-confessional Diplomacy and Diplomatic Intermediaries in the Early Modern Mediterranean," *Journal of Early Modern History* 19, no. 2–3 (April 2015): 93–105.

7. Mattingly, *Renaissance Diplomacy*, 55–59; Garrett Mattingly, "The First Resident Embassies: Mediaeval Italian Origins of Modern Diplomacy," *Speculum* 12, no. 4 (October 1937): 426.

8. Bruno Simon, "I rappresentanti diplomatici veneziani a Costantinopoli," in *Venezia e i Turchi: Scontri e confronti di due civiltà*, ed. Anna Della Valle (Milan: Electa, 1985), 56.

9. On the terms of the 1454 Ottoman-Venetian treaty, see Stanford J. Shaw, *History of the Ottoman Empire and Modern Turkey*, vol. 1: *Empire of the Gazis: The Rise and Decline of the Ottoman Empire 1280–1808* (Cambridge: Cambridge University Press, 1976), 62. The Ottomans, for their part, did not establish permanent diplomatic missions in Venice or other European capitals before the eighteenth century. Although they did send frequent temporary envoys to Venice, there was no Ottoman equivalent of the bailo. Goffman, "Negotiating with the Renaissance State"; Maria Pia Pedani Fabris, *In nome del Gran Signore: Inviati ottomani a Venezia dalla caduta di Costantinopoli alla guerra di Candia* (Venice: Deputazione Editrice, 1994), 10–11.

10. Antonio Fabris, "From Adrianople to Constantinople: Venetian-Ottoman Diplomatic Missions, 1360–1453," *Mediterranean Historical Review* 7, no. 2 (1992), 156; Pedani Fabris, "Venetian Consuls in Egypt and Syria in the Ottoman Age," *Mediterranean World* 18 (2006): 7–8.

11. Paolo Preto, "Le relazioni dei baili veneziani a Costantinopoli," *Il Veltro* 23, no. 2–4 (1979): 129; Andrea Zannini, "Economic and Social Aspects of the Crisis of Venetian Diplomacy in the Seventeenth and Eighteenth Centuries," in *Politics and Diplomacy in Early Modern Italy: The Structure of Diplomatic Practice, 1450–1800*, ed. Daniela Frigo (Cambridge: Cambridge University Press, 2000), 116.

12. Eric Dursteler, "The Bailo in Constantinople: Crisis and Career in Venice's Early Modern Diplomatic Corps," *Mediterranean Historical Review* 16, no. 2 (2001): 1–30; Zannini, "Economic and Social Aspects," 118; Valensi, *Birth of the Despot*, 16–17.

13. Although the year of Daniele Barbarigo's birth is unknown, Franz Babinger suggests that he may actually have been a relatively young man when he was elected consul in 1549. Franz Babinger, "Barbarigo, Daniele," in *Dizionario Biografico degli Italiani*, 1964, http://www.treccani.it/enciclopedia/daniele-barbarigo_(Dizionario-Biografico)/.

14. Extraordinary ambassadors were sent to the Ottoman court for specific missions of finite durations—for example, the negotiation of a treaty or the congratulation of a sultan on his accession or marriage. In periods when an extraordinary ambassador was present in Istanbul, the bailo would vacate his household in favor of the ambassador in recognition of the latter's supremacy. Dursteler, "Bailo in Constantinople," 3.

15. Paul Marcus Dover, "Deciphering the Diplomatic Archives of Fifteenth-Century Italy," *Archival Science* 7, no. 4 (2007): 299. On the organization of diplomatic material in the archive of the Venetian republic, see Filippo De Vivo, "Ordering the Archive in Early Modern Venice (1400–1650)," *Archival Science* 10, no. 3 (2010): 231–248. On the range of documents produced in the course of diplomatic activity, see Lazzarini, *Communication and Conflict*, 49–66.

16. John-Paul Ghobrial, *Whispers of Cities: Information Flows in Istanbul, London, and Paris in the Age of William Trumbull* (Oxford: Oxford University Press, 2013); Lazzarini, *Communication and Conflict*, 69–85; Michael Mallett, "Ambassadors and Their Audiences in Renaissance Italy," *Renaissance Studies* 8, no. 3 (1994): 229–243; Fletcher, *Diplomacy*, 105–121.

17. Archivio di Stato di Venezia (ASVe), Senato, Dispacci, Costantinopoli, Filze, 1a.

18. Stiffoni, "La scoperta e la conquista dell'America," 352.

19. It should be noted that there were a variety of genres of early modern writing that bore the title *relazione* or one of its cognates in other European languages. For the sake of clarity, unless otherwise noted, I use the term *relazioni* here to refer to the final reports delivered by diplomats and other Venetian officials following their return from their missions. For an introduction to the various genres of early modern relations, see Thomas V. Cohen and Germaine Warkentin, "Things Not Easily Believed: Introducing the Early Modern Relation," *Renaissance and Reformation/Renaissance et réforme* 34, no. 1–2 (2011): 8–10; Andreas Motsch, "Relations of Travel: Itinerary of a Practice," *Renaissance and Reformation/Renaissance et réforme* 34, no. 1–2 (2011): 207–236.

20. Quoted in Eric Dursteler, "Describing or Distorting the 'Turk'? The Relazioni of the Venetian Ambassadors in Constantinople as Historical Source," *Acta Histriae* 19, no. 1–2 (2011): 238.

21. Angelo Ventura, "Scrittori politici e scritture di governo," in *Storia della cultura veneta*, ed. Girolamo Arnaldi and Manlio Pastore Stocchi (Vicenza: Nera Pozza, 1981), 3:553–554.

22. Albèri, *Relazioni*, 3rd ser., 3:1–44.

23. Andrea Da Mosto, *L'Archivio di stato di Venezia: Indice generale, storico, descrittivo ed analitico* (Rome: Biblioteca d'arte editrice, 1937–1940), 1:47–48.

24. Francesca Antonibon, *Le relazioni a stampa di ambasciatori veneti* (Padua: Tipografia del seminario, 1939).

25. "Ciascheduno che ritorni da qualche legazione venga a questo sapientissimo senato, non a rendergli ragione delle azioni sue (che dalle medesime lettere di tempo in tempo scritte da lui si possono avere chiaramente comprese) ma a riferire se alcuna cosa del paese dal quale viene ha, negoziando o altrimenti investigando, conosciuta degna di esser da prudenti senatori udita e ponderata in benefizio della patria." Albèri, *Relazioni*, 1st ser., 1:34.

26. On the Venetian government's efforts to prevent the circulation of relazioni, see Filippo De Vivo, *Information and Communication: Rethinking Early Modern Politics* (Oxford: Oxford University Press, 2009), 63–70.

27. Marin Sanudo, *I diarii (1496–1533)*, ed. Rinaldo Fulin, Federico Stefani, Nicolò Barozzi, Guglielmo Berchet, and Marco Allegri (Venice: F. Visentini, 1879–1903), 47: coll. 63–64.

28. Biblioteca del Museo Correr (hereafter BCV), Donà, ms. 23, 211r.

29. These figures exclude the summaries of relazioni included in the edition. Albèri, *Relazioni*, 1st and 3rd ser.

30. In his entry on Gasparo Contarini's 1525 relazione following his embassy to Charles V, for example, Sanudo notes that Contarini was dressed "in black velvet [and] he went up to the speaker's stand and delivered his relazioni in a very low voice, such that he was poorly understood, but he spoke at great length. . . . He was at the speaker's stand for three and a half hours." Sanudo, *Diarii*, 40:285–286.

31. BCV, Donà, ms. 41, c. 169r.

32. Paolo Preto, *Venezia e i Turchi*, 2nd ed. (Rome: Viella, 2013), 92.

33. Andrei Pippidi, *Visions of the Ottoman World in Renaissance Europe* (New York: Columbia University Press, 2013), 56.

34. Robert Mantran, "Venise, centre d'informations sur les turcs," in *Venezia, centro di mediazione tra Oriente e Occidente, secoli XV–XVI: Aspetti e problemi*, ed. Hans Georg Beck, Manoussos Manoussacas, and Agostino Pertusi (Florence: L. S. Olschki, 1977), 1:115–116.

35. Franco Gaeta, introduction to *Relations des ambassadeurs vénitiens*, ed. Franco Gaeta (Paris: Éditions Klincksieck, 1969), v.

36. Carlo Morandi, introduction to *Relazioni di ambasciatori sabaudi, genovesi e veneti durante il periodo della grande alleanza e della successione di Spagna (1693–1713)*, ed. Carlo Morandi (Bologna: Nicola Zanichelli, 1935), xxii–xxiii.

37. For example, Ottaviano Maggi's *De legato*, while praising the practice of having ambassadors deliver relazioni before the Senate, does not specifically address the composition of the reports. Ottaviano Maggi, *De legato libri duo* (Venice: [Lodovico Avanzi], 1566), 25r–v. On advice literature for ambassadors, see Mattingly, *Renaissance Diplomacy*, 181–191; Douglas Biow, *Doctors, Ambassadors, Secretaries: Humanism and Professions in Renaissance Italy* (Chicago: University of Chicago Press, 2002), 101–127.

38. "Ricordi per ambasciatori, con un epilogo breve di quelle cose che si ricercano per fare una relazione." BNM Ital. VI, 187 (6039), cc. 245r–249v.

39. Donald E. Queller, "How to Succeed as an Ambassador: A Sixteenth Century Venetian Document," in *Post Scripta: Essays on Medieval Law and the Emergence of the European State in Honor of Gaines Post*, ed. Donald E. Queller and Joseph R. Strayer (Rome: Libreria Ateneo Salesiano, 1972), 657.

40. BNM, Ital. VI, 187 (6039), cc. 248v–249v.

41. "Terzo. Conviene ragionare degli habitatori suoi, mostrando gli loro costumi et habito. Di che colore, statura ò dispositione siano, se sono Religiosi, superstitiosi, et di altra particolare Religione. . . . Delle nature et conditioni della Plebe." BNM, Ital. VI, 187 (6039), cc. 249r–v.

42. Albèri, *Relazioni*, 1st ser., 3:3.

43. See, for example, Nicolò Tiepolo's 1532 relazione of his embassy to Charles V, which contains a preamble laying out an agenda similar to Falier's. Albèri, *Relazioni*, 1st ser., 1:33.

44. Da Mula's full agenda for ambassadorial relazioni reads as follows: "Nell' ultimo atto delle legazioni suoleno li ambasciatori referir a Vostra Serenità e alle SS. VV. EE. delle cose proprie de' principi, come sono i parentati, le origini, le parti del corpo, le qualità

dell'animo, i costumi e le operazioni loro; delli stati e regni, come sono i siti, i confini, la gente, i costumi e le volontà de' popoli." Albèri, *Relazioni*, 1st ser., 3:393.

45. Albèri, *Relazioni*, 1st ser., 2:21, 44.

46. Albèri, *Relazioni*, 1st ser., 2:227, 242–250.

47. See Benjamin J. Kaplan, *Divided by Faith: Religious Conflict and the Practice of Toleration in Early Modern Europe* (Cambridge, MA: Harvard University Press, 2007), 99–124. For Venetian patricians' views on the relationship between religious conformity and political stability, see Elisabeth G. Gleason, *Gasparo Contarini: Venice, Rome, and Reform* (Berkeley: University of California Press, 1993), 75–128.

48. The date and the attribution of authorship is taken from Maria Pia Pedani's edition of the account in Maria Pia Pedani, ed., *Costantinopoli relazioni inedite (1512–1789)* (Padua: Bottega d'Erasmo, 1996), 87–88.

49. "Non potrebbe un principe regger il Stato se ne' popoli non vi fusse alcuna religione; et quanto più sono osservanti delle cerimonie tanto sono più obediente al principe et ostinati nella difesa della sua fede." Pedani, *Costantinopoli relazioni*, 122.

50. Pedani, *Costantinopoli relazioni*, 122–123.

51. "La religione è come il cuor dell'uomo, da cui pende la vita, essendo quella un ottimo mezzo, come si è veduto in tutte le repubbliche e governi, massime nei principi, per moderare gli animi e farli conoscere Dio donatore degli stati e della vittorie; il che non accade agl'Inglesi, presso i quali nessuna cosa è più incostante dei decreti loro circa la religione, perché oggi fan no una cosa e dimani un'altra." Albèri, *Relazioni*, 1st ser., 2:242.

52. "Soddisfano all'obbligo de'sudditi Verso il principe, vivendo come egli vive, credendo ciò che egli crede, e finalmente facendo tutto ciò ch'egli comanda, con servirsene più per mostra esteriore, per non incorrere in sua disgrazia, che per zelo interiore, perché il medesimo fariano della religione maomettana o della giudaica, purchè il re mostrasse di credere, e volesse così, ed accomoderiansi a tutte, ma a quella più facilmente, dalla quale ne sperassero ovvero maggior licenza e libertà di vivere, ovvero qualche utile." Albèri, *Relazioni*, 1st ser., 2:362.

53. Rawdon Brown, ed., *Calendar of State Papers and Manuscripts, Relating to English Affairs, Existing in the Archives and Collections of Venice and in the Other Libraries of Northern Italy* (London: Longman, 1862), 6.2:1074. This remark concerning the age of English adherents of Catholicism is absent from Albèri's edition of Michiel's relazione.

54. In a statement echoing that of Daniele Barbaro's 1551 relazione on England, Soranzo writes that religious change "leva il rispetto del timor di Dio, il quale deve esser sempre preposto a tutti gli altri rispetti; perché in quello conste la regola della vita, la concordia degli uomini e la conservazione dello stato e d'ogni grandezza." Albèri, *Relazioni*, 1st ser., 4:137.

55. "L'altro mal effetto che fa quest'alterazione della religione, è che distrugge la polizia e l'ordine del governo, perché da quella nasce la mutazione dei costumi e del modo consueto di vivere, da quella il dispregio delle leggi e dell'autorità de' magistrati, e finalmente anco del principe." Albèri, *Relazioni*, 1st ser., 4:137.

56. "Di qua è nata la mutazione della fede, che è la maggiore alterazione che possa nascere in un regno, perchè oltre l'offesa che si fa a N.S. Iddio, ne segue la mutazione de'costumi, delle leggi, dell'obbedienza, e finalmente dello stato, come si vede esser successo in Asia, in Africa, in Grecia ed in gran parte dell'Europa." Soriano's relazione was actually

delivered following his embassy to Spain, but Philip II's marriage to Mary, who died during Soriano's time as ambassador to Spain, provided him with occasion to reflect on the situation in England. Albèri, *Relazioni*, 1st ser., 3:359.

57. Although in Albèri's published edition of the summary, the year of the relazione is listed as 1576, Tron in fact remained in Germany through all of the following year, making 1578 a more plausible date for the delivery of the relazione. Albèri, *Relazioni*, 1st ser., 6:181–192.

58. Antonibon, *Le relazioni a stampa di ambasciatori veneti*, 68.

59. "Come tutti questi popoli di Germania sono differenti di lingua, così in molte cose di nature e di costumi discordano." Albèri, *Relazioni*, 1st ser., 6:187.

60. "Gli Ungari sono arditi e valorosi, ma sediziosi, inobbedienti, nè reputano disonesto l'utile. I Tedeschi sono avari, sospettosi, ostinati e superbi. I Boemi non han fede nè religione, e sono instabili e creduli." Albèri, *Relazioni*, 1st ser., 6:188.

61. "Difetto comune del bere: i poveri quando possono, i ricchi in ogni tempo." This assessment of Germans is widespread in the reports of Venetian ambassadors, although Tron is one of the few to apply it to Hungarians and Bohemians as well. Albèri, *Relazioni*, 1st ser., 6:188. On the Venetian penchant for reporting on German drinking habits, see Donald E. Queller, "The Development of Ambassadorial Relazioni," in *Renaissance Venice*, ed. J. R. Hale (London: Rowman & Littlefield, 1973), 183.

62. "Ma questi popoli s'accordano tutti in non stimar altra nazione che la propria, e odiar le straniere." Albèri, *Relazioni*, 1st ser., 6:188.

63. As is the case with many late fifteenth- and early sixteenth-century relazioni, Mocenigo's and Contarini's relazioni survive only as summaries in the diaries of Marin Sanudo. The summaries of Mocenigo's and Contarini's relazioni, delivered in 1518 and 1519, respectively, are edited in Albèri, *Relazioni*, 3rd ser., 3:51–68.

64. Rudi Matthee, "The Safavids under Western Eyes: Seventeenth-Century European Travelers to Iran," *Journal of Early Modern History* 13, no. 2 (2009): 137–139; Roger Stevens, "European Visitors to the Safavid Court," *Iranian Studies* 7, no. 3–4 (1974): 421; Chloë Houston, "'Thou Glorious Kingdome, Thou Chiefe of Empires': Persia in Early Seventeenth-Century Travel Literature," *Studies in Travel Writing* 13, no. 2 (June 2009): 143–144; Palmira Brummett, "The Myth of Shah Ismail Safavi: Political Rhetoric and 'Divine' Kingship," in *Medieval Christian Perceptions of Islam*, ed. John Victor Tolan (New York: Garland, 1996), 345.

65. Pier Cesare Ioly Zorattini, *I nomi degli altri: Conversioni a Venezia e nel Friuli Veneto in età moderna* (Florence: L. S. Olschki, 2008), 315; E. Natalie Rothman, "Becoming Venetian: Conversion and Transformation in the Seventeenth-Century Mediterranean," *Mediterranean Historical Review* 21 (June 2006): 39–75; Stephen Ortega, "'Pleading for Help': Gender Relations and Cross-cultural Logic in the Early Modern Mediterranean," *Gender & History* 20, no. 2 (2008): 332–348.

66. "Tutti li popoli soggetti sono nemici loro, e massimamente quella parte che risguarda a ponente, la quale non solo confina con i principi cristiani, ma è anco tutta abitata da gente della medesima religione, così come non è loro manco nemica tutta la parte di levante; poichè e quelli che sono Turchi sono della setta persiana, e li Mori hanno anch'essi molta diversità nella legge con quelli della Porta." Albèri, *Relazioni*, 3rd ser., 1:314–315.

67. See, for example, Matteo Zane's 1594 report and Leonardo Donà's 1597 report, edited respectively in Albèri, *Relazioni*, 3rd ser., 3:381–344; Federico Seneca, *Il doge Leonardo Donà, la sua vita e la sua preparazione politica prima del dogado* (Padua: Antenore, 1959), 263–321.

68. "Hora la religion fra loro è molto divisa, seguitando quasi tutta l'Asia la religion persiana, secondo la dottrina d'Alì discepolo di Maometto loro comun profeta, e quelli che seguitano quell'opinione sono da Turchi chiamati chisillas, cioè cresta rossa, perché questi tali sogliono portare in testa certa fascia rossa per esser conosciuti dagl'altri. In Africa poi vi sono gli Arabi e Mori li quali, se bene sono Maomettani come sono li Turchi, sono però in molte cose differenti d'opinione, ed ognuno di loro stima essere della sua opinione vera. Gl'Arabi però non vogliono entrare nelle moschee de Turchi d'Europa per far loro orazione, stimando che siano di religione corrotta, e come si suol dire bastarda." Pedani, *Costantinopoli relazioni*, 350.

69. Bernardo returned to Istanbul in 1591–1592 charged with the highly unusual mission of retrieving the bailo Girolamo Lippomano, who was accused of treason, and securing his return to Venice. Although he was not formally sent as an ambassador, Bernardo nevertheless delivered a relazione following his return from the mission. On the charges against Lippomano and Bernardo's mission, see Maria Pia Pedani Fabris, *Elenco degli inviati diplomatici veneziani presso i sovrani ottomani* (Venice: n.p., 2000), 29–30; Paolo Preto, *I servizi segreti di Venezia* (Milan: Il Saggiatore, 1994), 76–78; Giuseppe Gullino, "Lippomano, Girolamo," in *Dizionario Biografico degli Italiani*, 2005, http://www.treccani.it/enciclopedia/girolamo-lippomano_(Dizionario-Biografico)/; Giovanni Pillinini, "Bernardo, Lorenzo," in *Dizionario Biografico degli Italiani*, 1967, http://www.treccani.it/enciclopedia/lorenzo-bernardo_(Dizionario-Biografico)/.

70. Preto, *Venezia e i Turchi*, 101–104.

71. Albèri, *Relazioni*, 3rd ser., 2:367.

72. Giorgio Rota, *Under Two Lions: On the Knowledge of Persia in the Republic of Venice (ca. 1450–1797)* (Vienna: Österreichischen Akademie der Wissenschaften, 2009), 26–46; Giorgio Rota, "Safavid Persia and Its Diplomatic Relations with Venice," in *Iran and the World in the Safavid Age*, ed. William Floor and Edmund Herzig (London: I. B. Tauris, 2012), 149–160.

73. The three envoys were Costantino Lascari during the war of 1499–1503, Michele Membré during the war of 1537–1540, and Vincenzo degli Alessandri during the war of 1570–1573. All three were unsuccessful in their missions to negotiate an anti-Ottoman alliance. In a departure from typical Venetian diplomatic practice, none of the three men were patricians, and only one of them, Vincenzo degli Alessandri, was a Venetian citizen. Although the use of citizen diplomats would become more common in the seventeenth century, it remained relatively rare in the sixteenth century. In the case of Lascari and Membré, who spent much of his career as a Venetian dragoman, it seems clear that they were selected partly for their linguistic ability. On the use of citizen diplomats, see Zannini, "Economic and Social Aspects," 133–134; on the use of noncitizen dragomans as diplomats, see E. Natalie Rothman, "Interpreting Dragomans: Boundaries and Crossings in the Early Modern Mediterranean," *Comparative Studies in Society and History* 51, no. 4 (September 2009): 782–783; E. Natalie Rothman, *The Dragoman Renaissance: Diplomatic Interpreters and the Routes of Orientalism* (Ithaca, NY: Cornell University Press, 2021), 80–112.

74. On early reports on Ismail, see Margaret Meserve, *Empires of Islam in Renaissance Historical Thought* (Cambridge, MA: Harvard University Press, 2009), 231–237; Margaret Meserve, "The Sophy: News of Shah Ismail Safavi in Renaissance Europe," *Journal of Early Modern History* 18, no. 6 (2014): 579–590.

75. Meserve, *Empires of Islam*, 232; Meserve, "Sophy," 583.

76. "Come heretichi dalle fede macometana, et usurpatori del stato di molti signori macometani." Guglielmo Berchet, ed., *La Repubblica di Venezia e la Persia* (Turin: G. B. Paravia, 1865–1866), 1:154.

77. "Questo signor Sophì è molto afezionato a questa sua setta che è una certa religione catholica a lor modo, in discordantia de la opinion del suo propheta Macometto et Omar, che fo suo discipulo, et questo Sophì aderisse ala opinion de Alì che fu pure discipol del profeta. Tamen in articulo di loro fede erano dissidenti come se pol dir fosseno al tempo di san Pietro et de altri pontifici gli Ariani, che benchè cristiani, tamen erano eretici." Berchet, *La Repubblica di Venezia e la Persia*, 1:155.

78. Pedani, *Costantinopoli relazioni*, 292.

79. "Sono li Persiani piuttosto genti povere che altrimenti. Nella città e ville non usano molti adornamenti. Dorme ognuno in terra, e quelli che sono in qualche condizione usano lo stramazzo sopra tappeti, gli altri un feltro semplice. Le donne sono per l'ordinario tutte brutte, ma di bellissimi lineamenti e nobili cere, sebbene i loro abiti non sono cosi attillati come quelli delle Turche. Usano però di vestire di seta, portando in testa il caffetano, lasciandosi veder la faccia a chi esse vogliono; e a chi non vogliono l'ascondono." Albèri, *Relazioni*, 3rd ser., 2:120.

80. Albèri, *Relazioni*, 3rd ser., 3:270–271.

81. Seneca, *Il doge Leonardo Donà*, 264.

82. "È stata cavata la religione de Turchi da quelli, che nel principio suo artifiosamente la inventarono con fine di dominare, dalla vecchia legge mosaica delli hebrei, et da quello di Christo redemptor nostro, pigliando da cadauna di esse et lasciando quello, che conferiva alla loro intentione, et che facilmente giudicarono dovere essere ricevuto da gli animi delli suoi seguaci." Seneca, *Il doge Leonardo Donà*, 312–313.

83. Nicolò Barozzi and Guglielmo Berchet, eds., *Relazioni degli stati europei lette al Senato dagli ambasciatori veneti nel secolo decimosettimo: Turchia* (Venice: P. Naratovich, 1871), 36, 178.

84. Seneca, *Il doge Leonardo Donà*, 313.

85. Barozzi and Berchet, *Relazioni: Turchia*, 36, 178.

86. Seneca, *Il doge Leonardo Donà*, 313.

87. Although Nani's full relazione does not survive, a summary was prepared by his successor as bailo, Francesco Contarini. All references to Nani's relazione are from the published edition of Contarini's summary. Barozzi and Berchet, *Relazioni: Turchia*, 36.

88. Nancy Bisaha, *Creating East and West: Renaissance Humanists and the Ottoman Turks* (Philadelphia: University of Pennsylvania Press, 2004), 167–168.

89. "Nec fefellit eum opinio in hac parte: placuit nova lex et brevi tempore ita coaluit, ut in multis populis gentibus ac linguis reciperetur, cuius fundamenta in voluptate iacta fuerunt." Aeneas Silvius Piccolomini, *Epistola ad Mahomatem II*, ed. Albert R. Baca (New York: Peter Lang, 1990), 76.

90. Giorgio Spini, *Ricerca dei libertini: La teoria dell'impostura delle religioni nel Seicento italiano*, 2nd ed. (Rome: Editrice Universale, 1983), 62.

91. Albèri, *Relazioni*, 1st ser., 2:361–362.

92. Norman Daniel, *Islam and the West: The Making of an Image*, rev. ed (Oxford: Oneworld Publications, 1993), 105.

93. Daniel J. Sahas, *John of Damascus on Islam: The "Heresy of the Ishmaelites"* (Leiden: Brill, 1972), 132; On the reception of John's account of Aryan influence, see Barbara Roggema, *The Legend of Sergius Baḥīrā: Eastern Christian Apologetics and Apocalyptic in Response to Islam* (Leiden: Brill, 2009), 168; Reinhold F. Glei, "John of Damascus," in *Christian-Muslim Relations: A Bibliographical History*, ed. David Thomas and Barbara Roggema (Leiden: Brill, 2009), 1:297–299.

94. Roggema, *The Legend of Sergius Baḥīrā*, 173.

95. Theodore Bibliander, ed., *Machumetis Saracenorum principis, eiusque successorum vitae, ac doctrina, ipseque Alcoran* (Basel: Ioannis Oporini, 1543), 1:3–4. On the reception of the Summa totius haeresis saracenorum, see Dominique Iogna-Prat and John Tolan, "Peter of Cluny," in *Christian-Muslim Relations: A Bibliographical History*, ed. David Thomas and Alex Mallett (Leiden: Brill, 2011), 3:606–607.

96. "Sectam habent ex iudaismo, christianismo, paganismo, et Arianorum haeresi commixtam." Desiderius Erasmus, *Utilissima consultatio de bello Turcis inferendo, et obiter enarratus Psalmus XXVIII*, ed. A. G. Weiler and C.S.M. Rademaker, Opera Omnia, 4.3 (Amsterdam: Elsevier, 1986), 76, lines 984–985.

97. On Nicholas of Cusa's understanding of Islam as a syncretic religion, see Morimichi Watanabe, "Cusanus, Islam, and Religious Tolerance," in *Nicholas of Cusa and Islam: Polemic and Dialogue in the Late Middle Ages*, ed. Ian Christopher Levy, Rita George-Tvrtković, and Donald Duclow (Leiden: Brill, 2014), 9–19; Carina L. Johnson, *Cultural Hierarchy in Sixteenth-Century Europe: The Ottomans and Mexicans* (Cambridge: Cambridge University Press, 2011), 63–64.

98. Aeneas Silvius Piccolomini, *Commentaries*, ed. Margaret Meserve and Marcello Simonetta (Cambridge, MA: Harvard University Press, 2003), 1:211. On the correspondence between Nicholas of Cusa and Pius II, see Meserve, *Empires of Islam*, 1, 100–103; Bisaha, *Creating East and West*, 67–68.

99. Luigi Bassano, *I costumi et i modi particolari de la vita de' Turchi* (Rome: Antonio Blado Asolano, 1545), 11v–12r; *L'Alcorano di Macometto, nel qual si contiene la dottrina, la vita, i costumi et le leggi sve* ([Venice]: Andrea Arrivabene, 1547), iiir–v, vv.

100. In his inventory of his library, Donà lists the title of the work simply as *De Turchi*, but his attribution of the work's authorship to "Bassano da Zara" and his inclusion of the year of publication leave no doubt as to the book's identity. BCV, Provenienze Diverse, ms. 2735, fasc. 2, c. 2v.

101. Gianfrancesco Morosini's earlier 1585 relazione is an exception. Morosini not only mentions both Aryan and Nestorian influences in Islam, like Cusanus and Pius, but he also attributes the latter to Mohammed's relationship with the monk Sergius Baḥīra. Albèri, *Relazioni*, 3rd ser., 3:270; On the history of medieval Christian interpretations of Baḥīra, see Roggema, *The Legend of Sergius Baḥīrā*, 151–201.

102. On secretaries, see Dover, "Deciphering the Diplomatic Archives of Fifteenth-Century Italy"; on physicians, see Johnson, *Cultural Hierarchy in Sixteenth-Century Europe*,

173–174; Benjamin Arbel, *Trading Nations: Jews and Venetians in the Early-Modern Eastern Mediterranean* (Leiden: Brill, 1995), 77–86.

103. De Vivo, *Information and Communication*, 74–75.

104. Eric Dursteler, "Speaking in Tongues: Language and Communication in the Early Modern Mediterranean," *Past & Present*, no. 217 (November 2012): 61.

105. Rothman, *The Dragoman Renaissance*.

106. Anderson, *The Rise of Modern Diplomacy 1450–1919*, 13; Tommaso Bertelè, *Il palazzo degli ambasciatori di Venezia a Costantinopoli e le sue antiche memorie: Ricerche storiche con documenti inediti e 185 illustrazioni* (Bologna: Appolo, 1932), 95; Keith Hamilton and Richard Langhorne, *The Practice of Diplomacy: Its Evolution, Theory, and Administration*, 2nd ed. (New York: Routledge, 2011), 58.

107. ASVe, Capi del Consiglio dei Dieci, Licenze di visitare ambasciatori e personaggi esteri, reg. 1–2.

108. Albèri, *Relazioni*, 1st ser., 6:361.

109. This is the same Giovanni Michiel whose relazione following his embassy to England is discussed earlier in the chapter.

110. "Mi ristringerò in alcune cose solamente, che mi sono parse degne da esser conosciute da homeni di stato." Joseph Fiedler, ed., *Relationen venetianischer Botschafter über Deutschland und Österreich im sechzehnten Jahrhundert* (Vienna: Kaiserlich-Königlichen Hof- und Staatsdruckerei, 1870), 227.

111. The attribution of authorship to Donà is made by Filippo De Vivo based on the hand of the document. De Vivo, *Information and Communication*, 59. An excerpt from Duodo's report on Poland appears at the beginning of this chapter.

112. The document is dated September 17, 1592. Donà notes that the relazione had been delivered earlier in the same evening in which he was writing. Leonardo Donà, *Relazioni de prencipi e molti stati*, BCV, Donà, ms. 41, c. 169r.

113. Donà's copy is bound alongside his notes on Duodo's relazione in the codex. BCV, Donà, ms. 41, cc. 170r–181v.

114. For a more traditional summary of Duodo's relazione (without any commentary), see the copy prepared by Giovanni Tiepolo, the future Patriarch of Venice. Giovanni Tiepolo, *Sommario della relatione del Clar.o Signor Pietro Duodo*, BCV, Wcovich Lazzari, b. 21, fasc. 3. Giovanni Tiepolo, "Sommario della relatione del Clar.o Signor Pietro Duodo" (Venice, 1596), Wcovich Lazzari, b. 21, fasc. 3, Museo Civico Correr. Giovanni Tiepolo, "Sommario della relatione del Clar.o Signor Pietro Duodo" (Venice, 1596), Wcovich Lazzari, b. 21, fasc. 3, Museo Civico Correr.

115. Donà was particularly impressed with Duodo's ability to name the provinces, principal cities, and major castles of Poland from memory. BCV, Donà, ms. 41, c. 169r.

116. "Molte altre circonstanze, più conveniente a Historia, che a Relatione, nelle quali e più proprio le considerationi di stato, che altre curiosita che possono massime esser vedute ne libri." BCV, Donà, ms. 41, c. 169r.

117. "Ha detto che in certa parte di quel Regno alcuni popoli sono idolatri . . . che adorano un certo serpente, et altre favolose cose, che si legono pur ne libri." BCV, Donà, ms. 41, c. 169v.

118. Martin Kromer, *De origine et rebus gestis Polonorum* (Basel, 1555), 61; Olaus Magnus, *Historia de gentibus septentrionalibus* (Rome, 1555), 776–777. BCV, Donà, 447, 10v.

119. By 1592, Donà had served as ambassador to Spain, the Holy Roman Empire, and four times as ambassador to Rome. For a summary of the offices Donà held before his election as doge, see Paul F. Grendler, "The Tre Savii Sopra Eresia 1547–1605: A Prosopographical Study," *Studi Veneziani* n.s. 3 (1979): 338.

120. Tommaso Contarini, "Relazione di Fiandra (1610)," in *Relazioni veneziane: Venetiaansche berichten over de Vereenigde Nederlanden van 1600–1795*, ed. P. J. Blok (The Hague: M. Nijhoff, 1909), 28.

121. Contarini, "Relazione di Fiandra (1610)," 33.

122. "Promettendogli di compensare ogni molestia con la brevità, lascierò la desscrizione, l'istorie, le trattazioni dei negozii finiti, e la superfluità, delle parole, dovendo il fine della relazione essere l'utile, e non l'ambizione; attenderò alle cose reali e necessarie." Barozzi and Berchet, *Relazioni: Turchia*, 263.

123. On the importance of the relazione to an ambassador's career, see Ventura, "Scrittori politici," 553; Valensi, *Birth of the Despot*, 13–17; Dursteler, "Describing or Distorting," 237.

124. On the reception of Bernardo's report, see Preto, "Le relazioni dei baili veneziani a Costantinopoli," 130; Dursteler, "Describing or Distorting," 240. On the reception of Querini's report, see Ventura, "Scrittori politici," 559.

125. ASVe, Senato Terra, reg. 23, cc. 149v–150r. Published in Maria Francesca Tiepolo, ed., *Aspetti e momenti della diplomazia veneziana: Catalogo della mostra documentaria, 26 giugno-26 settembre, 1982* (Venice: Archivio di Stato di Venezia, 1982), 84–85.

126. Amelio Tagliaferri, ed., *Relazioni dei rettori veneti in terraferma* (Milan: A. Giuffrè, 1973–1979).

127. ASVe, Collegio, Relazioni, b. 61, cc. 69v–71r

128. Pedani Fabris, "Venetian Consuls in Egypt and Syria."

129. ASVe, Collegio, Relazioni, b. 61, 69v–71r.

130. ASVe, Collegio, Relazioni, b. 31. Published in Guglielmo Berchet, ed., *Relazioni dei consoli veneti nella Siria* (Turin: G. B. Paravia, 1866), 74–78.

131. ASVe, Collegio, Relazioni, b. 31. Published in Berchet, *Relazioni dei consoli veneti nella Siria*, 100–109.

132. "L'uffizio del console è di aver principal cura e protezione del negozio della mercanzia, che viene trattato dai mercanti veneziani in quelle parti." Berchet, *Relazioni dei consoli veneti nella Siria*, 79.

133. ASVe, Collegio, Relazioni, b. 62, cc. 31r–37r.

134. Barbarigo's full agenda reads as follows: "Narrandoli nel stato ch'io ho ritrovato quel consolato, et quanto che per me si ha operato à honore suo, et beneficio delli mercanto fino al giongere del Mag.co Tiepolo mio successore, non lasciando de dire in che stato se ritrovano in quelle parte le cose del S.or Turco, et la compagnia ch'ho havuto dal Mag.co Ali Bassà, ch[e] era al governo dell'Egitto, racordandoli reverentemente quello che mi pare dovere essere honore de V[ost]ra Ser[ereni]tà et utile de Mercanti sudditi suoi." ASVe, Collegio, Relazioni, b. 62, c. 31v.

135. ASVe, Collegio, Relazioni, b. 1, reg. 2, 56v–80r. Barbarigo's relazione is published in Albèri, *Relazioni*, 3rd ser., 2:1–59.

136. Albèri, *Relazioni*, 3rd ser., 2:17–18, 9. It is worth noting that the ethnographic information in Barbarigo's relazione is not presented in a discrete section, an organizational practice that would become increasingly common in later sixteenth-century relazioni.

137. Michael Knapton, "'Dico in scrittura . . . quel ch'a boca ho riferto': La trasmissione delle conoscenze nelle relazioni dei rettori veneziani in terraferma, secoli XVI–XVII," in *L'Italia dell'inquisitore: Storia e geografia dell'Italia del Cinquecento nella Descrittione di Leandro Alberti: Atti del convegno internazionale di studi, Bologna, 27–29 maggio 2004*, ed. Massimo Donattini (Bologna: Bononia University Press, 2007), 543; Gerassimos D. Pagratis, ed., *Oi ektheseis tōn benetōn bailōn kai pronoētōn tēs Kerkyras (16. aiōnas)* (Athens: Ethnico Idryma Ereynōn. Institouto Byzantinōn Ereynōn, 2008), 463–464; Gino Barbieri, "Introduzione alle relazioni dei provveditori di Legnago," in *Provveditorato di Legnago*, ed. Amelio Tagliaferri, Relazioni dei rettori veneti in Terraferma, VIII (Milan: A. Giuffrè, 1977), xvi.

138. Pagratis, *Oi ektheseis*, 464–465.

139. For examples from the terraferma, see Tagliaferri, *Relazioni dei rettori*, 8:19, 10:93, 11:15, 12:32, 12:194.

140. Dimitris Arvanitakis, ed., *Oi anaphores ton beneton problepton tes Zakinthou: 16os–18os ai* [The reports of the Venetian provveditori of Zante: 16th to 18th centuries] (Venice: Elleniko institouto byzantinon, 2000), 59–60.

141. Arvanitakis, *Oi anaphores ton beneton problepton tes Zakinthou*, 222–223.

142. Simeon Ljubic, ed., *Commissiones et relationes venetae*, Monumenta spectantia historiam Slavorum meridionalium (Zagreb: Academia Scientiarum et Artium Slavorum Meridionalium, 1876), 2:205.

143. Ljubic, *Commissiones et relationes venetae*, 3:30–41.

144. Matteo Melchiorre, *Conoscere per governare: Le relazioni dei sindici inquisitori e il dominio veneziano in terraferma (1543–1626)* (Udine: Forum, 2013), 61.

145. Bon's report is edited in Melchiorre, *Conoscere per governare*, 265–277.

146. For introductions to the "new diplomatic history," see Watkins, "Toward a New Diplomatic History of Medieval and Early Modern Europe"; Mary Lindemann, "The Discreet Charm of the Diplomatic Archive," *German History* 29, no. 2 (June 2011): 283–304.

147. For recent studies, see Toby Osborne and Joan-Pau Rubiés, eds., "Diplomacy and Cultural Translation in the Early Modern World," special issue, *Journal of Early Modern History* 20, no. 4 (2016).

148. Mattingly, *Renaissance Diplomacy*.

149. *Thesoro politico cioè relationi instruttioni trattati, discorsi varii d'ambasciatori* (Cologne: Alberto Coloresco nell'Academia italiana di Colonia, 1589). On the Tesoro politico, see Simone Testa, "Per una interpretazione del Thesoro politico (1589)," *Nuova rivista storica* 85 (2001): 347–362; Simone Testa, "Alcune riflessioni sul Thesoro politico (1598)," *Bibliothèque d'humanisme et renaissance* 64 (2002): 679–687.

150. De Vivo, "How to Read Venetian Relazioni," 47; Ginevra Crosignani, "Raviglio Rosso, Giulio," in *Dizionario Biografico degli Italiani*, 2016, http://www.treccani.it//enciclopedia/giulio-raviglio-rosso_(Dizionario-Biografico).

151. De Vivo, "How to Read Venetian Relazioni," 47.

152. Brian Richardson, "A Scribal Publisher of Political Information: Francesco Marcaldi," *Italian Studies* 64, no. 2 (June 2009): 302.

153. On the relationship between the relazioni and the ars apodemica, see Noah Millstone, "Seeing like a Statesman in Early Stuart England," *Past & Present* 223, no. 1

(May 2014): 101–103; Joan-Pau Rubiés, "Instructions for Travellers: Teaching the Eye to See," *History and Anthropology* 9, no. 2–3 (1996): 149–150.

154. Preto, *Venezia e i turchi*, 178–179; Dursteler, "Describing or Distorting," 138.

155. Lazzaro Soranzo, *L'Ottomanno* (Ferrara: Vittorio Baldini, 1598), A1r–v.

156. Soranzo, *L'Ottomanno*, A2r.

157. Fiedler, *Relationen*, 227.

Chapter 3 Ethnography and the Venetian State

1. On other European states' use of diplomats in news gathering, see Mark Netzloff, "The Ambassador's Household: Sir Henry Wotton, Domesticity, and Diplomatic Writing," in *Diplomacy and Early Modern Culture*, ed. Robyn Adams and Rosanna Cox (New York: Palgrave Macmillan, 2011), 156–159; Michael Mallett, "Ambassadors and Their Audiences in Renaissance Italy," *Renaissance Studies* 8, no. 3 (1994): 229–243; Garrett Mattingly, *Renaissance Diplomacy* (New York: Dover, 1988), 97–99; John-Paul Ghobrial, *Whispers of Cities: Information Flows in Istanbul, London, and Paris in the Age of William Trumbull* (Oxford: Oxford University Press, 2013).

2. Pierre Sardella, *Nouvelles et spéculations à Venise au début du XVIe siècle* (Paris: A. Colin, 1948).

3. Sanudo's entry does not specify where the Frenchman had accompanied Ismail, although the date of the man's arrival in Venice suggests southeastern Anatolia.

4. Marin Sanudo, *I diarii (1496–1533)*, ed. Rinaldo Fulin, Federico Stefani, Nicolò Barozzi, Guglielmo Berchet, and Marco Allegri (Venice: F. Visentini, 1879–1903), 7: coll. 269–270.

5. Palmira Brummett, *Ottoman Seapower and Levantine Diplomacy in the Age of Discovery* (Albany: State University of New York Press, 1994), 67–68.

6. Sanudo, *Diarii*, 33: coll. 184.

7. "Referite zercha queste cosse [i.e., concerning India] longamente: siché Soa Serenità e tutti che l'aldite rimaseno stupefati di quelle cosse sono in India." Sanudo, *Diarii*, 35: coll. 173.

8. Sanudo, for example, used a very similar vocabulary in his entry on Ludovico de Varthema's address to the Collegio, discussed below, which contained an elaborate account of Indian customs. On the discourse of wonder in early modern European accounts of the Americas, see Stephen Greenblatt, *Marvelous Possessions: The Wonder of the New World* (Chicago: University of Chicago Press, 1991).

9. Giustinian's voyage obviously took him not only to India but to regions better covered by Venice's diplomatic intelligence network. Sanudo is not particularly forthcoming about what precisely Giustinian discussed, but the wording of his entry suggests that Giustinian's reporting on India was of central importance. The entry reads as follows: "Il Serenissimo con il Collegio et li Cai di X si reduseno ad aldir sier Zuan Francesco Justinian qu. Sier Nicolò da san Barnaba, stato 9 anni fuora, et è stato in India, et steteno ad aldirlo fino hore . . . di notte." The hour at which the address concluded is left blank in Sanudo's diary. Sanudo, *Diarii*, 53: coll. 73. On Giustinian's voyage, see Frederic Chapin Lane, *Venetian Ships and Shipbuilders of the Renaissance* (Baltimore: Johns Hopkins University Press, 1992), 116–117.

10. Joan-Pau Rubiés, *Travel and Ethnology in the Renaissance: South India through European Eyes, 1250–1625* (Cambridge: Cambridge University Press, 2002), 127; Kim M. Phillips, *Before Orientalism: Asian Peoples and Cultures in European Travel Writing, 1245–1510* (Philadelphia: University of Pennsylvania Press, 2014), 44; Albrecht Fuess, "Ludovico de Varthema," in *Christian-Muslim Relations. A Bibliographical History*, ed. David Thomas and John A. Chesworth (Leiden: Brill, 2014), 6:405–406.

11. Ludovico de Varthema, *Itinerario* (Rome: Etienne Guillery & Ercole Nani ad instantia de Ludovico degli Arrighi, 1510).

12. Fuess, "Ludovico de Varthema," 405; Carla Forti, "Varthema, Ludovico de," in *Dizionario biografico degli Italiani*, 2020, https://www.treccani.it/enciclopedia/ludovico-de-varthema_(Dizionario-Biografico).

13. "In questo zorno fo in colegio, da poi disnar, uno bolognese, venuto di Coloqut. Referì molte cosse di quelle parte; *adeo* tutti rimaseno stupidi di li ritti e costumi de India. Et per colegio li fo donato ducali 25 per il suo referir." Although the wording of Sanudo's entry suggests that Varthema had returned directly from Calicut to Venice, this was not in fact the case. Varthema had returned to Europe via Lisbon in the summer of 1508. Sanudo, *Diarii*, 7: coll. 662.

14. Andrea Da Mosto, *L'Archivio di stato di Venezia: Indice generale, storico, descrittivo ed analitico* (Rome: Biblioteca d'arte editrice, 1937–1940), 1:23.

15. Patricia H. Labalme and Laura Sanguineti White, "Appendix A: Money, Wealth, and Wages," in *Venice, Cità Excelentissima: Selections from the Renaissance Diaries of Marin Sanudo*, ed. Patricia H. Labalme and Laura Sanguineti White (Baltimore: Johns Hopkins University Press, 2008), 542.

16. Eric Dursteler, "Reverberations of the Voyages of Discovery in Venice, ca. 1501: The Trevisan Manuscript in the Library of Congress," *Mediterranean Studies* 9 (2000): 45–47; Robert Finlay, "Crisis and Crusade in the Mediterranean: Venice, Portugal, and the Cape Route to India (1498–1509)," *Studi veneziani* 28 (1994): 57; Sanjay Subrahmanyam, "The Birth-Pangs of Portuguese Asia: Revisiting the Fateful 'Long Decade' 1498–1509," *Journal of Global History* 2, no. 3 (November 2007): 265–270; Vincenzo Marchesi, "Le relazioni tra la repubblica Veneta e il Portogallo dall'anno 1522 al 1797," *Archivio veneto* 33 (1887): 12.

17. Quoted in Bailey W. Diffie and George D. Winius, *Foundations of the Portuguese Empire, 1415–1580* (Minneapolis: University of Minnesota Press, 1977), 208.

18. "Le remote parte e gente meridionale e orientale, siti e costume loro." Ludovico de Varthema, *Itinerario*, ed. Valentina Martino (Alessandria: Edizioni dell'Orso, 2011), 29.

19. On issues of authority in relation to late-medieval and early modern travel literature, see Daniel Carey, "The Problem of Credibility in Early Modern Travel," *Renaissance Studies* 33, no. 4 (2019): 524–547; Christine R. Johnson, "Buying Stories: Ancient Tales, Renaissance Travelers, and the Market for the Marvelous," *Journal of Early Modern History* 11, no. 6 (2007): 405–446; Joan-Pau Rubiés, "Instructions for Travellers: Teaching the Eye to See," *History and Anthropology* 9, no. 2–3 (1996): 148–149; Surekha Davies, "The Wondrous East in the Renaissance Geographical Imagination: Marco Polo, Fra Mauro and Giovanni Battista Ramusio," *History and Anthropology* 23, no. 2 (June 2012): 224–232.

20. Boemus's project in *Omnium gentium mores* has been interpreted as a reaction against contemporary travel writing and an effort to reclaim ethnographic discourse for

humanist authors—an argument that Boemus's letter to Grimm would seem to support. Vogel, "Cultural Variety in a Renaissance Perspective: Johannes Boemus on 'The Manners, Laws and Customs of All People' (1520)," in *Shifting Cultures: Interaction and Discourse in the Expansion of Europe*, ed. Joan-Pau Rubiés and Henriette Bugge (Münster: Lit Verlag, 1995), 17–34; for an alternate interpretation of Boemus's engagement with contemporary travel literature, see Anthony Grafton, *Inky Fingers: The Making of Books in Early Modern Europe* (Cambridge, MA: Harvard University Press, 2020), 11–25.

21. "Licet non ex levibus circulatoribus, non ex vagis mendicis, qui ut vulgo admiratiores acceptioresq[ue] sint, adeo nefandissime absq[ue] omni verecundia plaerunq[ue] mentiuntur: ut non ipsis modo non fides etiam minima habeatur, verum omnibus iuxta, qui aliquid de hi saut scribunt aut recitant: Sed ex gravium fidedignissimorum autorum scriptis." Johannes Boemus, *Omnium gentium mores, leges et ritus ex multis clarissimis rerum scriptoribus* (Lyon: Apud Haeredes Simonis Vincentii, 1535), 4.

22. Carla Forti, "Sull'itinerario di Ludovico di Varthema," in *Per Adriano Prosperi: L'Europa divisa e i nuovi mondi*, ed. Massimo Donattini, Giuseppe Marcocci, and Stefania Pastore (Pisa: Edizioni della Normale, 2011), 2:21.

23. The *Coloquios* is written in the form of a dialogue in which Orta is himself one of the interlocutors; this criticism of Varthema is articulated by Orta the interlocutor. Garcia da Orta, *Colloquies on the Simples and Drugs of India*, trans. Clements Markham (London: Henry Sotheran, 1913), 61–62.

24. Orta also offered some more concrete reasons that Varthema's *Itinerario* should not be believed. Varthema, for example, wrote that the water surrounding Hormuz is some of the softest in the world, when in fact, according to Orta, it was brackish. Orta also disputed Varthema's claim that in Malacca there is neither good water nor timber. Rubiés, *Travel and Ethnology in the Renaissance*, 145; Orta, *Colloquies on the Simples and Drugs of India*, 62.

25. For Donà's library, see BCV, Donà, ms. 447, no. 24, c. 16v; for Pinelli's library, see BNM, It. X 61 (6601), c. 100r.

26. Giovanni Battista Ramusio, ed., *Primo volume delle navigationi et viaggi* (Venice: Appresso gli heredi di Lucantonio Giunti, 1550), 158v.

27. For a list of editions of the *Itinerario*, see Varthema, *Itinerario* (2011), 89–103.

28. Ludovico de Varthema, "The Trauels of Lewis Barthema or Vertoman into Egypt, Syria, Arabia, Persia, and India," in *Purchas His Pilgrimes in Fiue Bookes*, ed. Samuel Purchas (London: Printed by William Stansby for Henrie Fetherstone, 1625), 2:1483.

29. Ramusio reported that "li iudei veramente lo adorano come un messia." Sanudo, *Diarii*, 54: coll. 148.

30. Sanudo, *Diarii*, 54: coll. 145–149.

31. On the figure of David ha-Reuveni, see Miriam Eliav-Feldon, *Renaissance Impostors and Proofs of Identity* (New York: Palgrave Macmillan, 2012), 68–91; Harris Lenowitz, *The Jewish Messiahs: From Galilee to Crown Heights* (Oxford: Oxford University Press, 1998), 93–124; Lea Sestieri, *David Reubeni: Un Ebreo d'Arabia in missione segreta nell'Europa del '500* (Genoa: Marietti, 1991).

32. Eliav-Feldon, *Renaissance Impostors*, 93–94.

33. Sanudo noted that it had been widely reported that Reuveni was a scoundrel and that his claims were false. "Si dice è una iotonia e non è vero quello el dice." Sanudo, *Diarii*, 54: coll. 144.

34. Emmanuele Antonio Cicogna, *Delle inscrizioni veneziane* (Venice: Giuseppe Picotti, 1853), 2:316n3.

35. Eliav-Feldon, *Renaissance Impostors*, 72.

36. Marica Milanesi, introduction to *Navigazioni e viaggi*, ed. Marica Milanesi (Turin: Einaudi, 1978), 1:xv.

37. Milanesi, "Introduction," xv.

38. "Et essendo . . . homo dottissimo nella leze hebrea." According to Ramusio's report, Reuveni described the kingdom of Prester John as being home to many Jewish tribes. Sanudo, *Diarii*, 54: coll. 146.

39. "Par che sopra li monti che divideno la arabia deserta dalla felice et dalla petrosa non molte giornate lontani del monte Synai se ritrovi una multitudine grande de Judei da forsi 300 milla anime, che viveno al modo et costumi de arabi, zoe da star ala campagna cavalcano a redosso con una sella di bambaso sulle carne et portano una canna per lanza . . . et ogni volta che la caravana de mori, che conduse le speciarie dalla Mecha et porto del Ziden verso Damasco et Aleppo, se affirma lì, essendoli necessario a ditta caravana star uno giorno apresso ditti monti per tuor aqua dovendo poi passar li deserti arenosi, ditti iudei armati *ut supra*, et molte volte insieme con arabi sui vicini, assaltano ditta caravana." Sanudo, *Diarii*, 54: coll. 145.

40. "Nui trovassemo una montagna laqual mostra d[i] circuito diece o vero xii miglia. In laqual mo[n]tagna habitano q[ua]tro o cinque milia iudei: liq[ua]li va[n]no nudi & sono di gra[n]deza de V palmi luno o vero VI & ha[n]no la voce feminile & sono piu nigri ch[e] de altro colore. Et non viveno d[']altra carne che de castrati & no[n] d[']altra cosa & sono circo[n]cisi & confessano loro essere iudei: & se possono havere un moro nelle mani loro lo scorticano vivo. Al pede de dicta montagna trovassimo uno reducto d[']acq[ua] laquale e acqua che piove alli te[m]pi. Noi carigassimo de dicta acqua XVI milia Cambelli de ch[e] li iudei forno mal co[n]tenti & andavano p[er] quello mo[n]te come caprioli & p[er] nie[n]te volevano desce[n]dere nel piano perch[é] son inimici mortali de mori." Ludovico de Varthema, *Itinerario* (Venice: per gli heredi di Giorgio di Rusconi, 1522), Biv.

41. Eliav-Feldon, *Renaissance Impostors*, 94.

42. Valentino Martino, the editor of the critical edition of Varthema's *Itinerario*, identifies the mountain as Harrat Khaybar in present-day Saudi Arabia. Varthema, *Itinerario* (2011), 247.

43. Varthema, *Itinerario* (1522), Bir.

44. Eliav-Feldon, *Renaissance Impostors*, 69.

45. "Costui, *re vera*, è arabo, perchè alla forma della persona et al color dimostra non esser di paesi nostri, è molto asciuto et simille alli indiani del Prete Giani." Sanudo, *Diarii*, 54: coll. 146.

46. Ramusio was also familiar with and had access to Sanudo's diaries before publishing his *Navigazioni e viaggi*. From 1530, Sanudo's diaries were made available to official historiographers of the republic, who also served as librarians of the city's public library. Although Ramusio himself never held the position, this did not, apparently, impede his access to the diaries. The Venetian patrician Pietro Bembo's surviving correspondence with Ramusio makes clear that Ramusio assisted Bembo in the administration of the library, particularly after Bembo was made a cardinal and relocated to Rome in 1539. On several occasions, Bembo wrote to Ramusio from Rome asking for assistance in obtaining volumes

of Sanudo's diaries, which he sought as source material for his history of Venice. Fiona Lejosne, "Un secrétaire vénitien entre archives et livres imprimés: Giovanni Battista Ramusio (1485–1557)," *Laboratoire italien. Politique et société*, no. 23 (October 2019): 8; Sardella, *Nouvelles*, 17.

47. Mattingly, *Renaissance Diplomacy*, 88; Keith Hamilton and Richard Langhorne, *The Practice of Diplomacy: Its Evolution, Theory, and Administration*, 2nd ed. (New York: Routledge, 2011), 59; Carla Coco and Flora Manzonetto, *Baili veneziani alla Sublime Porta: Storia e caratteristiche dell'ambasciata veneta a Costantinopoli* (Venice: Stamperia di Venezia, 1985), 66; Gerrit Verhoeven, *Europe within Reach: Netherlandish Travellers on the Grand Tour and beyond (1585–1750)*, trans. Diane Webb (Leiden: Brill, 2015), 56–61.

48. John Wansbrough, "A Mamluk Ambassador to Venice in 913/1507," *Bulletin of the School of Oriental and African Studies* 26, no. 3 (1963): 514; Maria Pia Pedani Fabris, *In nome del Gran Signore: Inviati ottomani a Venezia dalla caduta di Costantinopoli alla guerra di Candia* (Venice: Deputazione Editrice, 1994), 53–54; Stephen Ortega, *Negotiating Transcultural Relations in the Early Modern Mediterranean: Ottoman-Venetian Encounters* (Farnham, UK: Ashgate, 2014), 109.

49. Pedani Fabris, *In nome del Gran Signore*, 53–56.

50. Nicolas de Nicolay, *Les quatre premiers livres des Navigations et peregrinations orientales* (Lyon: Guillaume Rouillé, 1568), 11.

51. Robert Finlay, "The Venetian Republic as a Gerontocracy: Age and Politics in the Renaissance," *Journal of Medieval and Renaissance Studies* 8, no. 2 (1978): 157–178.

52. Andrea Zannini, "Economic and Social Aspects of the Crisis of Venetian Diplomacy in the Seventeenth and Eighteenth Centuries," in *Politics and Diplomacy in Early Modern Italy: The Structure of Diplomatic Practice, 1450–1800*, ed. Daniela Frigo (Cambridge: Cambridge University Press, 2000), 116; Eric Dursteler, "The Bailo in Constantinople: Crisis and Career in Venice's Early Modern Diplomatic Corps," *Mediterranean Historical Review* 16, no. 2 (2001): 9–10.

53. Giovanni Pillinini, "Bernardo, Lorenzo," in *Dizionario biografico degli Italiani*, vol. 9, 1967, http://www.treccani.it/enciclopedia/lorenzo-bernardo_(Dizionario-Biografico)/.

54. Quoted in Gino Benzoni, "Contarini, Francesco," in *Dizionario biografico degli Italiani*, 1983, http://www.treccani.it/enciclopedia/francesco-contarini_(Dizionario-Biografico)/.

55. Marino Cavalli, *Informatione dell'offitio dell'ambasciatore: 1550*, ed. Tommaso Bertelè (Florence: L. S. Olschki, 1935), 78.

56. On evolving requirements of this grade of citizenship, see Andrea Zannini, *Burocrazia e burocrati a Venezia in età moderna: I cittadini originari (sec. XVI–XVIII)* (Venice: Istituto veneto di scienze, lettere ed arti, 1993), 23–60; James S. Grubb, "Elite Citizens," in *Venice Reconsidered*, ed. John Martin and Denis Romano (Baltimore: Johns Hopkins University Press, 2008), 339–364.

57. Giuseppe Trebbi, "La cancelleria veneta nei secoli XVI e XVII," *Annali della Fondazione Luigi Einaudi* 14 (1980): 99.

58. In 1577, the number of chancellery secretaries was increased from 81 to 101. Mary Neff estimates that in a given year, 10 percent of chancellery secretaries would serve in diplomatic posts. Mary Frances Neff, "Chancellery Secretaries in Venetian Politics and Society, 1480–1533" (PhD diss., University of California, Los Angeles, 1985), 130.

59. Trebbi, "La cancelleria veneta," 108.

60. ASVe, Consiglio di Dieci, Deliberazioni, Comuni, Filze 233 (August 31, 1601). This order dealt specifically with material seized from the library of Gian Vincenzo Pinelli, discussed below and in chapter 4.

61. The 1425 *parte* of the Senate is reproduced in Maria Francesca Tiepolo, ed., *Aspetti e momenti della diplomazia veneziana: Catalogo della mostra documentaria, 26 giugno–26 settembre, 1982* (Venice: Archivio di Stato di Venezia, 1982), 23.

62. Michiel's account is held in ASVe, Collegio, Relazioni, b. 4. The second journal, written by Livo Cellini, is held in ASVe, Collegio, Relazioni, b. 5. Also preserved in ASVe, Collegio, Relazioni, b. 4 is an anonymous diary documenting the period of the bailo Marcantonio Barbaro's house arrest during the Ottoman-Venetian war of 1570–1573. Like the travel journal held alongside it in the *busta*, the diary was seized from the library of Gian Vincenzo Pinelli. Although the diary is not, strictly speaking, a diplomatic *travel* journal, its presence and location in the archive illustrates that a variety of genres were aligned with relazione.

63. ASVe, Collegio, Relazioni, b. 25.

64. Filippo De Vivo, *Information and Communication in Venice: Rethinking Early Modern Politics* (Oxford: Oxford University Press, 2009).

65. For an introduction to Pinelli's library, see Marcella Grendler, "Book Collecting in Counter-Reformation Italy: The Library of Gian Vincenzo Pinelli (1535–1601)," *Journal of Library History* 16, no. 1 (January 1981): 143–151; Angela Nuovo, "The Creation and Dispersal of the Library of Gian Vincenzo Pinelli," in *Books on the Move: Tracking Copies through Collections and the Book Trade*, ed. Robin Myers, Michael Harris, and Giles Mandelbrote (New Castle, DE: Oak Knoll Press, 2007), 39–67.

66. On the development of the Cancelleria secreta, see Filippo De Vivo, "Ordering the Archive in Early Modern Venice (1400–1650)," *Archival Science* 10, no. 3 (2010): 231–248.

67. Paolo Gualdo, *Vita Ioannis Vincentii Pinelli, patricii Genuensis, in qua studiosis bonarum artium, proponitur typus viri probi & eruditi* (Augsburg: Christophorus Mangus, 1607).

68. "Non vi è libraria così abietta, che per la maggior parte non le habbia, et son state raccolte dal signor Gio. Vincenzo in tempo che ciò non era prohibito, dico di darle fuori da gli stessi Ambasciatori." Gualdo's letter, dated July 21, 1601, is edited in Roberta Ferro, "Per la storia del fondo Pinelli all'Ambrosiana: Notizie dalle lettere di Paolo Gualdo," in *Tra i fondi dell'Ambrosiana: Manoscritti italiani antichi e moderni*, ed. Marco Ballarini et al. (Milan: Cisalpino, 2008), 1:285.

69. The secretaries did not inventory the entire library; rather, they looked exclusively at Pinelli's unbound manuscripts. This was a sensible and time-saving approach, since Pinelli tended to keep occasional writings such as relazioni and diplomatic travel journals in unbound fascicles grouped by subject. Evidently, the secretaries were unable even to inventory all of these materials, since some of the documents had been stolen before they arrived in the Cancelleria secreta. Their final inventory is titled "Inventario delle scritture, che si ritrovano nella presente Cassella, eccettuate alcune, che sono state rubbate fuori del studio del S[ign]or Pinelli." ASVe, Secreta, Archivio proprio Pinelli, b. 1, cc. 1r–18v. On the organization of Pinelli's library, see Nuovo, "Creation," 49–50.

70. "Essendo la maggior parte delle scritture, che furono del q[uondam] Gio[vani] Vincenzo Pinelli, et fatto venir di quì da Padoa per li Capi di questo Cons[igli]o in materie diverse di stato con poche altre di materia privata, ò di dottrine, et altro non pertineati all'interesse pub[li]co. L'anderà parte, che la Cassella di tutte esse scritture sia portata, et conservata nel secreto del Senato nostro, dovendo dalli Secretarii deputati ad esso secreto esser fatto un nuovo inventari di tutte esse scritture publiche, et in materia di stato, con ordinarle in modo, che con l'facilità possano bisognando trovarsi col detto inventario, et quelle altre poche concernenti materie private, se di poco rilievo, siano poste da parte, et consegnate alli heredi del d[ett]o Pinelli." ASVe, Consiglio di Dieci, Deliberazioni, Comuni, Filze 233 (August 31, 1601).

71. ASVe, Archivio proprio Pinelli, b. 1, cc. 1r–18v.

72. The Council of Ten's order includes no mention of how they were made aware of the presence of state documents in Pinelli's library. Pinelli, however, frequently invited guests, including many Venetian patricians, to use his library, so its contents would have been something of an open secret. On visitors to Pinelli's library, see Jaska Kainulainen, *Paolo Sarpi: A Servant of God and State* (Leiden: Brill, 2014), 40; Angela Nuovo, "Private Libraries in Sixteenth-Century Italy," in *Early Printed Books as Material Objects*, ed. Bettina Wagner and Marcia Reed (Berlin: De Gruyter, 2010), 234–235.

73. Maria Pia Pedani suggests that although Michiel's journey with Barbarigo's was undertaken in 1556, Michiel's account itself dates from 1558. Maria Pia Pedani Fabris, *Costantinopoli relazioni inedite (1512–1789)*. Relazioni di ambasciatori veneti al Senato 14 (Padua: Bottega d'Erasmo, 1996), 87.

74. "Conoscendo io quanta utilità soglia apportar agl'huomini nell'attioni l'esperienza delle cose, deliberai fra me stesso di abracciare la prima occasione la quale mi potesse dar comodità di vedere et conoscere diligentemente la corte e i costumi di alcuno principe di gran forze et potere . . . io pensava che ad un gentil'huomo veneziano, il quale si havesse proposto nell'animo di adoperarsi sempre ai essercicii della sua patria, fosse in ogni modo necessario non solo l'intendere i costumi et conoscere le forze de Turchi, ma etiandio cercare di vedere co' gl'occhi proprii quello che fosse possibile." [Nicolò Michiel], "Relatione di Constantinopoli di un nobile venetiano che ando in compagnia di Antonio Barbarigo, bailo." ASVe, Collegio, Relazioni, b. 4, fasc. 3, c. 1r.

75. "Lasciavo tuttavia di parlare di alcune cose, le quali satisfano piu tosto alla curiosita degl'huomini, et dilettano alquanto di quello che siano atte a insegnare et amaestrare alcuno negli negotii di qualche importanza." ASVe, Collegio, Relazioni, b. 4, fasc. 3, c. 15r.

76. ASVe, Consiglio di Dieci, Deliberazioni, Comuni, Filze 233 (August 31, 1601), c. 4r.

77. Donà was particularly committed to the practice of keeping a journal of all the diplomatic missions in which he participated. Autograph journals survive from his embassies to Spain (1570 and 1573), Vienna (1577), Rome (1589 and 1592), and Istanbul (1595). He also kept journals for travel he undertook as part of his nondiplomatic offices first in Friuli (1593) and then more widely in the terraferma (1601). Donà had evidently developed this habit in his youth. As a young man, Donà traveled to Cyprus with his father, who served as the Venetian governor of the island (1556–1558). A journal from this voyage also survives. Donà's diplomatic travel journals are found respectively in BCV, Donà, ms. 48, cc. 228r–245v; BCV, Donà, ms. 447/II; BCV, Donà, ms. 447/VI; Donà, 23; ASVe, Miscellanea Codici, IV, Codici Papadopoli, ms. 12, cc. 216r–237r; BCV, Donà, 447/V. A partial list of Donà's

travel journals and related writings can be found in Pietro Donazzolo, *I viaggiatori veneti minori: Studio bio-bibliografico* (Rome: Società geografica italiana, 1927), 129–130.

78. Andrea Navagero, *Il viaggio fatto in Spagna, et in Francia . . . con la descrittione particolare delli luochi, et costumi delli popoli di quelle provincie* (Venice: Domenico Farri, 1563), A2v.

79. BCV, Wcovich-Lazzari, b. 21, fasc. 6.

80. BCV, Donà, ms. 47, cc. 1–26.

81. Giovanni Carlo Scaramelli, "Ricordi a sé stesso," BNM, Ital. VII 1640 (7983), c. 5v. On Scaramelli's career, see Giuseppe Trebbi, "Il segretario veneziano," *Archivio storico italiano* 144 (1986): 55–56.

82. Rubiés, "Instructions for Travellers," 139–147; Justin Stagl, *A History of Curiosity: The Theory of Travel, 1550–1800* (Chur, Switzerland: Harwood Academic Publishers, 1994), 47–94; Peter Burke, *Varieties of Cultural History* (Ithaca, NY: Cornell University Press, 1997), 95–97.

83. "Co' suoi libri potrà acconciamente haver trattenimento, e scoprendo di mano in mano alcuna Isola, ò luogo di terra ferma, so ch'ella sarà diligente investigatrice delle cose piu notabili." Porcacchi was writing to William Malim, the former headmaster of Eton College. The edition of the letter published by Porcacchi is undated, but it was in 1564 that Malim traveled to Venice, Cyprus, and various parts of the Ottoman Empire. Although Porcacchi, unlike Scaramelli, did not give specific recommendations as to what the traveler should read, his inclusion of the ancient and modern names of cities and islands among the "cose piu notabili" that Malim should investigate suggests that he too intended Malim to read works of history and geography. Tommaso Porcacchi, *Lettere di XIII huomini illustri* (Venice: Appresso gli heredi Giovanni Maria Bonelli, 1571), 469v.

84. "Il Cairo è una città molto minore in ogni cosa di quello che risuona la sua fama. Ben è vero che è ricchissima ed abbondantissima di denaro, e grande due volte come Padova, assai più lunga che larga." Zaccaria Pagani, *Viaggio di Domenico Trevisan, ambasciatore veneto al gran sultano del Cairo nell'anno 1512*, ed. Nicolò Barozzi (Venice: Antonelli, 1875), 39–40.

85. "Gran popolo vi si trova, ma non tanto quanto si dice; si crede esser un milione e mezzo di anime, ma non è neanche la metà, e la maggior parte tutta canaglia e persone senza alcun costume." Pagani, *Viaggio di Domenico Trevisan*, 40.

86. This was reported, for example, by Vasco Díaz Tanco. The Venetian secretary Benedetto Ramberti also repeated the claim but conceded that only a portion of the church had been converted to stables. Vasco Díaz Tanco, *Libro dell'origine et successione dell'imperio de' Turchi*, trans. Alfonso de Ulloa (Venice: Gabriel Giolito de' Ferrari, 1558), 57; Benedetto Ramberti, *Libri tre delle cose de Turchi* (Venice: In casa haer. Aldo I Manuzio, 1539), 12r.

87. "La chiesa di Santa Sophia, opera invero eccellentissima, la quale non in tuto è integra, et questi l'hanno ridotta in moschea alla loro usanza, se bene alcuni hano scritto che questo Signore havea fatto stalla di cavali, il che è in tutto falso." Pedani Fabris, *Costantinopoli relazioni*, 101.

88. On the prevalence of this idea in the early modern Mediterranean, see Giuseppina Minchella, *Frontiere aperte: Musulmani, Ebrei e Cristiani nella Repubblica di Venezia* (Rome: Viella, 2014), 84–85.

89. "Non è vero che un giud[e]o non possa farsi Turcho se prima non diventi christiano, ma ben è vero che tenendo li Turchi in istima minore la Relig[ion]e Hebrea che la Christiana stimano anche più uno che di Christiano si faccia Turco che di Giudeo Turco." ASVe, Collegio, Relazioni, b. 4, fasc. 10, c. 17r.

90. "Esser piu da extimare uno visivo testimonio che diece de audito." Varthema, *Itinerario* (1522), aiir.

91. From the time of its first appearance in print, Menavino's account lacked a stable title. It was published in 1548, for example, as both *I cinque libri* and *Trattato de costumi et vita de Turchi*. Different titles still were used for later editions. For the sake of clarity, I refer to the work as *I cinque libri*.

92. Although the earliest printed edition of the *Cinque libri* is usually dated to 1548, it was actually printed a year earlier without any attribution to Menavino in the Italian translation of the Qur'an published in Venice by Andrea Arrivabene. Menavino's account was included among the prefatory texts dealing with Muslim theology and religious customs. Part of the reason why the *Alcorano* has been neglected in treatments of Menavino is that its editor not only published the text without any attribution of authorship, he also did away with Menavino's distinctive structure, thereby making the text more difficult for scholars to identify. The chapter divisions are kept intact, but the text, which is given the title "Della legge Mahomet[ana]," does away with Menavino's division of the work into books. *L'Alcorano di Macometto nel qual si contiene la dottrina, la vita, i costumi et le leggi sve* ([Venice]: Andrea Arrivabene, 1547), xxxixr–xlviiiv.

93. Pia Schwarz Lausten, "Giovanni Antonio Menavino," in *Christian-Muslim Relations: A Bibliographical History*, ed. David Thomas and John A. Chesworth (Leiden: Brill, 2014), 6:516; Wolfgang Schweickard, "Giovan Antonio Menavino's Account of His Captivity in the Ottoman Empire: A Revaluation," *Zeitschrift für romanische Philologie* 132, no. 1 (2016): 81–82.

94. "La turchesca legge è principalmente fondata ne' commandamenti d'un libro detto Musaph, il quale dicono esser stato mandato da Iddio per l'angelo a Mahometto, al quale portano tanto honore che nol toccano se non lavati et con un panno avolto alle mani, come cosa sacra." Pedani Fabris, *Costantinopoli relazioni*, 102.

95. The corresponding passage in Menavino's *Cinque libri*, which is slightly more detailed than Michiel's, reads as follows: "La Turchesca legge si trova da principio esser fondata ne' comandamenti del sopradetto libro Musaph, il quale dicono esser stato mandato in diverse parti da Dio per l'Angelo Gabriello à Mahometto; & che egli co i suoi Sculper, che vuol dire discepoli, l'hanno cosi distesamente composto, & messo insieme; al quale portano tanta veneratione, che toccare no'l possono, se non sono ben mondi, & lavati dalla cima del capo alle piante, overamente con uno panno alle mani involuto, come se cosa sacrata fusse." Giovanni Antonio Menavino, *I cinque libri della legge, religione, et vita de' Turchi* (Venice: Vincenzo Valgrisi, 1548), 16–17.

96. Pedani Fabris, *Costantinopoli relazioni*, 122; Menavino, *Cinque libri*, 17–18.

97. "Hanno sopra questi le loro espositioni, le quali s'io scrivessi sarei troppo longo et uscirei dal mio proposito." Pedani Fabris, *Costantinopoli relazioni*, 122.

98. Upon arriving in the port of Ragusa, the author recalls that "tutti noi giovani senza il clarissimo [Giacomo Soranzo]" disembarked and entered the city. The author, then, was clearly not the only young man in Soranzo's party. Carlo Ranzo, who also traveled with

Soranzo and kept a journal that was later published, noted that the ambassador traveled with forty men, many of whom were not Venetian noblemen but rather, men from the terraferma or other Italian states. Added to Soranzo's large party would have been the men accompanying the recently elected bailo Giovanni Correr. Because their elections fell so close together, Soranzo and Correr traveled together to Istanbul. Ranzo himself was from Vercelli in the Duchy of Savoy and it is certainly possible that the anonymous diary author was also neither a Venetian nor a Venetian subject. *Diario del viaggio da Venezia a Costantinopoli fatto da M. Jacopo Soranzo al Sultano Murad III in compagnia di M. Giovanni Correr bailo alla Porta Ottomana descritto da anonimo che fu al seguito del Soranzo, 1575* (Venice: Giambattista Merlo, 1856), 21; Carlo Ranzo, *Relatione di Carlo Ranzo gentil'hvomo di Vercelli d'vn viaggio fatto da Venetia in Constantinopoli: ritornato, che fù dalla battaglia Nauale assai curioso per i molti accidenti occorsi, oue si possono imparare stratagemme di guerra, humori d'huomini, e diuersita di genti, & di paesi* (Turin: Fratelli Cavaleri, 1616), 4.

99. The report is held in ASVe, Commemoriali, Memorie antiche importanti di vario argomento, 2, cc. 49–59. An edition of the report is published in Simeon Ljubic, *Commissiones et relationes venetae* (Zagreb: Academia Scientiarum et Artium Slavorum Meridionalium, 1876), 3:69–78.

100. The 1555 report in turn borrowed heavily from an earlier diplomatic travel journal by the Venetian secretary Benedetto Ramberti, which was published in 1539 as the *Libri tre delle cose de Turchi*. Ramberti's account will be discussed in the following section of this chapter. It is also possible that the 1575 journal author had also read Ramberti's *Libri tre*, although the language in his journal hews much more closely to that of the 1555 report.

101. Mosto, *L'Archivio di stato di Venezia*, 2:249; Maria Francesca Tiepolo, "Archivio di Stato di Venezia," in *Guida generale degli archivi di stato italiani* (Rome: Ministero per i Beni Culturali e Ambientali, 1994), 4:907–908.

102. Tiepolo, "Archivio di Stato di Venezia," 908.

103. "Qui i[n]comi[n]cia il parlar italiano, ma ta[n]to mescolato co'l Fra[n]cese, ch[e] difficil cose è, ch[e] o l'uno, o l'altro l'i[n]te[n]da." [Costantino Garzoni], "Relazione del viaggio di Antonio Tiepolo in Spagna e in Portogallo," BNM, Ital. XI 182 (7361), c. 78r. The attribution of authorship to Garzoni is drawn from Pietro Zorzanello and Giulio Zorzanello, eds., *Inventari dei manoscritti delle biblioteche d'Italia*, vol. 87 (Florence: L. S. Olschki, 1967), 61.

104. "Questa città parla tutta italiano, ma una contrada che è abitata da tedeschi ed è chiamata la contrada tedesca parla l'idioma tedesco insieme con l'italiano. I tedeschi considerano questa una città della Germania, ma non lo è né la sua lingua né il suo sito, che è posto di qua dalle Alpi, ed anche le sue radici la portano verso l'Italia." Leonardo Donà, *Il viaggio a Vienna di Leonardo Donà, ambasciatore della Repubblica veneta, nell'anno 1577: Diario*, ed. Umberto Chiaromanni (Padua: CLEUP, 2004), 127.

105. Donà, *Il viaggio a Vienna di Leonardo Donà*, 128.

106. See chapter 2. On Mediterranean multilingualism more generally, see Eric Dursteler, "Speaking in Tongues: Language and Communication in the Early Modern Mediterranean," *Past & Present*, no. 217 (November 2012): 47–77.

107. "Leur plus commun langage, est Esclavon: vray est qu'ils parlent aussi un certain Italien corrompu, encores plus goffe, que celuy des Venitiens." Nicolay, *Les quatre premiers livres des Navigations*, 155r.

108. "Usano le donne la lingua dalmatina con la quale parlando li altri della Dalmazia si servono, ma gli uomini e questa e la italiana, questa con li forestieri e l'altra fra di loro, con tutto che la lingua loro natia sia la schiava con vocaboli corotti, usando parte di essi molti vocaboli toscani, molti veneziani ed altri lombardi e pugliesi." *Diario del viaggio da Venezia a Costantinopoli*, 25.

109. Respectively, "la lingua dalmatina" and "la lingua schiavona." The corresponding section of the 1555 report reads as follows: "Usano le donne la lingua schiavona, con la quale parlano li altri Dalmatici, ma li huomeni et questa et la italiana. La lingua loro natia è schiava, con la quale parlano li altri Dalmatini; parlano etiam la lingua italiana con vocaboli corotti, perciochè parte usano puri vocaboli Toscani parte puri Venetiani antiqui, parte Lombardi et parte Pujesi." Ljubic, *Commissiones et relationes venetae*, 3:73–74.

110. The party arrived in Ragusa on May 11, 1575, seven days after leaving Venice, and departed the following day. *Diario del viaggio da Venezia a Costantinopoli*, 21, 31.

111. *Diario del viaggio da Venezia a Costantinopoli*, 31.

112. *Diario del viaggio da Venezia a Costantinopoli*, 28–31; Ljubic, *Commissiones et relationes venetae*, 3:69–71.

113. On Ramberti's career trajectory, see Marino Zorzi, *La libreria di San Marco: Libri, lettori, società nella Venezia dei dogi* (Milan: A. Mondadori, 1987), 111; Donazzolo, *Viaggiatori veneti*, 101.

114. On Ludovici's mission, see Eugenio Albèri, ed., *Relazioni degli ambasciatori veneti al senato* (Florence: Società editrice fiorentina, 1839–1863), p. ser. III, 1:2; Maria Pia Pedani Fabris, *Elenco degli inviati diplomatici veneziani presso i sovrani ottoman* (Venice: n.p., 2000), 21.

115. This explanation of the purpose of the mission is absent from printed editions of Ramberti's work. Benedetto Ramberti, "Viaggio et ritti del stato et imperio del Turco," BCV, Provenienze Diverse, ms. 394 c, vol. 2, fasc. 14.2, c. 1r.

116. Giosafat Barbaro, Ambrogio Contarini, Benedetto Ramberti, and Luigi Roncinotto, *Viaggi fatti da Vinetia, alla Tana, in Persia, in India, et in Costantinopoli: Con la descrittione particolare di citta, luoghi, siti, costumi, et della porta del gran Turco* (Venice: nelle case haer. Aldo I Manuzio, 1543).

117. Francesco Sansovino, *Dell'historia universale dell'origine et imperio de Turchi: Nella quali si Contengono Gli offici, i leggi, i costumi di quella natione, cosi in tempo di pace, come di guerra* (Venice: Francesco Sansovino & C., 1560), 107r–125.

118. Antoine Geuffroy and Benedetto Ramberti, *Estat de la court du grant Turc, Lordre de sa gendarmerie, et de ses finances: Avec ung brief discours de leurs conquestes depues le premier de ceste race* (Antwerp: Jehan Steels, 1542); Antoine Geuffroy and Benedetto Ramberti, *The Order of the Greate Turckes Courte, of Hys Menne of Warre, and of All Hys Conquestes, with the Summe of Mahumetes Doctryne. Translated out of Frenche* (London: Ricardus Grafton, 1542); On the relationship between the Italian, French, and English editions, see Anders Ingram, *Writing the Ottomans: Turkish History in Early Modern England* (New York: Palgrave Macmillan, 2015), 24; Palmira Brummett, *Mapping the Ottomans: Sovereignty, Territory, and Identity in the Early Modern Mediterranean* (Cambridge: Cambridge University Press, 2015), 56–57.

119. Certain manuscript copies contain an alternate introduction in which Ramberti names himself as the author and explains the purpose of the diplomatic mission. This in-

troduction is absent from all printed editions of the work. BCV, Provenienze Diverse, ms. 394 c, vol. 2, fasc. 14.2, c. 1r; BCV, Correr, ms. 1205/2625, c. 1r.

120. BNM, Lt. XIV 243 (4070), fasc. 7, c. 2v; Benedetto Ramberti, "Viaggio a Costantinopoli nel 1533," BAM, O 69 sup.

121. Donà's conjecture must have been based on the date of Ramberti's journey, since any mention of the author's connection to Daniele de' Ludovici was stripped from printed editions of the account. BCV, Provenienze Diverse, ms. 2735 c, fasc. 2, c. 2v.

122. Ramberti's passage on Ragusan dress reads, "Le donne non sono molto belle, & vesteno male, cioè habiti nelli quali compreno male. Portano in capo una cosa lunga di panno de lino, & se son nobili di sete bianca in forma di piramide, & vanno con le calze calate fino alli schinchi." Nicolay offers a nearly word-for-word translation: "Leurs femmes ne sont gueres belles, & s'habillent assez mal porprement, portans ordinairement un ornement de teste eslevé en coqueluche, faite de finetoile de lin. Mais les femmes nobles le portent de soye blanche, ayans leurs chausses avallées iusques aux tallons." Ramberti, *Libri tre*, 4r; Nicolay, *Les quatre premiers livres des Navigations*, 155r.

123. "Hora, che uscito delle fatiche del longo viaggio mi trovo ocioso, scriverò brievemente quelle cose che mi pareno degne di memoria: perche, se la fortuna, o'l tempo fara mutatione di quel stato, come è di sua natura, & come ha fatto di Alessandro Magno, delli Romani patroni de'l mondo, & alli giorni nostri de'l Soldano, li quali della infinita loro grandezza il nome solo hanno lasciato alla posterita, possa io delli costumi, delle forze, governo, & leggi di tal natione rendere conto à quelli, che non l'havessero vedute." Ramberti, *Libri tre*, 2r.

124. Marina Formica, *Lo specchio turco: Immagini dell'altro e riflessi del sé nella cultura italiana d'età moderna* (Rome: Donzelli Editore, 2012), 35–36.

125. Ramberti, *Libri tre*, 4r–5r.

126. Ramberti, *Libri tre*, 2v.

127. Ramberti, *Libri tre*, 12v–13r.

128. "Poi nella terzo notarò alcune considerationi pertinenti alla perfetta cognitione del suo governo." Ramberti, *Libri tre*, 2v.

129. "Gia havendo io circa la corte di questo Signore notate quelle cose, che ho giudicate degne di memoria; venirò mo à quelle altre, che sono pertinenti alla compita cognitione delli costumi di tal natione, & del modo di viver & governo loro." Ramberti, *Libri tre*, 26v.

130. "Una cosa hanno di bene che dispreggiano la morte, essendo persuasi che sia scritto in fronte à cadauno il giorno della morte sua: laqual openione però è solamente nella plebe bassa, & che non ha molto che perdere morendo: ma quelli che hanno ufficii, & che sono ben ricchi, raro ò non mai si mettono à i pericoli, & hanno molto cara la lor vita, mantenendo tale persuasione ne i Soldati." Ramberti, *Libri tre*, 29r.

131. In the late sixteenth and early seventeenth centuries, the connection between occasionalism and military prowess was also drawn in Venetian relazioni. See, for example, the dragoman Giovanni Battista Salvago's 1625 report on North Africa. Giovanni Battista Salvago, *"Africa Overo Barbarìa." Relazione al doge di Venezia sulle reggenze di Algeri e di Tunisi del dragomanno G. B. Salvago, 1625. Introduzione e note di Alberto Sacerdoti*, ed. Alberto Sacerdoti (Padua: A. Milani, 1937), 64–65.

132. Ramberti, *Libri tre*, 28v.

133. Ramberti, *Libri tre*, 27r–v.

134. Elisabeth G. Gleason, *Gasparo Contarini: Venice, Rome, and Reform* (Berkeley: University of California Press, 1993), 111–112.

135. Bruno Basile, "Introduzione e nota bio-bibliografica," in *Il serraglio del gransignore*, ed. Bruno Basile (Rome: Salerno, 2002), 8–9. In suggesting that Bon may have been influenced by Donà, Basile points to the two men's shared interest the religion, customs, and daily life of the Turks. Although this is true of Donà's notebook and is, indeed, the distinguishing feature of Bon's *Descrizione*, it is also a shared feature of most late sixteenth-century Venetian accounts of the Ottoman Empire, particularly those accounts produced in a diplomatic context.

136. Leonardo Donà, "Libreto di alcune memorie tenute nell'ambasceria mia di Costantinopoli," BCV, Donà, ms. 23, 157r–169r, 177r–181r, 188r–209r, 211r–325v.

137. My dating of the work to the 1580s is based on the fact that Donini (as one of the two interlocutors in the dialogue) discussed appointments he held as a diplomatic secretary through 1579. The manuscript copy in the library of the Museo Correr—the only surviving copy I have been able to locate—was copied by the future patriarch Giovanni Tiepolo at the age of twenty. Tiepolo dated the copy December 9, 1591. Marcantonio Donini, "Tre dialoghi di Marc'Antonio Donini già secretario veneto delle cose dei Turchi," BCV, Wcovich Lazzari, b. 31, fasc. 10, 30–32, 139. For an alternate dating of the work, see Piotr Chmiel, *Rethinking the Concept of Antemurale: Venetian Diplomacy in Respect of the Ottoman World (1573–1645)* (Rome: Accademia Polacca Roma, 2019), 14.

138. BCV, Wcovich Lazzari, b. 31, fasc. 10, 34–39, 95. Some of the interlocutor's other questions include why Muslims abstain from pork (125), whether they go to bed early and what kinds of beds they sleep on (128), whether their men wear beards (139), and whether the Turkish language is "rich in words and in concepts" (144).

139. Maria Pia Pedani Fabris, *Venezia porta d'oriente* (Bologna: Il Mulino, 2010), 264; Filippo De Vivo, "How to Read Venetian Relazioni," *Renaissance and Reformation/Renaissance et réforme* 34, no. 1–2 (2011): 46; Paolo Preto, *Venezia e i turchi*, 2nd ed. (Rome: Viella, 2013), 192–193.

140. Pedani Fabris, *Costantinopoli relazioni*, 487–488.

141. Nicolò Barozzi and Guglielmo Berchet, eds., *Relazioni degli stati europei lette al Senato dagli ambasciatori veneti nel secolo decimosettimo: Turchia* (Venice: P. Naratovich, 1871), 96–97.

142. Barozzi and Berchet, *Relazioni: Turchia*, 63–64.

143. Ramberti, *Libri tre*, 28v.

144. After returning from Istanbul, Bon became involved with a project to found an academy to educate boys from poor patrician families, pledging the significant sum of 5,000 ducats to help secure its establishment. Ottaviano Bon, *Lettera a Luigi Lollino vescovo di Belluno* (Rovigo: A. Minelli, 1844), 8; Margherita Pasdera, "Bon, Ottaviano," in *Dizionario biografico degli Italiani*, 1969, http://www.treccani.it/enciclopedia/ottaviano-bon_(Dizionario-Biografico)/. On the institution of the Enderun Mektebi, see Colin Imber, *The Ottoman Empire, 1300–1650: The Structure of Power* (New York: Palgrave Macmillan, 2009), 149–151.

145. Menavino, *Cinque libri*, 96–97; Barozzi and Berchet, *Relazioni: Turchia*, 81–83.

146. Barozzi and Berchet, *Relazioni: Turchia*, 82.

Chapter 4 Reading Ethnography in Early Modern Venice

1. "Le quali sono non solamente state dette da molti, ma scritti anche, e stampate, di modo che con pochi soldi ogni uno le può vedere." BCV, Donà, ms. 146, 170r. Navagero made this remark in the introductory section of his relazione. As is the case with his editions of other relazioni, Albèri's edition of Navagero's report omits the entire introductory section. I have thus quoted from a copy originally belonging to the library of Leonardo Donà.

2. Paul F. Grendler, *Schooling in Renaissance Italy: Literacy and Learning, 1300–1600* (Baltimore: Johns Hopkins University Press, 1989), 43–46.

3. R. A. Houston, *Literacy in Early Modern Europe: Its Growth, Uses and Impact, 1500–1800*, 2nd ed. (London: Routledge, 2002), 142, 144–145.

4. As Grendler's figures reveal, female attendance at formal schools was virtually nonexistent. Only 0.2 percent of Venetian girls attended formal schools (compared to the more robust figure of 26 percent of boys), while 7 percent of girls and 6 percent of boys attended Schools of Christian Doctrine. Grendler, *Schooling in Renaissance Italy*, 46.

5. See Sara T. Nalle, "Literacy and Culture in Early Modern Castile," *Past & Present*, no. 125 (November 1989): 65–96; Peter Burke, "Oral Culture and Print Culture in Renaissance Italy," *ARV: Scandinavian Yearbook of Folklore* 54 (1998): 7–18; Houston, *Literacy in Early Modern Europe*, 141–171; Jonathan Barry, "Literacy and Literature in Popular Culture: Reading and Writing in Historical Perspective," in *Popular Culture in England, 1500–1800*, ed. Tim Harris (London: Macmillan, 1995), 69–94.

6. Armando Petrucci, "Scrittura, alfabetismo ed educazione grafica nella Roma del primo Cinquecento: Da un libretto di conti di Maddalena pizzicarola in Trastevere," *Scrittura e civiltà* 2 (1978): 184.

7. Richard Mackenney, *Tradesmen and Traders: The World of the Guilds in Venice and Europe, c. 1250–c. 1650* (Totowa, NJ: Barnes & Noble Books, 1987), 182–184, 193–194.

8. Isabelle Palumbo-Fossati, "Livres et lecteurs dans la Venise du XVI siècle," *Revue française d'histoire du livre* 54, no. 49 (1985): 488.

9. Peter Clark, "The Ownership of Books in England, 1560–1640: The Example of Some Kentish Townsfolk," in *Schooling and Society: Studies in the History of Education*, ed. Lawrence Stone (Baltimore: Johns Hopkins University Press, 1976), 95–111; Houston, *Literacy in Early Modern Europe*, 204; Lyndan Warner, *The Ideas of Man and Woman in Renaissance France: Print, Rhetoric, and Law* (London: Routledge, 2016), 179.

10. It should be noted that Zorzi's inventories cover a slightly longer period than do Palumbo-Fossati's, which may partly explain the consistently lower rates of book ownership he found across all segments of the population. While Zorzi's records begin in 1527, Palumbo-Fossati's cover only the second half of the century. Marino Zorzi, "La circolazione del libro a Venezia nel Cinquecento: Biblioteche private e pubbliche," *Ateneo veneto* 177 (1990): 129.

11. Sarah Gwyneth Ross, *Everyday Renaissances: The Quest for Cultural Legitimacy in Venice* (Cambridge, MA: Harvard University Press, 2016), 31.

12. Houston, *Literacy in Early Modern Europe*, 204–208.

13. The corresponding figures in Zorzi's study were 5 and 23 percent. Palumbo-Fossati, "Livres et lecteurs," 488, 504; Zorzi, "La circolazione del libro," 117–18, 126.

14. Palumbo-Fossati, "Livres et lecteurs," 498; Ross, *Everyday Renaissances*, 32.

15. Ross, *Everyday Renaissances*, 36–37.

16. Thirty percent of the nonpatrician merchant inventories examined by Palumbo-Fossati included books. Palumbo-Fossati, "Livres et lecteurs," 500–501.

17. On the methodological challenges involved in the study of cheap print, see David Rosenthal and Rosa Salzberg, "Rosa Salzberg: 'Print Saturated the Lives of Ordinary People,'" *Earlymoderncommunities* (blog), June 2011, http://earlymoderncommunities.org/home/interviews-2/rosa-salzberg-print-saturated-the-lives-of-ordinary-people/; Rosa Salzberg, *Ephemeral City: Cheap Print and Urban Culture in Renaissance Venice* (Manchester: Manchester University Press, 2014), 1–17.

18. Pietro Martire d'Anghiera, *De rebus Oceanicis et orbe novo decades tres* (Basel: Johann Bebel, 1533); Pedro Fernandes de Queirós, *Relatione d'vn memoriale che ha presentato a sva maesta il Capitano Pietro Ferdinando de Quir, sopra la popolanza scoperta nella quarta parte del mondo australe incognita, con le sue richezze, & fertilità scoperte per il medemo capitano.* (Milan: Padolfo Malatesta, 1611). Donà records his copy of d'Anghiera (including the printer and date of publication) in BCV, Donà, ms. 447/24, 16v. Donà's copy of Queirós's pamphlet is bound alongside his writings and notes on Spain and its empire in BCV, Donà, ms. 48, at c. 273.

19. Thomas N. Corns, "The Early Modern Search Engine: Indices, Title Pages, Marginalia and Contents," in *The Renaissance Computer: Knowledge Technology in the First Age of Print*, ed. Neil Rhodes and Jonathan Sawday (London: Routledge, 2000), 93–102; Brian Richardson, *Printing, Writers and Readers in Renaissance Italy* (Cambridge: Cambridge University Press, 1999), 129–135; Ann Blair, *Too Much to Know: Managing Scholarly Information before the Modern Age* (New Haven, CT: Yale University Press, 2010), 53–54.

20. On the sources of the prefatory material in the *Alcorano*, see Pier Mattia Tommasino, *The Venetian Qur'an: A Renaissance Companion to Islam*, trans. Sylvia Notini (Philadelphia: University of Pennsylvania Press, 2018), 24–42.

21. ASVe, Senato Terra, reg. 35, 129v.

22. Modena's writing on Jewish customs predates his reading of the *Alcorano* (or at least his surviving notes on the book). According to Adelman, the notebook containing Modena's reading notes on the *Alcorano* dates from the 1640s. Leon Modena, *Historia de gli riti hebraici* (Paris, 1637); Howard Adelman, "A Rabbi Reads the Qur'an in the Venetian Ghetto," *Jewish History* 26, no. 1–2 (May 2012): 125.

23. Adelman, "A Rabbi Reads the Qur'an," 134.

24. BNM, D 086D 095.

25. In his study of the Friulian miller Menocchio, another famous (likely) reader of the *Alcorano*, Carlo Ginzburg suggests that like Modena, Menocchio drew little apparent distinction between the text of the Qur'an and the accompanying paratextual material. Adelman, "A Rabbi Reads the Qur'an," 125–126, 131–134; Carlo Ginzburg, *The Cheese and the Worms: The Cosmos of a Sixteenth-Century Miller*, trans. John A. Tedeschi and Anne Tedeschi (Baltimore: Johns Hopkins University Press, 1980), 107.

26. Scholars have used a variety of terms to describe the sort of nonlinear reading discussed here, including *segmental* (Darnton), *nonserial* (Corns), and *consultation* (Blair). My preference is for "consultation" or "consultative" reading since it draws attention to the editorial interventions that facilitated and encouraged such reading. Robert Darnton,

"Extraordinary Commonplaces," *New York Review of Books* 47, no. 20 (December 2000): 82–87; Corns, "The Early Modern Search Engine"; Blair, *Too Much to Know*, 1–9.

27. Blair, *Too Much to Know*, 53.

28. The 1572 and 1590 editions list both Simone Gagliano and Girolamo Porro, the Paduan printer and engraver responsible for the isolario's island maps, as the publishers. All subsequent editions were published by Gagliano's heirs.

29. On the development of the isolario, see Marziano Guglielminetti, "Per un sottogenere della letteratura di viaggio: Gl'isolari fra quattro e cinquecento," in *La letteratura di viaggio dal Medioevo al Rinascimento: Generi e problemi* (Alessandria: Edizioni dell'orso, 1989), 107–117; George Tolias, "Isolarii, Fifteenth to Seventeenth Century," in *Cartography in the European Renaissance*, ed. David Woodward, trans. Timothy Cullen (Chicago: University Of Chicago Press, 2007), 23:63–84; Denis E. Cosgrove, *Apollo's Eye: A Cartographic Genealogy of the Earth in the Western Imagination* (Baltimore: Johns Hopkins University Press, 2001), 79–101; Bronwen Wilson, "Assembling the Archipelago: Isolarii and the Horizons of Early Modern Public Making," in *Making Space Public in Early Modern Europe: Geography, Performance, Privacy*, ed. Angela Vanhaelen and Joseph P. Ward (London: Routledge, 2013), 101–126; Anastasia Stouraiti, "Talk, Script and Print: The Making of Island Books in Early Modern Venice," *Historical Research* 86, no. 232 (May 2013): 207–229.

30. Tolias, "Isolarii," 264.

31. "Tute le isole del mondo . . . cum loro nomi antichi et moderni, siti, costumi, historie, fabule, et ogni altra cosa a quelle pertinenti ordinatamente ne li lor lochi poste." Rinaldo Fulin, ed., "Documenti per servire alla storia della tipografia veneziana," *Archivio veneto* 23 (1882): 206.

32. Benedetto Bordone, *Libro di Benedetto Bordone nel qual si ragiona de tutte l'isole del mondo con li lor nomi antichi & moderni, historie, favole, & modi del loro vivere, & in qual parte del mare stanno, & in qual parallelo & clima giacciono* (Venice: Niccolò Zoppino, 1528).

33. Tommaso Porcacchi, *L'isole piu famose del mondo* (Venice: Simone Galignani & Girolamo Porro, 1572), a2v; Tommaso Porcacchi, *L'isole piu famose del mondo* (Venice: Simone Galignani & Girolamo Porro, 1576), a5r.

34. Porcacchi, *L'isole* (1576), a5r.

35. Francesco Sansovino, ed., *Historia universale dell'origine, et imperio de' turchi* (Venice: Michel Bonelli, 1573), +7v, ++2r.

36. "Venice: June 1618, 16–30," in Calendar of State Papers Relating to English Affairs in the Archives of Venice, Volume 15, 1617–1619, ed. Allen B. Hinds (London: His Majesty's Stationery Office, 1909), 236–251, http://www.british-history.ac.uk/cal-state-papers/venice/vol15/pp236-251.

37. Filipo de Vivo, "How to Read Venetian Relazioni," *Renaissance and Reformation/Renaissance et réforme* 34, no. 1–2 (2011): 33.

38. On the history of the Inquisitors of State, see for a case study of the circulation of Venetian reports in England, see Paolo Preto, *I servizi segreti di Venezia* (Milan: Il Saggiatore, 1994), 59–74; for a case study of the circulation of Venetian reports in England, see Diego Pirillo, *The Refugee-Diplomat: Venice, England, and the Reformation* (Ithaca, NY: Cornell University Press, 2018), 118–141.

39. "La *relatione fatta dall'ambasciator Contarini venuto novamente d'Inghilterra,* la quale consiste in narratione delli costumi et qualità del Re et Regina et filioli, et sin dove si estendono le forze sue, et il sito dell'Isola et altre cose curiose che con dieci ducati la si haverà." Quoted in Armand Baschet, *Les archives de Venise: Histoire de la chancellerie secrète, le sènat, le cabinet des ministres, le Conseil des Dix, et les Inquisiteurs d'état dans leurs rapports avec la France* (Paris: Henri Plon, 1870), 353. Although Baschet suggests that the letter dates from July 1609, the fact that Francesco Contarini was not named as ambassador until September 1609 and only returned to Venice the following year makes 1610 a more plausible year for the letter. Gino Benzoni, "Contarini, Francesco," in *Dizionario biografico degli Italiani* 28 (1983), http://www.treccani.it/enciclopedia/francesco-contarini_(Dizionario-Biografico)/.

40. The list is undated, but Donà's mention of the availability of a relatively recent 1595 report on Savoy allows us to date the document to Donà's third and final embassy to Rome in 1598. BCV, Donà, ms. 216, 259v.

41. BCV, Donà, ms. 216, 259r–260r.

42. Franco Gaeta, introduction to *Relations des ambassadeurs vénitiens,* edited by Franco Gaeta (Paris: Éditions Klincksieck, 1969), vii. At the end of the sixteenth century, one Venetian ducat was worth approximately ten lire, or slightly less than the value of fifteen Roman paoli. It is possible that the discrepancy between the price of relazioni in Rome and that of the relazione mentioned by the agent was partly a function of the relative novelty of the reports. Although, as the Mantuan agent emphasized, Contarini's report on England was very recent, the reports listed by Donà were considerably older.

43. It is not possible to date all fifty-three of the relazioni. Donà does not himself list the dates of the relazioni, but he does list the state treated by each report and, in most cases, the name of the ambassador who wrote it. These two pieces of information are usually sufficient to date a given report. Where Donà does not list the author, however, it is impossible to assign a date to the relazione.

44. On the relationship between relazioni and news, see Mario Infelise, "News Networks between Italy and Europe," in *The Dissemination of News and the Emergence of Contemporaneity in Early Modern Europe,* ed. Brendan Maurice Dooley (Farnham, UK: Ashgate, 2010), 58–59; Mario Infelise, "Book Publishing and the Circulation of Information," in *A Companion to Venetian History, 1400–1797,* ed. Eric R. Dursteler (Leiden: Brill, 2013), 656.

45. Robert Mantran, "Venise, centre d'informations sur les turcs," in *Venezia, centro di mediazione tra Oriente e Occidente, secoli XV–XVI: Aspetti e problemi,* ed. Hans Georg Beck, Manoussos Manoussacas, and Agostino Pertusi (Florence: L. S. Olschki, 1977); Gino Benzoni, "Il 'farsi turco,' ossia l'ombra del rinnegato," in *Venezia e i Turchi: Scontri e confronti di due civilità,* ed. Anna Della Valle (Milan: Electra, 1985),123; Paolo Preto, "Turchi e la cultura veneziana del seicento," in *Il seicento,* vol. 2, Storia della cultura veneta 4 (Vicenza: N. Pozza, 1984), 91.

46. John-Paul Ghobrial, *The Whispers of Cities: Information Flows in Istanbul, London, and Paris in the Age of William Trumbull* (Oxford: Oxford University Press, 2013), 61–62.

47. Ghobrial, *Whispers of Cities,* 57–62.

48. The turn away from Venetian relazioni in the later seventeenth century was less pronounced in the Italian Peninsula than elsewhere. In the early eighteenth century, the

Venetian ambassador to Rome, Lorenzo Tiepolo, was still complaining of the existence of an open market for relazioni in the city. Particularly upsetting to him was the fact that the pool of available relazioni was not limited to older reports of merely historical interest but also included the most recent ambassadorial reports. Gaeta, "Introduction," vii.

49. For one of these exceptions, see Filippo de Vivo's discussion of the Venetian Inquisitors of State's investigation of Cesare Prata, a professional scribe accused of selling copies of ambassadorial relazioni. De Vivo, "How to Read Venetian Relazioni," 34.

50. ASVe, Miscellanea codici, Storia veneta, Genealogie Barbaro, vol. VII, b. 23, fol. 27.

51. BNM, Ital. VII 1573 (7970). On rhetoric and patrician education in Venice more generally, see Filippo de Vivo, "Rhetoric and Government in Sixteenth-Century Venice: Some Paradoxes," *The Italianist* 27 (2007): 192–195.

52. All of the members of the academy listed in the minute book were Venetian patricians. BNM, Ital. VII 705 (7955), 35v, 44v.

53. For example, in the entry dated January 27, 1601, the unnamed secretary noted the departure from the academy's usual activities, recording "q[uest]a sera non vi è stata consulta, ma io hò portato la relatione di Germania." BNM, Ital. VII 705 (7955), 35v.

54. Margherita Pasdera, "Bon, Ottaviano," in *Dizionario Biografico degli Italiani* 11 (1969), http://www.treccani.it/enciclopedia/ottaviano-bon_(Dizionario-Biografico)/; Bruno Basile, "Introduzione e nota bio-bibliografica," in *Il serraglio del gransignore*, ed. Bruno Basile (Rome: Salerno, 2002), 19–20.

55. Filipo de Vivo, *Information and Communication in Venice: Rethinking Early Modern Politics* (Oxford: Oxford University Press, 2009), 63–70.

56. De Vivo, *Information and Communication*, 66.

57. ASVe, Quarantia Criminale, b. 137, 22r, 25r.

58. ASVe, Quarantia Criminale, b. 137, 26v.

59. "[È] da credere, che sia occorso à me quello, che occorre à tutti in questi casi di relationi, come cose curiose et desiderate." ASVe, Quarantia Criminale, b. 137, 27r.

60. ASVe, Quarantia Criminale, b. 137, 26v, 49r.

61. "Io l'ho scritta per relatione, et quanto ad haverla fatta in terza persona, dico che dovendo rappresentare attione di due Amb[asciato]ri mi pareva che meglio potesse comparir così, che in prima persona." ASVe, Quarantia Criminale, b. 137, 26r.

62. "Questa scrittura che vi si mostra non ha forma di relatione, essendo scritta in terza persona, et come scritta per dar notitià al mondo, et non al principe di quel negotio, però non può restar satisfatta à giustitia di quello, che dite, ciò è di haverla fatta per presentare, come relatione." ASVe, Quarantia Criminale, b. 137, 25v–26r.

63. "La scrittura è stata data in mano non solo à senatori ma à persone, che non entrano in senato et che non sono neanco nel n[umer]o de Nobeli di questa Rep[ubbli]ca." ASVe, Quarantia Criminale, b. 137, 27r.

64. Francis Bacon famously listed print, gunpowder, and the compass as the three inventions that had most profoundly transformed the modern world. Closer to Venice, the Paduan jurist and antiquarian Guido Panciroli had also included print in his list of the most significant modern inventions that set the modern world apart from that of the ancients. Francis Bacon, *The New Organon*, ed. Lisa Jardine and Michael Silverthorne (Cambridge: Cambridge University Press, 2000), 100; Guido Panciroli, *Rerum memorabilium, iam olim*

deperditarum: & contrà recens atque ingeniosè inuentarum: Libri duo, trans. Heinrich Salmuth (Hamburg: Forsterianis, 1602), 2:278–288.

65. Venetian baili and ambassadors frequently commented in their relazioni on the absence of printed books in the Ottoman Empire. See, for example, the 1592 relazione of Lorenzo Bernardo. Eugenio Albèri, ed., *Relazioni degli ambasciatori veneti al senato* (Florence: Società editrice fiorentina, 1839–1863), 3rd ser., 2:364–365.

66. The major exception to the manuscript circulation of Venetian relazioni came at the end of the sixteenth century with the publication of an anthology of political and diplomatic writing from across the Italian states under the title of *Tesoro politico*. Although the various editions of the *Tesoro* certainly contained a great deal of ethnographic information, they framed the relazioni in terms of the insights they offered into affairs of state and not the customs of those states' inhabitants. On the history of the *Tesori politici*, see Simone Testa, "Alcune riflessioni sul Thesoro Politico (1598)," *Bibliothèque d'humanisme et renaissance* 64, no. 3 (January 2002): 679–687; Simone Testa, "Per una interpretazione del Thesoro politico (1589)," *Nuova rivista storica* 85 (2001): 347–362; Mario Infelise, *Prima dei giornali: Alle origini della pubblica informazione, secoli XVI e XVII* (Rome: Laterza, 2002), 157–158; a partial bibliography of the *Tesori politici* is offered in Tommaso Bozza, *Scrittori politici italiani dal 1550 al 1650, saggio di bibliografia* (Rome: Edizioni di "Storia e letteratura," 1949), 68–71.

67. Brian Richardson, *Manuscript Culture in Renaissance Italy* (Cambridge: Cambridge University Press, 2009); David McKitterick, *Print, Manuscript and the Search for Order, 1450–1830* (Cambridge: Cambridge University Press, 2003).

68. McKitterick, *Print, Manuscript and the Search for Order*, 30.

69. See, for example, Almut Höfert, "The Order of Things and the Discourse of the Turkish Threat: The Conceptualisation of Islam in the Rise of Occidental Anthropology in the Fifteenth and Sixteenth Centuries," in *Between Europe and Islam: Shaping Modernity in a Transcultural Space*, ed. Almut Höfert and Armando Salvatore (Brussels: Peter Lang, 2000), 52; Justin Stagl, *A History of Curiosity: The Theory of Travel, 1550–1800* (Chur, Switzerland: Harwood Academic Publishers, 1994), 52.

70. Richardson, *Manuscript Culture*, 2–10; Yaacob Dweck, *The Scandal of Kabbalah: Leon Modena, Jewish Mysticism, Early Modern Venice* (Princeton, NJ: Princeton University Press, 2011), 19–20; Brian Richardson, "A Scribal Publisher of Political Information: Francesco Marcaldi," *Italian Studies* 64, no. 2 (June 2009): 309–310.

71. Ross, *Everyday Renaissances*.

72. "Lascerò da parte la considerazione di molte cose, se bene curiose, niente di manco superflue, potendosi come cose ordinarie cavar da diversi libri e informazioni che vanno attorno." Albèri, *Relazioni*, p. ser. I, 4:409.

73. Martin Lowry, *The World of Aldus Manutius: Business and Scholarship in Renaissance Venice* (Ithaca, NY: Cornell University Press, 1979), 7–47.

74. BCV, Donà, ms. 146, 170r.

75. Quoted in Elisabeth G. Gleason, *Gasparo Contarini: Venice, Rome, and Reform* (Berkeley: University of California Press, 1993), 27.

76. On the broader phenomenon of Venetian patricians preserving state documents in family archives, see Dorit Raines, "L'archivio familiare strumento di formazione politica del patriziato veneziano," *Accademie e biblioteche d'Italia* 64 (1996): 5–36; Dorit Raines,

"L'arte di ben informarsi: Carriera politica e pratiche documentarie nell'archivio familiare di patrizi veneziani: I Molin di San Pantalon," in *Archivi nobiliari e domestici. Conservazione, metodologie di riordino e prospettive di ricerca storica. Atti del Convegno di Studi, Udine* (Udine: Forum, 2000), 1–21; Dorit Raines, "The Private Political Archives of the Venetian Patriciate: Storing, Retrieving and Recordkeeping in Fifteenth-Eighteenth Centuries," *Journal of the Society of Archivists* 32, no. 1 (2011): 131–142.

77. BCV, Donà, ms. 23, 177r–179v.

78. BCV, Donà, ms. 23, 108r–134v.

79. BCV, Donà, ms. 48, 274r–296r.

80. BCV, Donà, ms. 23, 111v.

81. BCV, Donà, ms. 23, 111v, 115r–v; Federico Seneca, *Il doge Leonardo Donà, la sua vita e la sua preparazione politica prima del dogado* (Padua: Antenore, 1959), 292, 297, 306, 313.

82. Paolo Preto, *Venezia e i turchi*, 2nd ed. (Rome: Viella, 2013), 141–142.

83. "Non permettono Turchi la stampa d[e] libri nel loro stato, la caggione alc[uni] dicevano esser p[er] non levar il viver a molti ch[e] dalle copie d[e]l scriver a mano vivono." BCV, Donà, ms. 23, 111v.

84. Albèri, *Relazioni*, 3rd ser., 2:364–.

85. *L'Alcorano di Macometto nel qual si contiene la dottrina, la vita, i costumi et le leggi sve* ([Venice]: Andrea Arrivabene, 1547), xxxiiir.

86. "Piu vero dicesi che sia p[er]che ad essendo lecito a p[er]sona alc[un]a ch[e] s'habbia mescolato con do[n]na . . . di toccare scrittura, dove sia nominato il nome di Dio et della lor legge, cio no[n] havrebbe luoco nelli stampati, ch[e] p[er] varii modi stampando et maneggiando li caratteri della stampa contravenireano al sudetto instituto." BCV, Donà, ms. 23, 111v.

87. On the multilingual nature of the Ottoman court, see Linda T. Darling, "Ottoman Turkish: Written Language and Scribal Practice, 13th to 20th Centuries," in *Literacy in the Persianate World: Writing and the Social Order*, ed. Brian Spooner and William L. Hanaway (Philadelphia: University of Pennsylvania Press, 2012), 171–195.

88. BCV, Donà, ms. 23, 76v.

89. Although, as a rule, sixteenth- and early seventeenth-century Venetians did not study Turkish, Arabic, or for that matter, Persian, there were some exceptions. Teodoro Dandolo, a native of Bukhara located today in Uzbekistan, worked as a Turkish-language tutor in the homes of several Venetians. Teodoro Dandolo and his trial before the Inquisition will be discussed in further detail in the following chapter. ASVe, Santo Ufficio, b. 72, proc. "Teodoro Persico, ovvero Teodolo Tartaro."

90. "A Costantinopoli non è dubbio che bisogna che sappino la lengua schiava, la greca et la turca, altramenti li huomeni sono come mutti, et si patiria estremamente, anzi non saria possibile andarvi nè starve nè far cosa alcuna." Marino Cavalli, *Informatione dell'offitio dell'ambasciatore: 1550*, ed. Tommaso Bertelè (Florence: L. S. Olschki, 1935), 85.

91. Marcella Grendler, "A Greek Collection in Padua: The Library of Gian Vincenzo Pinelli (1535–1601)," *Renaissance Quarterly* 33, no. 3 (1980): 386.

92. Angela Nuovo, "Private Libraries in Sixteenth-Century Italy," in *Early Printed Books as Material Objects*, ed. Bettina Wagner and Marcia Reed (Berlin: De Gruyter, 2010); Angela Nuovo, "'Et amicorum': Costruzione e circolazione del sapere nelle biblioteche private del cinquecento," in *Libri, biblioteche e cultura degli ordini regolari nell'Italia moderna*

attraverso la documentazione della Congregazione dell'indice, ed. Rosa Marisa Borraccini Verducci and Roberto Rusconi (Vatican City: Biblioteca apostolica Vaticana, 2006), 105–127; Angela Nuovo, "A proposito del carteggio Pinelli-Dupuy," *Biblioteca: Rivista di studi bibliografici* 1 (2002): 96–97; Zorzi, "La circolazione del libro," 151.

93. Paul F. Grendler, *The Roman Inquisition and the Venetian Press, 1540–1605* (Princeton, NJ: Princeton University Press, 1977), 288; Paolo Gualdo, *Vita Ioannis Vincentii Pinelli, patricii Genuensis, in qua studiosis bonarum artium, proponitur typus viri probi & eruditi* (Augsburg: Christophorus Mangus, 1607), 19; John-Mark Philo, "English and Scottish Scholars at the Library of Gian Vincenzo Pinelli (1565–1601)," *Renaissance and Reformation/Renaissance et réforme* 42, no. 2 (2019): 51–80.

94. Jaska Kainulainen, *Paolo Sarpi: A Servant of God and State* (Leiden: Brill, 2014), 40.

95. On the production of the two posthumous inventories of the library, see Grendler, "A Greek Collection in Padua," 391–392; Roberta Ferro, "Per la storia del fondo Pinelli all'Ambrosiana: notizie dalle lettere di Paolo Gualdo," in *Tra i fondi dell'Ambrosiana: Manoscritti italiani antichi e moderni*, ed. Marco Ballarini, Gennaro Barbarisi, Claudia Berra, and Giuseppe Frasso (Milan: Cisalpino, 2008), 1:274; Anna Maria Raugei, "Tra gli scaffali di una biblioteca italiana: Gian Vincenzo Pinelli e la letteratura francese sul Nuovo Mondo," in *La scoperta dell'America e le lettere francese*, ed. Enea Balmas (Milan: Cisalpino, 1992), 182–184.

96. In executing the Council of Ten's order, the council's secretaries also produced a partial inventory of Pinelli's manuscripts focused on his collection of Venetian state writings. "Inventario delle scritture, che si ritrovano nella presente Cassella, eccettuate alcune, che sono state rubbate fuori del studio del Signor Pinelli," ASVe, Archivio proprio Pinelli, n. 1, 1r–18v.

97. Raugei, "Tra gli scaffali di una biblioteca italiana," 182–183.

98. Marcella Grendler, "Book Collecting in Counter-Reformation Italy: The Library of Gian Vincenzo Pinelli (1535–1601)," *Journal of Library History* 16, no. 1 (January 1981): 144–146.

99. "Index librorum bibliothecae Pinellae secundum ordinem arcarum, in quibus libri inclusi sunt iuxta formam traditam ab Antonio Olgiato," BAM, B 311 suss., 6v, 9r, 33v, 131v, 135r. Curiously, neither of the inventories suggest that Pinelli owned an independent print edition of Ramberti's *Libri tre* (although the account was included in the 1564 Sansovino collection in his library). He did, however, own a manuscript copy of the account. Its current shelfmark is BAM, O 69 sup.

100. "Inventario della libreria di Gio. Vicenzo Pinelli ereditata da Francesco Pinelli," BNM, Ital. X 61 (6601), 5r, 9v–10v, 12r, 29c, 83r, 84r.

101. BAM, R 100 sup.

102. The estimate that Pinelli's library originally contained 10,000 printed titles is drawn from Angela Nuovo. The manuscript figure is drawn from the 1609 inventory of Pinelli's library. Despite having been drawn up *after* the losses at sea, this later inventory actually lists more manuscripts than the 1604 inventory—a reflection of its producers' more careful cataloging practices. BAM, B 311 suss; Nuovo, "Private Libraries in Sixteenth-Century Italy," 235.

103. Filippo Pigafetta and Duarte Lopez, *Relatione del reame di Congo et delle circonvicine contrade, tratta dalla scritti & ragionamenti di Odoardo Lopez Portoghese per Filippo Pigafetta*

(Rome: Bartolomeo Grassi, 1591). On Pigafetta's career, see Anne Wolff, *How Many Miles to Babylon? Travels and Adventures to Egypt and Beyond, 1300 to 1640* (Liverpool: Liverpool University Press, 2003), 90–93; Daria Perocco, "Pigafetta, Filippo," in *Dizionario biografico degli Italiani*, 2015, https://www.treccani.it/enciclopedia/filippo-pigafetta_(Dizionario-Biografico).

104. In a letter dated December 21, 1580, for example, Pigafetta offered Pinelli a copy of a Venetian relazione of "Portugal and the Indies," which he sent to Padua the following month. BAM, D 34 inf., 80r, 86v.

105. This was the case in an undated letter in which Pigafetta provided Pinelli with a summary of the bailo Giacomo Soranzo's relazione. Pigafetta also took the occasion to inform Pinelli of the Council of Ten's investigation of Soranzo for treason, which helps date the letter to 1584. BAM, D 34 inf., 32r–v.

106. ASVe, Consiglio di Dieci, Deliberazioni, Comuni, Filze 233 (August 31, 1601), 3r–v; "Della natura degli Inglesi," BAM, C 64 inf., 2r–9v.

107. Several of the non-Venetian diplomatic manuscripts originally from mazzo Q are currently bound in BAM, D 484 inf. These include anonymous accounts of the differences between Islam as practiced in the Persian and Ottoman Empires (75r–v) and of the early history of Islam (29r–30r).

108. Much of the original mazzo CC is currently bound in BAM, R 100 sup.

109. As one might expect, these mazzi were of special interest to the secretaries charged with seizing Venetian state documents from Pinelli's collection. As a result, a significant portion of Pinelli's Venetian materials are inventoried in ASVe, Consiglio di Dieci, Deliberazioni, Comuni, Filze 233 (August 31, 1601), 8r–10v.

110. "Qui vor[r]ei," Pinelli wrote, "che si descrivesse la citta del Cairo cioe di che lunghezza et larghezza, et circuito si trova, et che n[umer]o de genti può contenere et che vittovaglia vi si trova in abodanza." Pellegrino Brocardo, "Relatione del Cairo," BNM, Ital. XI 28 (6790), 273. Although most of the documents seized from Pinelli's library under order of the Council of Ten are currently held in Venice in the Archivio di Stato, a small portion of these, including Brocardo's journal, were eventually transferred to the Biblioteca Marciana. On the eighteenth-century transfer of the Council of Ten's manuscripts to the Marciana, see Marino Zorzi, *La libreria di San Marco: Libri, lettori, società nella Venezia dei dogi* (Milan: A. Mondadori, 1987), 296–298.

111. For example, Pinelli's entries under the headings "Heresies" and "The Bible" were in the vernacular. BAM, O 150 sup., 76v–78r, 207r–212r. On the relationship between commonplace books and sixteenth- and seventeenth-century Latin rhetorical education, see Ann Moss, *Printed Commonplace-Books and the Structuring of Renaissance Thought* (New York: Clarendon, 1996), 134–185; Ann Moss, "Commonplace-Rhetoric and Thought-Patterns in Early Modern Culture," in *The Recovery of Rhetoric: Persuasive Discourse and Disciplinarity in the Human Sciences*, ed. R. H. Roberts and James M. M. Good (Charlottesville: University of Virginia Press, 1993), 53; Zachary S. Schiffman, *The Birth of the Past* (Baltimore: Johns Hopkins University Press, 2011), 172–183.

112. BAM, O 150 sup., 62r–64v.

113. These topics are dealt with respectively in BAM, O 150 sup., 63r, 63v, 64r, 63v.

114. BAM, O 150 sup., 62r.

115. Pinelli's entry, which reads "quelli de la China co[n] dir una parola medesima q.n un alta voce, q.n con mezzana, q.n con bascia denotano tre cose diverse" bears a strong

resemblance to a letter in his collection written by Matteo Ricci in which Ricci discusses the difficulties of the Chinese language and the problems they posed to the missionary effort. The language, Ricci wrote, "è altra cosa, che ne la greca ne la todesca, quanto al parlare è tanto equivoca che tiene molte parole che significano piu di mille cose et alle volte non vi è altra differentia tra 'luna e l'ultra, che pron[n]unciarsi un voce piu alta ò piu bassa . . . e cosi quando parlano alle volte tra loro per potersi intendere scrivono quello che vogliono dire p[er]che nella l[ette]ra sono differenti l'una dal'altra." BAM, O 150 sup., 63v; Matteo Ricci, Letter to Martino de Fornari, February 13, 1583, BAM, R 100 sup., 266r.

116. Angela Caracciolo Aricò, "Il Nuovo Mondo e l'umanesimo: Imagini e miti dell'editoria venezia," in *L'impatto della scoperta dell'America nella cultura veneziana*, ed. Angela Caracciolo Aricò (Rome: Bulzoni, 1990), 25; John Huxtable Elliott, *The Old World and the New 1492–1650* (Cambridge: Cambridge University Press, 1970), 28–53.

117. For example, in response to a letter from Filippo Pigafetta dated March 19, 1584, in which Pigafetta mentioned several books that he had recently read on the New World, Pinelli drew up a detailed list of questions inquiring about the precise publication information for each of the editions. BAM, D 34 inf., 20r–22r. On Pinelli's collection of printed books on the Americas, see Raugei, "Tra gli scaffali di una biblioteca italiana."

118. BAM, O 150 sup., 64v.

119. BAM, O 150 sup., 62r–v.

120. "In Babilonia et in Venetia anticam[en]te si adunavano tutte le donne di marito ogni anno le belle s'incantavano le mediocri si casavano senza dinari, e le brutte delli dineri havute dalle belle si casavano." BAM, O 150 sup., 62r–v.

Chapter 5 Ethnography, the City, and the Place of Religious Minorities

1. Tellingly, Thomas included these observations in a subsection of his account of Venice titled "The Liberty of Strangers," a heading that he omitted from his accounts of all other Italian cities. William Thomas, *The Historie of Italie a Boke Excedyng Profitable to Be Redde: Because It Intreateth of the Astate of Many and Diuers Common Weales, How Thei Haue Ben, [and] Now Be Gouerned* (London, 1549), 85r–v.

2. Benjamin Ravid, "Between the Myth of Venice and the Lachrymose Conception of Jewish History: The Case of the Jews of Venice," in *The Jews of Italy: Memory and Identity*, ed. Bernard Dov Cooperman and Barbara Garvin (Bethesda: University Press of Maryland, 2000), 151–192.

3. On the sixteenth-century competition between Venice and the papal port of Ancona to attract Jews and other Ottoman merchants, see Benjamin J. Kaplan, *Divided by Faith: Religious Conflict and the Practice of Toleration in Early Modern Europe* (Cambridge, MA: Harvard University Press, 2007), 303–304; Benjamin Ravid, "Jews in International Trade: The Emergence of the Levantine and Ponentines," in *The Jews of Early Modern Venice*, ed. Robert C. Davis and Benjamin Ravid (Baltimore: Johns Hopkins University Press, 2001), 73–96; Benjamin Ravid, "The Legal Status of the Jewish Merchants of Venice, 1541–1638," *Journal of Economic History* 35, no. 1 (1975): 274–279.

4. For a comparative view of early modern restrictions on noblemen's direct involvement with commerce, see Jonathan Dewald, *The European Nobility, 1400–1800* (Cambridge: Cambridge University Press, 1996), 93–97.

5. Although citizenship was necessary for membership in Amsterdam's guilds, this could be purchased regardless of an individual's length of residency in the city. Maartje van Gelder, *Trading Places: The Netherlandish Merchants in Early Modern Venice* (Leiden: Brill, 2009), 36.

6. Luciano Pezzolo, "The Venetian Economy," in *A Companion to Venetian History, 1400–1797*, ed. Eric R. Dursteler (Leiden: Brill, 2013), 259.

7. Maria Fusaro, *Political Economies of Empire in the Early Modern Mediterranean: The Decline of Venice and the Rise of England 1450–1700* (Cambridge: Cambridge University Press, 2015), 175–177.

8. Brian Pullan, "The Occupations and the Investments of the Venetian Nobility in the Middle and Late Sixteenth Century," in *Renaissance Venice*, ed. John R. Hale (London: Rowman & Littlefield, 1973), 379–408; Ugo Tucci, "The Psychology of the Venetian Merchant in the Sixteenth Century," in *Renaissance Venice*, ed. J. R. Hale (London: Rowman & Littlefield, 1973).

9. Fusaro, *Political Economies of Empire*, 176; Pezzolo, "The Venetian Economy," 267–268.

10. Andrea Da Mosto, *L'Archivio di stato di Venezia: Indice generale, storico, descrittivo ed analitico* (Rome: Biblioteca d'arte editrice, 1937–1940), 1:196–197; Fusaro, *Political Economies of Empire*, 180–181.

11. Maria Borgherini-Scarabellin, *Il magistrato dei Cinque Savi alla Mercanzia dalla istituzione alla caduta della repubblica: Studio storico su documenti d'archivio* (Venice: Deputazione di storia patria, 1925), 16.

12. Borgherini-Scarabellin, *Il magistrato dei Cinque Savi*, 13.

13. E. Natalie Rothman, *Brokering Empire: Trans-imperial Subjects between Venice and Istanbul* (Ithaca, NY: Cornell University Press, 2012), 198–204; Ennio Concina, *Fondaci: Architettura, arte, e mercatura tra Levante, Venezia, e Alemagna* (Venice: Marsilio, 1997), 229–230, 238–239.

14. ASVe, Cinque Savi alla Mercanzia (hereafter VS), ser. I, b. 187, fasc. 1 (March 29, 1621 and May 25, 1621).

15. Benjamin Ravid, "'Kosher Bread' in Baroque Venice," *Italia* 6, no. 1–2 (1987): 22.

16. ASVe, VS, ser. II, b. 62, fasc. 165 (August 9, 1594 and December 18, 1596).

17. ASVe, VS, ser. II, b. 62, fasc. 165 (December 18, 1596).

18. For an interpretation of this episode as an instance of minority communities strategically claiming linguistic incompetence to secure collective privileges, see Rothman, *Brokering Empire*, 195.

19. Quoted in Rothman, *Brokering Empire*, 195.

20. Shlomo Simonsohn, "La condizione giuridica degli Ebrei nell'Italia centrale e settentrionale (secoli XII–XVI)," in *Gli Ebrei in Italia*, ed. Corrado Vivanti (Turin: Einaudi, 1996), 1:103; Robert Bonfil, *Jewish Life in Renaissance Italy*, trans. Anthony Oldcorn (Berkeley: University of California Press, 1994), 89; Bernard Cooperman, "Venetian Policy toward Levantine Jews and Its Broader Italian Context," in *Gli Ebrei a Venezia: Secoli XIV–XVIII*, ed. Gaetano Cozzi (Milan: Edizioni Comunità, 1987), 65–84. For a contemporary condotta offering similar protections for the observance of rites and customs, see the 1553 Ancona charter edited in Moritz Stern, *Urkundliche Beiträge über die Stellung*

der Päpste zu den Juden: mit Benutzung des päpstlichen Geheimarchivs zu Rom (Kiel: Fiencke, 1893), 111–112.

21. The relevant article of the charter reads in its entirety: "L'anderà parte, che per anni dieci prossimi venturi sia concesso salvo condotto à qualunque Ebreo Mercante Levantino et Ponentino di poter venir ad habitar in questa nostra città con le loro famiglie, star, et in esse praticar liberamente, portando la sessa, over baretta gialla da Ebrei, et facendo la sua habitazione nel ghetto novo con li altri Ebrei, nel qual possano far, et usar li loro riti, precetti, cerimonie, et tenere sinagoghe secondo l'uso loro, sicuri per detto tempo di non esser molestati p[er] causa di religione da qual si voglia Magistrato." Benjamin Ravid, "The First Charter of the Jewish Merchants of Venice, 1589," *AJS Review* 1 (1976): 220.

22. ASVe, VS, ser. II, b. 62, fasc. 165 (December 18, 1596).

23. ASVe, VS, ser. I, b. 137, 30v (March 4, 1588).

24. "Ogn'altro giorno vanno procurando essi Ebrei cose nove." ASVe, VS, ser. II, b. 62, fasc. 165 (December 18, 1596).

25. "Sotto pretesto di quelle loro cerimonie non osservate dalli altri Ebrei di questa Città, e pur vivono sotto una medema Legge, vanno procurando d'introdurre, che da questo deputato sia dispensato, et venduto à loro modo il Pane sop[radet]to, et che per questa via sia fatta una nova Pistoria in esso Ghetto." ASVe, VS, ser. II, b. 62, fasc. 165 (December 18, 1596).

26. ASVe, VS, ser. II, b. 62, fasc. 165 (December 18, 1596).

27. ASVe, VS, ser. II, b. 62, fasc. 165 (December 18, 1596).

28. On the introduction of sumptuary laws governing Jews in other Italian cities, see Diane Owen Hughes, "Distinguishing Signs: Ear-Rings, Jews and Franciscan Rhetoric in the Italian Renaissance City," *Past & Present*, no. 112 (1986): 3–59; Flora Cassen, *Marking the Jews in Renaissance Italy: Politics, Religion, and the Power of Symbols* (Cambridge: Cambridge University Press, 2017).

29. There had also been an attempt in Venice to require distinguishing signs for Jewish women, although, as with the early legislation aimed at Jewish men, the law did not seem to have been enforced. In 1443, at a time in which Jewish men were distinguished by a yellow badge attached to their clothing, the Venetian Senate passed a law requiring Jewish women to wear the same badge. Benjamin Ravid, "From Yellow to Red: On the Distinguishing Head-Covering of the Jews of Venice," *Jewish History* 6, no. 1 (1992): 182–183.

30. Carla Boccato, "Processi ad Ebrei nell'archivio degli ufficiali al Cattaver a Venezia," *Rassegna mensile di Israel* 41, no. 3 (1975): 167; Ravid, "From Yellow to Red," 179–182.

31. Mosto, *L'Archivio di stato di Venezia*, 101.

32. ASVe, VS, ser. II, b. 62, fasc. 163 (December 15, 1609).

33. ASVe, VS, ser. I, b. 142, 31r–32r (September 19, 1607).

34. "Nelli privilege delle loro condotte vien dechiarito, che debbano portare la sessa ò baretta Giala p[er] distinguerli dalli Christiani, ne vien giustificato che ditta sessa debba esser più vergata, o non vergata, non facendo questo effetto alcuno, ò alterat[io]ne ma restano con dette sesse distinti et conosciuti dalli Christiani." ASVe, VS, ser. I, b. 146, 111v–112r.

35. "Per relat[ion]e del Nores, dragomano, et de Persiani che s'attrovano in questa città, habbiamo che li hebrei persiani nel loro paese portano le sesse vergate in capo, et pare l'anno pass[at]o sono capitati in questa Città hebrei persiani al n[ume]ro di X.ci con loro

m[ercan]tie, che hanno sempre portato in capo le sesse vergate: si che parendo à noi, che questa ritentione sia senza delitto." ASVe, VS, ser. I, b. 146, 112r–112v.

36. Rothman, *Brokering Empire*, 174–175, 185–186.

37. Rothman has published a transcription and translation of De Nores's 1594 petition requesting an appointment as public dragoman. In it, he lists among his qualifications his extensive period of residence in the Ottoman Empire and Persia and the familiarity with the customs of those nations that he gained during his time as a slave. Rothman, *Brokering Empire*, 260–263.

38. Although in contemporary English the term *Mohammedanism* is at best awkward and at worst offensive, I have opted to retain it. As will become apparent, the charge of maomettanismo encompassed a wide variety of behaviors, ranging from clandestine conversion to Islam, to uttering words in praise of Mohammed, to failing to observe regular Catholic abstentions from the consumption of meat. It was not fully coextensive with crypto-Muslim belief and practice. I have used the anglicization of maomettanismo to foreground the elasticity of the charge in a way that more familiar terms would not.

39. From 1547 to 1585, out of a total of 1,229 cases, the Venetian tribunal dealt with 717 cases of Lutheranism but only 34 cases of Judaizing and 10 cases of Mohammedanism. John Tedeschi and William Monter, "Toward a Statistical Profile of the Italian Inquisitions, Sixteenth to Eighteenth Centuries," in *The Prosecution of Heresy: Collected Studies on the Inquisition in Early Modern Italy* (Binghamton, NY: Medieval and Renaissance Texts and Studies, 1986), 105.

40. Although Venice had technically had an inquisitorial office since the thirteenth century, it was moribund for a century before its reestablishment. For an overview of the sixteenth-century reestablishment of the Venetian Inquisition, see Andrea Del Col, *L'inquisizione in Italia: Dal XII al XXI secolo* (Milan: Oscar Mondadori, 2006), 341–347; Paul F. Grendler, *The Roman Inquisition and the Venetian Press, 1540–1605* (Princeton, NJ: Princeton University Press, 1977), 35–42.

41. On the negotiation of the Venetian Inquisition's mixed constitution, see Pullan, *The Jews of Europe and the Inquisition of Venice, 1550–1670* (Oxford: Blackwell, 1983), 26–44.

42. Nicholas Davidson, "Rome and the Venetian Inquisition," *The Journal of Ecclesiastical History* 39 (1988): 23–34.

43. Carlo Ginzburg, "The Inquisitor as Anthropologist," in *Clues, Myths, and the Historical Method*, trans. John Tedeschi and Anne Tedeschi (Baltimore: Johns Hopkins University Press, 1989), 156–164. On the monologic nature of inquisitorial testimony, see also Andrea Del Col, "I criteri dello storico nell'uso delle fonti inquisitoriali moderne," in *L'inquisizione romana: Metodologia delle fonti e storia istituzionale*, ed. Andrea Del Col and Giovanna Paolin (Trieste: Edizioni Università di Trieste, 2000), 51–72; Gian Paolo Gri, "L'Uso delle fonti inquisitoriali in ambito demo-anthropologico," in *L'Inquisizione romana: metodologia delle fonti e storia istituzionale*, ed. Andrea Del Col and Giovanna Paolin (Trieste: Edizioni Università di Trieste, 2000), 73–89.

44. Anne Jacobson Schutte, "Un inquisitore al lavoro: Fra Marino da Venezia e l'Inquisizione veneziana," in *I francescani in Europa tra Riforma e Controriforma* (Perugia: Università degli studi di Perugia, 1987), 173.

45. "Non est hereticus, qui male vivit, sed qui male credit." Diego Simancas, *De catholicis institutionibus* (Rome, 1575), 228.

46. "Exteriora demonstrant interiora, & per ea iudicantur." Pietro Vendramin, ed., *Repertorium inquisitorium pravitatis haereticae* (Venice: Damianum Zenarum, 1575), 327. On the publication history of the work, see Thomas F. Mayer, *The Roman Inquisition: A Papal Bureaucracy and Its Laws in the Age of Galileo* (Philadelphia: University of Pennsylvania Press, 2013), 164; Andrea Errera, "Repertorium inquisitorum," in *Dizionario storico dell'Inquisizione*, ed. Adriano Prosperi (Florence: Scuola normale superiore, 2010), 3:1313.

47. Del Col, *L'inquisizione in Italia*, 770; Andrea Errera, *Processus in causa fidei: L'evoluzione dei manuali inquisitoriali nei secoli XVI–XVIII e il manuale inedito di un inquisitore perugino* (Bologna: Monduzzi, 2000), 86–87; Edward Peters, "Editing Inquisitors' Manuals in the Sixteenth Century: Francisco Peña and the Directorium Inquisitorum of Nicholas Eymeric," *Library Chronicle* 40 (1974): 95–107.

48. Although Peña, like Eymeric, was a Spaniard, he worked in Rome from 1573 and wrote his commentary in the context of the Roman rather than the Spanish Inquisition. Errera, *Processus in causa fidei*, 119, 134.

49. Following the establishment of the Roman Inquisition, the *Directorium inquisitorum* went through four editions by the end of the sixteenth century followed by another three editions in the seventeenth century, one of which was heavily abridged. The final edition was published in Rome in 1628.

50. Nicolau Eymerich and Francesco Peña, *Directorium inquisitorum* (Venice: Marcum Antonium Zalterium, 1607), 440–441.

51. "Reiudaiza[n]tes haeretici, seu co[n]versi de iudaismo, & reversi mente & secrete ad Iudaismu[m], huiusmodi signis exterioribus dignoscu[n]tur; Raro Ecclesia[m] intrant; Iudaismu[m] sive locum, in quo mora[n]tur Iudaei, frequentant; Iudaeis se associant; a Christianorum consortio se elongant; cum Iudaeis in eoru[m] festivitatibus, ubi co[m]mode possunt, comedu[n]t; carnes porcinas no[n] edunt; diebus veneris carnes comedu[n]t; sabbatu[m] colunt; diebus Dominicis secrete in domibus suis operibus servilibus se exponent." Nicolau Eymerich and Francesco Peña, *Directorium inquisitorum* (Rome, 1585), 474.

52. Eymerich and Peña, *Directorium Inquisitorum* (1585), 474.

53. On the role of fama in the Roman Inquisition, see Jane K. Wickersham, *Rituals of Prosecution: The Roman Inquisition and the Prosecution of Philo-Protestants in Sixteenth-Century Italy* (Toronto: University of Toronto Press, 2012), 94–95; Mayer, *The Roman Inquisition*, 155–168; Thomas F. Mayer, *The Roman Inquisition on the Stage of Italy, c. 1590–1640* (Philadelphia: University of Pennsylvania Press, 2014), 6–7.

54. Pullan, *The Jews of Europe*, 102.

55. "Ho inteso dire per detto generale che il detto Pacifico è hebreo fatto christiano." Pier Cesare Ioly Zorattini, ed., *Processi del S. Uffizio di Venezia contro Ebrei e giudaizzanti*, Storia dell'ebraismo in Italia: Studi e testi (Florence: L. S. Olschki, 1980–1997), 6:121.

56. The record of the tribunal's questioning of Scarpogiato reveals that although the tribunal explicitly asked him about Pacifico's reputation in the neighborhood, Scarpogiato was unprompted in his reflections on observing Pacifico on Saturdays. "Io ho osservato et li ho posto mente che venere, venendo il sabbato alli venti hore et per tutto il sabbato non lavora che egli non faceva cosa alcuna né manco vendeva le sue merce né lavorava, essendo solito gli altri giorni lavorare et fare li corali falsi." Ioly Zorattini, *Processi*, 6:121.

57. The original tenancy agreement, dated November 22, 1584, was copied into the trial record. Ioly Zorattini, *Processi*, 7:99–100; Fusaro, *Political Economies of Empire*, 226.

58. On the parochial nature of Venetian gossip and information sharing, see Alexander Cowan, "Gossip and Street Culture in Early Modern Venice," *Journal of Early Modern History* 12, no. 3 (2008): 313–333.

59. "Interrogata se lei cognosce nella sua contrada alcuno che viva alla lutherana o marana, respondit." Ioly Zorattini, *Processi*, 7:81.

60. "Io non li ho mai visto andar in chiesa né mancho quando passano da la giesia a cavarse la beretta et, perché io haveva inteso dir che erano Marani dava a mente quando sonava l'Ave Maria, né mai ghe ho visto né inzenochiarse né cavarse la beretta né dir l'Ave Maria. Et a questo ci ho advertito più volte." Ioly Zorattini, *Processi*, 7:81.

61. "Interrogata se lei sa che li ditti Philippi habino o tengano in casa inmagini del Signor, de la Madona o d'altri santi, respondit: Caro signor, io ho inteso a dir che i non tengono imagine né del Signor né de la Madona né di santi, et so che, quando i sono venuti a star là, in su la piatta de le robbe non ghe era alcuna imagine né de la Madonna né di santi perché mi le haveria visti et per la contrada se dice che in casa loro non ci è imagine de sorte nissuna perché mi le haveria visti." Ioly Zorattini, *Processi*, 7:83.

62. "Interrogata, chi li fano la cusina alli ditti Philippi, respondit: Quella mora che i ha in casa et quando portano polli a casa sempre li portano vivi et il venere portano polli assai ma de la carne non si puol veder perché i porta la robba in quelle so sportelle." Ioly Zorattini, *Processi*, 7:83.

63. During her appearance before the tribunal, Dominica also reported that the Filippi's former servant had told her that he left the family's service because they were Jews who ate meat at prohibited times. She revealed this in response to a direct question from the tribunal about whether the family ate meat on Fridays and Saturdays. "Interrogata se lei sa in che modo vivano li detti Philippi in casa loro, se manzano carne de venere o de sabbado, respondit: Mi non son stata mai in casa sua ma ho ben inteso a dir da un loro garzon che gia 3 o 4 mesi in circa è stato con loro et, essendoli stato tolto un sechio da trazer aqua a detti suoi patroni, incolpavano el putto predetto et lui scampo via et quando el fu scampà via el diseva che i sono pezo che Zudei che manzavano la carne el venere et il sabbato." Ioly Zorattini, *Processi*, 7:83.

64. The question of ritual slaughter was also raised in a 1555 investigation for Judaizing. In the earlier case, however, it was introduced by members of the tribunal. While questioning Elena de Freschi Olivi, who was suspected of Judaizing, members of the tribunal asked her if she had ever slaughtered chickens in the Jewish manner. Ioly Zorattini, *Processi*, 1:195–196.

65. "All'incontro della mia habitation de là del canal ve habitano alcuni che per inteso a dir son Marani. Io non li conosco de nome ma, se il vedesse, li conosceria di facia, massime quello che è capo de la casa. Io ho advertito più volte che'l venere da sera come è verso le 23 hore in circa acendere alcune lume che hano 7 o 8 boche et fano 7 o 8 lumi et inmediate serano le finestre ma, con tuto che serano li veri, perché non ci sono schuri li lumi si veggono fino alla matina e il giorno non si può così vedere ma el sabbado da sera si vede che ardeno ancor essi lumi. Et questi lumi non gli ho visti nelli altri giorni de la settimana ma solamente el venere a sera per fino al sabbato da sera. Et ho advertito anco che nella casa di questi ch'io li ho per mercanti, li altri giorni de la settimana ci praticano Christiani et Hebrei

ma il sabbato non ci praticano Christiani ma solamente Hebrei, massimamente donne che vano a visitare le donne de la casa." Ioly Zorattini, *Processi*, 7:84–85.

66. "Et ad interrogationem dixit: in casa del mio patron non si acendono lumi per la festa." Ioly Zorattini, *Processi*, 7:86.

67. It is unclear from Guato's testimony whether he was identifying a menorah or Shabbat candles. In his edition of the trial dossier, Pier Cesare Ioly Zorattini suggests that Guato was likely referring to a menorah. Ioly Zorattini, *Processi*, 7:84.

68. For an overview of rates of literacy and formal schooling in sixteenth-century Venice, see Grendler, *Schooling in Renaissance Italy*, 43–46.

69. Unlike some other Italian cities, Venice never established a Monte di Pietà, making Jewish pawn broking an essential source of credit for the poor. Benjamin Ravid, "Venice and Its Minorities," in *A Companion to Venetian History, 1400–1797*, ed. Eric R. Dursteler (Leiden: Brill, 2013), 480–481; David Joshua Malkiel, "The Ghetto Republic," in *The Jews of Early Modern Venice*, ed. Robert C. Davis and Benjamin Ravid (Baltimore: Johns Hopkins University Press, 2001), 118–119; Benjamin Ravid, "The Venetian Government and the Jews," in *The Jews of Early Modern Venice*, ed. Robert C. Davis and Benjamin Ravid (Baltimore: Johns Hopkins University Press, 2001), 3–14.

70. Ravid, "The First Charter of the Jewish Merchants of Venice, 1589," 220.

71. Benjamin Ravid, "Christian Travelers in the Ghetto of Venice: Some Preliminary Observations," in *Between History and Literature: Studies in Honor of Isaac Barzilay*, ed. Stanley Nash (Bnei Brak, Israel: Hakibbutz Hameuchad, 1997), 111–117; Abraham Melamed, "English Travelers and Venetian Jewish Scholars: The Case of Simone Luzzatto and James Harrington," in *Gli Ebrei e Venezia: Secoli XIV–XVIII*, ed. Gaetano Cozzi (Milan: Edizioni Comunità, 1987), 512. For a broader discussion of the Venetian ghetto and the Christian gaze, see Dana E. Katz, *The Jewish Ghetto and the Visual Imagination of Early Modern Venice* (Cambridge: Cambridge University Press, 2017).

72. For broader examinations of cosmopolitanism in early modern Europe, see Margaret C. Jacob, *Strangers Nowhere in the World: The Rise of Cosmopolitanism in Early Modern Europe* (Philadelphia: University of Pennsylvania Press, 2006); Alison Games, *The Web of Empire: English Cosmopolitans in an Age of Expansion, 1560–1660* (Oxford: Oxford University Press, 2008).

73. Here, I draw on Benjamin Kaplan's distinction between tolerance (seen as an ideal) and toleration (seen as a practice of religious coexistence). It should be noted that historians have offered varying definitions of tolerance. In contrast with Kaplan, for example, who places tolerance in the realm of ideas, Alexandra Walsham treats tolerance as a form of behavior. Kaplan, *Divided by Faith*, 8–11; Alexandra Walsham, *Charitable Hatred: Tolerance and Intolerance in England, 1500–1700* (Manchester: Manchester University Press, 2006), 29.

74. For a discussion of the 1589 charter and a comparison of Venetian and papal policy regarding the reversion of new Christians, see Benjamin Ravid, "Venice, Rome, and the Reversion of New Christians to Judaism: A Study in Ragione di Stato," in *L'identità dissimulata: Giudaizzanti iberici nell'Europa cristiana dell'età moderna*, ed. Pier Cesare Ioly Zorattini (Florence: L. S. Olschki, 2000), 151–193.

75. Tedeschi and Monter, "Toward a Statistical Profile of the Italian Inquisitions," 105.

76. Christopher F. Black, *The Italian Inquisition* (New Haven, CT: Yale University Press, 2009), 60–63.

77. ASVe, Santo Ufficio (hereafter SU), b. 35, proc. "Giorgio." On the use of summary procedure by the tribunals of the Roman Inquisition, see Elena Brambilla, "Spontanea comparizione (Procedura sommaria)," in *Dizionario storico dell'Inquisizione*, ed. Adriano Prosperi (Florence: Scuola normale superiore, 2010), 3:1474–1475.

78. For a discussion of some of the broad outlines of the biographies of Muslim converts who appeared before the Venetian tribunal, see Georgios Plakotos, "Christian and Muslim Converts from the Balkans in Early Modern Venice: Patterns of Social and Cultural Mobility and Identities," in *Developing Cultural Identity in the Balkans: Convergence vs. Divergence*, ed. Raymond Detrez and Pieter Plas (New York: Peter Lang, 2005), 125–145.

79. This phenomenon was particularly evident in situations where converts could not communicate effectively in either Italian or Latin and thus required the assistance of an interpreter during their appearance before the tribunal. In such instances, a given interpreter would often interpret for multiple converts who needed his services on the same day. See, for example, ASVe, SU, b. 69, proc. "Fiorenza Podocataro" and "Demetrio Bagga" (October 22, 1592); ASVe, SU, b. 87, proc. "Giorgio Sigismondo Suarz" and "Jacopo Copoman" (January 15, 1630).

80. ASVe, SU, b. 57, proc. "Mustafa Balirai."

81. Bronwen Wilson, "Reflecting on the Turk in Late Sixteenth-Century Venetian Portrait Books," *Word & Image* 19, no. 1–2 (January 2003): 48; Maria Pia Pedani, *The Ottoman-Venetian Border (15th–18th Centuries)*, trans. Mariateresa Sala (Venice: Edizioni Ca' Foscari, 2017), 103–104.

82. Carlo Ranzo, *Relatione di Carlo Ranzo gentil'hvomo di Vercelli d'vn viaggio fatto da Venetia in Constantinopoli: Ritornato, che fù dalla battaglia Nauale assai curioso per i molti accidenti occorsi, oue si possono imparare stratagemme di guerra, humori d'huomini, e diuersita di genti, & di paesi* (Turin: Fratelli Cavaleri, 1616), 6.

83. ASVe, SU, b. 89, proc. "Giuseppe Struppiolo."

84. The literature on the relationship between dress and religious identity in the early modern world is now vast. For discussions particular to the early modern Mediterranean, see Giuseppina Minchella, *Frontiere aperte: Musulmani, Ebrei e Cristiani nella Repubblica di Venezia* (Rome: Viella, 2014), 25–26; Wilson, "Reflecting on the Turk in Late Sixteenth-Century Venetian Portrait Books"; Bronwen Wilson, *The World in Venice: Print, the City, and Early Modern Identity* (Toronto: University of Toronto Press, 2005), 70–132; Linda Colley, "Going Native, Telling Tales: Captivity, Collaborations and Empire," *Past & Present*, no. 168 (2000): 178; Hughes, "Distinguishing Signs"; Olivia Remie Constable, *To Live like a Moor: Christian Perceptions of Muslim Identity in Medieval and Early Modern Spain*, ed. Robin Vose (Philadelphia: University of Pennsylvania Press, 2018), 15–62.

85. "Mi son apogliato habito di Christiano vestendomi l'habito Turchescho, facendomi radere et ponendomi el Turbante in testa et entrato in nave per andare in Constantinopoli: et essendo constituito avanti questo S[an]to Tribunale, hò con la bocca mia piu volte rinegato la fede di Christo dicendo che sempre son stato Turcho: della qual cosa io me son dolente e penteso et me domando p[er]dono, à Dio et à questo S[an]to Officio et assolutione dall'Apostasia dalla fede." ASVe, SU, b. 57, proc. "Mustafa Balirai."

86. "Ei dictum che li schiavi vanno rasi e lui ha la barba molto grande, e che essendo venuto con barba vestito da Franco, mostra che lui sia fatto christiano." The questioner's language here is itself worth noting since it highlights the way in which members of the

tribunal were willing to modulate and reframe their questions depending on the background of the accused. The category of "Frankish" dress was one that had little resonance in Venice but would certainly have carried greater significance for a man like Balirai who was staying in Venice only temporarily and whose life had unfolded against a broader Mediterranean backdrop. ASVe, SU, b. 57, proc. "Mustafa Balirai."

87. "Respondit: Io non servivo p[er] schiavo in galera, ma servivo in casa." ASVe, SU, b. 57, proc. "Mustafa Balirai."

88. "Int[erogatu]s come potrà provare che egli sia turco et non [christ]iano, havendo li segni et l'habito da [christ]iano." The rosary and cross were found among Bartolomeo's effects when he was arrested. ASVe, SU, b. 88, proc. "Fra Giovanni Fecondo, Giovanni Lopes, Bartolomeo Derera" (questioning of Bartolomeo Derera, May 24, 1631).

89. On early modern conceptions of Granadine Moriscos as a nation, see Antonio Feros, *Speaking of Spain: The Evolution of Race and Nation in the Hispanic World* (Cambridge, MA: Harvard University Press, 2017), 94–104.

90. "Tutti li Granatini caminano così, perche andando in altro modo sarebbero castigati, et alcuni de nostri portano adosso reliquie, et sentono messa le d[o]meniche per forza per parer [christ]iani. Io non sono [christ]iano. . . . Non so che cosa sia fede [christ]iana. È vero che li turchi granatini sono astretti à battezzarse, ma usano questo inganno, che mandano un fig[lio]lo ad esser battezzatto più volte con fingerlo che sia il fig[lio]lo non battizzato. Et mia madre mi disse che io non son stato mai battezzato, ma che lei usò questo inganno di mandar un altro fig[lio]lo à battezzarse in luogo mio." In response to this last claim, an unnamed member of the tribunal sharply reproached Derea, stating that it was not credible that Spanish priests would show such negligence in their duties that they would fail to realize that they had baptized the same child multiple times. It should be noted that since the presence of an interpreter was not recorded, we can assume that Derera spoke Italian well enough to give testimony before the tribunal. ASVe, SU, b. 88, proc. "Fecondo, Lopes, Derera" (questioning of Bartolomeo Derera, May 24, 1631).

91. "Int[erogatu]s se esso sia circonciso. R[espondi]t S[igno]ri nò. Niun Moisco è tagliato ne circunciso, perche vivono tutti come [christ]iani. Quelli Morischi che restano [christ]iani vivevano come [Christ]iani." ASVe, SU, b. 88, proc. "Fecondo, Lopes, Derera" (questioning of Bartolomeo Derera, May 24, 1631).

92. "Io hò detto di haver vissuto da [christ]iano come per ceremonia nel modo che li altri Granatini vivevano." ASVe, SU, b. 88, proc. "Fecondo, Lopes, Derera" (May 27, 1631).

93. ASVe, SU, b. 88, proc. "Fecondo, Lopes, Derera" (June 17, 1631).

94. "Ti lasciasti indurre ad entrare nella loro Casa [i.e., the Fondaco dei Turchi], ove asserendogli di esser Turco Granatino, et chiamati per nome Mustaffa, et voler andare in Constantinopoli à vivere alla Turchesca, hai consentito che ti sia rasa la testa con lasciarti nel mezzo il zaffo all'usanza de Turchi." ASVe, SU, b. 88, proc. "Fecondo, Lopes, Derera" (June 17, 1631).

95. Rothman, *Brokering Empire*, 30; Borgherini-Scarabellin, *Il magistrato dei Cinque Savi*, 54–55.

96. Rothman, *Brokering Empire*, 29–60.

97. Rothman, *Brokering Empire*; E. Natalie Rothman, "Interpreting Dragomans: Boundaries and Crossings in the Early Modern Mediterranean," *Comparative Studies in Society and History* 51, no. 4 (September 2009): 771–800; E. Natalie Rothman, "Dragomans

and 'Turkish Literature': The Making of a Field of Inquiry," *Oriente moderno* 93, no. 2 (January 2013): 390–421; Stephen Ortega, "Across Religious and Ethnic Boundaries: Ottoman Networks and Spaces in Early Modern Venice," *Mediterranean Studies* 18, no. 1 (December 2009): 66–89; Stephen Ortega, *Negotiating Transcultural Relations in the Early Modern Mediterranean: Ottoman-Venetian Encounters* (Farnham, UK: Ashgate, 2014).

98. Giorgio Rota, *Under Two Lions: On the Knowledge of Persia in the Republic of Venice (ca. 1450–1797)* (Vienna: Österreichischen Akademie der Wissenschaften, 2009), 21.

99. ASVe, SU, b. 72, proc. "Teodoro Persico" (January 20, 1621 and July 27, 1624).

100. It is unclear whether Benedetto had received the patronage of a member of the patrician Soriano family and hence adopted the Soriano family name (in the same way that Teodoro had adopted the Dandolo name) or whether Soriano was a toponymic surname.

101. "Int[erogatu]s, respondit. . . . Mi tengo che lui sia poco buon [Christ]iano, perche con li turchi si fa turco, con li hebrei si fa hebreo, et con li [Christ]iani si fa christiano, et così fanno tutti li tartari nel pratticare." ASVe, SU, b. 72, proc. "Teodoro Persico," 7v (June 30, 1620).

102. "Mi credo che facesse questo per sprezzo della n[ost]ra fede, perche lui p[rim]a era . . . de quei Tartari, che sono cativa natione et nemici grandi di [Christ]iani." ASVe, SU, b. 72, proc. "Teodoro Persico," 17r (September 24, 1620).

103. "Int[erogatu]s che dica se in varie occ[asi]oni hà detto male del battesimo, riprendendo anco alcuni che attendono alli Cathecumeni, et dicendo parole disprezzo del d[et]to battesimo et delli evangeli nostri. R[espondi]t: S[igno]ri, no. Li Persiani et Turchi credono nell'Evangelio." ASVe, SU, b. 72, proc. "Teodoro Persico" (January 19, 1621).

104. "Int[erogatu]s se in occ[asi]one de inviti fatti da Meemet à qualche della sua p[ro]fess[ion]e, esso Const.o habbia mai detto parole indecente, affermando di esser uscite dalla bocca di N[ostro] S[igno]r Giesu [Christ]o. R[espondi]t S[igno]ri no. Et se hò detto hò detto bene, perche su l'Alcoran si no[m]i[n]a la gloriosa Vergine Maria et li Santi Ap[osto]li con molte laudi." ASVe, SU, b. 72, proc. "Teodoro Persico" (May 14, 1624).

105. ASVe, SU, b. 72, proc. "Teodoro Persico" (June 11, 1620).

106. Flaminio had petitioned the Cinque Savi for an appointment as a commercial broker in 1611. ASVe, VS, ser. I, b. 143, 87r–88r.

107. ASVe, SU, b. 85, proc. "Giovanni Battista Flaminio," 1v.

108. "[À] tutte l'hore pratica con turchi persiani, sempre mangia, et conversa con loro, et è (si può dire) con essi una stessa cosa hà per p[er] predelletti quelli ritti et costumi detestando et abhomenvoli." ASVe, SU, b. 85, proc. "Giovanni Battista Flaminio," 1r.

109. "Che molte volte li Turchi dispensano dalla circoncisione, q[ue]lli che si vogliono far turchi nasc[ostamen]te." ASVe, SU, b. 85, proc. "Giovanni Battista Flaminio," 1v.

110. "Voglio dire, che le navi de' gl'alberi, e gl'alberi delle navi conducono ogni merce a Vinegia. Mirabile è ne gl'habitatori. Laonde non si discerne, se Vinegia è nel mondo, ò il mondo in Vinegia." Luigi Groto, *Le orationi volgari* (Venice: Fabio & Agostino Zoppini, 1586), 9r.

Conclusion

1. Elisheva Carlebach, *Divided Souls: Converts from Judaism in Germany, 1500–1750* (New Haven, CT: Yale University Press, 2001), 182; Yaacov Deutsch, "'A View of the Jewish Religion': Conceptions of Jewish Practice and Ritual in Early Modern Europe," *Archiv*

für Religionsgeschichte 3 (2001): 273–295; Yaacov Deutsch, *Judaism in Christian Eye: Ethnographic Descriptions of Jews and Judaism in Early Modern Europe*, trans. Avi Aronsky (Oxford: Oxford University Press, 2012), 1.

2. Joan-Pau Rubiés, "New Worlds and Renaissance Ethnology," *History and Anthropology* 6, no. 2–3 (1993): 161; James Hankins, "Renaissance Crusaders: Humanist Crusade Literature in the Age of Mehmed II," *Dumbarton Oaks Papers* 49 (1995): 121–123; Yaacov Deutsch, "Religious Rituals and Ethnographic Knowledge: Sixteenth-Century Descriptions of Circumcision," in *Knowledge and Religion in Early Modern Europe: Studies in Honor of Michael Heyd*, ed. Asaph Ben-Tov, Yaacov Deutsch, Tamar Herzig, and Michael Heyd (Leiden: Brill, 2013), 119–134.

3. Jonathan Sheehan, "Sacred and Profane: Idolatry, Antiquarianism and the Polemics of Distinction in the Seventeenth Century," *Past & Present*, no. 192 (2006): 35–66; Roger A. Johnson, "Natural Religion, Common Notions, and the Study of Religions: Lord Herbert of Cherbury (1583–1648)," *Religion* 24, no. 3 (1994): 213–224.

4. Samuel Purchas, *Purchas His Pilgrimage. Or Relations of the World and the Religions Obserued in All Ages and Places Discouered, from the Creation vnto This Present in Foure Partes* (London: William Stansby for Henrie Fetherstone, 1613), A6r–8v, 16.

5. Sheehan, "Sacred and Profane"; Guy A. Stroumsa, *A New Science: The Discovery of Religion in the Age of Reason* (Cambridge, MA: Harvard University Press, 2010).

6. "Diversae nationes populorum inter se discrepant genere, moribus, lingua, legibus." Regino of Prüm, *Reginonis abbatis prumiensis Chronicon*, ed. Friedrich Kurze, Scriptores rerum Germanicarum in usum scholarum (Hanover: impensis bibliopolii Hahniani, 1890), xx.

7. Anthony D. Smith, *The Ethnic Origins of Nations* (Oxford: Blackwell, 1986); Patrick Geary, "Power and Ethnicity: History and Anthropology," *History and Anthropology* 26, no. 1 (January 2015): 8–17; Robert Bartlett, "Medieval and Modern Concepts of Race and Ethnicity," *Journal of Medieval and Early Modern Studies* 31, no. 1 (2001): 39–56; Robert Bartlett, *The Making of Europe: Conquest, Colonization, and Cultural Change, 950–1350* (Princeton, NJ: Princeton University Press, 1993).

8. Carmen Nocentelli, *Empires of Love: Europe, Asia, and the Making of Early Modern Identity* (Philadelphia: University of Pennsylvania Press, 2013), 4–13; Francisco Bethencourt, *Racisms: From the Crusades to the Twentieth Century* (Princeton, NJ: Princeton University Press, 2013); David Nirenberg, "Was There Race before Modernity? The Example of 'Jewish' Blood in Late Medieval Spain," in *The Origins of Racism in the West*, ed. Miriam Eliav-Feldon, Benjamin Isaac, and Joseph Ziegler (Cambridge: Cambridge University Press, 2009), 232–264.

9. Joan-Pau Rubiés, "Travel Writing as a Genre: Facts, Fictions and the Invention of a Scientific Discourse in Early Modern Europe," *Journeys: The International Journal of Travel and Travel Writing* 1, no. 1/2 (2000): 24.

Bibliography

Archival and Manuscript Sources

Archivio di Stato di Venezia (ASVe)
- Archivio proprio di Gian Vincenzo Pinelli
- Capi del Consiglio di Dieci
- Cinque Savi alla Mercanzia
- Collegio, Relazioni
- Consiglio di Dieci, Deliberazioni
- Miscellanea Codici
- Quarantia Criminales
- Santo Ufficio
- Senato, Dispacci, Costantinopoli
- Senato Terra

Biblioteca Ambrosiana, Milan (BAM)

Biblioteca del Museo Correr, Venice (BCV)
- Correr
- Donà dalle Rose (Donà)
- Provenienze Diverse
- Wcovich Lazzari

Biblioteca Nazionale Marciana, Venice (BNM)
- Manoscritti Italiani
  - Classe VI
  - Classe VII
  - Classe X
  - Classe XI
- Manoscritti Latini
  - Classe XIV

Primary Sources

Albèri, Eugenio, ed. *Relazioni degli ambasciatori veneti al Senato.* 15 vols. Florence: Società editrice fiorentina, 1839–1863.

Ammirato, Scipione. *Discorsi del signor Scipione Ammirato sopra Cornelio Tacito. Nuovamente posti in luce con due tavole, una dei discorsi, e luoghi di Cornelio sopra i quali son fondati, l'altra delle cose più notabili.* Florence: Filippo II Giunta, 1594.

Anghiera, Pietro Martire d'. *De rebus Oceanicis et orbe novo decades tres.* Basel: Johann Bebel, 1533.

Arvanitakis, Dimitris, ed. *Oi anaphores ton beneton problepton tes Zakinthou: 160s–180s ai* (The reports of the Venetian provveditori of Zante: 16th to 18th centuries). Venice: Elleniko institouto byzantinon, 2000.

Bacon, Francis. *The New Organon.* Edited by Lisa Jardine and Michael Silverthorne. Cambridge: Cambridge University Press, 2000.

Barbaro, Giosafat, Ambrogio Contarini, Benedetto Ramberti, and Luigi Roncinotto. *Viaggi fatti da Vinetia, alla Tana, in Persia, in India, et in Costantinopoli: Con la descrittione particolare di citta, luoghi, siti, costumi, et della porta del gran turco.* Venice: Nelle case haer. Aldo I Manuzio, 1543.

Barozzi, Nicolò, and Guglielmo Berchet, eds. *Relazioni degli stati Europei lette al senato dagli ambasciatori veneti nel secolo decimosettimo: Turchia.* Venice: P. Naratovich, 1871.

Baschet, Armand. *Les archives de Venise: Histoire de la chancellerie secrète, le sénat, le cabinet des ministres, le Conseil des Dix, et les Inquisiteurs d'état dans leurs rapports avec la France.* Paris: Henri Plon, 1870.

Bassano, Luigi. *I costumi et i modi particolari de la vita de' Turchi.* Rome: Antonio Blado Asolano, 1545.

Berchet, Guglielmo, ed. *La repubblica di Venezia e la Persia.* 2 vols. Turin: G. B. Paravia, 1865–1866.

———. *Relazioni dei consoli veneti nella Siria.* Turin: G. B. Paravia, 1866.

Bertelli, Ferdinando. *Omnium fere gentium nostrae aetatis habitus.* Venice: Ferdinando Bertelli typis excudebat, 1563.

———. *Omnium fere gentium nostrae aetatis habitus.* Venice: Ferdinando Bertelli typis excudebat, 1569.

Bertelli, Pietro. *Diversarum nationum habitus.* Padua: Alciato Alciati & Pietro Bertelli, 1594.

Bibliander, Theodore, ed. *Machumetis Saracenorum principis, eiusque successorum vitae, ac doctrina, ipseque Alcoran.* Basel: Ioannis Oporini, 1543.

Boemus, Johannes. *Gli costumi, le leggi et l'usanze di tutte le genti.* Translated by Lucio Fauno. Venice: Michele Tramezzino, 1542.

———. *Omnium gentium mores leges et ritus.* Augsburg: Sigismund Grimm and Marcus Wirsung, 1520.

———. *Omnium gentium mores, leges et ritus ex multis clarissimis rerum scriptoribus.* Lyon: Simonis Vincentii, 1535.

Bon, Ottaviano. *Lettera a Luigi Lollino vescovo di Belluno.* Rovigo: A. Minelli, 1844.

Bordone, Benedetto. *Libro di Benedetto Bordone nel qual si ragiona de tutte l'isole del mondo con li lor nomi antichi & moderni, historie, favole, & modi del loro vivere, & in qual parte del mare stanno, & in qual parallelo & clima giacciono.* Venice: Niccolò Zoppino, 1528.

Brown, Rawdon, ed. *Calendar of State Papers and Manuscripts, Relating to English Affairs, Existing in the Archives and Collections of Venice and in the Other Libraries of Northern Italy.* 38 vols. London: Longman, 1862.

Cavalli, Marino. *Informatione dell'offitio dell'ambasciatore: 1550*. Edited by Tommaso Bertelè. Florence: L. S. Olschki, 1935.

Cicogna, Emmanuele Antonio. *Delle inscrizioni veneziane*. 6 vols. Venice: Giuseppe Picotti, 1853.

Contarini, Gasparo. *De magistratibus & republica venetorum*. Paris: Michel de Vascosan, 1543.

Contarini, Tommaso. "Relazione di Fiandra (1610)." In *Relazioni veneziane: Venetiaansche berichten over de Vereenigde Nederlanden van 1600–1795*, edited by P. J. Blok, 28–68. The Hague: M. Nijhoff, 1909.

Coryate, Thomas. *Coryats Crudities*. London: William Stansby, 1611.

De Solis, Giulio Cesare. *Descrittione di molte isole famosissime nella quale breuemente si narrano le cose principali di quelle*. Padua: Lorenzo Pasquati stampatore della magnifica Vniuersita dei legisti, 1596.

Diario del viaggio da Venezia a Costantinopoli fatto da M. Jacopo Soranzo al Sultano Murad III in compagnia di M. Giovanni Correr bailo alla Porta Ottomana descritto da anonimo che fu al seguito del Soranzo, 1575. Venice: Giambattista Merlo, 1856.

Díaz Tanco, Vasco. *Libro dell'origine et successione dell'imperio de'Turchi*. Translated by Alfonso de Ulloa. Venice: Gabriel Giolito de' Ferrari, 1558.

Donà, Leonardo. *Il viaggio a Vienna di Leonardo Donà, ambasciatore della Repubblica veneta, nell'anno 1577: Diario*. Edited by Umberto Chiaromanni. Padua: CLEUP, 2004.

Erasmus, Desiderius. *Utilissima consultatio de bello turcis inferendo, et obiter enarratus Psalmus XXVIII*. Edited by A. G. Weiler and C.S.M. Rademaker. Opera Omnia, 4.3. Amsterdam: Elsevier, 1986.

Eymerich, Nicolau, and Francesco Peña. *Directorium inquisitorum*. Rome, 1585.

———. *Directorium inquisitorum*. Venice: Marcum Antonium Zalterium, 1607.

Fausto, Sebastiano. *Delle nozze trattato del Fausto da Longiano in cui si leggono i riti, i costumi, gl'instituti, le cerimonie etc. di diversi antichi popoli aggiuntivi e precetti matrimoniali di Plutarco*. Venice: Plinio Pietrasanta, 1554.

Fiedler, Joseph, ed. *Relationen venetianischer Botschafter über Deutschland und Österreich im sechzehnten Jahrhundert*. Vienna: Kaiserlich-Königlichen Hof- und Staatsdruckerei, 1870.

Franceschi, Andrea de. "Itinerario di Germania dell'anno 1492." Edited by Enrico Simonsfeld. *Miscellanea di storia veneta* Ser. II, 9 (1903): 275–345.

———. *Two Italian Accounts of Tudor England: A Journey to London in 1497; a Picture of English Life under Queen Mary*. Edited by Cesare V. Malfatti. Barcelona, 1953.

François Desprez. *Recueil de la diversité des habits qui sont de present en usaige, tant es pays d'Europe, Asie, Affrique et illes sauvages*. Paris: Richard Breton, 1562.

Fulin, Rinaldo, ed. "Documenti per servire alla storia della tipografia veneziana." *Archivio veneto* 23 (1882): 84–212, 390–405.

Geuffroy, Antoine, and Benedetto Ramberti. *Estat de la court du grant turc, lordre de sa gendarmerie, et de ses finances: Avec ung brief discours de leurs conquestes depues le premier de ceste race*. Antwerp: Jehan Steels, 1542.

———. *The Order of the Greate Turckes Courte, of Hys Menne of Warre, and of All Hys Conquestes, with the Summe of Mahumetes Doctryne. Translated out of Frenche*. London: Ricardus Grafton excudebat, 1542.

Giraldi, Lilio Gregorio. *De sepulchris et vario sepeliendi ritu.* Basel: Michael Isengrin, 1539.

Gratian. *The Treatise on Laws: Decretum DD. 1–20.* Translated by Augustine Thompson and James Gordley. Washington, DC: Catholic University of America Press, 1993.

Groto, Luigi. *Le orationi volgari.* Venice: Fabio & Agostino Zoppini, 1586.

Gualdo, Paolo. *Vita Ioannis Vincentii Pinelli, patricii Genuensis, in qua studiosis bonarum artium, proponitur typus viri probi & eruditi.* Augsburg: Christophorus Mangus, 1607.

Ioly Zorattini, Pier Cesare, ed. *Processi del S. Uffizio di Venezia contro Ebrei e giudaizzanti.* 14 vols. Storia dell'ebraismo in Italia: Studi e testi. Florence: L. S. Olschki, 1980–1997.

Kromer, Martin. *Martini Cromeri De origine et rebus gestis polonorum libri XXX: Adiecta est in fine eiusdem autoris funebris oratio, Sigismundi regis uitam compendiose complexa.* Basel: Ioannem Oporinum, 1555.

L'Alcorano di Macometto, nel qual si contiene la dottrina, la vita, i costumi et le leggi sve. [Venice]: Andrea Arrivabene, 1547.

León, Pedro de Cieza de. *Cronica del gran regno del Perù: Con la descrittione di tutte le prouincie, costumi, e riti: Con le nuove città edificate, & altre strane & marauigliose notitie: Parte prima.* Translated by Agostino di Cravaliz. Venice: Camillo Franceschini, 1576.

Maffei, Raffaele. *Commentariorum urbanorum libri XXXVIII.* Rome: Ioannem Besicken Alemanum, 1506.

Maggi, Ottaviano. *De legato libri duo.* Venice: [Lodovico Avanzi], 1566.

Magnus, Olaus. *Ain kurze auslegung und verklerung der neuen mappen von den alten Göttenreich und andern nordlenden sampt mit den uunderlichen dingen in land und uasser darinnen begriffen biss her also klerlich nieintuuelt geschriben.* Venice: [Giovanni Tommaso], 1539.

———. *Carta marina et descriptio septemtrionalium terrarum ac mirabilium rerum in eis contentarum diligentissime elaborata anno domini 1539.* [Venice]: Thomas de Rubis, 1539.

———. *Historia de gentibus septentrionalibus, earumque diversis statibus, conditionibus, moribus, ritibus, superstitionibus.* Rome: Giovanni Maria Viotti in aedibus Sanctae Brigittae, 1555.

———. *Opera breve, la quale demonstra, e dechiara, overo da il modo facile de intendere la charta, over delle terre frigidissime di settentrione: Oltra il mare germanico, dove si contengono le cose mirabilissime de quelli paesi, fin'a quest'hora non cognosciute, ne da greci, ne da latini.* Venice: Giovanni Tommaso, 1539.

Menavino, Giovanni Antonio. *I cinque libri della legge, religione, et vita de' Turchi.* Venice: Vincenzo Valgrisi, 1548.

Montaigne, Michel de. *The Complete Essays.* Translated by J. M. Cohen. London: Penguin, 1993.

———. *The Complete Essays.* Translated by M. A. Screech. London: Penguin, 2003.

Navagero, Andrea. *Il viaggio fatto in Spagna, et in Francia . . . con la descrittione particolare delli luochi, et costumi delli popoli di quelle provincie.* Venice: Domenico Farri, 1563.

Nicolay, Nicolas de. *Les quatre premiers livres des Navigations et peregrinations orientales.* Lyon: Guillaume Rouillé, 1568.

Orta, Garcia da. *Colloquies on the Simples and Drugs of India.* Translated by Clements Markham. London: Henry Sotheran, 1913.

Pagani, Zaccaria. *Viaggio di Domenico Trevisan, ambasciatore veneto al gran sultano del Cairo nell'anno 1512.* Edited by Nicolò Barozzi. Venice: Tipografia Antonelli, 1875.

Pagratis, Gerassimos D., ed. *Oi ektheseis tōn benetōn bailōn kai pronoētōn tēs Kerkyras (16. aiōnas).* Athens: Ethnico Idryma Ereynōn, Institouto Byzantinōn Ereynōn, 2008.

Panciroli, Guido. *Rerum memorabilium, iam olim deperditarum: & contrà recens atque ingeniosè inuentarum: libri duo.* Translated by Heinrich Salmuth. Vol. 2. Hamburg: Forsterianis, 1602.

Panciroli, Guido, and Flavio Gualtieri. *Raccolta breue d'alcune cose piu segnalate c'hebbero gli antichi, e d'alcune altre trouate da moderni.* Venice: Bernardo Giunti, Gio. Battista Ciotti, & compagni, 1612.

Pedani Fabris, Maria Pia, ed. *Costantinopoli relazioni inedite (1512–1789).* Relazioni di ambasciatori veneti al Senato 14. Padua: Bottega d'Erasmo, 1996.

Pian del Carpine, Giovanni da. *Opera dilettevole da intendere, nella qual si contiene doi Itinerarii in Tartaria, per alcuni Frati dell'ordine minore, è di S. Dominico, mandati da Papa Innocento IIII nella detta Provincia de Scithia per Ambasciatori, non più vulgarizata.* Venice: Giovanni Antonio de Nicolini da Sabio, 1537.

Pian del Carpine, Giovanni da, and Willem van Ruysbroek. *The Texts and Versions of John de Plano Carpini and William de Rubruquis, as Printed for the First Time by Hakluyt in 1598, Together with Some Shorter Pieces.* Edited by C. Raymond Beazley. London: Hakluyt Society, 1903.

Piccolomini, Aeneas Silvius. *Commentaries.* Edited by Margaret Meserve and Marcello Simonetta. Vol. 1. Cambridge, MA: Harvard University Press, 2003.

———. *Epistola ad Mahomatem II.* Edited by Albert R. Baca. New York: Peter Lang, 1990.

Pigafetta, Filippo, and Duarte Lopez. *Relatione del reame di Congo et delle circonvicine contrade, tratta dalla scritti & ragionamenti di Odoardo Lopez Portoghese per Filippo Pigafetta.* Rome: Bartolomeo Grassi, 1591.

Poliziano, Angelo. *Opera.* Venice: Aldo I Manuzio, 1498.

Porcacchi, Tommaso. *Funerali antichi di diversi popoli, et nationi; forma, ordine, et pompa di sepolture, di essequie, di consecrationi antiche et d'altro, descritti in dialogo da Thomaso Porcacchi da Castiglione Arretino. Con le figure in rame di Girolamo Porro padouano.* Venice: Simone Galignani, 1574.

———, ed. *Lettere di XIII huomini illustri.* Venice: Appresso gli heredi Giovanni Maria Bonelli, 1571.

———. *L'isole piu famose del mondo.* Venice: Simone Galignani & Girolamo Porro, 1572.

———. *L'isole piu famose del mondo.* Venice: Simone Galignani & Girolamo Porro, 1576.

Priuli, Mafio. *Copia di una lettera venuta d'India, indrizzata al magnifico M. Costantino di Priuli nella quale si leggono cose maravigliose e varie di quelli paesie, scritta nel 1537 - ricevuta nel 1539.* Venice: Alvisopoli, 1824.

Purchas, Samuel. *Purchas His Pilgrimage. Or Relations of the World and the Religions Obserued in All Ages and Places Discouered, from the Creation Vnto This Present in Foure Partes.* London: Printed by William Stansby for Henrie Fetherstone, 1613.

Queirós, Pedro Fernandes de. *Relatione d'vn memoriale che ha presentato a sva maesta il Capitano Pietro Ferdinando de Quir, sopra la popolanza scoperta nella quarta parte del mondo australe incognita, con le sue richezze, & fertilità scoperte per il medemo capitano.* Milan: Padolfo Malatesta, 1611.

Ramberti, Benedetto. *Libri tre delle cose de Turchi.* Venice: Aldo I. Manuzio, 1539.

Ramusio, Giovanni Battista, ed. *Primo volume delle navigationi et viaggi*. Venice: Appresso gli heredi di Lucantonio Giunti, 1550.

Ranzo, Carlo. *Relatione di Carlo Ranzo gentil'hvomo di Vercelli d'vn viaggio fatto da Venetia in Constantinopoli: Ritornato, che fù dalla battaglia Nauale assai curioso per i molti accidenti occorsi, oue si possono imparare stratagemme di guerra, humori d'huomini, e diuersita di genti, & di paesi*. Turin: Fratelli Cavaleri, 1616.

Regino of Prüm. *Reginonis abbatis prumiensis Chronicon*. Edited by Friedrich Kurze. Scriptores rerum Germanicarum in usum scholarum. Hanover: Impensis bibliopolii Hahniani, 1890.

Robortello, Francesco. *De historica facultate*. Florence: Lorenzo Torrentino, 1548.

Salvago, Giovanni Battista. "*Africa Overo Barbarìa.*" *Relazione al doge di Venezia sulle reggenze di Algeri e di Tunisi del dragomanno G. B. Salvago, 1625. Introduzione e note di Alberto Sacerdoti*. Edited by Alberto Sacerdoti. Padua: A. Milani, 1937.

Sansovino, Francesco. *Dell'historia universale dell'origine et imperio de Turchi: Nella quali si contengono gli offici, i leggi, i costumi di quella natione, cosi in tempo di pace, come di guerra*. Venice: Francesco Sansovino & C., 1560.

———, ed. *Historia universale dell'origine, et imperio de' Turchi*. Venice: Michel Bonelli, 1573.

Sanudo, Marin. *I diarii (1496–1533)*. Edited by Rinaldo Fulin, Federico Stefani, Nicolò Barozzi, Guglielmo Berchet, and Marco Allegri. 58 vols. Venice: F. Visentini, 1879–1903.

Simancas, Diego. *De catholicis institutionibus*. Rome, 1575.

Soranzo, Lazzaro. *L'Ottomanno di Lazaro Soranzo*. Ferrara: Vittorio Baldini, 1598.

Stern, Moritz. *Urkundliche Beiträge über die Stellung der Päpste zu den Juden: mit Benutzung des päpstlichen Geheimarchivs zu Rom*. Kiel: Fiencke, 1893.

Tagliaferri, Amelio, ed. *Relazioni dei rettori veneti in terraferma*. Milan: A. Giuffrè, 1973–1979.

Thesoro politico cioè relationi instruttioni trattati, discorsi varii d'ambasciatori. Pertinenti alla cognitione, & intelligenza delli stati, interessi, & dipendenze de più gran principi del mondo. Nuovamente impresso a beneficio di chi si diletta intendere, & pertinentemente discorrere li negotii di stato. Cologne: Alberto Coloresco nell'Academia italiana di Colonia, 1589.

Thomas, William. *The Historie of Italie a Boke Excedyng Profitable to Be Redde: Because It Intreateth of the Astate of Many and Diuers Common Weales, How Thei Haue Ben, [and] Now Be Gouerned*. London, 1549.

Varthema, Ludovico de. *Itinerario*. Rome: Etienne Guillery & Ercole Nani ad instantia de Ludovico degli Arrighi, 1510.

———. *Itinerario*. Venice: Per gli heredi di Giorgio di Rusconi, 1522.

———. *Itinerario*. Edited by Valentina Martino. Alessandria: Edizioni dell'Orso, 2011.

———. "The Trauels of Lewis Barthema or Vertoman into Egypt, Syria, Arabia, Persia, and India." In *Purchas His Pilgrimes in Fiue Bookes*, edited by Samuel Purchas, 2:1483–1495. London: Printed by William Stansby for Henrie Fetherstone, 1625.

Vasari, Giorgio. *Le vite de piu eccellenti architetti, pittori, et scultori italiani da Cimabue insino a' tempi nostri*. Florence: Lorenzo Torrentino, 1550.

Vecellio, Cesare. *De gli habiti antichi, et moderni di diverse parti del mondo*. Venice: Damiano Zenaro, 1590.

———. *Habiti antichi et moderni di tutto il mondo*. Translated by Sulstatius Gratilianus. Venice: Appresso haer. Melchiorre I Sessa: Giovanni Bernardo Sessa, 1598.

Vendramin, Pietro, ed. *Repertorium inquisitorium pravitatis haereticae*. Venice: Damianum Zenarum, 1575.

Weigel, Hans, and Jost Amman. *Habitus praecipuorum populorum tam virorum quam feminarum singulari arte depicti: Trachtenbuch*. Nuremberg, 1577.

Zen, Nicolò. *De i commentarii del viaggio in Persia di m. Caterino Zeno il K. et delle guerre fatte nell'imperio Persiano, dal tempo di Ussuncassano in quà. Libri due. Et dello scoprimento dell'isole Frislanda, Eslanda, Engrovelanda, Estotilanda, et Icaria, fatto sotto il Polo Artico, da due fratelli Zeni, m. Nicolò il K. e m. Antonio. Libro uno. Con un disegno particolare di tutte le dette parte di tramontana da lor scoperte*. Venice: Francesco Marcolini, 1558.

Zen, Pietro. "Itinerario di Pietro Zeno oratore a Costantinopoli compendiato da Marino Sanuto." Edited by Rinaldo Fulin. *Archivio veneto* XXII (1881): 104–136.

Secondary Sources

Abulafia, David. *The Discovery of Mankind: Atlantic Encounters in the Age of Columbus*. New Haven, CT: Yale University Press, 2008.

Acciarino, Damiano. "De Re Vestiaria: Renaissance Discovery of Ancient Clothing." *La rivista di Engramma*, no. 154 (2018): 111–140.

Adelman, Howard. "A Rabbi Reads the Qur'an in the Venetian Ghetto." *Jewish History* 26, no. 1–2 (May 2012): 125–137.

———. "Rabbi Leon Modena and the Christian Kabbalists." In *Renaissance Rereadings: Intertext and Context*, edited by Maryanne Cline Horowitz, Anne J. Cruz, and Wendy Ann Furman, 271–286. Urbana: University of Illinois Press, 1988.

———. "Success and Failure in the Seventeenth-Century Ghetto of Venice: The Life and Thought of Leon Modena, 1571–1648." PhD diss., Brandeis University, 1985.

Ambrosini, Federica. "Venetian Diplomacy, Spanish Gold, and the New World in the Sixteenth Century." In *The New World in Early Modern Italy, 1492–1750*, edited by Elizabeth Horodowich and Lia Markey, 47–60. Cambridge: Cambridge University Press, 2017.

Anderson, Matthew S. *The Rise of Modern Diplomacy 1450–1919*. London: Longman, 1993.

Antonibon, Francesca. *Le relazioni a stampa di ambasciatori veneti*. Padua: Tipografia del seminario, 1939.

Arbel, Benjamin. *Trading Nations: Jews and Venetians in the Early-Modern Eastern Mediterranean*. Leiden: Brill, 1995.

Aricò, Angela Caracciolo. "Il Nuovo Mondo e l'umanesimo: Imagini e miti dell'editoria venezia." In *L'impatto della scoperta dell'America nella cultura veneziana*, edited by Angela Caracciolo Aricò, 25–33. Rome: Bulzoni, 1990.

Arnold, Rafael. "Neutral or Natural Relater? Some Remarks on Rabbi Leone da Modena's Historia de Riti Hebraici." *Zutot* 4, no. 1 (2004): 107–112.

Banerjee, Pompa. *Burning Women: Widows, Witches, and Early Modern European Travelers in India*. New York: Palgrave Macmillan, 2003.

Barbieri, Gino. "Introduzione alle relazioni dei provveditori di Legnago." In *Provveditorato di Legnago*, edited by Amelio Tagliaferri, xv–lxiv. Relazioni dei rettori veneti in terraferma, VIII. Milan: A. Giuffrè, 1977.

Bareggi, Claudia Di Filippo. *Il mestiere di scrivere: Lavoro intellettuale e mercato librario a Venezia nel Cinquecento.* Rome: Bulzoni, 1988.

Barry, Jonathan. "Literacy and Literature in Popular Culture: Reading and Writing in Historical Perspective." In *Popular Culture in England, 1500–1800*, edited by Tim Harris, 69–94. London: Macmillan, 1995.

Bartlett, Robert. "Medieval and Modern Concepts of Race and Ethnicity." *Journal of Medieval and Early Modern Studies* 31, no. 1 (2001): 39–56.

———. *The Making of Europe: Conquest, Colonization, and Cultural Change, 950–1350.* Princeton, NJ: Princeton University Press, 1993.

Basile, Bruno. "Introduzione e nota bio-bibliografica." In *Il serraglio del gransignore*, edited by Bruno Basile, 1–22. Rome: Salerno, 2002.

Bellavitis, Anna. "'Per cittadini metterete': La stratifiazione della società veneziana cinquecentesca tra norma giuridica e riconoscimento sociale." *Quaderni storici* 30, no. 2 (1995): 359–383.

———. "Il 'farsi turco,' ossia l'ombra del rinnegato." In *Venezia e i Turchi: Scontri e confronti di due civilità*, edited by Anna Della Valle, 91–133. Milan: Electra, 1985.

———. "Ranke's Favorite Source: The Venetian Relazioni: Impressions with Allusions to Later Historiography." In *Leopold von Ranke and the Shaping of the Historical Discipline*, edited by Georg G. Iggers and James M. Powell, 45–57. Syracuse, NY: Syracuse University Press, 1990.

Bertelè, Tommaso. *Il palazzo degli ambasciatori di Venezia a Costantinopoli e le sue antiche memorie: Ricerche storiche con documenti inediti e 185 illustrazioni.* Bologna: Appolo, 1932.

Bethencourt, Francisco. *Racisms: From the Crusades to the Twentieth Century.* Princeton, NJ: Princeton University Press, 2013.

Bevilacqua, Eugenia. "Geografi e cosmografi." In *Storia della cultura veneta: Dal primo Quattrocento al Concilio di Trento*, edited by Girolamo Arnaldi and Manlio Pastore Stocchi, 2:355–374. Vicenza: Neri Pozza, 1980.

Biow, Douglas. *Doctors, Ambassadors, Secretaries: Humanism and Professions in Renaissance Italy.* Chicago: University of Chicago Press, 2002.

Bisaha, Nancy. *Creating East and West: Renaissance Humanists and the Ottoman Turks.* Philadelphia: University of Pennsylvania Press, 2004.

Black, Christopher F. *The Italian Inquisition.* New Haven, CT: Yale University Press, 2009.

Blair, Ann. *Too Much to Know: Managing Scholarly Information before the Modern Age.* New Haven, CT: Yale University Press, 2010.

Blanc, Odile. "Images du monde et portraits d'habits: Les recueils de costumes de la Renaissance." *Bulletin du bibliophile*, no. 2 (1995): 221–261.

Bleichmar, Daniela. *Visible Empire: Botanical Expeditions and Visual Culture in the Hispanic Enlightenment.* Chicago: University of Chicago Press, 2012.

Boccato, Carla. "Processi ad Ebrei nell'archivio degli ufficiali al Cattaver a Venezia." *Rassegna mensile di Israel* 41, no. 3 (1975): 164–180.

Bonfil, Robert. *Jewish Life in Renaissance Italy.* Translated by Anthony Oldcorn. Berkeley: University of California Press, 1994.

Borgherini-Scarabellin, Maria. *Il magistrato dei Cinque Savi alla Mercanzia dalla istituzione alla caduta della repubblica: Studio storico su documenti d'archivio.* Venice: Deputazione di storia patria, 1925.

Boruchoff, David. "Indians, Cannibals, and Barbarians: Hernan Cortes and Early Modern Cultural Relativism." *Ethnohistory* 62, no. 1 (January 2015): 17–38.

Bowd, Stephen D. *Venice's Most Loyal City: Civic Identity in Renaissance Brescia*. Cambridge, MA: Harvard University Press, 2010.

Bozza, Tommaso. *Scrittori politici italiani dal 1550 al 1650, saggio di bibliografia*. Rome: Edizioni di "Storia e letteratura," 1949.

Brummett, Palmira. *Mapping the Ottomans: Sovereignty, Territory, and Identity in the Early Modern Mediterranean*. Cambridge: Cambridge University Press, 2015.

———. *Ottoman Seapower and Levantine Diplomacy in the Age of Discovery*. Albany: State University of New York Press, 1994.

———. "The Myth of Shah Ismail Safavi: Political Rhetoric and 'Divine' Kingship." In *Medieval Christian Perceptions of Islam*, edited by John Victor Tolan, 331–360. New York: Garland, 1996.

Burke, Peter. *A Social History of Knowledge: From Gutenberg to Diderot*. Cambridge: Polity Press, 2000.

———. "Early Modern Venice as a Center of Information and Communication." In *Venice Reconsidered*, edited by John Martin and Denis Romano, 389–419. Baltimore: Johns Hopkins University Press, 2008.

———. "From Antiquarianism to Anthropology." In *Momigliano and Antiquarianism: Foundations of the Modern Cultural Sciences*, edited by Peter N. Miller, 229–247. Toronto: University of Toronto Press, 2007.

———. "Oral Culture and Print Culture in Renaissance Italy." *ARV: Scandinavian Yearbook of Folklore* 54 (1998): 7–18.

———. *Varieties of Cultural History*. Ithaca, NY: Cornell University Press, 1997.

Burnett, Stephen G. *From Christian Hebraism to Jewish Studies: Johannes Buxtorf (1564–1629) and Hebrew Learning in the Seventeenth Century*. Leiden: Brill, 1996.

Campigotto, Luca. "Veneziani in India nel XVI secolo." *Studi veneziani* 22 (1991): 75–116.

Carey, Daniel. "The Problem of Credibility in Early Modern Travel." *Renaissance Studies* 33, no. 4 (2019): 524–547.

Carlebach, Elisheva. *Divided Souls: Converts from Judaism in Germany, 1500–1750*. New Haven, CT: Yale University Press, 2001.

Cassen, Flora. *Marking the Jews in Renaissance Italy: Politics, Religion, and the Power of Symbols*. Cambridge: Cambridge University Press, 2017.

Chmiel, Piotr. *Rethinking the Concept of Antemurale: Venetian Diplomacy in Respect of the Ottoman World (1573–1645)*. Rome: Accademia Polacca Roma, 2019.

Clark, Peter. "The Ownership of Books in England, 1560–1640: The Example of Some Kentish Townsfolk." In *Schooling and Society: Studies in the History of Education*, edited by Lawrence Stone, 95–111. Baltimore: Johns Hopkins University Press, 1976.

Coco, Carla, and Flora Manzonetto. *Baili veneziani alla Sublime Porta: Storia e caratteristiche dell'ambasciata veneta a Costantinopoli*. Venice: Stamperia di Venezia, 1985.

Cohen, Jeremy. "Scholarship and Intolerance in the Medieval Academy: The Study and Evaluation of Judaism in European Christendom." *American Historical Review* 91, no. 3 (June 1986): 592–613.

———. *The Friars and the Jews: The Evolution of Medieval Anti-Judaism*. Ithaca, NY: Cornell University Press, 1982.

Cohen, Mark R. "Leone da Modena's Riti: A Seventeenth-Century Plea for Social Toleration of Jews." *Jewish Social Studies* 33, no. 4 (1972): 287–321.

Cohen, Thomas V., and Germaine Warkentin. "Things Not Easily Believed: Introducing the Early Modern Relation." *Renaissance and Reformation/Renaissance et réforme* 34, no. 1–2 (2011): 7–23.

Colley, Linda. "Going Native, Telling Tales: Captivity, Collaborations and Empire." *Past & Present*, no. 168 (2000): 170–193.

Concina, Ennio. *Fondaci: Architettura, arte, e mercatura tra Levante, Venezia, e Alemagna.* Venice: Marsilio, 1997.

Constable, Olivia Remie. *To Live like a Moor: Christian Perceptions of Muslim Identity in Medieval and Early Modern Spain.* Edited by Robin Vose. Philadelphia: University of Pennsylvania Press, 2018.

Cooperman, Bernard. "Venetian Policy toward Levantine Jews and Its Broader Italian Context." In *Gli Ebrei a Venezia: Secoli XIV–XVIII*, edited by Gaetano Cozzi, 65–84. Milan: Edizioni Comunità, 1987.

Corns, Thomas N. "The Early Modern Search Engine: Indices, Title Pages, Marginalia and Contents." In *The Renaissance Computer: Knowledge Technology in the First Age of Print*, edited by Neil Rhodes and Jonathan Sawday, 93–102. London: Routledge, 2000.

Cosgrove, Denis E. *Apollo's Eye: A Cartographic Genealogy of the Earth in the Western Imagination.* Baltimore: Johns Hopkins University Press, 2001.

Costantini, Vera. "Dalla laguna al deserto: I rapporti tra Venezia ed Aleppo." *Levante* 49 (2002): 15–31.

Cowan, Alexander. "Gossip and Street Culture in Early Modern Venice." *Journal of Early Modern History* 12, no. 3 (2008): 313–333.

Crick, Julia, and Alexandra Walsham. "Script, Print, and History." In *The Uses of Script and Print, 1300–1700*, edited by Alexandra Walsham and Julia Crick, 1–26. Cambridge: Cambridge University Press, 2004.

Daniel, Norman. *Islam and the West: The Making of an Image.* Rev. ed. Oxford: Oneworld Publications, 1993.

Darling, Linda T. "Ottoman Turkish: Written Language and Scribal Practice, 13th to 20th Centuries." In *Literacy in the Persianate World: Writing and the Social Order*, edited by Brian Spooner and William L. Hanaway, 171–195. Philadelphia: University of Pennsylvania Press, 2012.

Darnton, Robert. "Extraordinary Commonplaces." *New York Review of Books* 47, no. 20 (December 2000): 82–87.

Davidson, Nicholas. "Rome and the Venetian Inquisition in the Sixteenth Century." *The Journal of Ecclesiastical History* 39 (1988): 16–36.

Davies, Surekha. *Renaissance Ethnography and the Invention of the Human: New Worlds, Maps and Monsters.* Cambridge: Cambridge University Press, 2016.

———. "The Wondrous East in the Renaissance Geographical Imagination: Marco Polo, Fra Mauro and Giovanni Battista Ramusio." *History and Anthropology* 23, no. 2 (June 2012): 215–234.

Davis, Natalie Zemon. "Fame and Secrecy: Leon Modena's Life as an Early Modern Autobiography." *History and Theory* 27, no. 4 (December 1988): 103–118.

De Vivo, Filippo. "How to Read Venetian Relazioni." *Renaissance and Reformation/Renaissance et réforme* 34, no. 1–2 (2011): 25–59.

———. *Information and Communication in Venice: Rethinking Early Modern Politics.* Oxford: Oxford University Press, 2009.

———. "Ordering the Archive in Early Modern Venice (1400–1650)." *Archival Science* 10, no. 3 (2010): 231–248.

———. "Rhetoric and Government in Sixteenth-Century Venice: Some Paradoxes." *The Italianist* 27 (2007): 188–205.

Defert, Daniel. "Un genre ethnographique profane au XVIe: Les livres d'habits." In *Histoires de l'anthropologie (XVI–XIXe siècles)*, edited by Britta Rupp-Eisenreich, 25–41. Paris: Klincksieck, 1984.

Del Col, Andrea. "I criteri dello storico nell'uso delle fonti inquisitoriali moderne." In *L'inquisizione romana: Metodologia delle fonti e storia istituzionale*, edited by Andrea Del Col and Giovanna Paolin, 51–72. Trieste: Edizioni Università di Trieste, 2000.

———. *L'inquisizione in Italia: Dal XII al XXI secolo.* Milan: Oscar Mondadori, 2006.

Deutsch, Yaacov. "'A View of the Jewish Religion': Conceptions of Jewish Practice and Ritual in Early Modern Europe." *Archiv für Religionsgeschichte* 3 (2001): 273–295.

———. *Judaism in Christian Eyes: Ethnographic Descriptions of Jews and Judaism in Early Modern Europe.* Translated by Avi Aronsky. Oxford: Oxford University Press, 2012.

———. "Religious Rituals and Ethnographic Knowledge: Sixteenth-Century Descriptions of Circumcision." In *Knowledge and Religion in Early Modern Europe: Studies in Honor of Michael Heyd*, edited by Asaph Ben-Tov, Yaacov Deutsch, Tamar Herzig, and Michael Heyd, 119–134. Leiden: Brill, 2013.

Dewald, Jonathan. *The European Nobility, 1400–1800.* Cambridge: Cambridge University Press, 1996.

Diffie, Bailey W., and George D. Winius. *Foundations of the Portuguese Empire, 1415–1580.* Minneapolis: University of Minnesota Press, 1977.

Donattini, Massimo. "Giovanni Battista Ramusio." In *Christian-Muslim Relations: A Bibliographical History*, edited by David Thomas and John A. Chesworth, 6:528–537. Leiden: Brill, 2014.

Donazzolo, Pietro. *I viaggiatori veneti minori, studio bio-bibliografico.* Rome: Società geografica italiana, 1927.

Dover, Paul Marcus. "Deciphering the Diplomatic Archives of Fifteenth-Century Italy." *Archival Science* 7, no. 4 (2007): 297–316.

Dursteler, Eric. "Describing or Distorting the 'Turk'? The Relazioni of the Venetian Ambassadors in Constantinople as Historical Source." *Acta Histriae* 19, no. 1–2 (2011): 231–248.

———. "Identity and Coexistence in the Eastern Mediterranean, ca. 1600." *New Perspectives on Turkey*, no. 18 (1998): 113–130.

———. "Reverberations of the Voyages of Discovery in Venice, ca. 1501: The Trevisan Manuscript in the Library of Congress." *Mediterranean Studies* 9 (2000): 43–64.

———. "Speaking in Tongues: Language and Communication in the Early Modern Mediterranean." *Past & Present*, no. 217 (November 2012): 47–77.

———. "The Bailo in Constantinople: Crisis and Career in Venice's Early Modern Diplomatic Corps." *Mediterranean Historical Review* 16, no. 2 (2001): 1–30.

Dweck, Yaacob. *The Scandal of Kabbalah: Leon Modena, Jewish Mysticism, Early Modern Venice*. Princeton, NJ: Princeton University Press, 2011.

Eliav-Feldon, Miriam. *Renaissance Impostors and Proofs of Identity*. New York: Palgrave Macmillan, 2012.

Elliott, John Huxtable. "The Discovery of America and the Discovery of Man." In *Spain and Its World, 1500–1700: Selected Essays*, 42–64. New Haven, CT: Yale University Press, 1989.

———. *The Old World and the New 1492–1650*. Cambridge: Cambridge University Press, 1970.

Errera, Andrea. *Processus in causa fidei: L'evoluzione dei manuali inquisitoriali nei secoli XVI–XVIII e il manuale inedito di un inquisitore perugino*. Bologna: Monduzzi, 2000.

Fabris, Antonio. "From Adrianople to Constantinople: Venetian-Ottoman Diplomatic Missions, 1360–1453." *Mediterranean Historical Review* 7, no. 2 (1992): 154–200.

Feros, Antonio. *Speaking of Spain: The Evolution of Race and Nation in the Hispanic World*. Cambridge, MA: Harvard University Press, 2017.

Ferro, Roberta. "Per la storia del fondo Pinelli all'Ambrosiana: Notizie dalle lettere di Paolo Gualdo." In *Tra i fondi dell'Ambrosiana: Manoscritti italiani antichi e moderni*, edited by Marco Ballarini, Gennaro Barbarisi, Claudia Berra, and Giuseppe Frasso, 1:255–288. Milan: Cisalpino, 2008.

Finlay, Robert. "Crisis and Crusade in the Mediterranean: Venice, Portugal, and the Cape Route to India (1498–1509)." *Studi veneziani* 28 (1994): 45–90.

———. "The Venetian Republic as a Gerontocracy: Age and Politics in the Renaissance." *Journal of Medieval and Renaissance Studies* 8, no. 2 (1978): 157–178.

Fletcher, Catherine. *Diplomacy in Renaissance Rome: The Rise of the Resident Ambassador*. Cambridge: Cambridge University Press, 2015.

———. "Mere Emulators of Italy: The Spanish-Italian Diplomatic Discourse, 1492–1550." In *The Spanish Presence in Sixteenth-Century Italy: Images of Iberia*, edited by Piers Baker-Bates and Miles Pattenden, 11–28. Aldershot, UK: Ashgate, 2015.

Formica, Marina. *Lo specchio turco: Immagini dell'altro e riflessi del sé nella cultura italiana d'età moderna*. Rome: Donzelli Editore, 2012.

Forti, Carla. "Sull'itinerario di Ludovico di Varthema." In *Per Adriano Prosperi: L'Europa divisa e i nuovi mondi*, edited by Massimo Donattini, Giuseppe Marcocci, and Stefania Pastore, 2:21–31. Pisa: Edizioni della Normale, 2011.

Fuess, Albrecht. "Ludovico de Varthema." In *Christian-Muslim Relations. A Bibliographical History*, edited by David Thomas and John A. Chesworth, 6:405–409. Leiden: Brill, 2014.

Fusaro, Maria. *Political Economies of Empire in the Early Modern Mediterranean: The Decline of Venice and the Rise of England 1450–1700*. Cambridge: Cambridge University Press, 2015.

Gaeta, Franco. Introduction to *Relations des ambassadeurs vénitiens*, i–xxiii. Edited by Franco Gaeta. Paris: Éditions Klincksieck, 1969.

Games, Alison. *The Web of Empire: English Cosmopolitans in an Age of Expansion, 1560–1660*. Oxford: Oxford University Press, 2008.

Gaudio, Michael. *Engraving the Savage: The New World and Techniques of Civilization*. Minneapolis: University of Minnesota Press, 2008.

Geary, Patrick. "Power and Ethnicity: History and Anthropology." *History and Anthropology* 26, no. 1 (January 2015): 8–17.

Gelder, Maartje van. *Trading Places: The Netherlandish Merchants in Early Modern Venice.* Leiden: Brill, 2009.

Ghobrial, John-Paul. *The Whispers of Cities: Information Flows in Istanbul, London, and Paris in the Age of William Trumbull.* Oxford: Oxford University Press, 2013.

Ginzburg, Carlo. "Provincializing the World: Europeans, Indians, Jews (1704)." *Postcolonial Studies* 14, no. 2 (2011): 135–150.

———. *The Cheese and the Worms: The Cosmos of a Sixteenth-Century Miller.* Translated by John A. Tedeschi and Anne Tedeschi. Baltimore: Johns Hopkins University Press, 1980.

———. "The Inquisitor as Anthropologist." In *Clues, Myths, and the Historical Method,* translated by John Tedeschi and Anne Tedeschi, 156–164. Baltimore: Johns Hopkins University Press, 1989.

Gleason, Elisabeth G. *Gasparo Contarini: Venice, Rome, and Reform.* Berkeley: University of California Press, 1993.

Glei, Reinhold F. "John of Damascus." In *Christian-Muslim Relations: A Bibliographical History,* edited by David Thomas and Barbara Roggema, 1:295–301. Leiden: Brill, 2009.

Gliozzi, Giuliano. *Adamo e il nuovo mondo: La nascita dell'antropologia come ideologia coloniale: Dalle genealogie bibliche alle teorie razziali (1500–1700).* Florence: La nuova Italia, 1977.

Goffman, Daniel. "Negotiating with the Renaissance State: The Ottoman Empire and the New Diplomacy." In *The Early Modern Ottomans: Remapping the Empire,* edited by Virginia Aksan and Daniel Goffman, 61–74. Cambridge: Cambridge University Press, 2007.

Göl, Ayla. "Europe, Islam and the Pax Ottomana, 1453–1774." In *International Orders in the Early Modern World: Before the Rise of the West,* edited by Shogo Suzuki, Yongjin Zhang, and Joel Quirk, 34–54. London: Routledge, 2013.

Grafton, Anthony. *Inky Fingers: The Making of Books in Early Modern Europe.* Cambridge, MA: Harvard University Press, 2020.

———. *New Worlds, Ancient Texts: The Power of Tradition and the Shock of Discovery.* Cambridge, MA: Belknap, 1992.

Granlund, John. "The Carta Marina of Olaus Magnus." *Imago Mundi* 8, no. 1 (1951): 35–43.

Greenblatt, Stephen. *Marvelous Possessions: The Wonder of the New World.* Chicago: University of Chicago Press, 1991.

Grendler, Marcella. "A Greek Collection in Padua: The Library of Gian Vincenzo Pinelli (1535–1601)." *Renaissance Quarterly* 33, no. 3 (1980): 386–416.

———. "Book Collecting in Counter-Reformation Italy: The Library of Gian Vincenzo Pinelli (1535–1601)." *Journal of Library History* 16, no. 1 (January 1981): 143–151.

Grendler, Paul F. "Francesco Sansovino and Italian Popular History 1560–1600." *Studies in the Renaissance* 16 (1969): 139–180.

———. *Schooling in Renaissance Italy: Literacy and Learning, 1300–1600.* Baltimore: Johns Hopkins University Press, 1989.

———. *The Roman Inquisition and the Venetian Press, 1540–1605.* Princeton, NJ: Princeton University Press, 1977.

———. "The Tre Savii Sopra Eresia 1547–1605: A Prosopographical Study." *Studi veneziani* n.s. 3 (1979): 283–340.

———. *The Universities of the Italian Renaissance.* Baltimore: Johns Hopkins University Press, 2002.

Gri, Gian Paolo. "L'uso delle fonti inquisitoriali in ambito demo-anthropologico." In *L'inquisizione romana: Metodologia delle fonti e storia istituzionale*, edited by Andrea Del Col and Giovanna Paolin, 73–89. Trieste: Edizioni Università di Trieste, 2000.

Grubb, James S. "Elite Citizens." In *Venice Reconsidered*, edited by John Martin and Denis Romano, 339–364. Baltimore: Johns Hopkins University Press, 2008.

Guglielminetti, Marziano. "Per un sottogenere della letteratura di viaggio: Gl'isolari fra Quattro e Cinquecento." In *La letteratura di viaggio dal Medioevo al Rinascimento: Generi e problemi*, 107–117. Alessandria: Edizioni dell'orso, 1989.

Hamilton, Keith, and Richard Langhorne. *The Practice of Diplomacy: Its Evolution, Theory, and Administration*. 2nd ed. New York: Routledge, 2011.

Hamlin, William M. "Attributions of Divinity in Renaissance Ethnography and Romance; or, Making Religion of Wonder." *Journal of Medieval and Renaissance Studies* 24, no. 3 (1994): 415–447.

———. "On Continuities between Skepticism and Early Ethnography; or, Montaigne's Providential Diversity." *Sixteenth Century Journal* 31, no. 2 (2000): 361–379.

Hankins, James. "Renaissance Crusaders: Humanist Crusade Literature in the Age of Mehmed II." *Dumbarton Oaks Papers* 49 (1995): 111–207.

Harris, Steven J. "Mapping Jesuit Science: The Role of Travel in the Geography of Knowledge." In *The Jesuits: Cultures, Sciences, and the Arts*, edited by John W. O'Malley, Gauvin Alexander Bailey, Steven J. Harris, and T. Frank Kennedy, 212–240. Toronto: University of Toronto Press, 1999.

Heater, Derek Benjamin. *World Citizenship and Government: Cosmopolitan Ideas in the History of Western Political Thought*. New York: St. Martin's, 1996.

Hodgen, Margaret T. *Early Anthropology in the Sixteenth and Seventeenth Centuries*. Philadelphia: University of Pennsylvania Press, 1964.

———. "Sebastian Muenster (1489–1552): A Sixteenth-Century Ethnographer." *Osiris* (1954):504–529.

Höfert, Almut. "The Order of Things and the Discourse of the Turkish Threat: The Conceptualisation of Islam in the Rise of Occidental Anthropology in the Fifteenth and Sixteenth Centuries." In *Between Europe and Islam: Shaping Modernity in a Transcultural Space*, edited by Almut Höfert and Armando Salvatore, 39–69. Brussels: Peter Lang, 2000.

Horodowich, Elizabeth. *The Venetian Discovery of America: Geographic Imagination in the Age of Encounters*. Cambridge: Cambridge University Press, 2018.

Houston, Chloë. "'Thou Glorious Kingdome, Thou Chiefe of Empires': Persia in Early Seventeenth-Century Travel Literature." *Studies in Travel Writing* 13, no. 2 (June 2009): 141–152.

Houston, R. A. *Literacy in Early Modern Europe: Its Growth, Uses and Impact, 1500–1800*. 2nd ed. London: Routledge, 2002.

Howard, Deborah. "The Status of the Oriental Traveler in Renaissance Venice." In *Reorienting the Renaissance: Cultural Exchanges with the East*, edited by Gerald Maclean, 29–49. New York: Palgrave Macmillan, 2005.

Hughes, Diane Owen. "Distinguishing Signs: Ear-Rings, Jews and Franciscan Rhetoric in the Italian Renaissance City." *Past & Present*, no. 112 (1986): 3–59.

Imber, Colin. *The Ottoman Empire, 1300–1650: The Structure of Power*. New York: Palgrave Macmillan, 2009.

Infelise, Mario. "Book Publishing and the Circulation of Information." In *A Companion to Venetian History, 1400–1797*, edited by Eric R. Dursteler, 651–674. Leiden: Brill, 2013.

———. *I padroni dei libri: Il controllo sulla stampa nella prima età moderna*. Rome: Laterza, 2014.

———. "News Networks between Italy and Europe." In *The Dissemination of News and the Emergence of Contemporaneity in Early Modern Europe*, edited by Brendan Maurice Dooley, 51–67. Farnham, UK: Ashgate, 2010.

———. *Prima dei giornali: Alle origini della pubblica informazione, secoli XVI e XVII*. Rome: Laterza, 2002.

Ingram, Anders. *Writing the Ottomans: Turkish History in Early Modern England*. New York: Palgrave Macmillan, 2015.

Iogna-Prat, Dominique, and John Tolan. "Peter of Cluny." In *Christian-Muslim Relations: A Bibliographical History*, edited by David Thomas and Alex Mallett, 3:604–610. Leiden: Brill, 2011.

Iordanou, Ioanna. "What News on the Rialto? The Trade of Information and Early Modern Venice's Centralized Intelligence Organization." *Intelligence and National Security* 31, no. 3 (April 2016): 305–326.

Jacob, Margaret C. *Strangers Nowhere in the World: The Rise of Cosmopolitanism in Early Modern Europe*. Philadelphia: University of Pennsylvania Press, 2006.

Jed, Stephanie. "The Tenth Muse: Gender, Rationality, and the Marketing of Knowledge." In *Women, "Race," and Writing in the Early Modern Period*, edited by Margo Hendricks and Patricia A. Parker, 195–208. London: Routledge, 1994.

Johnson, Carina L. *Cultural Hierarchy in Sixteenth-Century Europe: The Ottomans and Mexicans*. Cambridge: Cambridge University Press, 2011.

Johnson, Christine R. "Buying Stories: Ancient Tales, Renaissance Travelers, and the Market for the Marvelous." *Journal of Early Modern History* 11, no. 6 (2007): 405–446.

Johnson, Roger A. "Natural Religion, Common Notions, and the Study of Religions: Lord Herbert of Cherbury (1583–1648)." *Religion* 24, no. 3 (1994): 213–224.

Kainulainen, Jaska. *Paolo Sarpi: A Servant of God and State*. Leiden: Brill, 2014.

Kaplan, Benjamin J. *Divided by Faith: Religious Conflict and the Practice of Toleration in Early Modern Europe*. Cambridge, MA: Harvard University Press, 2007.

Katz, Dana E. *The Jewish Ghetto and the Visual Imagination of Early Modern Venice*. Cambridge: Cambridge University Press, 2017.

Kelley, Donald R. "'Second Nature': The Idea of Custom in European Law, Society, and Culture." In *The Transmission of Culture in Early Modern Europe*, edited by Ann Blair and Anthony Grafton, 131–172. Philadelphia: University of Pennsylvania Press, 1990.

Khanmohamadi, Shirin A. *In Light of Another's Word: European Ethnography in the Middle Ages*. Philadelphia: University of Pennsylvania Press, 2013.

Knapton, Michael. "'Dico in scrittura . . . quel ch'a boca ho rifertto': La trasmissione delle conoscenze nelle relazioni dei rettori veneziani in terraferma, secoli XVI–XVII." In *L'Italia dell'inquisitore: Storia e geografia dell'Italia del Cinquecento nella Descrittione di Leandro Alberti: Atti del convegno internazionale di studi, Bologna, 27–29 maggio 2004*, edited by Massimo Donattini, 531–554. Bologna: Bononia University Press, 2007.

Krstić, Tijana, and Maartje van Gelder. "Introduction: Cross-confessional Diplomacy and Diplomatic Intermediaries in the Early Modern Mediterranean." *Journal of Early Modern History* 19, no. 2–3 (April 2015): 93–105.

Labalme, Patricia H., and Laura Sanguineti White. "Appendix A: Money, Wealth, and Wages." In *Venice, Cità Excelentissima: Selections from the Renaissance Diaries of Marin Sanudo*, edited by Patricia H. Labalme and Laura Sanguineti White, 541–543. Baltimore: Johns Hopkins University Press, 2008.

Lane, Frederic Chapin. *Venetian Ships and Shipbuilders of the Renaissance*. Baltimore: Johns Hopkins University Press, 1992.

Lazzarini, Isabella. *Communication and Conflict: Italian Diplomacy in the Early Renaissance, 1350–1520*. Oxford: Oxford University Press, 2015.

Lejosne, Fiona. "Un secrétaire vénitien entre archives et livres imprimés: Giovanni Battista Ramusio (1485–1557)." *Laboratoire italien. Politique et société*, no. 23 (October 2019).

Lenowitz, Harris. *The Jewish Messiahs: From Galilee to Crown Heights*. Oxford: Oxford University Press, 1998.

Lindemann, Mary. "The Discreet Charm of the Diplomatic Archive." *German History* 29, no. 2 (June 2011): 283–304.

Ljubic, Simeon, ed. *Commissiones et relationes venetae*. 3 vols. Monumenta spectantia historiam Slavorum meridionalium. Zagreb: Academia Scientiarum et Artium Slavorum Meridionalium, 1876.

Lockhart, Laurence. "European Contacts with Persia, 1350–1736." In *The Cambridge History of Iran*, edited by Peter Jackson and Laurence Lockhart, 6:373–412. Cambridge: Cambridge University Press, 1986.

Lowry, Martin. *The World of Aldus Manutius: Business and Scholarship in Renaissance Venice*. Ithaca, NY: Cornell University Press, 1979.

Lucchetta, Giuliano. "Viaggiatori e racconti di viaggi nel Cinquecento." In *Storia della cultura veneta: Dal primo Quattrocento al Concilio di Trento*, edited by Girolamo Arnaldi and Manlio Pastore Stocchi, 2:433–489. Vicenza: Neri Pozza, 1980.

MacCormack, Sabine. "Limits of Understanding: Perceptions of Greco-Roman and Amerindian Paganism in Early Modern Europe." In *America in European Consciousness*, edited by Karen Ordahl Kupperman, 79–129. Chapel Hill: University of North Carolina Press, 1995.

Mackenney, Richard. *Tradesmen and Traders: The World of the Guilds in Venice and Europe, c. 1250–c. 1650*. Totowa, NJ: Barnes & Noble Books, 1987.

MagLaque, Erin. "Humanism and Colonial Governance in the Venetian Ageaen: The Case of Giovanni Bembo." *Journal of Early Modern History* 19, no. 1 (January 2015): 45–70.

Malkiel, David Joshua. "The Ghetto Republic." In *The Jews of Early Modern Venice*, edited by Robert C. Davis and Benjamin Ravid, 117–142. Baltimore: Johns Hopkins University Press, 2001.

Mallett, Michael. "Ambassadors and Their Audiences in Renaissance Italy." *Renaissance Studies* 8, no. 3 (1994): 229–243.

Mantran, Robert. "Venise, centre d'informations sur les turcs." In *Venezia, centro di mediazione tra Oriente e Occidente, secoli XV–XVI: Aspetti e problemi*, edited by Hans Georg Beck, Manoussos Manoussacas, and Agostino Pertusi, 1:111–116. Florence: L. S. Olschki, 1977.

Marchesi, Vincenzo. "Le relazioni tra la repubblica Veneta e il Portogallo dall'anno 1522 al 1797." *Archivio veneto* 33 (1887): 1–42, 283–307.

Mason, Peter. "Classical Ethnography and Its Influence on the European Perception of the Peoples of the New World." In *The Classical Tradition and the Americas: European Images of the Americas and the Classical Tradition*, edited by Wolfgang Hasse and Meyer Reinhold, 135–172. Berlin: de Gruyter, 1994.

Matthee, Rudi. "The Safavids under Western Eyes: Seventeenth-Century European Travelers to Iran." *Journal of Early Modern History* 13, no. 2 (2009): 137–171.

Mattingly, Garrett. *Renaissance Diplomacy*. New York: Dover, 1988.

———. "The First Resident Embassies: Mediaeval Italian Origins of Modern Diplomacy." *Speculum* 12, no. 4 (October 1937): 423–439.

Mayer, Thomas F. *The Roman Inquisition: A Papal Bureaucracy and Its Laws in the Age of Galileo*. Philadelphia: University of Pennsylvania Press, 2013.

———. *The Roman Inquisition on the Stage of Italy, c. 1590–1640*. Philadelphia: University of Pennsylvania Press, 2014.

McKenzie, D. F. "Speech-Manuscript-Print." In *Making Meaning: "Printers of the Mind" and Other Essays*, edited by Peter D. McDonald and Michael Felix Suarez, 237–258. Amherst: University of Massachusetts Press, 2002.

McKitterick, David. *Print, Manuscript and the Search for Order, 1450–1830*. Cambridge: Cambridge University Press, 2003.

McLean, Matthew. *The Cosmographia of Sebastian Münster: Describing the World in the Reformation*. Aldershot, UK: Ashgate, 2013.

Melamed, Abraham. "English Travelers and Venetian Jewish Scholars: The Case of Simone Luzzatto and James Harrington." In *Gli Ebrei e Venezia: Secoli XIV–XVIII*, edited by Gaetano Cozzi, 507–527. Milan: Edizioni Comunità, 1987.

Melchiorre, Matteo. *Conoscere per governare: Le relazioni dei sindici inquisitori e il dominio veneziano in terraferma (1543–1626)*. Udine: Forum, 2013.

Meserve, Margaret. *Empires of Islam in Renaissance Historical Thought*. Cambridge, MA: Harvard University Press, 2009.

———. "The Sophy: News of Shah Ismail Safavi in Renaissance Europe." *Journal of Early Modern History* 18, no. 6 (2014): 579–608.

Miekkavaara, Leena. "Unknown Europe: The Mapping of the Northern Countries by Olaus Magnus in 1539." *Belgeo. Revue belge de géographie*, no. 3–4 (2008): 307–324.

Milanesi, Marica. Introduction to *Navigazioni e viaggi*, edited by Marica Milanesi, 1:xii–xxxvi. Turin: Einaudi, 1978.

———. *Tolomeo sostituito: Studi di storia delle conoscenze geografiche nel XVI secolo*. Milan: Unicopli, 1984.

Millstone, Noah. "Seeing like a Statesman in Early Stuart England." *Past & Present* 223, no. 1 (May 2014): 77–127.

Minchella, Giuseppina. *Frontiere aperte: Musulmani, Ebrei e Cristiani nella Repubblica di Venezia*. Rome: Viella, 2014.

Modell, Judith. "From Ethnographies to Encounters: Differences and Others." *Journal of Interdisciplinary History* 27, no. 3 (Winter 1997): 481–495.

Modena, Leon. *Historia de gli riti hebraici*. Paris, 1637.

Momigliano, Arnaldo. "Ancient History and the Antiquarian." *Journal of the Warburg and Courtauld Institutes* 13, no. 3/4 (1950): 285–315.

———. *The Classical Foundations of Modern Historiography*. Berkeley: University of California Press, 1990.

Morandi, Carlo. Introduction to *Relazioni di ambasciatori sabaudi, genovesi e veneti durante il periodo della grande alleanza e della successione di Spagna (1693–1713)*, xi–lxiv. Edited by Carlo Morandi. Bologna: Nicola Zanichelli, 1935.

Moss, Ann. "Commonplace-Rhetoric and Thought-Patterns in Early Modern Culture." In *The Recovery of Rhetoric: Persuasive Discourse and Disciplinarity in the Human Sciences*, edited by R. H. Roberts and James M. M. Good, 49–60. Charlottesville: University of Virginia Press, 1993.

———. *Printed Commonplace-Books and the Structuring of Renaissance Thought*. New York: Clarendon, 1996.

Mosto, Andrea Da. *L'archivio di stato di Venezia: Indice generale, storico, descrittivo ed analitico*. 2 vols. Rome: Biblioteca d'arte editrice, 1937–1940.

Motsch, Andreas. "Relations of Travel: Itinerary of a Practice." *Renaissance and Reformation/Renaissance et réforme* 34, no. 1–2 (2011): 207–236.

Nalle, Sara T. "Literacy and Culture in Early Modern Castile." *Past & Present*, no. 125 (November 1989): 65–96.

Nederman, Cary J. *Worlds of Difference: European Discourses of Toleration, c. 1100–c. 1550*. University Park: Pennsylvania State University Press, 2010.

Neff, Mary Frances. "Chancellery Secretaries in Venetian Politics and Society, 1480–1533." PhD diss., University of California, Los Angeles, 1985.

Netzloff, Mark. "The Ambassador's Household: Sir Henry Wotton, Domesticity, and Diplomatic Writing." In *Diplomacy and Early Modern Culture*, edited by Robyn Adams and Rosanna Cox, 155–171. New York: Palgrave Macmillan, 2011.

Nirenberg, David. "Was There Race before Modernity? The Example of 'Jewish' Blood in Late Medieval Spain." In *The Origins of Racism in the West*, edited by Miriam Eliav-Feldon, Benjamin Isaac, and Joseph Ziegler, 232–264. Cambridge: Cambridge University Press, 2009.

Nocentelli, Carmen. *Empires of Love: Europe, Asia, and the Making of Early Modern Identity*. Philadelphia: University of Pennsylvania Press, 2013.

Nuovo, Angela. "A proposito del carteggio Pinelli-Dupuy." *Biblioteca: Rivista di studi bibliografici* 1 (2002): 96–115.

———. "'Et amicorum': Costruzione e circolazione del sapere nelle biblioteche private del Cinquecento." In *Libri, biblioteche e cultura degli ordini regolari nell'Italia moderna attraverso la documentazione della Congregazione dell'indice*, edited by Rosa Marisa Borraccini Verducci and Roberto Rusconi, 105–127. Vatican City: Biblioteca apostolica Vaticana, 2006.

———. "Private Libraries in Sixteenth-Century Italy." In *Early Printed Books as Material Objects*, edited by Bettina Wagner and Marcia Reed, 229–240. Berlin: de Gruyter, 2010.

———. *The Book Trade in the Italian Renaissance*. Translated by Lydia G. Cochrane. Leiden: Brill, 2013.

———. "The Creation and Dispersal of the Library of Gian Vincenzo Pinelli." In *Books on the Move: Tracking Copies through Collections and the Book Trade*, edited by Robin

Myers, Michael Harris, and Giles Mandelbrote, 39–67. New Castle, DE: Oak Knoll Press, 2007.

Ortega, Stephen. "Across Religious and Ethnic Boundaries: Ottoman Networks and Spaces in Early Modern Venice." *Mediterranean Studies* 18, no. 1 (December 2009): 66–89.

———. *Negotiating Transcultural Relations in the Early Modern Mediterranean: Ottoman-Venetian Encounters*. Farnham, UK: Ashgate, 2014.

———. "'Pleading for Help': Gender Relations and Cross-cultural Logic in the Early Modern Mediterranean." *Gender & History* 20, no. 2 (2008): 332–348.

Osborne, Toby, and Joan-Pau Rubiés, eds. "Introduction: Diplomacy and Cultural Translation in the Early Modern World." *Journal of Early Modern History* 20, no. 4 (2016): 313–330.

Pagden, Anthony. *The Fall of Natural Man: The American Indian and the Origins of Comparative Ethnology*. Cambridge: Cambridge University Press, 1982.

Palumbo-Fossati, Isabelle. "Livres et lecteurs dans la Venise du XVI siècle." *Revue française d'histoire du livre* 54, no. 49 (1985): 481–513.

Pedani Fabris, Maria Pia. *Elenco degli inviati diplomatici veneziani presso i sovrani ottomani*. Venice: n.p., 2000.

———. *In nome del gran signore: Inviati ottomani a Venezia dalla caduta di Costantinopoli alla guerra di Candia*. Venice: Deputazione Editrice, 1994.

———. "Venetian Consuls in Egypt and Syria in the Ottoman Age." *Mediterranean World* 18 (2006): 7–21.

———. *Venezia porta d'Oriente*. Bologna: Il Mulino, 2010.

———. *The Ottoman-Venetian Border (15th–18th Centuries)*. Translated by Mariateresa Sala. Venice: Edizioni Ca' Foscari, 2017.

Peters, Edward. "Editing Inquisitors' Manuals in the Sixteenth Century: Francisco Peña and the Directorium inquisitorum of Nicholas Eymeric." *Library Chronicle* 40 (1974): 95–107.

Petrucci, Armando. "Scrittura, alfabetismo ed educazione grafica nella Roma del primo Cinquecento: Da un libretto di conti di Maddalena pizzicarola in Trastevere." *Scrittura e civiltà* 2 (1978): 163–207.

Pezzolo, Luciano. "The Venetian Economy." In *A Companion to Venetian History, 1400–1797*, edited by Eric R. Dursteler, 255–290. Leiden: Brill, 2013.

Phillips, Kim M. *Before Orientalism: Asian Peoples and Cultures in European Travel Writing, 1245–1510*. Philadelphia: University of Pennsylvania Press, 2014.

Philo, John-Mark. "English and Scottish Scholars at the Library of Gian Vincenzo Pinelli (1565–1601)." *Renaissance and Reformation/Renaissance et réforme* 42, no. 2 (2019): 51–80.

Pippidi, Andrei. *Visions of the Ottoman World in Renaissance Europe*. New York: Columbia University Press, 2013.

Pirillo, Diego. *The Refugee-Diplomat: Venice, England, and the Reformation*. Ithaca, NY: Cornell University Press, 2018.

Plakotos, Georgios. "Christian and Muslim Converts from the Balkans in Early Modern Venice: Patterns of Social and Cultural Mobility and Identities." In *Developing Cultural Identity in the Balkans: Convergence vs. Divergence*, edited by Raymond Detrez and Pieter Plas, 125–145. New York: Peter Lang, 2005.

Pratt, Mary Louise. "Arts of the Contact Zone." *Profession* 91 (1998): 171–185.

———. *Imperial Eyes: Travel Writing and Transculturation.* 2nd ed. London: Routledge, 2007.

Preto, Paolo. *I servizi segreti di Venezia.* Milan: Il Saggiatore, 1994.

———. "Le relazioni dei baili veneziani a Costantinopoli." *Il veltro* 23, no. 2–4 (1979): 125–131.

———. "Turchi e la cultura veneziana del Seicento." In *Il Seicento*, 2:313–241. Storia della cultura veneta 4. Vicenza: N. Pozza, 1984.

———. *Venezia e i Turchi.* 2nd ed. Rome: Viella, 2013.

Pullan, Brian. *The Jews of Europe and the Inquisition of Venice, 1550–1670.* Oxford: Blackwell, 1983.

———. "The Occupations and the Investments of the Venetian Nobility in the Middle and Late Sixteenth Century." In *Renaissance Venice*, edited by John R. Hale, 379–408. London: Rowman & Littlefield, 1973.

———. "'Three Orders of Inhabitants': Social Hierarchies in the Republic of Venice." In *Orders and Hierarchies in Late Medieval and Renaissance Europe*, edited by Jeffrey Howard Denton, 147–168. Toronto: University of Toronto Press, 1999.

Queller, Donald E. "How to Succeed as an Ambassador: A Sixteenth Century Venetian Document." In *Post Scripta: Essays on Medieval Law and the Emergence of the European State in Honor of Gaines Post*, edited by Donald E. Queller and Joseph R. Strayer, 655–671. Rome: Libreria Ateneo Salesiano, 1972.

———. "The Development of Ambassadorial Relazioni." In *Renaissance Venice*, edited by J. R. Hale, 174–196. London: Rowman & Littlefield, 1973.

Raines, Dorit. "L'archivio familiare strumento di formazione politica del patriziato veneziano." *Accademie e biblioteche d'Italia* 64 (1996): 5–36.

———. "L'arte di ben informarsi: Carriera politica e pratiche documentarie nell'archivio familiare di patrizi veneziani: I Molin di San Pantalon." In *Archivi nobiliari e domestici. Conservazione, metodologie di riordino e prospettive di ricerca storica. Atti del Convegno di Studi, Udine*, 1–21. Udine: Forum, 2000.

———. "The Private Political Archives of the Venetian Patriciate: Storing, Retrieving and Recordkeeping in Fifteenth-Eighteenth Centuries." *Journal of the Society of Archivists* 32, no. 1 (2011): 131–142.

Raugei, Anna Maria. "Tra gli scaffali di una biblioteca italiana: Gian Vincenzo Pinelli e la letteratura francese sul Nuovo Mondo." In *La scoperta dell'America e le lettere francese*, edited by Enea Balmas, 181–192. Milan: Cisalpino, 1992.

Ravid, Benjamin. "Between the Myth of Venice and the Lachrymose Conception of Jewish History: The Case of the Jews of Venice." In *The Jews of Italy: Memory and Identity*, edited by Bernard Dov Cooperman and Barbara Garvin, 151–192. Bethesda: University Press of Maryland, 2000.

———. "Christian Travelers in the Ghetto of Venice: Some Preliminary Observations." In *Between History and Literature: Studies in Honor of Isaac Barzilay*, edited by Stanley Nash, 111–150. Bnei Brak, Israel: Hakibbutz Hameuchad, 1997.

———. "From Yellow to Red: On the Distinguishing Head-Covering of the Jews of Venice." *Jewish History* 6, no. 1 (1992): 179–210.

———. "Jews in International Trade: The Emergence of the Levantine and Ponentines." In *The Jews of Early Modern Venice*, edited by Robert C. Davis and Benjamin Ravid, 73–96. Baltimore: Johns Hopkins University Press, 2001.

———. "'Kosher Bread' in Baroque Venice." *Italia* 6, no. 1–2 (1987): 20–29.

———. "The First Charter of the Jewish Merchants of Venice, 1589." *AJS Review* 1 (1976): 187–222.

———. "The Legal Status of the Jewish Merchants of Venice, 1541–1638." *Journal of Economic History* 35, no. 1 (1975): 274–279.

———. "The Venetian Government and the Jews." In *The Jews of Early Modern Venice*, edited by Robert C. Davis and Benjamin Ravid, 3–30. Baltimore: Johns Hopkins University Press, 2001.

———. "Venice and Its Minorities." In *A Companion to Venetian History, 1400–1797*, edited by Eric R. Dursteler, 449–485. Leiden: Brill, 2013.

———. "Venice, Rome, and the Reversion of New Christians to Judaism: A Study in Ragione di Stato." In *L'identità dissimulata: Giudaizzanti iberici nell'Europa cristiana dell'età moderna*, edited by Pier Cesare Ioly Zorattini, 151–193. Florence: L. S. Olschki, 2000.

Richardson, Brian. "A Scribal Publisher of Political Information: Francesco Marcaldi." *Italian Studies* 64, no. 2 (June 2009): 296–313.

———. *Manuscript Culture in Renaissance Italy*. Cambridge: Cambridge University Press, 2009.

———. *Printing, Writers and Readers in Renaissance Italy*. Cambridge: Cambridge University Press, 1999.

Roggema, Barbara. *The Legend of Sergius Baḥīrā: Eastern Christian Apologetics and Apocalyptic in Response to Islam*. Leiden: Brill, 2009.

Rosenthal, David, and Rosa Salzberg. "Rosa Salzberg: 'Print Saturated the Lives of Ordinary People.'" *Earlymoderncommunities* (blog), June 2011. http://earlymoderncommunities.org/home/interviews-2/rosa-salzberg-print-saturated-the-lives-of-ordinary-people/.

Rosenthal, Margaret F. "Clothing, Fashion, Dress, and Costume in Venice (c. 1450–1650)." In *A Companion to Venetian History, 1400–1797*, edited by Eric R. Dursteler, 889–928. Leiden: Brill, 2013.

Rosenthal, Margaret F., and Ann Rosalind Jones. "Vecellio and His World." In *The Clothing of the Renaissance World: Europe, Asia, Africa, the Americas: Cesare Vecellio's Habiti Antichi et Moderni*, edited by Margaret F. Rosenthal and Ann Rosalind Jones, 8–44. London: Thames & Hudson, 2008.

Ross, Sarah Gwyneth. *Everyday Renaissances: The Quest for Cultural Legitimacy in Venice*. Cambridge, MA: Harvard University Press, 2016.

Ross, Tricia M. "Anthropologia: An (Almost) Forgotten Early Modern History." *Journal of the History of Ideas* 79, no. 1 (January 2018): 1–22.

Rota, Giorgio. "Safavid Persia and Its Diplomatic Relations with Venice." In *Iran and the World in the Safavid Age*, edited by William Floor and Edmund Herzig, 149–160. London: I. B. Tauris, 2012.

———. *Under Two Lions: On the Knowledge of Persia in the Republic of Venice (ca. 1450–1797)*. Vienna: Österreichischen Akademie der Wissenschaften, 2009.

Roth, Cecil. "Leone Da Modena and the Christian Hebraists of His Age." In *Jewish Studies in Memory of Israel Abrahams*, edited by George Alexander Kohut, 384–401. New York: Press of the Jewish Institute of Religion, 1927.

Rothman, E. Natalie. "Becoming Venetian: Conversion and Transformation in the Seventeenth-Century Mediterranean." *Mediterranean Historical Review* 21 (June 2006): 39–75.

———. *Brokering Empire: Trans-imperial Subjects between Venice and Istanbul*. Ithaca, NY: Cornell University Press, 2012.

———. "Dragomans and 'Turkish Literature': The Making of a Field of Inquiry." *Oriente moderno* 93, no. 2 (January 2013): 390–421.

———. "Interpreting Dragomans: Boundaries and Crossings in the Early Modern Mediterranean." *Comparative Studies in Society and History* 51, no. 4 (September 2009): 771–800.

———. *The Dragoman Renaissance: Diplomatic Interpreters and the Routes of Orientalism*. Ithaca, NY: Cornell University Press, 2021.

Rowe, John H. "Ethnography and Ethnology in the Sixteenth Century." *Kroeber Anthropological Society Papers* 30 (1964): 1–19.

Rozzo, Ugo. *Linee per una storia dell'editoria religiosa in Italia (1465–1600)*. Udine: Arti Grafiche Friulane, 1993.

Rubiés, Joan-Pau. "Instructions for Travellers: Teaching the Eye to See." *History and Anthropology* 9, no. 2–3 (1996): 139–190.

———. "New Worlds and Renaissance Ethnology." *History and Anthropology* 6, no. 2–3 (1993): 157–197.

———. *Travel and Ethnology in the Renaissance: South India through European Eyes, 1250–1625*. Cambridge: Cambridge University Press, 2002.

———. "Travel Writing as a Genre: Facts, Fictions and the Invention of a Scientific Discourse in Early Modern Europe." *Journeys: The International Journal of Travel and Travel Writing* 1, no. 1/2 (2000): 5–35.

Rublack, Ulinka. *Dressing Up: Cultural Identity in Renaissance Europe*. Oxford: Oxford University Press, 2010.

Ryan, Michael T. "Assimilating New Worlds in the Sixteenth and Seventeenth Centuries." *Comparative Studies in Society and History* 23, no. 4 (October 1981): 519–538.

Sahas, Daniel J. *John of Damascus on Islam: The "Heresy of the Ishmaelites."* Leiden: Brill, 1972.

Salzberg, Rosa. *Ephemeral City: Cheap Print and Urban Culture in Renaissance Venice*. Manchester: Manchester University Press, 2014.

Sardella, Pierre. *Nouvelles et spéculations à Venise au début du XVIe siècle*. Paris: A. Colin, 1948.

Schiffman, Zachary S. *The Birth of the Past*. Baltimore: Johns Hopkins University Press, 2011.

Schutte, Anne Jacobson. "Un inquisitore al lavoro: Fra Marino da Venezia e l'Inquisizione veneziana." In *I francescani in Europa tra Riforma e Controriforma*, 165–196. Perugia: Università degli studi di Perugia, 1987.

Schwartz, Stuart B., ed. *Implicit Understandings: Observing, Reporting and Reflecting on the Encounters between Europeans and Other Peoples in the Early Modern Era*. Cambridge: Cambridge University Press, 1994.

Schwarz Lausten, Pia. "Giovanni Antonio Menavino." In *Christian-Muslim Relations: A Bibliographical History*, edited by David Thomas and John A. Chesworth, 6:512–522. Leiden: Brill, 2014.

Schweickard, Wolfgang. "Giovan Antonio Menavino's Account of His Captivity in the Ottoman Empire: A Revaluation." *Zeitschrift für romanische Philologie* 132, no. 1 (2016): 180–205.

Seneca, Federico. *Il doge Leonardo Donà, la sua vita e la sua preparazione politica prima del dogado*. Padua: Antenore, 1959.

Sestieri, Lea. *David Reubeni: Un Ebreo d'Arabia in missione segreta nell'Europa del '500*. Genoa: Marietti, 1991.

Shaw, Stanford J. *History of the Ottoman Empire and Modern Turkey*. Vol. 1: *Empire of the Gazis: The Rise and Decline of the Ottoman Empire 1280–1808*. Cambridge: Cambridge University Press, 1976.

Sheehan, Jonathan. "Sacred and Profane: Idolatry, Antiquarianism and the Polemics of Distinction in the Seventeenth Century." *Past & Present*, no. 192 (2006): 35–66.

Simon, Bruno. "I rappresentanti diplomatici veneziani a Costantinopoli." In *Venezia e i Turchi: Scontri e confronti di due civiltà*, edited by Anna Della Valle, 56–69. Milan: Electa, 1985.

Simonsohn, Shlomo. "La condizione giuridica degli Ebrei nell'Italia centrale e settentrionale (secoli XII–XVI)." In *Gli Ebrei in Italia*, edited by Corrado Vivanti, 1:95–120. Turin: Einaudi, 1996.

Small, Margaret. "Displacing Ptolemy? The Textual Geographies of Ramusio's Navigazioni e Viaggi." In *Mapping Medieval Geographies: Geographical Encounters in the Latin West and Beyond, 300–1600*, edited by Keith D. Lilley, 152–174. Cambridge: Cambridge University Press, 2014.

Smith, Anthony D. *The Ethnic Origins of Nations*. Oxford: Blackwell, 1986.

Smith, Stefan Halikowski. "Gasparo Contarini's Relazione of November 1525 to the Venetian Senate on the Divergent Dynamics of the Spanish and Portuguese World Empires." *Mediterranean Historical Review* 32, no. 2 (July 2017): 189–235.

Sperling, Jutta. "The Paradox of Perfection: Reproducing the Body Politic in Late Renaissance Venice." *Comparative Studies in Society and History* 41, no. 1 (January 1999): 3–32.

Spini, Giorgio. *Ricerca dei libertini: La teoria dell'impostura delle religioni nel Seicento italiano*. 2nd ed. Rome: Editrice Universale, 1983.

Stagl, Justin. *A History of Curiosity: The Theory of Travel, 1550–1800*. Chur, Switzerland: Harwood Academic Publishers, 1994.

Stevens, Roger. "European Visitors to the Safavid Court." *Iranian Studies* 7, no. 3–4 (1974): 421–457.

Stiffoni, Giovanni. "La scoperta e la conquista dell'America nelle prime relazioni degli ambasciatori veneziani (1497–1559)." In *L'impatto della scoperta dell'America nella cultura veneziana*, edited by Angela Caracciolo Arico, 351–364. Rome: Bulzoni, 1990.

Stouraiti, Anastasia. "Talk, Script and Print: The Making of Island Books in Early Modern Venice." *Historical Research* 86, no. 232 (May 2013): 207–229.

Stroumsa, Guy G. *A New Science: The Discovery of Religion in the Age of Reason*. Cambridge, MA: Harvard University Press, 2010.

Subrahmanyam, Sanjay. "The Birth-Pangs of Portuguese Asia: Revisiting the Fateful 'Long Decade' 1498–1509." *Journal of Global History* 2, no. 3 (November 2007): 261–280.

Taylor, Kathryn. "Ancients and Moderns in Sixteenth-Century Ethnography." *History of European Ideas* 46, no. 2 (February 2020): 113–130.

———. "Making Statesmen, Writing Culture: Ethnography, Observation, and Diplomatic Travel in Early Modern Venice." *Journal of Early Modern History* 22, no. 4 (August 2018): 279–298.

Tedeschi, John, and William Monter. "Toward a Statistical Profile of the Italian Inquisitions, Sixteenth to Eighteenth Centuries." In *The Prosecution of Heresy: Collected Studies on the Inquisition in Early Modern Italy*, 89–126. Binghamton, NY: Medieval and Renaissance Texts and Studies, 1986.

Testa, Simone. "Alcune riflessioni sul Thesoro politico (1598)." *Bibliothèque d'humanisme et renaissance* 64, no. 3 (January 2002): 679–687.

———. "Per una interpretazione del Thesoro politico (1589)." *Nuova rivista storica* 85 (2001): 347–362.

Tiepolo, Maria Francesca. "Archivio di Stato di Venezia." In *Guida generale degli archivi di stato Italiani*, 4:859–1148. Rome: Ministero per i Beni Culturali e Ambientali, 1994.

———, ed. *Aspetti e momenti della diplomazia veneziana: Catalogo della mostra documentaria, 26 giugno–26 settembre, 1982*. Venice: Archivio di Stato di Venezia, 1982.

Tolias, George. "Isolarii, Fifteenth to Seventeenth Century." In *Cartography in the European Renaissance*, edited by David Woodward, translated by Timothy Cullen, 3:263–284. Chicago: University of Chicago Press, 2007.

Tommasino, Pier Mattia. *The Venetian Qur'an: A Renaissance Companion to Islam*. Translated by Sylvia Notini. Philadelphia: University of Pennsylvania Press, 2018.

Trebbi, Giuseppe. "Il segretario veneziano." *Archivio storico italiano* 144 (1986): 35–73.

———. "La cancelleria veneta nei secoli XVI e XVII." *Annali della Fondazione Luigi Einaudi* 14 (1980): 65–125.

True, Micah. *Masters and Students: Jesuit Mission Ethnography in Seventeenth-Century New France*. Montreal: McGill-Queen's University Press, 2015.

Tucci, Ugo. "Il patrizio veneziano mercante e umanista." In *Venezia, centro di mediazione tra Oriente e Occidente, secoli XV–XVI: Aspetti e problemi*, edited by Hans Georg Beck, Manoussos Manoussacas, and Agostino Pertusi, 1:335–357. Florence: L. S. Olschki, 1977.

———. "The Psychology of the Venetian Merchant in the Sixteenth Century." In *Renaissance Venice*, edited by J. R. Hale, 346–378. London: Rowman & Littlefield, 1973.

Valensi, Lucette. *The Birth of the Despot: Venice and the Sublime Porte*. Translated by Arthur Denner. Ithaca, NY: Cornell University Press, 1993.

Veneri, Toni. "Giovanni Battista Ramusio, molto più di uno spettatore. Le quinte delle 'Navigationi et viaggi.'" *Italica* 89, no. 2 (2012): 162–201.

Ventura, Angelo. "Scrittori politici e scritture di governo." In *Storia della cultura veneta*, edited by Girolamo Arnaldi and Manlio Pastore Stocchi, 3:513–563. Vicenza: Nera Pozza, 1981.

Verhoeven, Gerrit. *Europe within Reach: Netherlandish Travellers on the Grand Tour and Beyond (1585–1750)*. Translated by Diane Webb. Leiden: Brill, 2015.

Vermeulen, Han. *Before Boas: The Genesis of Ethnography and Ethnology in the German Enlightenment*. Lincoln: University of Nebraska Press, 2015.

———. "The German Invention of Völkerkunde: Ethnological Discourse in Europe and Asia, 1740–1798." In *German Invention of Race*, edited by Sara Eigen and Mark Larrimore, 123–145. Albany: State University of New York Press, 2012.

Vogel, Klaus. "Cultural Variety in a Renaissance Perspective: Johannes Boemus on 'The Manners, Laws and Customs of All People' (1520)." In *Shifting Cultures: Interaction and Discourse in the Expansion of Europe*, edited by Joan-Pau Rubiés and Henriette Bugge, 17–34. Münster: Lit Verlag, 1995.

Walsham, Alexandra. *Charitable Hatred: Tolerance and Intolerance in England, 1500–1700*. Manchester: Manchester University Press, 2006.

Wansbrough, John. "A Mamluk Ambassador to Venice in 913/1507." *Bulletin of the School of Oriental and African Studies* 26, no. 3 (1963): 503–530.

Warner, Lyndan. *The Ideas of Man and Woman in Renaissance France: Print, Rhetoric, and Law*. London: Routledge, 2016.

Watanabe, Morimichi. "Cusanus, Islam, and Religious Tolerance." In *Nicholas of Cusa and Islam: Polemic and Dialogue in the Late Middle Ages*, edited by Ian Christopher Levy, Rita George-Tvrtković, and Donald Duclow, 9–19. Leiden: Brill, 2014.

Watkins, John. "Toward a New Diplomatic History of Medieval and Early Modern Europe." *Journal of Medieval and Early Modern Studies* 38, no. 1 (2008): 1–14.

Wickersham, Jane K. *Rituals of Prosecution: The Roman Inquisition and the Prosecution of Philo-Protestants in Sixteenth-Century Italy*. Toronto: University of Toronto Press, 2012.

Wilson, Bronwen. "Assembling the Archipelago: Isolarii and the Horizons of Early Modern Public Making." In *Making Space Public in Early Modern Europe: Geography, Performance, Privacy*, edited by Angela Vanhaelen and Joseph P. Ward, 101–126. London: Routledge, 2013.

———. "Reflecting on the Turk in Late Sixteenth-Century Venetian Portrait Books." *Word & Image* 19, no. 1–2 (January 2003): 38–58.

———. *The World in Venice: Print, the City, and Early Modern Identity*. Toronto: University of Toronto Press, 2005.

Wolff, Anne. *How Many Miles to Babylon? Travels and Adventures to Egypt and Beyond, 1300 to 1640*. Liverpool: Liverpool University Press, 2003.

Wolff, Larry. *Venice and the Slavs: The Discovery of Dalmatia in the Age of Enlightenment*. Stanford, CA: Stanford University Press, 2002.

Yurdusev, A. Nuri. "The Middle East Encounter with the Expansion of European International Society." In *International Society and the Middle East: English School Theory at the Regional Level*, edited by Barry Buzan and A. Gonzalez-Pelaez, 70–91. Basingstoke, UK: Palgrave Macmillan, 2009.

Zannini, Andrea. *Burocrazia e burocrati a Venezia in età moderna: I cittadini originari (sec. XVI–XVIII)*. Venice: Istituto veneto di scienze, lettere ed arti, 1993.

———. "Economic and Social Aspects of the Crisis of Venetian Diplomacy in the Seventeenth and Eighteenth Centuries." In *Politics and Diplomacy in Early Modern Italy: The Structure of Diplomatic Practice, 1450–1800*, edited by Daniela Frigo, 109–146. Cambridge: Cambridge University Press, 2000.

Zorattini, Pier Cesare Ioly. *I nomi degli altri: Conversioni a Venezia e nel Friuli Veneto in età moderna*. Florence: L. S. Olschki, 2008.

Zorzanello, Pietro, and Giulio Zorzanello, eds. *Inventari dei manoscritti delle Biblioteche d'Italia*. Vol. 87. Florence: L. S. Olschki, 1967.

Zorzi, Marino. "La circolazione del libro a Venezia nel Cinquecento: Biblioteche private e pubbliche." *Ateneo veneto* 177 (1990): 117–189.

———. *La libreria di San Marco: Libri, lettori, società nella Venezia dei dogi*. Milan: A. Mondadori, 1987.

Index

About the Author

KATHRYN TAYLOR is assistant professor of history at the University of Tennessee at Chattanooga. A scholar of the cultural and intellectual history of early modern Italy and the Mediterranean, their articles have appeared in *History of European Ideas*, *Sixteenth Century Journal*, and *Journal of Early Modern History*.

